starring SHERLOCK HOLMES

A CENTURY OF THE MASTER DETECTIVE ON SCREEN

DAVID STUART DAVIES

FOREWORD BY
IAN RICHARDSON

TITAN BOOKS

LONDON

STARRING SHERLOCK HOLMES

ISBN 1 84576 537 0
ISBN-13 9781845765378

Published by
Titan Books
A division of
Titan Publishing Group Ltd
144 Southwark St
London
SE1 0UP

First edition 2001. Revised edition October 2007
10 9 8 7 6 5 4 3 2 1

Starring Sherlock Holmes text copyright © 2001, 2007 David Stuart Davies. All rights reserved.

Foreword copyright © 2001 Ian Richardson.

Designed by Caroline Grimshaw.

Front cover image: Jeremy Brett as Sherlock Holmes. Courtesy of Granada Picture Library. Copyright © Granada Television.
Back cover image: Copyright © Universal Pictures.

www.titanbooks.com

Did you enjoy this book? We love to hear from our readers. Please e-mail us at: readerfeedback@titanemail.com or write to Reader Feedback at the above address.

To subscribe to our regular newsletter for up-to-the-minute news, great offers and competitions, email: booksezine@titanemail.com

A CIP catalogue record for this title is available from the British Library.

Printed in China by C&C Offset Printing Co., Ltd.

DEDICATION

To
The Baker Street Irregulars
A group of remarkable individuals whose love of Sherlock Holmes helps to make this world a happier place.

AUTHOR'S ACKNOWLEDGEMENTS

It has been a great pleasure for me to re-visit the world of Sherlock Holmes in order to update this volume detailing the many screen appearances, along with those on stage and radio, of this great iconoclastic figure. However, the task was tinged with sadness, for two individuals who helped me with the original book have died since the first edition was published in 2001. Richard Lancelyn Green, who I was proud to call a friend, was the foremost Holmes/Doyle collector and scholar in the world. Very generously he allowed me to plunder his vast collection of stills and cinema memorabilia to help illustrate this book. Certainly *Starring Sherlock Holmes* would not be as pictorially exciting without the gems from Richard's collection.

That excellent actor Ian Richardson, who kindly and graciously penned the Foreword, has also passed on. His acting career encompassed the classics as well as modern dramas, but he remains unique as a Sherlockian performer in having portrayed not only Sherlock Holmes, but also Joseph Bell, the man generally regarded as the inspiration for the character. We met several times and he was a wonderful man with a warmth that came, like Bell's, from his Scottish roots and a sharpness of mind and an attention to detail that was reminiscent of Mr Holmes himself.

Other friends and colleagues who have provided me with images or information include: Tony Earnshaw, whose book *Peter Cushing — An Actor and a Rare One* is a must for all Holmes fans, Roger Johnson, editor of *The Sherlock Holmes Journal*, Charles Prepolec who placed his knowledge and stock of images at my disposal, Linda Pritchard, Jean Upton and Richard Valley. I would also like to thank my editors at Titan, David Barraclough and Adam Newell, whose enthusiasm, good humour and kindness helped enormously to spur me on when the going got tough.

I must also raise a toast to thank those past writers who have travelled similar roads and whose work made my research easier than it might have been: Michael Pointer, Chris Steinbrunner & Norman Michaels, Robert W. Pohle & Douglas C. Hart, Gordon E. Kelley, Allan Eyles, Ron Haydock and Ron De Waal. Finally, yet another big hug for my wonderful wife Kathryn whose love, constructive observations, encouragement, and her unwavering belief in me and this project were invaluable.

David Stuart Davies, June 2007

The publishers would also like to thank Roseanne Boyce, Jonathan Clements, Marcus Hearn, The Tony Hillman Collection, Stephen Jones, Bob Kelly, Kate Pankhurst, Dr Ben Newell, Christine Rimmer and Roseanne Boyle at Granada, and David Williams.

PICTURE CREDITS

Page 3: *Basil Rathbone in* The Adventures of Sherlock Holmes *(1939).*
Pages 4 and 5: *Some of the many faces of the Great Detective and his associate Doctor Watson: Clive Brook and Reginald Owen, Basil Rathbone and Nigel Bruce, Peter Cushing and Nigel Stock, Robert Stephens and Colin Blakely, Jeremy Brett and Edward Hardwicke, Matt Frewer and Kenneth Welsh.*
Page 6: *Ian Richardson as Sherlock Holmes.*
Page 7 (below right): *Richardson as Doyle's inspiration for Holmes, Dr Joseph Bell.*

CONTENTS

FOREWORD

OFFER ANY ACTOR IN THE WORLD THE PART OF Sherlock Holmes, and I am willing to wager that you will get an affirmative response. No matter whether they be too short, too old, or too fat, the lure of the Great Detective is irresistible. Part of the attraction lies in those traits which, while not admirable in themselves, are those we would secretly love to have. Holmes may possess an encyclopaedic knowledge of the cigar ashes of the world, recognise different types of earth on the edges of trousers, be capable of writing monographs on a dozen abstruse subjects and using his brain, as sharp as a gimlet, and as fast as lightning, to produce deductions of startling accuracy. These qualities we admire legitimately. The secret admiration and envy is for his indifference to women, his casual cruelty — not intentional, but springing from a nature not prone to emotion in itself and slow to realise its existence in others — his disregard for the conventional, and his refusal to do anything that he finds boring. A very great number of things bore him. His only true passions are crime and music. We do not, of course, desire to follow him into his deepest depressive troughs, nor the desperate tedium that leads him to the needle.

So, though a 'hero', he escapes the dullness of having to be a good person. He is allowed to behave badly because you are led to believe that without his faults he would not have his virtues. He is to be forgiven because of the brilliance of his brain, and cannot be expected to be as other men.

When you think of Holmes in visual terms, it is always the original Paget illustrations that come first into your mind. The tall, deerstalkered figure with the long sensitive fingers, aquiline profile, and the dark piercing eyes. Next probably comes into your head all these qualities in the person of Basil Rathbone.

As children, during the Second World War, my sister and I would walk to the Roxy cinema in the purlieus of Edinburgh to see the Sherlock Holmes films in which he starred. Some were full length (such as *The Hound of the Baskervilles*) and others were much shorter, occupying the slot of the B-film which always accompanied the main feature film in those days. These 'programmers' had been produced in the early forties, and had been subtly updated from their Victorian settings to incorporate patriotic and anti-fascist messages that fitted the times and inspired the audience to acts of heroism against the enemies of King and Country. I loved them. I thought Basil Rathbone the most wonderful actor I'd ever seen. Much, much later, when I played Sherlock Holmes myself, it was always he that I had in mind, try though I might to get out of his shadow.

By strange coincidence, I find myself, twenty years on (and too old for Holmes), playing Doctor Joseph Bell, Arthur Conan Doyle's tutor at the Medical Faculty of Edinburgh University, and one of his prime models for the fictional creation. It was Bell's brilliant displays of logical deduction for the benefit of his pupils, tossed off insouciantly with some self-deprecating introduction such as, 'I really can tell you almost nothing about this patient, other than...' and then would come the details of the subject's home-town, job, marital and financial status, and so on, all gleaned from that long first look at hands, feet and faces.

Holmes weaves his fascination yet. Hence this book.

Ian Richardson

Ian Richardson
London, April 2001

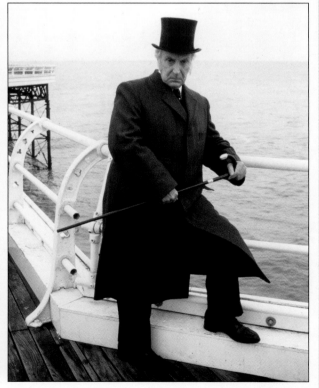

ARTHUR CONAN DOYLE

ART IN THE BLOOD

Arthur Conan Doyle is chiefly remembered as the creator of Sherlock Holmes, the world's first consulting detective — a character who leapt off the page and developed an independent existence in film, on stage, radio and other media. But Holmes was only one of the multi-faceted strings to Doyle's bow.

ARTHUR IGNATIUS CONAN DOYLE WAS BORN IN Edinburgh on 22 May 1859. His mother, Mary, was of Irish extraction, and could trace her ancestry back to the famous Percy family of Northumberland and from there to the Plantagenet line. It is little wonder then that the young Doyle was told tales of history, high adventure and heroic deeds, all of which were to be the seeds of inspiration in his later writing career.

The family was large — Arthur was one of ten children — and life was difficult for his mother, who struggled to bring them up on the meagre income provided by her unambitious husband Charles Altamont Doyle, a civil servant and sometime artist. Doyle's father was prone to bouts of depression, epilepsy and alcoholism that eventually led to him being institutionalised in 1893.

To help Arthur escape the depressing home background, Mrs Doyle scraped enough money together to send him to Stonyhurst College, a strict Jesuit establishment situated in an isolated part of Lancashire. It was here that he began to examine his religious beliefs, and by the time he left the school in 1875 Doyle had firmly rejected Christianity and embraced agnosticism. After studying a further year with the Jesuits in Feldkirch in Austria, Doyle surprised his artistic family by choosing to study medicine at Edinburgh University.

It was during his time at the University — 1876 to 1881 — that he encountered two professors who would later serve as models for his characters. Doyle was a literary beachcomber on the shore of life, collecting many things from his experiences to use later in his fiction. In his autobiography, *Memories and Adventures* (1924), Doyle describes Professor Rutherford with his 'Assyrian beard, his prodigious voice, his enormous chest and his singular manner', characteristics that

later found themselves assigned to the colourful Professor George Edward Challenger, the central character in his famous science fiction novel *The Lost World* (1912). More significant was his association with Dr Joseph Bell, whose method of deducing the history and circumstances of his patients appeared little short of magical. Here was the model and inspiration for Sherlock Holmes, and it is interesting to note that the first collection of short stories, *The Adventures of Sherlock Holmes* (1892), is dedicated 'To My Old Teacher Joseph Bell'. It has been said that Doyle looked upon Bell as a father figure, as he lacked one at home.

To raise money for his fees while at university and assist his mother with the upkeep of the family, Doyle took on many part-time jobs, including that of medical assistant in such locations as Birmingham, Sheffield and Shropshire. He even served as a ship's doctor on an Arctic whaler, another experience that provided material for his writing, in particular the eerie ghost story 'The Captain of the 'Pole-Star'' (1883).

After graduating, in 1882 he became a partner in a medical practice in Plymouth with Dr George Turnaville Budd, who had been a fellow student at Edinburgh. Budd was an eccentric and volatile man and the partnership soon disintegrated, leaving Doyle to pack his bags and set up practice on his own in Southsea. By this time he had already started writing fiction, but it was at Southsea that Doyle made a more determined effort to be published. As he slowly built up his medical practice, Doyle tried his hand at a series of short stories, later toying with the idea of creating a tale in which a detective — a character first named Sherrinford Holmes — solved a crime by deductive reasoning in the same manner as Joseph Bell. This idea materialised as the novella *A Study in Scarlet*,

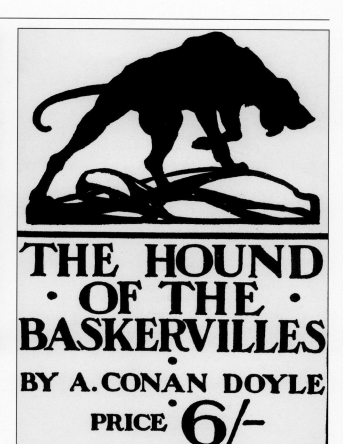

THE HOUND · OF · THE · BASKERVILLES ·

BY A. CONAN DOYLE

PRICE 6/-

GEORGE NEWNES LTD.

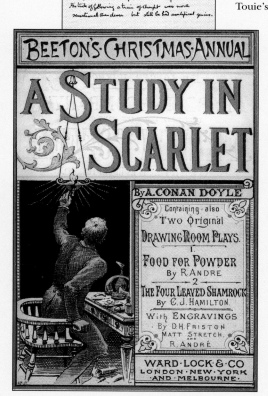

with, of course, Sherrinford becoming Sherlock, and thus a legend was born. *A Study in Scarlet* finally appeared in *Beeton's Christmas Annual* for 1887. Doyle accepted the meagre fee of £25 and in doing so relinquished all claims to the copyright. Meanwhile, in 1885, Doyle had married Louise Hawkins ('Touie'), the sister of one of his patients, but it was a union dogged by Touie's constant ill health.

Buoyed up by the publication of his detective story, Doyle now switched to historical fiction, his first love, inspired by the stories told to him as a child by his mother, and his admiration for the works of Sir Walter Scott. The result was *Micah Clarke* (1889), a tale based on the Monmouth rebellion. It was a great critical and financial success, and it was this novel that convinced Arthur Conan Doyle that his future lay in writing. The American based *Lippincott's Magazine* commissioned a second Sherlock Holmes novel in 1890 and he produced *The Sign of Four* in less than six weeks. However, it wasn't until 1891, when *The Strand Magazine* in London began the celebrated series of twelve short stories later collected as *The Adventures of Sherlock Holmes*, that the character of Holmes really captured the imagination of the reading public. It was Doyle who had approached *The Strand* in the first instance: 'It had struck me that a single character running through

a series, if it only engaged the reader, would bind the reader to that magazine.' And that is exactly what happened. Within six months of the first appearance of the Baker Street detective in the pages of *The Strand,* in the story 'A Scandal in Bohemia', the main selling point of the magazine was the new Sherlock Holmes adventure.

Despite the success of the first series of twelve tales, Doyle quickly became bored with his creation, and although he succumbed to the offer of an increased fee for a second series, was determined that this should be the last. He wanted to spend more time writing historical fiction, which he saw as a more worthy pursuit and one that would gain him greater recognition as an author. So in the last story of the second series (later collected as *The Memoirs of Sherlock Holmes* [1894]), he consigned his hero to the watery depths of the Reichenbach Falls in Switzerland, locked in the arms of the criminal mastermind Professor Moriarty.

Ignoring the public howls of complaint about his brutal murder of Holmes, Doyle concentrated on a wide variety of other literary projects, including *Rodney Stone*

Previous page (above): *The young Conan Doyle.*
Previous page (below): *The charismatic and inspirational Dr Joseph Bell.*
Top left: *Doyle married Jean Leckie at St Margaret's, Westminster, on 18 September 1907. Doyle's brother Innes (right) was his best man.*
Middle left: *The first page of notes for A Study in Scarlet featuring the early names Sherrinford Holmes and Ormond Sacker (later John H. Watson).*
Bottom left: *Front cover of Beeton's Christmas Annual, which featured the first Sherlock Holmes story.*

(1896, a tale of Regency life), *Uncle Bernac* (1897, a novel of the Napoleonic wars) and numerous short stories. It was around this time that he created one of his own favourite characters, Brigadier Gerard, a wily and comically pompous French officer serving under Napoleon. As with Holmes, Gerard first appeared in a series of stories in *The Strand* and then later in book form.

As Doyle's stature as a writer grew, he became more and more involved in public life. He was actively engaged in the Boer War (1899-1902), offering medical assistance at the Langman field hospital in Bloemfontein, and writing the history of the war and a pamphlet vindicating the actions of the British Army.

It was at the turn of the century that Doyle hit upon a plot for a mystery involving a spectral hound. Constructing the framework of the story with the aid of his friend Fletcher Robinson, the author realised that he needed a central character to play detective, and so resurrected Holmes for *The Hound of the Baskervilles*, which first appeared in *The Strand* in August 1901. The following year, Doyle was

successful) and similarly, he protested the innocence of Oscar Slater, a German Jew accused of murder. Thanks to Doyle's efforts, Slater was finally released in 1927 after serving eighteen years of a life sentence.

With the outbreak of the First World War in 1914, Doyle was instrumental in forming the local volunteer force — a forerunner of the Home Guard — and acted as a war correspondent, visiting the battlefronts.

Perhaps it was the senseless slaughter of so many young lives that revitalised his interest in spiritualism, for in 1916 he became convinced that he should devote his final years to the advancement of this belief. The decision was further strengthened by the death of his son, Kingsley, who succumbed to pneumonia after being badly wounded in the Somme. In the last decade of his life Doyle poured most of his time and energies into lecturing on spiritualism in Australia, America, Canada and South Africa. He was careful and thorough in testing mediums, but there were occasions when he was deceived.

Sherlock Holmes once observed, 'Art in the blood is liable to take the strangest forms.' He could well have been referring to the life and career of his creator.

offered a knighthood for his services in the Boer War — although many felt that it was more of a thank you for bringing about the return of Sherlock Holmes. In 1903 he succumbed to the offers of large fees from both Britain and America, and began writing more Holmes short stories.

Touie died in 1906 and Doyle married Jean Leckie, the real love of his life, a year later. It was during this period that he became involved in a personal fight to establish the innocence of a Parsee, George Edalji, convicted of horse and cattle maiming in Warwickshire. Using the methods of his detective hero, which helped prove that because of his very poor eyesight, Edalji could not have performed the savage attacks on the animals, Doyle effected his release from a seven-year sentence.

There were other causes that Doyle took up when he felt injustice had been wrought. Notably he campaigned to have the death penalty lifted from Roger Casement, a traitor during the First World War (though in this case he was not

These were seized upon by his critics to justify what they regarded as his credulity. Certainly in 1922, when he declared the famous Cottingley Fairy photographs to be genuine, he appeared naïvely gullible. Two Yorkshire girls claimed not only to have seen fairies in a watery dell near their home in Cottingley, but to have taken photographs of them as well. Edward Gardiner, a leading theosophist, was convinced of the photographs' authenticity and Doyle supported this view.

It was Doyle's obsession with spiritualism and his search for irrefutable proof of a life beyond death that led him into a brief friendship with the magician Houdini, who was also a spiritualist. The two men eventually fell out after a séance in which Lady Jean Conan Doyle, acting as a medium, apparently received a written message from Houdini's dead mother. As the magician's mother was Jewish and couldn't speak or write a word of English, Houdini denounced the séance as being false. The magician later wrote a mocking

MR. PUNCH'S PERSONALITIES.
XII.—SIR ARTHUR CONAN DOYLE.

article about it, thus widening the rift between the two men.

Following a lecture tour of Scandinavia and Holland in 1929, Doyle returned home exhausted, and suffered a heart attack. He never fully recovered, and died at his home in Crowborough, Sussex, on 7 July 1930.

Arthur Conan Doyle was a remarkable man in all areas of his life. His literary output covers perhaps a wider range than any other writer of the nineteenth and early twentieth centuries: he wrote poetry, plays, sea stories, domestic dramas, historical romances, supernatural chillers, medical tales, spiritualist tracts and, of course, detective stories. But as well as being a remarkable author, he was also a brilliant, energetic, innovative man with strong personal visions, attitudes and ideas — a Victorian with a twentieth century outlook. His passion drove him to pursue many activities: he ran for Parliament (unsuccessfully); he played cricket for the MCC, once capturing the wicket of the great W. G. Grace; he introduced cross country ski-ing to Switzerland; he had a keen interest in photography and contributed articles on the subject to *The British Journal of Photography*; and, of course, he was also a doctor, a title which he prized above all others.

With so many outstanding and fascinating qualities it is not surprising then that his most famous literary creation, Sherlock Holmes, was imbued with a similar kind of brilliance.

Previous page (above): *Doyle with Jackie Coogan, c1923.*
Previous page (below): *Denis, Lady Conan Doyle, Jean, Sir Arthur and Adrian in 1923.*
Above left: *Doyle with Eille Norwood.*
Top right: *Satirical cartoon in* Punch, *1926.*

SILENT SHERLOCKS

LIGHTS! CAMERA! DEDUCTION!

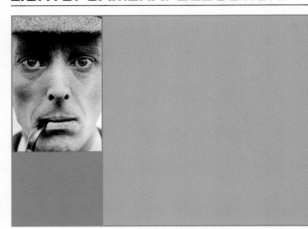

Strangely, Sherlock Holmes, the essentially English eccentric detective, was brought to the screen with great enthusiasm by foreign film-makers well before the British studios showed any interest.

SHERLOCK HOLMES BECAME A CINEMA ICON almost as soon as the movies were up and projecting onto silver screens. The first known film to feature the sleuth was *Sherlock Holmes Baffled*, made by the American Mutoscope and Bioscope Company in 1900. This humorous movie, which lasts less than one minute, is little more than an exercise in primitive trick photography. We are shown a dressing-gowned Holmes (played by an unnamed actor — probably a studio employee) outwitted by a burglar who has broken into the Baker Street rooms. Apparently, the burglar has special powers allowing him to disappear and reappear at will, a skill that baffles the detective — hence the title.

Sherlock Holmes Baffled is of historic interest not just because it is the first known Holmes film, but it also reveals that even at this early stage in the medium's development, the use of the name Sherlock Holmes was seen as a selling point. And so it has remained.

Holmes' second screen exploit came in 1905, and also originated from an American studio, Vitagraph. It is known under two titles: *Held for Ransom* and *The Adventures of Sherlock Holmes*. Lasting eight minutes, it was a great improvement on the previous film and claimed to have been based on *The Sign of Four*. The production also gave us the first screen Holmes who can be positively identified: Maurice Costello.

During the latter half of the twentieth century's first decade there were a confusing number of short Sherlock Holmes films. In Italy in 1908 Societa Anonima Ambrosio produced *Un Rivale de Sherlock Holmes* (known as *Rival Sherlock Holmes* in America), while in the same year in the States, Crescent Films, one of the rapidly proliferating but generally short-lived independent film companies in New York, came up with *Sherlock Holmes and the*

Great Murder Mystery. The plot appears to have been inspired by Poe's *Murders in the Rue Morgue* and involved a homicidal gorilla.

While Sherlock Holmes was ignored by his own country's infant film industry, movie-makers in Europe embraced the character wholeheartedly. The Danish Nordisk Company embarked on a whole series of Holmes films. This is a bewildering bunch of movies, with some titles also involving the gentleman crook Raffles, created by E. W. Hornung, Conan Doyle's brother-in-law. To add to the confusion, Holmes was portrayed by different actors throughout the series.

Viggo Larsen appears to have been the leading light in this venture, for not only did he play Sherlock in most of the films

of a large luminous dog, a strange spectral lady who brings death to members of the Baskerville family.

After releasing their final Holmes film, *Sherlock Holmes' Last Exploit*, Nordisk remained in Baker Street, but they tried to disguise the fact. Although the studio used Doyle's plot from 'The Adventure of the Norwood Builder', they called their 1912 movie *The Hypnotic Detective* and introduced their own master sleuth, Professor Locksley. Confusingly, Locksley was played by the studio's last Holmes, Holger Rasmusson. Then, in 1913, Nordisk featured Locksley in *The Stolen Treaty*, a lightly disguised version of the Holmes story 'The Naval Treaty'.

Meanwhile, the Germans had been working on their own Holmes films. Viggo Larsen had joined Berlin's Vitascope Company in 1910, and began appearing as the detective in a series of their two-reelers in which Holmes pitted his wits against Arsène Lupin, the French jewel thief created by Maurice Leblanc, a kind of Gallic Raffles, played by Paul Otto. There were five titles: *The Old Secretaire*, *The Blue Diamond*, *The Fake Rembrandts*, *Arsène Lupin's Escape* and *The Finish of Arsène Lupin*. Following the successful imprisonment of Lupin in this feature, Vitascope made *Sherlock Holmes contra Professor Moriarty* with Larsen as Holmes and Paul Otto, Arsène Lupin himself, as the Professor. This cross-referencing of actors must have been as puzzling as the mysteries for

but he also wrote and directed them. Other Holmes included Alwin Neuss, who was promoted from the Watson role, Forest Holger-Madsen, who had also played Raffles, Otto Lagoni and Holger Rasmusson. There were thirteen films in this series produced between 1908 and 1911, including such titles as *Sherlock Holmes in the Gas Cellar*, *The Theft of the Diamonds*, *A Confidence Trick* and *The Grey Dame*, which was apparently based on *The Hound of the Baskervilles* but featured, instead

Previous page (below left): Holmes (Alwin Neuss) is Stapleton's prisoner in the first Der Hund von Baskerville *(1914).*

Previous page (above right): Sherlock Holmes Baffled (1900) — the first Holmes film ever.

Previous page (below right): Holmes (Viggo Larsen) grapples with Raffles (Holger Madsen) in Nordisk's 'Sherlock Holmes in Danger of His Life' (Sherlock Holmes i Livsfare; 1908).

Above left: Otto Lagoni — a rather plump Sherlock.

Top right: Holmes (Alwin Neuss) is pursued in Ein Schrei in Der Nacht (1915).

Above right: Holmes (Alwin Neuss) gets due respect from the police in Nordisk's 'The One Million Bond' (Millionobligation; 1910).

Bottom left: Detail from a brochure promoting the Éclair version of 'The Musgrave Ritual'.

the cinemagoers of the day.

And then came the highly successful, long-running German series of *The Hound of the Baskervilles* — seven films in all — which constituted a protracted sequence of sequels and prolongations of the original novel. Alwin Neuss began playing Holmes, but as the series wearied on other actors stepped into his shoes. Stapleton, the villain in the novel, emerges as a man of great resource and resilience. He does not die at the end of the first in the series, *Der Hund Von Baskerville* (June 1914), he is merely imprisoned, but in the second episode, *Das Einsame Haus* ('The Isolated House', October 1914), he escapes from Dartmoor Prison and repairs to a strange submersible house. Holmes is not without modern science on his side either: he has a pocket radio to aid him. At the end of this instalment, Stapleton is both drowned and blown to bits but, miraculously, manages to challenge Holmes again in the third entry, *Das Unheimliche* ('The Uncanny Room', April, 1915). And so the series trundled on, with the last episode, *Das House Ohne Fenster* ('The House Without Windows'), appearing after the First World War in 1920.

In 1912 Conan Doyle sold the film rights

feature, *A Study in Scarlet*, appeared in 1914 and was produced by Samuelson Film Mfg Co Ltd. The film followed Doyle's plot very closely, but instead of telling the Mormon sequence in flashback as in the novel, the story was told chronologically, with the result that Holmes becomes almost a supporting character, appearing fairly late in the proceedings.

The sleuth was played by James Bragington, who was not an actor but merely a studio employee who resembled the accepted image of Holmes. His actions were closely supervised by director George Pearson, who told Bragington how to behave while the scene was actually being filmed. The American scenes were shot on the expansive flat beach at Southport in Lancashire, doubling for the Salt Lake plains, and the rugged Cheddar Gorge in Somerset, which represented the Rocky Mountains.

In 1916, the same company had another shot at a Holmes novel, *The Valley of Fear*, which starred the actor H. A. Saintsbury, who had played the role of the great detective over a thousand times on stage before making this movie. Unfortunately, like *A Study in Scarlet*, this is a lost

'The glamour in which our imaginations have enshrouded Sherlock Holmes cannot be captured and presented in a film' — *Kinematograph Weekly* in 1913.

to Sherlock Holmes to the French film company Éclair, although he did not involve himself personally in the productions. The features were filmed in Britain that year with an almost all-British cast, the exception being Georges Treville, who played Holmes. The eight films in the series, billed as a Franco-British production, were only very loosely based on the Doyle tales. For example, in *The Speckled Band*, Holmes, in the disguise of a wealthy foreigner, visits Stoke Moran, home of the dastardly Grimesby Roylott, to ask for permission to marry Roylott's step-daughter; and in *The Adventure of the Copper Beeches*, the detective only makes an appearance in the final moments to rescue the heroine. The other titles in the series, which were all released in America first, are: *The Musgrave Ritual, Silver Blaze, The Reigate Squires, The Beryl Coronet, A Mystery of Boscombe Vale* and *The Stolen Papers* (based on 'The Naval Treaty').

The first full-length British Holmes

film, but reviews suggest that Saintsbury had difficulty adapting his stage mannerisms to the more natural techniques of cinema. Perhaps that's why this was his one and only screen appearance.

Sadly, the period of the silent movie is also the great era of lost films. So many celluloid gems have vanished without trace, or the nitrate stock on which they were made has crumbled to dust. Another of these casualties is the 1914 *A Study in Scarlet* made by Universal Film mfg — the forerunner of Universal Pictures — which starred Francis Ford, brother of the great film director John, as Holmes. Francis Ford also directed, and his wife Grace Cunard wrote the screenplay for this two-reeler that claimed to be true to the novel. Indeed, Sir Arthur Conan Doyle's name and picture were used freely to promote the film, although it is most probable that the author knew nothing about the project,

Previous page (top):
The Éclair version of 'The Speckled Band' was only loosely based on Doyle.
Previous page (middle): *Holmes (James Bragington) examines a corpse in the British* A Study in Scarlet *(1914).*
Previous page (bottom): *William Gillette's Holmes threatens the villains in the gas chamber scene from the lost* Sherlock Holmes *(1916).*
Far left: *James Bragington, a studio employee promoted to the role of Holmes because of his gaunt features and penetrating eyes.*
Left: *Edward Fielding (Watson) and William Gillette (Holmes) attend to a distressed client in* Sherlock Holmes *(1916).*

WILLIAM GILLETTE 1853-1937

In 1899, a script for a Holmes play written by Doyle came into the hands of the American actor William Gillette, who liked what he read but thought some re-writing would improve the drama. Doyle had lost interest in the project by the time he received a telegram from Gillette asking permission to introduce a romance in the play and 'to marry Holmes'. The author famously replied: 'You may marry or murder or do what you like with him.' But, on seeing Gillette's final version, Doyle gave his approval, telling the actor that he 'had turned it into a fine play.' *Sherlock Holmes* opened in New York on 6 November 1899 and the success it received sealed Gillette's fate, for he was to appear in the drama with amazing regularity until he retired in 1932. In 1916, at the age of sixty-two, he made a film version of the play, but it was on stage that Gillette really excelled as Holmes. American critic Booth Tarkington summed up the feelings of many when he said 'I would rather see you play Sherlock Holmes than be a child again on Christmas morning.'

having sold the rights to the Holmes stories to Éclair.

A missing silent movie of significance is a screen version of the play *Sherlock Holmes* starring William Gillette, who became *the* Holmes for a generation of theatregoers on both sides of the Atlantic in the first three decades of the twentieth century. The movie was made in 1916, a time when so many stage personalities were being sought by Hollywood to recreate their famous theatrical roles and, incidentally, to bring some prestige and respectability to the 'flickers', which were still considered a bastard art form. The company Essanay shot the film in April 1916 and when it was released in May to general acclaim, one reviewer expressed

his delight that Gillette was able 'to leave in a comparatively permanent form his Sherlock Holmes for the delight of future generations.' No doubt this reviewer was unaware of the sad irony in the phrase 'comparatively permanent'.

Between 1910 and 1920 there were over fifty silent Holmes movies produced. (Reference will be made to those not covered here in the Filmography.) Upon examining the large output of silent Holmes movies, one can see that they fell into one of two camps: either they attempted, with varying degrees of success, to be true to both the character and the plots of the stories, or they simply took the basic elements of Holmes and set him in

completely new, and sometimes inappropriate, scenarios. Already Sherlock Holmes was reduced to being just a puppet of the film-makers.

It was the character Kathy Selden in the movie *Singin' in the Rain* (1952) who criticised silent movies as 'a lot of dumb show'. And certainly these early productions were just that. They robbed Sherlock Holmes of his greatest attribute — his verbal demonstrations of intellectual superiority and deductive brilliance. Flash cards were not the same and in general movie-makers kept them to a minimum. Therefore, in the silent Sherlocks, the detective became more the action man than the thinker.

EILLE NORWOOD

THE SILENT SHERLOCK

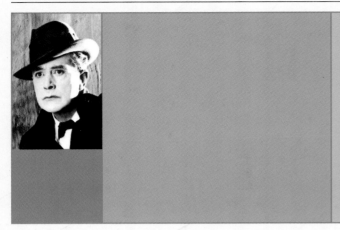

'Norwood had that rare quality which can only be described as glamour, which compels you to watch an actor eagerly, even when he is doing nothing. He has a quite unrivalled power of disguise' — Sir Arthur Conan Doyle.

THERE CAN BE NO DOUBT THAT EILLE Norwood was the silent movies' greatest Holmes. If only by the sheer volume of his output — starring in forty-seven titles in two years — he emerges as the champion. He was also a consummate player, and while not possessing the Paget-like gaunt, aquiline features, he convinced in all other departments, despite being sixty when he first played the role. His real name was Anthony Edward Brett, but he changed it for stage purposes to Eille Norwood — inspired by an unrequited love, Eileen, and his old address, in Norwood, south London.

When the Stoll film company embarked on a series of two-reelers featuring the famous detective in 1921 they asked Norwood, who had enjoyed modest success as an actor, largely on stage, to star. He took the challenge of playing Holmes very seriously, studying the stories closely, absorbing the various details of Holmes' mannerisms and dress. He even shaved his hairline to create the impression of the extra 'frontal development' associated with the sage of Baker Street. At first the director, Maurice Elvey, disagreed with Norwood's interpretation of the role, but the actor was insistent that his was the correct version. 'Let's film a scene your way, then mine,' he suggested to Elvey. On viewing the results, the director had to admit that his star was right.

While shooting the first two-reeler, *The Dying Detective*, Norwood made the following statement to the press: 'It is with no light spirit of bravado that I shoulder my responsibility, but with the full knowledge of its many difficulties. It is so easy to play the detective in private life, over the breakfast table and in the armchair — and so very much the reverse to play Sherlock Holmes on the screen. But I shall set about the task with a grim determination to work in earnestness, for success'.

His meticulous approach is evident in an incident which occurred early on during filming. Studying a script at home, Norwood had been horrified to read: 'Enter Sherlock Holmes in a white beard.' He protested strongly that Holmes 'would never have done that.' It was obvious that the film executives had little idea of the original Holmes character. When Norwood outlined his plans for disguises, the executives were dubious to say the least. Jeffrey Bernard, production chief at Stoll, told Norwood that it would be impossible for him to disguise his height and appearance. The next day Bernard noticed a small taxi driver standing on the set. As visitors were not allowed in the studios, he sent some minions to eject this interloper. The taxi driver protested in a strong Cockney accent and argued for several minutes until Bernard himself joined the fray, whereupon the taxi driver drew himself up to his full height and revealed himself to be — Eille Norwood. It was a *coup de théâtre* worthy of Holmes himself; and the actor had proved his point with great aplomb!

Norwood made three series of two-reelers (each film lasting about twenty-five minutes) between 1921 and 1923. The first series — *The Adventures of Sherlock Holmes* — contained fifteen films, each closely adapted from Doyle's stories. This was followed by a feature version of *The Hound of the Baskervilles* (1921), also directed by Maurice Elvey. Unfortunately, because of the fidelity to the originals and Elvey's unimaginative direction, these films tend to have too much 'dialogue', which affects the pace of the narrative. In particular, *The Hound* has a distinct lack of mood and atmosphere, and Elvey keeps most of the action indoors. Baskerville Hall is never seen in relation to its supposedly bleak surroundings, whilst forays onto Grimpen Mire suggest spare parkland or possibly early morning filming on Hampstead

Heath, but never a sense of desolation, of sweeping moorland and a treacherous quagmire. There is one touch of showmanship however: the film frames featuring the Hound itself are hand painted to create a luminous glow, ensuring that the spectral beast's infrequent appearances do carry a token shock value.

If the first series and the subsequent feature were regarded as a little disappointing, Norwood himself was con-sidered to be a splendid incarnation of Holmes, with many reviewers referring to his portrayal as 'an impersonation'. *The Moving Picture News* stated that 'Norwood *is* Holmes in countenance, personality and conduct.' Conan Doyle was also among the admirers and presented the actor with the jazzy dressing gown which he wore in most of the movies.

In fact, Norwood was so popular that he also played Holmes on stage in *The Return* of *Sherlock Holmes*, which opened at Princes Theatre, Shaftesbury Avenue, on 9 October 1923.

There were two more series of fifteen two-reelers: *The Further Adventures of Sherlock Holmes* (1922) and *The Last Adventures of Sherlock Holmes* (1923). These were directed by George Ridgewell, who also wrote some of the screenplays, but Maurice Elvey returned for Norwood's final celluloid outing, *The Sign of Four* (1923). For this, Hubert Willis, who had played Watson throughout the series, was replaced by the younger Arthur Cullin because Willis was regarded as too old to be romantically involved with Holmes' young female client, Mary Morstan.

It is interesting to note that all these films were presented as contemporary dramas. There was no attempt to reproduce the Victorian period, and so London was seen as a modern city with motorcars, buses and electric lighting.

Despite the short span of Eille Norwood's association with Sherlock Holmes — after 1924 he never played the character again — he nevertheless made a great impact on the general public and critics alike. Sadly, very few of his movies still exist and those that do are in poor condition. However, it is clear from these remaining fading strips of celluloid and the production stills that Eille Norwood was indeed a super silent Sherlock.

Previous page: Eille Norwood, the greatest screen Sherlock of the silent era.
Above left: Silver Blaze (1923).
Top right: Watson (Hubert Willis) and Inspector Hopkins (Teddy Arundell) view the precious pearl extracted from the debris of the smashed bust of Napoleon by Holmes (Eille Norwood) in The Six Napoleons (1922).
Above right: Holmes investigates in The Hound of the Baskervilles (1921).

EILLE NORWOOD
as
SHERLOCK HOLMES
in
SIR ARTHUR CONAN DOYLE'S
GREATEST MYSTERY DRAMA
IT'S AN R-C PICTURE
"THE HOUND OF THE BASKERVILLES"
DISTRIBUTED BY FILM BOOKING OFFICES of AMERICA

SHERLOCK HOLMES

UK title Moriarty
First screening 1 May 1922
Production company Goldwyn Pictures
Duration 136 minutes
Black and white
Director Albert Parker
Silent

At Cambridge University, where Holmes (John Barrymore) and Watson (Roland Young) are students, Prince Alexis (Reginald Denny) has been accused of theft. But the youthful sleuth establishes the guilt of another student, Forman Wells (William H. Powell), who, he finds out, is employed by Moriarty (Gustav von Seyffertitz) to spy on undergraduates with influential connections. On leaving Cambridge, Holmes sets up in Baker Street, devoting himself to the pursuit of Moriarty and helping 'the weary and mystery laden'. He has also fallen in love with Alice Faulkner (Carol Dempster), the sister of Rose, Alexis' fiancée who committed suicide when she learned she was deemed too common to marry the Prince. Alexis wishes to retrieve his love letters to Rose, which are now in Alice's possession. Holmes discovers that Alice is being kept prisoner by Moriarty's minions, the Larrabees (Hedda Hopper and Anders Randolf), whom he visits, insisting on seeing Alice. Once alone with her, Holmes declares his love and assures the girl that he will rescue her. Meanwhile 221B Baker Street is burned down by Moriarty. Finally, disguised as an old clergyman, Holmes traps Moriarty in Watson's office before setting off on honeymoon with Alice.

ALTHOUGH THE SCREENPLAY IS CREDITED TO Marion Fairfax and Earle Browne, the William Gillette play formed the basis for the latter half of the plot in *Sherlock Holmes*. At the time of production, the rights to the Holmes stories were owned by either Stoll or Samuelson, and the only major Sherlock property available for Goldwyn to buy was Gillette's play. The renowned stage actor John Barrymore merged his famous profile with that of the Great Detective to present a youthful version of the sleuth, which was a refreshing change after the pensionable Gillette and Norwood. Barrymore possessed a fine aquiline nose and dark good looks — rather like a tousled-haired Jeremy Brett — but he was not tall, so the rest of the cast were chosen carefully so as not to tower over the star.

Barrymore himself participated in the early pre-production stages with the director and Charles Cadwallader, the designer. In fact, his own sketches were the basis for the set representing Moriarty's underground lair, the brooding design and eerie lighting of which provides one of the picture's most memorable sequences.

Barrymore explained his approach to

as a weakness rather than a strength.

Other critics complained that the number of flashcards containing lengthy exchanges of dialogue slowed the flow of the narrative. In *America* Joseph Mulvaney wrote: 'Even with Barrymore concentrating until his brows became as corrugated as an accordion, the Great Detective could not get his stuff across to the spectators and the subtitles had to be made nearly continuous to let us know what it was all about.' Another reviewer observed that, 'There is none of the eccentric side of [Holmes] except that Barrymore certainly looks a bit extravagant when he runs.'

'If there is anyone who can successfully combine the story-book conception of Holmes with the hero of a romance it is John Barrymore' — *Mail*, 1922.

JOHN BARRYMORE
in
SHERLOCK HOLMES
Directed by ALBERT PARKER
Adapted from WILLIAM GILLETTE'S stage play founded on Sir CONAN DOYLE'S stories
A Goldwyn Picture

the character in the press at the time: 'My feeling is, that for film audiences scattered the world over, it is not sufficient merely to bring Sherlock and show him at work... to explain the conflict in the drama we are presenting, we desire to make it clear why Sherlock Holmes is what he his — to trace, in other words, his development as the Master Sleuth.'

At well over two hours' playing time and involving location shooting in England and Switzerland, *Sherlock Holmes* was a prestigious production, but it aroused mixed reactions upon release. One reviewer noted that 'despite Mr Barrymore and his co-workers, it is dull', while another observed that Barrymore 'thoroughly humanised the Conan Doyle creation' — a process which was regarded

Watson was played with great charm by Roland Young. Barrymore admitted that he was taken in somewhat by this 'modest, self-effacing' actor: 'I took a great liking to him; so much so that I began to feel sorry for him during our scenes together. For once in my life, I decided to be somewhat decent towards a colleague. I suggested a little stage business now and then, so that such a charming, agreeable thespian might not always be lost in the shuffle. When I saw the completed film I was flabbergasted, stunned, and almost became an atheist on the spot. That quiet agreeable bastard had stolen, not one, but every damned scene. The consummate artist and myself had been friends for years, but I wouldn't think of trusting him on any stage. He is such a cunning,

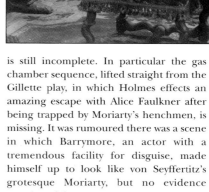

larcenous demon when on the boards.'

The film was released in Britain under the title of *Moriarty*. It was suggested that this was due to some obscure legal reasons, but it is more likely that the mediocrity of so many of the earlier Holmes films may well have been the deciding factor.

For many years *Sherlock Holmes* was a lost film, but in 1976 it was rediscovered. In fact what was found were rolls and rolls of negative sections, in which every take was jumbled out of order, with only a few single-frame flash titles for guidance. The task of reassembling the film in the correct sequence seemed an all but impossible one. However, with some help from director Albert Parker, whose memory of the movie was understandably vague, British film-maker and historian Kevin Brownlow did piece it together, replaced titles and made sense out of this celluloid jigsaw, although the newly-restored version is still incomplete. In particular the gas chamber sequence, lifted straight from the Gillette play, in which Holmes effects an amazing escape with Alice Faulkner after being trapped by Moriarty's henchmen, is missing. It was rumoured there was a scene in which Barrymore, an actor with a tremendous facility for disguise, made himself up to look like von Seyffertitz's grotesque Moriarty, but no evidence remains of the sequence.

Above left: Holmes (John Barrymore) and Watson (Roland Young).
Above right: The grotesque Moriarty (Gustav von Seyffertitz) challenges Holmes in his Baker Street rooms.
Far left: Location shooting in London.
Left: Holmes — licensed to kill!

SHERLOCK HOLMES

THE ULTIMATE HERO

Sherlock Holmes is the ultimate hero. He is both a thinker and a man of action, placing justice above the arbitrary infelicities of human law. Although the Victorian period is his natural milieu, he is a hero for all ages and remains a potent character in the twenty-first century.

THE FOG CLEARS FOR A WHILE AND, illuminated by the yellow glare of a gas lamp, we glimpse a tall, spare figure dressed in an Inverness cape and a deerstalker. In height he is rather over six feet, and so excessively lean that he seems considerably taller. His eyes are sharp and piercing and his thin hawk-like nose gives his whole expression an air of alertness and decision. His chin, too, has a prominence and squareness, which mark the man of determination.

This is Sherlock Holmes as Arthur Conan Doyle imagined him. A seminal portrait which was enhanced by the illustrations of Sidney Paget, who used his

Holmes proclaims that, 'Detection is, or ought to be an exact science, and should be treated in the same cold unemotional manner.'

Observation and deduction are Holmes' methods. Given an old felt hat, from which Watson can learn little, Sherlock Holmes is able to deduce that the owner is highly intellectual, was fairly well-to-do but is now poor, and whose health has been deteriorating, probably under the influence of drink, and that his wife has ceased to love him.

But Holmes is not merely an armchair academic playing detective, he is also very much a man of action, and it is through

'Men find Holmes fascinating because he is self-contained: women see him as a challenge — they want to expose the emotion beneath that icy demeanour' — Jeremy Brett.

brother, Walter, as a model, thus creating the definitive image of the Great Detective.

Initially, Holmes emerges from the Conan Doyle canon as a cerebral animal: 'I cannot live without brainwork, what else is there to live for?' His cognitive pursuits cover many areas: 'He spoke on a quick succession of subjects — on miracle plays, on mediaeval pottery, on Stradivarius violins, on the Buddhism of Ceylon and on warships of the future — handling each as though he had made a special study of it.'

Holmes is also presented as a man immune from the ordinary human weaknesses and emotions. Therefore he rejects such feelings as love and passion, since they would cloud his judgement.

this aspect that the potency of the character and the stories reach their full power. As Watson puts it: 'It was indeed like the old times when at that hour I found myself beside him in a hansom, my revolver in my pocket and the thrill of adventure in my heart'.

Holmes is physically agile and is, according to Watson, 'one of the finest boxers of his weight that I have ever seen.' He is an 'excellent' swordsman and singlestick player. Music is also a consuming passion. Holmes owns a Stradivarius — which he bought for fifty-five shillings in Tottenham Court Road — and is an expert player. He also writes monographs on a wide range of subjects

THE SIGN OF FOUR
Sir Arthur CONAN DOYLE

CONAN DOYLE CHARACTERS

SHERLOCK HOLMES DISGUISED

CONAN DOYLE CHARACTERS

SHERLOCK HOLMES

relating to his detective work, such as 'Upon the Distinction Between the Ashes of Various Tobaccos', and is a master of disguise, a skill that the cinema was quick to utilise. He cannot resist 'a touch of the dramatic', and after whipping off his disguise as an old sea dog in *The Sign of Four*, Inspector Athelney Jones observes: 'You would have made an actor — and a rare one.'

Sherlock Holmes is a Renaissance man then, but no really fascinating character is perfect. There must be flaws that enhance the charisma. Holmes' addiction to cocaine (injected in a seven per cent solution) has been well exploited in the movies, although his need of the drug does not spring from hedonism but simply the desperate desire to counteract the boredom of inactivity: 'My mind rebels against stagnation… I abhor the dull routine of existence. I crave for mental exaltation. That is why I have chosen my particular profession, or rather created it, for I am… the only unofficial consulting detective in the world. I am the last and highest court of appeal in detection.' As Watson notes on another occasion, 'Holmes did not rank modesty amongst his virtues.'

Holmes is a solitary man. Apart from Watson he has no friends, although he has an amicable relationship with his fatter, lazier and equally brilliant elder brother, Mycroft, who, when not acting on government business, spends most of his time at the Diogenes, a club for the 'most unsociable and unclubbable men in town.'

When Holmes met Watson in 1881 and they began sharing rooms at 221B Baker Street under the watchful eye of their landlady, Mrs Hudson, he was already practising as a detective. Watson, an ex-army doctor with time on his hands, began to accompany Holmes on his investigations, and his accounts of these adventures were published in *The Strand Magazine*. The pair became inseparable, investigating a series of bizarre and baffling mysteries involving deadly snakes, phantom hounds and stolen treaties. Inseparable that is until Professor Moriarty, the Napoleon of Crime and Holmes' nemesis, emerged on the scene.

On a ledge overlooking the terrible Reichenbach Falls in Switzerland, the two men fought, each hoping to end the other's life. As fate would have it, they both plunged into the roaring waters below. Or so Watson and the reading public were led to believe. In reality Holmes had escaped, and he took the opportunity to travel incognito around Europe and beyond for three years — even visiting the high Lama in Tibet. On his return to London, he nearly gave Watson a heart attack by appearing in the Doctor's consulting room, slipping out of his disguise as an old bookseller and announcing his return from the grave. And so the old firm set up again in Baker Street, until Holmes retired in 1904, and went to live on the south coast in a small cottage with a view of the English Channel.

Holmes came out of retirement briefly on the brink of the First World War when he and Watson captured a German spy. There is no record of the death of Sherlock Holmes. Indeed, how could there be? Surely, he is immortal.

Previous page (above):
Holmes as immortalised
by Sidney Paget.
Previous page (below):
Holmes looks down
from above the
Reichenbach falls in
'The Empty House'
by Frederick Dorr Steele.
Above left: Holmes in
'Black Peter' by
Dorr Steele.
Above right: Two of the
1923 series of 25 Turf
cigarette cards featuring
Doyle characters, drawn
by Alexander Bogulavsky.
Far left: Sidney Paget's
Holmes and Watson.
Left: The shooting of
the Hound of the
Baskervilles by Paget.

THE RETURN OF SHERLOCK HOLMES

First screening 25 October 1929
Production company Paramount
Duration 79 minutes
Black and white
Directors Basil Dean and Clive Brook
Silent/sound

Holmes (Clive Brook) is attending the wedding of Mary (Betty Lawford), the daughter of Watson (H. Reeves-Smith), when the groom's father is found murdered in his study. Holmes suspects poison after finding a trick cigarette case harbouring a sharp needle. Meanwhile Roger (Hubert Druce), the groom, is kidnapped. Acting on a few slender clues, Holmes rushes off to Cherbourg with Watson and Mary, where they board a liner for America. Holmes becomes suspicious of the ship's doctor (Donald Crisp), who is in fact Colonel Sebastian Moran. Using a variety of disguises, including that of a German musician who performs conjuring tricks, Holmes discovers that Roger is on board, being held prisoner by his old rival, Professor Moriarty (Harry T. Morey). A disguised Moriarty entertains Holmes to dinner and attempts to poison him using the trick cigarette case. Holmes feigns death only to revive in time to apprehend his enemy. To escape capture, Moriarty takes poison and vanishes over the side of the ship, whilst Mary is reunited with Roger.

Below left: Watson (H. Reeves-Smith), his daughter Mary (Betty Lawford) and Sherlock Holmes (Clive Brook).
***Below right:** Paramount on Parade: featuring Philo Vance (William Powell), Fu Manchu (Warner Oland) and Holmes (Clive Brook).*

THE RETURN OF SHERLOCK HOLMES marked the sound début of the Great Detective. However, as not all cinemas were equipped to show talkies at the time, reportedly a silent version was also made. The film was shot, according to the film's star, Clive Brook, very quickly and cheaply in a cramped studio in midtown Manhattan and on board an ocean liner sailing from England to New York. Apparently the studio had paid $5,000 for the use of the Holmes, Watson and Moriarty characters but was prevented from adapting a Conan Doyle tale. Therefore, it was rather mischievous of Basil Dean and Garret Fort, who wrote the screenplay, to interpolate ideas from 'The Adventure of the Dying Detective' and 'The Final Problem' into their script.

The shoot was a troubled one. Director Basil Dean's work had hitherto been mostly confined to the theatre and he had little experience of making movies — let alone taking on the intricacies of sound recording. He insisted on having four-sided sets constructed, to assist the actors in a feeling of reality, not understanding that cameramen and sound recordists could not operate effectively in such an environment. After many disagreements, Dean left the picture and Clive Brook finished directing it.

It was this production which started the trend for giving Holmes a much older and dimmer Watson in H. Reeves-Smith's, whose performance did not please the critics. *Variety* said: 'Too many "marvel-ouses" and "elementaries". And Doc Watson's enforced stupidity is too apparent.' These, of course, are all the failings that have dogged Watson's film career ever since.

In general reviewers liked Brooks' Holmes — although there were dissenters — but the film was given the thumbs down. *New York Times* critic Mordaunt Hall thought the movie was 'diffuse, complicated, unexciting and lacking in ingenuity'. One reader of *Film Weekly* was less restrained: 'The story was puerile, the setting was modernized… and worst of all Watson was given a daughter, so that the film might not lack "love interest".'

PARAMOUNT ON PARADE

At the time of Brook's *The Return of Sherlock Holmes*, Paramount was also enjoying success with two series of films, one featuring Philo Vance (William Powell), the dilettante American private detective, and the other Dr Fu Manchu (Warner Oland), the evil oriental mastermind. At the suggestion of David O. Selznick, they were included along with Brook as Holmes in a virtually plotless burlesque sketch — 'Murder Will Out' — in *Paramount on Parade* (1930). This was one of a number of revue features presented by the major studios at the beginning of the talkie era to showcase the talent they had under contract. Interestingly, William Powell made his screen début in Barrymore's *Sherlock Holmes* and was later replaced in the Philo Vance series by Basil Rathbone, while Warner Oland went on to play another great detective, Charlie Chan, in a series of B movies for Twentieth Century Fox. *Paramount on Parade* marks the only occasion when Sherlock Holmes dies on screen, shot by Fu Manchu. Perhaps it was a prophetic act, for Paramount did not make another Holmes movie for over thirty years.

THE SPECKLED BAND

First screening March 1931
Production company British and Dominion Studios
Duration 90 minutes
Black and white
Director Jack Raymond

Doctor Grimesby Rylott (Lyn Harding) has murdered one of his stepdaughters, Julia Stonor, in order to retain her inheritance. She died with the puzzling words 'it was the speckled band' on her lips. Doctor Watson (Athole Stewart), a friend of the dead girl's mother, attends the inquest, and his suspicions are sufficiently aroused for him to call upon his friend Sherlock Holmes (Raymond Massey) to investigate. Once his surviving stepdaughter, Helen (Angela Baddeley), announces her intention to marry, Rylott has to act quickly and, with the assistance of his housekeeper (Nancy Price), plans another murder. He forces Helen to move into her dead sister's bedroom because of some spurious building work taking place in her own quarters. Disguised as a workman, Holmes gains entry to the house and discovers evidence that convinces him that the girl is in great danger. That night, he and Watson stay in the bedroom and encounter the speckled band itself — a deadly snake that Rylott has introduced into the room through a ventilator. As the snake slithers down a dummy bell rope, the detective beats it with a stick, sending it back through the ventilator to attack its master.

Below left: Rylott (Lyn Harding) plots with his housekeeper (Nancy Price).

Below right: Watson (Athole Stewart) tries to persuade Holmes to attend the heroine's wedding.

THE SPECKLED BAND, STARRING RAYMOND Massey making his screen début, has the distinction of being the first British Holmes talkie. Producer Herbert Wilcox was determined to present a Sherlock Holmes for the new talking picture age, so the detective was given an ultra modern office with dictaphones, a typing pool of busy secretaries and an intercom. He even has a machine in his room that records conversations so that they can be filed for reference. The old Holmes simply scribbled notes down on his shirt cuff!

The screenwriter, W. P. Lipscomb, included elements from Conan Doyle's own stage version of *The Speckled Band*, as well as from the original story. Watson's involvement in the plot reflects that of the play: he was a friend of the Stonor girls' mother and thus it is he who brings the case to Holmes' notice, rather than Helen as in the story. (Also, for some unknown reason, when Doyle adapted his tale for the stage in 1910 he changed the names Stoner to Stonor and Roylott to Rylott.) Watson's

direct involvement with the plot is a useful device that prevents the character from being merely an onlooker or a comic foil: he is neither in this film. It is in the early scenes that Watson — a pleasant performance by Athole Stewart — establishes not only his level-headedness but also his courage in his ability to stand up to the villain's bullying nature. The bully in question, Doctor Grimesby Rylott, is performed in melodramatic fashion by Lyn Harding, who made a career out of playing villains. He had been Rylott in the original stage production, and later played Professor Moriarty to Arthur Wontner's Holmes in *The Triumph of Sherlock Holmes*. When he was in the stage version, Harding persuaded Conan Doyle to allow him to emphasise Rylott's 'neurotic nature'. This manifested itself in an over-the-top performance which Harding carried through to his screen portrayal. In particular, the famous scene from the story where Rylott visits Holmes in Baker Street to warn him off and bends a poker to demonstrate his

great strength is played with wild, barnstorming gusto.

While we have the benefit of one of cinema's youngest Holmes to date — he was only thirty-five — there is no light and shade in Massey's performance. He demonstrates no sense of excitement or urgency and exudes a perpetual mood of melancholy. This is highlighted in the closing moments during the film's happy ending, when Watson is trying to persuade Holmes to join him in attending Helen Stonor's wedding. Holmes says such an event is 'not my line.' Watson remonstrates with him. 'Rubbish. We all come to it, my dear fellow, we all come to it,' he says, and exits laughing. Holmes, staring miserably at the camera, replies, 'Not all.'

The hi-tech Holmes as presented in this movie pleased neither critics nor cinemagoers. *Picturegoer Weekly* stated: 'To try and modernise a famous character like Sherlock Holmes is asking for trouble. You cannot divorce Holmes from the period of hansoms and a Baker Street that is long past.'

ARTHUR WONTNER

THE CRITICS' CHOICE

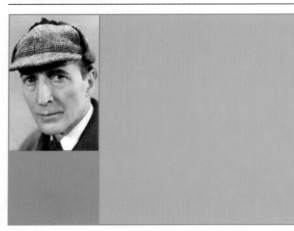

Although he starred in five popular Sherlock Holmes movies in seven years and was described by one film critic as the 'perfect Holmes', the actor Arthur Wontner is virtually unknown today.

Below: Arthur Wontner, a forgotten Sherlock.
Right: Holmes (Arthur Wontner) and Watson (Ian Fleming).

OF ALL THE MOVIE ACTORS TO PEER OUT FROM under the brim of a deerstalker and exclaim, 'Elementary, my dear Watson', none received more immediate acclaim from film critics and Holmes *aficionados* than Arthur Wontner. Vincent Starrett, doyen of American Sherlockian scholars, said of him: 'no better Sherlock Holmes than Wontner is likely to be seen and heard in pictures, in our time. Sentimentalised, as is imperative, his detective is the veritable fathomer of Baker Street in person. The keen worn kindly face and quiet prescient smile are out of the very pages of the book.' Conan Doyle's widow, Lady Jean, wrote to Wontner expressing her approval and delight at 'your really splendid acting… [and] masterly presentation of Sherlock Holmes'.

Arthur Wontner was born in London in 1875, only twelve years before Holmes himself made his literary début. He was first and foremost a stage actor but began appearing in movies in 1915. However, it was not until he starred as Holmes that he really caught the attention of cinema audiences. It was playing another famous sleuth, Sexton Blake — 'the office boy's Sherlock Holmes' — on stage in 1930 that helped Wontner secure the role of the Great Detective. A number of reviewers remarked on the actor's striking resemblance to the accepted image of Holmes as epitomised by the Paget drawings. These comments prompted producer Julius Hagen of Twickenham Film Studios Ltd to give Wontner a screen test in the December of that year, and he was duly cast as Sherlock Holmes in the company's forthcoming production, *The Sleeping Cardinal*.

In later life Wontner recalled some of the circumstances at Twickenham Studios: 'The studio wasn't much more than a big tin shed really, not like studios today. We used to start filming early in the morning and continued until pretty late at night with very few breaks. Of course we had to stop shooting quite often when a train went by, because of the noise. But we couldn't afford much time for retakes, and there were no elaborate rehearsals or anything like that'.

The movie was a great success, especially in America, where *The Bioscope* said that 'the poise and intelligence of Mr Arthur Wontner's characterisation of Sherlock Holmes makes it the most distinguished yet on screen, superior even to the interpretations of Clive Brook and John Barrymore.'

Over the next six years he made another four Sherlock sagas. While the quality of the films varied, as did their reception at the box office and by the

critics, there was always unanimous praise for Wontner's portrayal. As *Picturegoer* stated in their review of Wontner's third outing, *The Sign of Four*, 'Arthur Wontner is, as usual, a perfect Holmes'.

Time has not been kind to these early talkies and, viewed now, the series seems slow, with Wontner appearing rather too relaxed and avuncular. His delivery of the lines, while assuring the audience of the detective's intellectual prowess, was so casual that he failed to capture the quixotic nature of Sherlock Holmes.

While Wonter's last Holmes film, *Silver Blaze*, was made in 1937, he did play the character one more time — on radio. In 1943, approaching seventy, Wontner appeared on the BBC Home Service in an adaptation of 'The Boscombe Valley Mystery' with Carleton Hobbs as his Watson. Hobbs, of course, was later promoted to the role of Sherlock and became *the* radio Holmes of the fifties and sixties.

Wontner's portrayal of Holmes has now been eclipsed by that of Basil Rathbone who, metaphorically, was waiting in the wings. Today, the Wontner features are hardly ever shown on television, with the result that, sadly and unfairly, the actor who made such an impact in the role and was the 'perfect Holmes' to the cinemagoers of the thirties is now a forgotten Sherlock.

THE SLEEPING CARDINAL

US TITLE Sherlock Holmes' Fatal Hour
FIRST SCREENING March 1931
PRODUCTION COMPANY Twickenham Film Studios Ltd
DURATION 84 minutes
Black and white
DIRECTOR Leslie Hiscott

A bank is raided and a guard shot, but apparently nothing is taken. This is a cunning plan by master criminal Professor Moriarty (Norman McKinnell) who has arranged for the stolen banknotes to be substituted by counterfeit ones. To delay discovery further, the stolen money will be taken abroad by the Honourable Ronald Adair (Leslie Perrins), whose diplomatic immunity facilitates smuggling. Moriarty, hiding his identity by speaking from behind a painting of a sleeping cardinal, threatens Adair, who is a card cheat, with exposure if he does not agree to the trip. Holmes (Arthur Wontner) is sure that Professor Robert [sic] Moriarty, a master of disguise, is behind the raid and the murder of the bank guard, although Watson (Ian Fleming) and Lestrade (Philip Hewland) are far from convinced. After refusing to smuggle the bank notes, Adair is found shot and his sister Kathleen (Jane Welsh) is arrested. Moriarty now attempts to assassinate Holmes by shooting at him from the empty house opposite 221B, but fails and is captured by the detective, who reveals the villain to be a close friend of the Adairs.

Below: The effectively cluttered Baker Street sitting room with Holmes (Arthur Wontner), Watson (Ian Fleming) and the cheery Mrs Hudson (Minnie Rayner).

THE STORY OF *THE SLEEPING CARDINAL* claims to be based on two of Doyle's stories, 'The Adventure of the Empty House' and 'The Final Problem'. But in truth the screenwriters, Cyril Twyford and H. Fowler Mear, have merely snatched details from these stories to weave into a new plot of their own. We have the introduction of Moriarty from 'The Final Problem', and the Adair murder, along with the famous attempt on Holmes' life by shooting at his silhouetted form seen at the window of 221B, are taken from 'The Empty House'. The rest is original material. As well as changing Moriarty's name from James to Robert, the writers also made him a master of disguise. In the movie Holmes says, 'Oh, lots of people know Moriarty, but they don't know he *is* Moriarty. He has hundreds of disguises and hundreds of aliases.' This new facet to the Professor's character allows for the surprise ending, when he is unmasked and revealed to be a character who has hitherto been presented as an innocent and helpful fellow.

In many ways *The Sleeping Cardinal* is the best of the Wontner series, with Holmes' deductions arising naturally out of the plot and never going beyond the bounds of plausibility, as they tended to in the later entries. We are also introduced to the Baker Street regulars: the plump and coy Mrs Hudson played by Minnie Rayner, who appeared in all but one of the movies; the rather thick-headed Lestrade (Philip Hewland) and a dapper and vain Watson (Ian Fleming).

Released in America under the more dramatic title *Sherlock Holmes' Fatal Hour*, the film was a great success, winning the New York critics' Cinema Prize as the season's best mystery drama. The movie ran for over a month on Broadway — an unprecedented achievement for a British film in 1931. One American reviewer wrote: '[O]ne of the best of the English films to be shown on this side of the Atlantic. More than this, it is charged with deep suspense and excitement, and it is largely due to the poised and intelligent efforts of Mr Wontner that this is so.'

The only sour note seemed to be a mild dislike of Ian Fleming's portrayal, another in a long line of stupid Watsons. As one critic put it: 'Cast is up to par with the exception of Ian Fleming as Dr Watson who doesn't seem to fit.'

Regrettably, the American success of *Sherlock Holmes' Fatal Hour* did not benefit Twickenham. Warner Brothers, who distributed the film in Britain, didn't think the film was up to its own standard of production, so they sold the American distribution rights to First Division, a much smaller company, for the meagre sum of £800.

In Britain the film was released in March 1931, the same month as Raymond Massey's *The Speckled Band*, which it trounced at the box office.

THE HOUND OF THE BASKERVILLES

First screening July 1931
Production company Gainsborough Pictures
Duration 75 minutes
Black and white
Director V. Gareth Gundrey

The plot follows the main path of the Conan Doyle novel but within a contemporary setting. In a prologue we learn of the legend of the Hound which has haunted the Baskerville family for generations, before we move to Baker Street where Dr Mortimer (Wilfred Shine) asks Holmes (Robert Rendel) to look into the recent death, in strange circumstances, of Sir Charles Baskerville. Mortimer is also concerned for the welfare of young Sir Henry (John Stuart), newly arrived from Canada to take over the estate. Watson (Fred Lloyd) is despatched to Dartmoor to protect the baronet. While Watson makes notes concerning the various neighbours he encounters on the moor, including Stapleton (Reginald Bach) and his sister (Heather Angel), unbeknownst to him Holmes has also travelled down to Dartmoor and is camped in an old stone hut, watching events from afar. Eventually he is reunited with Watson in time to prevent the Hound from attacking Sir Henry. Holmes finally corners Stapleton in his house but, after a prolonged struggle, the villain escapes in his motor car. Driving recklessly in a desperate bid to get away, Stapleton careers over a cliff.

Below: The 'best actor in the film'. Champion Egmund of Send poses obligingly with the prone Sir Henry Baskerville (John Stuart).

THE SMALL BRITISH STUDIO, GAINSBOROUGH Pictures, in search of a sure-fire hit, conducted a poll in *Film Weekly*, a popular magazine, asking readers what kind of movie they would most like to see. There was overwhelming support for a talking version of *The Hound of the Baskervilles*. As this poll was conducted only months after the death of Sir Arthur Conan Doyle, during a period when the papers were full of articles about the author and his Holmes stories, one wonders whether this influenced the choice.

The project was placed in the hands of the young and dynamic Michael Balcon, who was to become one of the giants of British cinema, producing such movies as *The 39 Steps* (1935), *Dead of Night* (1945) and *The Ladykillers* (1955), amongst many others. The scenario was concocted by the director, V. Gareth Gundrey, but thriller writer Edgar Wallace, fresh from his chores on *King Kong* (1933), was brought in to beef up the dialogue and, to his credit, he attempted to introduce some of Doyle's original words into the script.

As with the Wontner movies, economy dictated that Sherlock Holmes would be a contemporary character — with no hansom cabs, period costume or gas lighting. However, this was the first production of *The Hound* to use real Dartmoor locations for its exterior shooting, with Lustleigh Hall near Hound Tor standing in for Baskerville Hall.

As if to emphasise the modernity of this version, Balcon engaged Robert Rendel, a rather bland actor who had never starred in a movie before, to play Holmes. It was a strange choice, for with his plump features and stout figure, Rendel looked nothing like the popular conception of Holmes. *Variety* recorded that '[Rendel] was far from the prepossessing figure of fiction'. But then this publication had little positive to say on any aspect of the picture: '[The film] was poorly cast, virtually none of the principals interpreting the Doyle characters as readers visualise them' and 'at times the film even seemed a comedy version of the famous story.'

Ironically, the Hound itself — a mastiff that gloried in the name of Champion Egmund of Send — was judged to be the best actor in the film, although *Variety* noted that 'it bounded over the rocks and walls like a big good natured mongrel rather than a ferocious maneater'. There was no attempt to make it glow like a phantom and its appearances were in very unconvincing day-for-night shots.

For many years this production of *The Hound of the Baskervilles* was regarded as a lost film. A print was in existence but it lacked a soundtrack. Then, incredibly, in the mid-1990s one was unearthed in America. Eventually picture and sound were married together to create a viewable film. In September 1999, it was shown to a gathering of the Sherlock Holmes Society of London at the Museum of London, and by the time the movie was into its final reel, the assembled Sherlockians were rocking in their seats with laughter at the preposterous shenanigans on screen. *Variety* had been right!

THE MISSING REMBRANDT

FIRST SCREENING August 1932
PRODUCTION COMPANY Twickenham Film Studios Ltd
DURATION 84 minutes
Black and white
DIRECTOR Leslie Hiscott

An unscrupulous millionaire art dealer, Baron von Guntermann (Francis L. Sullivan), is responsible for the theft of a Rembrandt from the Louvre. Commissioned to recover the painting, Holmes (Arthur Wontner) is also consulted by Lady Violet Lumsden (Jane Welsh), who is being blackmailed by von Guntermann over some compromising letters of hers. Disguised as a clergyman, Holmes visits von Guntermann's town house, but the Baron sees through his disguise and traps him in the vaults beneath an auction gallery. Von Guntermann believes Holmes is unarmed, but the detective opens the book of sermons he is carrying and pulls out an automatic pistol, allowing him to make good his escape. Holmes' next move is to burgle von Guntermann's safe for the incriminating letters, while Watson (Ian Fleming) waits outside in a two-seater getaway car. Holmes ultimately exposes the Baron for the crook he is and reveals the whereabouts of the stolen Rembrandt: with a sponge, he wipes a simple watercolour painting, uncovering the masterpiece beneath.

Right: The faithful Mrs Hudson (Minnie Rayner) attends Holmes (Arthur Wontner).
Below: Holmes, Watson (Ian Fleming) and Lady Violet Lumsden (Jane Welsh).

THE WARM RECEPTION GIVEN TO THEIR FIRST Holmes feature, *The Sleeping Cardinal* starring Arthur Wontner, prompted Twickenham to waste little time in preparing a follow-up, which arrived in the cinemas a year later. In fact, it was registered for release in February 1932, although it was not shown in British cinemas until the August of that year.

Although the screenplay is credited to H. Fowler Mear and Cyril Twyford, as was the first in the series, Arthur Wontner contributed much of his own dialogue to ensure 'Doyelian fidelity'. Supposedly based on Doyle's 'The Adventure of Charles Augustus Milverton', the story's slender plot is much altered and expanded in the film, so that little of the original remains, except the avaricious central character.

Directing duties were once again handled by the rather pedestrian Leslie

Hiscott, and several of the cast who had been seen in the previous movie returned, creating the sense of a movie repertory company. As well as Wontner and Fleming as Holmes and Watson, Minnie Rayner was back, playing for laughs as usual, as the blousy Mrs Hudson, as was Philip Hewland as the likeable but dim Inspector Lestrade. Jane Welsh, who had been the heroine Kathleen Adair in *The Sleeping Cardinal*, once again appeared as the female lead, playing Lady Violet.

Francis L. Sullivan, making his film début, was physically impressive as the Milverton character, Baron von Guntermann, but seemed less assured with his Teutonic vowels. As *Variety* noted: 'Sullivan, an Irish man with an English accent trying to do a German accent, is a bit hard on American ears.'

One of the young actors in a subsidiary role, Miles Mander, who played a broken down artist under the thrall of Guntermann, later went on to appear in several of the Rathbone Holmes movies, making a very impressive cold-hearted villain in *The Pearl of Death*.

Surprisingly, many contemporary reviews made mention of the modernisation of the setting. Of course, this was nothing new — all previous Holmes talkies and most of the silent movies had eschewed the Victorian period for budgetary reasons — and yet it still seemed to catch the reviewers unawares.

Sadly, *The Missing Rembrandt* is a lost film, and in judging it one has to rely on contemporary reviews, which suggest that it was not one of the best in the Wontner series. However, it would be interesting to see Wontner — not given to adopting disguises in his films — appearing as a hirsute clergyman and an old woman.

In *Picturegoer Weekly*, Lionel Collier wrote: 'Arthur Wontner *is* Sherlock Holmes and in this picture he is excellent, giving a characterisation which makes Conan Doyle's famous character "live" on the screen. Hiscott has, perhaps, failed to get much movement into the story, but this deficiency is amply made up by the excellent way he has directed Arthur Wontner, on whom the main interest is continually focused'.

SHERLOCK HOLMES

FIRST SCREENING November 1932
PRODUCTION COMPANY Fox
DURATION 68 minutes
Black and white
DIRECTOR William K. Howard

Professor Moriarty (Ernest Torrence) escapes from prison just as Sherlock Holmes (Clive Brook) is about to marry Alice Faulkner (Miriam Jordan), an attractive blonde whose father (Ivan Simpson) owns one of the wealthiest banks in London. Moriarty calls a meeting of the great criminals from all over the world, proposing to import gangster methods to London. In the meantime, Holmes is arrested for the (staged) killing of his old rival Inspector Gore-King (Alan Mowbray). The detective believes that if Moriarty thinks he is out of the way, it will be easier to flush out the evil mastermind. Holmes discovers that Moriarty's grand plan is to carry out a spectacular robbery of the Faulkner bank, with Alice and Billy the Page (Howard Leeds) held as hostages. In a climactic shootout in a tunnel under the bank, Holmes, in disguise as one of the gang, manages to dispatch Moriarty. The detective then sets off on honeymoon with Alice.

CLIVE BROOK TOOK ON THE ROLE OF SHERLOCK Holmes for the third and final time in this stylish production, but the actor was far from happy with the end result, branding it 'a terrible film.' He was on a long term contract with Paramount and was loaned out to Fox for this feature. 'I foolishly thought — Sherlock Holmes, fine! I'll do it,' Brook remembered. 'I didn't have a script which was unusual for me. I got on the set and began reading this thing and I discovered it was ghastly from my point of view, bringing it up to date with gangsters from America and Holmes engaged to that girl... The American director lacked any respect for Conan Doyle's characters, and ruthlessly introduced anything that he thought would be attractive at the box office. Nor had he any respect for the script, since he extemporised new scenes as he went along.' Interestingly, that script was written by Bertram Millhauser, who later became one of the regular writers on the Universal Holmes series.

The film's romance element, of course, was not new, having been taken from the Gillette play and introduced in several

previous movies. But the fact that Alice persuaded the Great Detective to abandon his dangerous life and retire to a farm to keep chickens was perhaps an infelicity too

would seem more appropriate to a Saturday matinée serial than a Sherlock Holmes mystery. *Picturegoer Weekly* observed 'the story has been brought up to date... and

'Old-fashioned artificial stage play with modern trimmings that only muddle it. The interpolated modern gangster angle will mystify the mugs who go for underworld' — *Variety*.

far for most enthusiasts. Similarly, the saloon bombings and gangster violence seemed at odds with the more restrained world of Baker Street. We are also presented with a Holmes who has invented a gadget that produces an electric ray to immobilise motor cars, something that

instead of incisive deduction and clever detail, there is all the paraphernalia of melodrama, with thrills of a popular order'.

However, despite these anomalies, the film is great fun, moves at a smart pace and is far glossier than its British counterparts. There are some beautifully composed and

CLIVE BROOK
1887-1974

Clive Brook was originally cast as the Great Detective in *The Return of Sherlock Holmes* because the producer David O. Selznick thought he looked liked the Paget drawings. Brook, along with most critics, failed to see the resemblance, but was happy to play the character: 'As far as I am concerned, Conan Doyle… made his Holmes larger than life; and that's how I played it and this permitted much comedy.' Brook was essentially a stage actor of the old school and in most of his roles he appeared as the perfect English gentleman, complete with rigid upper lip and rather priggish manner. He played Holmes in much the same way. Indeed, so stiff was his acting at times that one critic, seeing him playing the romantic lead in *The Laughing Lady* (1930), pretended to mistake him for the butler. Brook was not happy in Hollywood, likening working there to being on a chain gang: 'The links of the chain are forged not with cruelties but with luxuries.'

effectively lit shots throughout, none more so than a sequence near the beginning where George Barnes' smoothly flowing camera follows the guards as they race down the grim corridors of the prison where Moriarty is incarcerated. Eventually we reach the wall of a cellblock with a message scrawled across it: 'Tell Holmes I'm OUT.'

Clive Brook gained mixed reviews for his last attempt at Holmes. While one reviewer described him as 'a well nourished but otherwise engaging Holmes' another stated that 'Clive Brook presents a bumptious, obstinate character rather than a brilliant one.'

Watson was played by the versatile Reginald Owen, who a year later would swap his doctor's bag for the deerstalker and magnifying glass of Holmes himself in World Wide's *A Study in Scarlet* (1933). Owen's Watson has an insultingly low profile in the film, appearing in only two scenes, and serves no purpose by his presence except to utter absurd lines like, 'Great Heavens, Holmes! It is positively an ambuscade.' Owen was the third choice for the role, and the confusion over the casting may be the reason why the part was downsized. The character is treated shabbily throughout, failing to appear in the final scene to act as Holmes' best man because, as Billy the Page says, 'his wife's mother has had an attack of talking sickness.' Indeed, it is the obnoxious Billy who shares the most scenes with Holmes, which is a great pity, for the part was played by Howard Leeds, an American youngster who could not master any form of English accent and had limited acting ability.

Ernest Torrence, whom one

film critic referred to as 'a restrained volcano of hatred and violence behind a mask of obsequious innocence', proved one of the best screen Moriartys. *Picturegoer Weekly* stated that he gave 'the best performance.'

Previous page (right):
Holmes (Clive Brook) considers the prospect of running a chicken farm with his fiancée Alice Faulkner (Miriam Jordan).
Above left: Billy (Howard Leeds), seen here on the left, shared more scenes with Holmes than Watson did.
Far left: Holmes, disguised as an old woman, fools Moriarty (Ernest Torrence) and his associate.
Left: Ernest Torrence consults the script with the director, William K. Howard.

THE SIGN OF FOUR

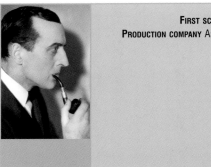

First screening September 1932
Production company Associated Radio Pictures
Duration 75 minutes
Black and white
Director Graham Cutts

The screenplay relies heavily on Conan Doyle's novel. Holmes (Arthur Wontner) is visited by a frightened Mary Morstan (Isla Bevan) who, alone in London after the disappearance of her father, Captain Morstan, has received a lustrous pearl from an unknown benefactor. Accepting the case, Holmes and Watson (Ian Hunter) encounter the eccentric Thaddeus Sholto (Miles Malleson), whose brother has been murdered. The detective then learns of the Great Agra Treasure which had been stolen by Sholto's father and Captain Morstan. Holmes realises that the murder was an act of revenge by an individual who was cheated out of his share of the stolen booty. The trail leads eventually to the one-legged Jonathan Small (Graham Soutten) and his grisly pygmy accomplice, Tonga (Togo), who are working in a sideshow at an amusement park. Small kidnaps Mary and the film climaxes, as in the novel, with a chase by police boat down the River Thames. The villains are killed and Watson eventually plucks up the courage to ask Mary to marry him. She accepts — a decision that Holmes considers, 'Amazing'.

Right: Wheelchair-bound Major Sholto (Herbert Lomas) reveals his secret to his two sons, Bartholemew (Kynaston Reeves) and Thaddeus (Miles Malleson).
Below: *Inspector Athelney Jones (Gilbert Davis), Holmes (Arthur Wontner) and his younger Watson (Ian Hunter).*

Shot at the new Ealing Studios in February and March 1932, *The Sign of Four* was the third Holmes movie to star Arthur Wontner, and yet it was not made by his usual production company, Twickenham Film Studios. Curiously, neither Wontner nor the character of Sherlock Holmes were under contract to Twickenham and so Associated Radio Pictures stepped in neatly and snapped up the star for their feature. Their presentation of Holmes was somewhat different, mainly because of the approach taken by the American producer, Rowland V. Lee. He stated at the time: 'Sherlock Holmes is to be a vivid hero, a tiger among men, a fighting detective, superhuman in every way. That is exactly what he was intended to be... Was the mighty Sherlock Holmes a man who simply played the violin and drugged himself when seeking inspiration? Not a bit of it.

He was a MAN! Humorous — what a sense of comedy; strong — look how he fought the great Moriarty; athletic — remember how he ran after the Hound of the Baskervilles. What a MAN! Sherlock Holmes has been pressed like a roseleaf in a book. Now I am going to make him the man he was... not the dreamy detective who spent his life back chatting with Watson'.

Certainly, the usually laconic Wontner does appear more alert and vital in this movie than in the previous two. He seems more energetic, actually indulging, for the first and last time, in a bout of fisticuffs with the villain. It was also noticeable that his delivery of dialogue is speedier, which caused one reviewer in the States to complain: 'The dialogue as spoken by the all-British cast is often unintelligible to American ears'.

Wontner was the only regular from the Twickenham pictures to be involved in this movie. Minnie Rayner, who had played Mrs Hudson with great comic charm, was replaced by Claire Greet. Ian Fleming was ousted from the role of Dr Watson because he was regarded as too old for the romantic scenes with Mary Morstan. The good Doctor was portrayed by Ian Hunter, a youthful thirty-two but, paired with fifty-seven year-old Wontner, he looked more like Holmes' son than his contemporary. It has been suggested that both Rowland V. Lee and executive producer Basil Dean (who directed most of *The Return of Sherlock Holmes* (1929) before his acrimonious departure) directed some scenes.

The film received mixed reviews. While some critics praised the evocation of the seamy atmosphere of the East End waterfront, others complained about poor lighting and photography. But, as usual, all critics were united in their praise for Wontner's portrayal of Holmes, with the *New York Times* classing it as an 'excellent interpretation'.

On its initial release in America, *The Sign of Four* was accompanied in cinemas by a short film entitled *Sherlock's Home.* This Vitaphone documentary, directed by Alf Goulding and written by Jack Henley, was a twenty-minute travelogue that explored the environs of London.

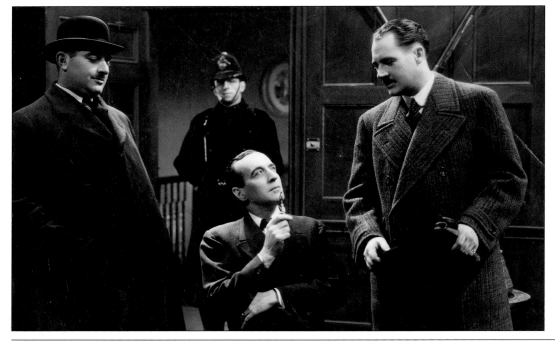

A STUDY IN SCARLET

First screening April 1933
Production company World Wide
Duration 75 minutes
Black and white
Director Edwin L. Marin

Merrydew (Alan Dinehart), a suave but crooked solicitor, is the brain behind The Scarlet Ring, a gang of jewel thieves who have all sworn to leave their estates to the surviving members in the event of death. With the assistance of the wily oriental, Ah Yet (Tetsu Komai), and Captain Pyke (Wyndham Standing) and his wife (Anna May Wong), Merrydew plans to murder the other members for their inheritance. Two of the gang have already been mysteriously despatched. Eileen Forrester (June Clyde), the innocent daughter of one of them, is invited by Merrydew to take her father's place in The Scarlet Ring, and he gradually involves her in his shady activities. The wife of the other victim visits Holmes (Reginald Owen) and Watson (Warburton Gamble) to seek their help. Holmes investigates and manages to save Eileen from harm by unmasking the murderer at an isolated old house. It is Captain Pyke, who had earlier faked his own death to escape suspicion. Merrydew, arriving too late to prevent the exposure of his plot, is arrested by Inspector Lestrade (Alan Mowbray).

Below: On the case in a low dive, Holmes (Reginald Owen, seated right) chats to the locals. Billy Bevan, a comedy star from the silent era, is standing next to the detective. He would turn up later in a minor role in Rathbone's Terror by Night *(1946).*

Despite using the title of the first Holmes novel, this film bears no resemblance to it at all. Indeed, while the plot is an original one, it includes elements from several of the short stories, the screenwriter Robert Florey seemingly having fun slipping Jabez Wilson, a character from Doyle's 'The Red-Headed League', into the melting pot. One of the motifs running through the film, a series of cunning little nursery-type rhymes, is similar to the device later used by Agatha Christie in her novel *Ten Little Niggers* (first published in 1939). The rhymes prophesy the death of another member of The Scarlet Ring: 'Six little black boys/playing with a hive/a bumble stung one/And then there were five.' Another similarity with the Christie novel is that the killer fakes his own murder, thus causing the suspicion to fall elsewhere. One wonders if the Queen of Crime saw this movie and was influenced by it.

Sherlock Holmes was played by the versatile British actor Reginald Owen, who would later add Scrooge to his gallery of screen characters. Having been promoted from the role of Watson in Clive Brook's *Sherlock Holmes* (1932), he threw himself into this venture with great enthusiasm, even being credited with 'continuity and dialogue'. In fact, Owen was hopeful that this would be the first in a series of Holmes movies starring and written by himself. While he gives a pleasing, studied performance, Owen's well-made frame and chubby features are far from ideal in representing the lean, hawk-faced detective. Trade paper *Kinematograph Weekly* noted, damning with faint praise, that 'It cannot be said Reginald Owen conforms to the popular conception of Sherlock Holmes, but his performance is not unsatisfactory'. The *New York Times* thought 'he was a good looking Holmes and speaks his lines with due reverence'.

Watson, played by the grandly named Warburton Gamble, is an older, slightly dim, insignificant character, contributing nothing to the main action of the movie. Sadly, this was so often the case with Watson in these early talkies. *Kinematograph Weekly* called Gamble 'feeble'. Similarly, Lestrade is presented as a pompous numbskull (as portrayed by Alan Mowbray, who had also appeared in Brook's

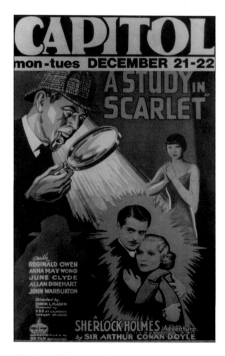

Sherlock Holmes and later turned up as Moriarty's henchman, Colonel Sebastian Moran, in Rathbone's *Terror by Night*).

The movie is filled with wry humour. For example, this whimsical interchange in the scene where Lestrade, stuck for ideas as usual, calls on Holmes for help. 'You come to see me professionally?' asks Holmes. 'Well… unofficially,' replies the Inspector. 'I see,' says the detective, 'heads you win, tails I lose.' Another amusing line occurs when Holmes visits the villainous Thaddeus Merrydew (a mixture of Charles Augustus Milverton and Professor Moriarty). Merrydew keeps the detective waiting for two hours because, 'I had to digest my lunch before seeing you.'

There is one very strange anomaly in this bland but nevertheless entertaining movie: Holmes' address is given as 221A Baker Street!

THE TRIUMPH OF SHERLOCK HOLMES

First screening February 1935
Production company Real Art Productions Ltd
Duration 84 minutes
Black and white
Director Leslie Hiscott

Watson (Ian Fleming) is visiting Holmes (Arthur Wontner), who has just retired to keep bees in Sussex, when the detective receives a note from an informant warning him that some dark deed is about to take place at Birlstone Manor. Then Lestrade (Charles Mortimer) turns up, seeking Holmes' help concerning the murder of John Douglas (Leslie Perrins), the owner of Birlstone, who has had his head blown off. Holmes is convinced that Moriarty (Lyn Harding) is behind the crime. At Birlstone, Holmes discovers that Douglas was a member of the Scowrers, 'a society of blackmail and murder' in the mining community of Vermissa Valley in Pennsylvania. We then learn in flashback how Douglas, actually the infamous Pinkerton agent Birdy Edwards, had, while working undercover, smashed the society — killing its leader, Boss McGinty (Roy Emerton) — and then escaped to England. Holmes explains that the dead man is not Douglas but one of Moriarty's men and that Douglas is still alive. Moriarty, who has been employed by the Scowrers to exact their revenge, then arrives. Following a confrontation, the Professor falls from the top of a ruined tower after being shot by Holmes.

Right: Ian Fleming returned as Watson to Wontner's Holmes.
Below: Moriarty (Lyn Harding) is apprehended by Holmes, assisted by Watson and the bowler-hatted Lestrade (Charles Mortimer).

THE TRIUMPH OF SHERLOCK HOLMES IS NOT only the most sophisticated and accomplished of the Wontner series, it is also a very effective retelling of *The Valley of Fear*, the fourth Holmes novel. In general, filmmakers have shied away from this story because it features a mid-section flashback set in America in which Holmes plays no part. This did not seem to concern Real Art Productions, which was actually Twickenham Film Studios, who had made the first two Wontner/Holmes features, under a new banner. The problem of presenting the great outdoors of the Vermissa Valley in Pennsylvania was solved by making them the great indoors: most of the American scenes were shot as interiors.

Moriarty, who is only referred to in the novel, is given an active role to play in the film, and in an early scene he even visits Holmes at Baker Street on the eve of the

detective's retirement. This moment relies heavily on a very similar confrontation in Conan Doyle's 'The Final Problem'. The film-makers may have overlooked the fact that there was also such an encounter in their first Wontner feature, *The Sleeping Cardinal*, four years earlier. Holmes regrets that he has 'failed to run [Moriarty] to earth', while the Professor wishes Holmes 'a pleasant retirement.' Obviously cinemagoers were expected to ignore the risible situation in which Holmes is apparently happy to toddle off to the country to keep bees while the Napoleon of Crime still flourishes as a criminal!

Moriarty was played with great relish by Lyn Harding, following on from his over-the-top Grimesby Rylott in *The Speckled Band* in 1931. Harding's very broad theatrical style contrasts greatly with Wontner's smooth, quiet delivery, but nevertheless it's a contrast that works effectively.

After missing out on *The Sign of Four* (1932), Ian Fleming was back as Watson. Looking and acting not unlike Charlie Chaplin's little brother, the character is presented as a figure of fun throughout. A good example can be seen in the film's running joke: whenever Holmes and Watson meet anyone new, Watson has to nudge Holmes in order to be introduced. Minnie Rayner also returned as Mrs Hudson, but is only seen briefly in the opening scene.

The screenplay is attributed to Twickenham regulars H. Fowler Mear and Cyril Twyford and, once again, Wontner was credited with his own dialogue, no doubt injecting the touches of sly humour that permeate the film. One suspects Wontner was responsible for this exchange after Moriarty has tumbled to his death from the top of the ruined tower: 'It's a long drop,' says Watson. 'Yes...' Holmes replies, 'rather more than is required by law, my dear Watson, but equally effective.'

The Triumph of Sherlock Holmes was generally well received by the critics, but as usual it was Wontner who came in for the greatest praise. The reviewer in the British Film Institute's *Monthly Film Bulletin* stated: 'the brisk American sequence is particularly effective — the photography is good, but the triumph is Arthur Wontner's.'

SILVER BLAZE

US TITLE Murder at the Baskervilles
FIRST SCREENING July 1937
PRODUCTION COMPANY Twickenham Film Productions Ltd
DURATION 71 minutes
Black and white
DIRECTOR Thomas Bentley

Holmes (Arthur Wontner), recuperating from overwork, is persuaded by Watson (Ian Fleming) to accept an invitation to stay with Sir Henry Baskerville (Lawrence Grossmith) on Dartmoor — it is now twenty years since the case of the phantom Hound. On arrival, Holmes learns that the racehorse Silver Blaze, the favourite for the Barchester Cup, has been stolen from a neighbouring stable and the horse's trainer has been killed. Jack Trevor (Arthur Macrae), the fiancé of Baskerville's daughter, is under suspicion and so Holmes agrees to investigate, believing that Moriarty (Lyn Harding) is behind the crime. To facilitate a betting scam, the Professor has been paid £10,000 to ensure that Silver Blaze does not run. Holmes tracks the horse down, and explains that the animal killed its trainer by kicking him in the head when he tried to cut the horse's tendon to stop it from racing. As Silver Blaze romps towards the finishing line, one of Moriarty's henchmen shoots the jockey, preventing the horse from winning. Holmes sets Watson on Moriarty's trail, but he is captured, and only rescued in the nick of time by Holmes and the police, who arrest the Professor.

Right: The injured jockey is questioned. Holmes (Arthur Wontner), with arms folded, remains aloof from the proceedings.
Below: The US poster.

SILVER BLAZE WAS WONTNER'S SWAN-SONG IN the role of Sherlock Holmes. Like many last entries in screen series, this film is not top drawer. Part of the problem lies in the attempt to adapt a short story for a feature-length movie, for despite the additions and expansions, the writers (H. Fowler Mear and Arthur Macrae — one of the film's featured players) could not disguise the slender plot line. Yet again Professor Moriarty was resurrected to be the criminal puppet master, despite the fact that we had seen him topple to his death in the previous film. One must also question the demotion of Doyle's criminal mastermind to horse nobbling. This activity seems far below the machinations of the character whom Holmes described as 'the organiser of half that is evil and nearly all that is undetected in this great city.' The Moriarty in this film, with his smart modern office and gangland heavies, is more like a second rate gangster.

In a kind of desperation, the script also

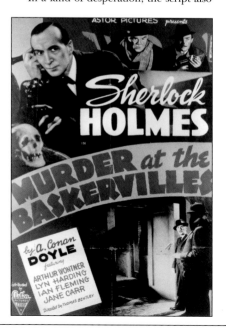

throws in Sir Henry Baskerville for good measure. This addition at least allowed the distributors to call the movie *Murder at the Baskervilles* in the United States, when it eventually opened there in 1941. No doubt it was finally released in the hope that it could bathe in the reflected glory of Rathbone's *The Hound of the Baskervilles* (1939).

In *Silver Blaze*, Wontner seems more than ever to emphasise the laconic humour that had become a trademark of his performance as Holmes. The detective treats Watson and Mrs Hudson (Minnie Rayner) with comic irony, but it is for Inspector Lestrade (or 'Less-trade' as Wontner calls him) that Holmes reserves his wittiest and most subtle put-downs. Lestrade: 'Any food containing sufficient poison can cause death.' Holmes: 'Can it really? I hadn't thought of that.' Lestrade: 'There are things in this case that completely baffle me.' Holmes: 'Really? You surprise me.'

But, despite these felicitous touches, on the whole this is a rather plodding affair, and while Wontner still gave value for money, he was looking all of his sixty-one years. The film's initial reception was not wholly positive. During the first London run of *Silver Blaze* in July 1937, a Friday night audience started to send the film up. A group who had, as the cinema manager commented euphemistically, 'dropped in after a good dinner', began to laugh in all the wrong places, and before long others began to join in. The result was that the film was removed from the programme for two days. The press reaction to the incident was indignant. *The Times* stated: 'It is hoped that the audience at the Regal will for the remainder of the week comport themselves with more respect when in the presence of the great man.' *The Bystander* was equally appalled: 'Nothing less than sacrilege… a miserable generation is growing up which appears to have no reverence for the immortal Sherlock Holmes.'

CONTINENTAL HOLMES

SHERLOCK STARS IN EUROPE

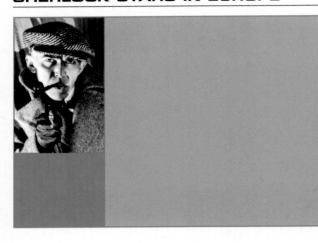

While British and American studios had, with the arrival of talking pictures, embraced the character of Sherlock Holmes with enthusiasm, producing ten features between 1929 and 1937, European film-makers, Germany in particular, had not forgotten the sleuth from Baker Street.

WITH THE DOMINANCE OF HOLLYWOOD AND the British studios in the years following the First World War, it is easy to forget that most developed countries had a cinema industry. Their output may not have been prolific or polished, but often it was as entertaining as anything America or Britain had to offer. And Sherlock Holmes, a character, it seems, whose appeal knows no boundaries or frontiers, remained a potent cinematic icon in Europe at this time.

In 1932, Czechoslovakia's Elekta Films produced *Lelicek Ve Sluzbach Sherlocka Holmese* ('Lelicek in the Service of Sherlock Holmes'). Directed by Karel Lamac and written by Vaclav Wasserman, it starred Martin Fric as Holmes and Vlasta Burian as

the secret agent Lelicek, whom the detective despatches on a mission to investigate a scandal at the Puerto Rican royal palace. The bulk of this seventy-five minute movie is taken up with Lelicek's adventures, and Holmes plays no significant role in the plot, appearing only briefly at the beginning. It is as though the producers used the detective's name merely as a marquee attraction, emphasising once again the international appeal of the character. Watson does not feature at all.

Germany had always shown a keen interest in Doyle's detective and produced three Sherlock Holmes features in 1937. This is somewhat surprising, for at this time the German film industry was under strict

Nazi control and heavily influenced by Goebbels' propaganda machine. To feature a free-spirited bohemian character like Sherlock Holmes in their movies seems very much at odds with the narrow dictatorial philosophy of the Hitler regime.

Der Hund Von Baskerville, an Ondra-Lamac-Film G.m.b.H production starring Bruno Guttner as Holmes and Fritz Odemar as Watson, was released in January 1937. Directed by Karel Lamac, who had worked on the earlier Czech movie, *Der Hund* was very much a modern Germanic interpretation of the Doyle story, with a rather humourless Holmes costumed in a flat cap, leather overcoat and a polo-necked jersey, packing a gun. The Baskervilles lived in a large castle rather than a modest manor house, and there seemed to be an underlying message within the movie concerning the decadence of the British aristocracy. This version of *The Hound* has the dubious distinction of being a favourite with Adolf Hitler, who had a print of it in his private collection — it was found in Berchtesgarden in 1945.

Released one month later was Neue Film KG's *Sherlock Holmes: Die Graue Dame* ('Sherlock Holmes: The Grey Lady'), produced and directed by Erich Engels, and written by Engels and Hans Heur. This ninety-minute film was not based on any Doyle story, but rather on a play by Muller-Puzika called *The Dead of the Unknown*, which did not feature Sherlock Holmes at all. The title of this movie, however, suggests that it may have been inspired, at least in part, by the Nordisk film of the same title made in 1909. The Germanic influence was felt once more in the interpretation of Holmes, for despite its British setting, he turns out to be working hand in hand with the Geheimpolizei, an organisation akin to the Gestapo, thus transforming the bourgeois independent detective of Baker Street into a cunning

secret policeman. This anomaly is compounded by another: Doctor Watson is absent from the movie, but Holmes is attended by a servant called John. Hermann Speelmans as Sherlock was somewhat plump and visually a far cry from the Paget drawings.

The third German offering in 1937 was *Der Mann, der Sherlock Holmes War* ('The Man Who Was Sherlock Holmes'), produced by UFA, directed by Karl Hartl, and written by Hartl and by R. A. Stemmle. This is essentially a comedy film featuring Hans Albers and Heinz Rühmann as two incompetent detectives who, because they are failing to attract clients, decide to dress and act like Sherlock Holmes and Doctor Watson in the hope that this will boost business. It does, but, although they fool many people with their charade, at various points in the story they keep running into one individual who knows that they are really impostors. At the end of the film this character, played by Paul Bildt — who is billed in the credits as The Man Who Laughed — reveals himself to be none other than Sir Arthur Conan Doyle.

The film is set in Paris during the 1936 World Exposition, where Mary and Jane Berry, daughters of the recently deceased Professor Berry, have just learned that their sole inheritance, a priceless Mauritius stamp, is a forgery. 'Sherlock' gallantly steps in to help, but, in his search for the real stamp, is arrested and ends up as the defendant in a trial that is the sensation of Paris. The charge against him: impersonating Sherlock Holmes! The climactic trial is as dramatic as it is amusing, and is fondly thought of by Sherlockian film enthusiasts.

Variety sent a correspondent resident in Berlin to review the film. He liked it, noting, 'it was chockfull of thrills and complications,' and saying of the star, 'It would be hard to find a face anywhere so suited to the role of Sherlock Holmes.'

Hans Albers was one of the greatest players in the German cinema, and was regarded as a kind of Teutonic Clark Gable at the time. Siegfried Kracaeur, in his psychological study of German film, *From Caligari to Hitler*, regards Albers as personifying the underlying theme of the German cinema of the thirties: that everyday life is a fairy tale. 'The Man Who Was Sherlock Holmes' seems to bear out this assertion very well.

THE HOUND OF THE BASKERVILLES

FIRST SCREENING 31 March 1939
PRODUCTION COMPANY Twentieth Ce ntury Fox
DURATION 80 minutes
Black and white
DIRECTOR Sidney Lanfield

In 1650 the wicked Sir Hugo Baskerville was attacked and killed by a great black beast out on the moors. Since that time all the members of the Baskerville family have met violent ends, the most recent being Sir Charles, whose death leaves the estate to young Sir Henry (Richard Greene). Doctor Mortimer (Lionel Atwill), a family friend, is worried about the welfare of the young baronet just arrived from Canada, and secures the services of Holmes (Basil Rathbone) and Watson (Nigel Bruce) to look after his safety. Watson travels down to Baskerville Hall with Sir Henry, while Holmes makes his way there secretly, camping on the moor disguised as an old beggar. Sir Henry encounters his near neighbours, Stapleton (Morton Lowry) and his sister Beryl (Wendy Barrie), with whom he falls in love. Meanwhile, the butler Barryman (John Carradine) has been leaving food and clothes for Selden, an escaped convict hiding on the moor. Watson challenges the butler, and learns that Selden is Mrs Barryman's brother. While wearing Sir Henry's old clothes, the convict is killed by the hound. Holmes now reveals his presence and, with Watson, foils the attempt to kill Sir Henry. The Hound is shot and the murderer is arrested.

PROBABLY STILL THE BEST OF THE MANY versions of *The Hound*, this classic production is an impressively mounted and energised Gothic romance, with Ernest Pascal's literate and focused script remaining respectfully close to the original story. It was also the first Sherlockian film to attempt to recreate the Victorian period and place the detective in his true milieu. However, there is a sequence not in the novel, featuring a seance in which Mrs Mortimer (Beryl Mercer), in a trance-like state, attempts to get in touch with the dead Sir Charles to find out, 'What happened that night on the moor.' The only reply is the low eerie howl of a hound, far out in the distance. This scene enhances the mood of supernatural foreboding and menace which effectively permeates the whole film. The sense that the powers of rational man are threatened in this godforsaken part of England is remarkably potent in this movie and contributes greatly to its effectiveness. This aspect of the story is so often neglected by film-makers, many of whom seem to forget about the phantom Hound until the last

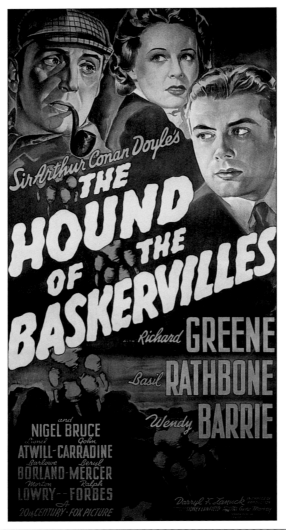

place of mystery. No wonder the people hereabout have such odd beliefs. Some will tell you that nothing ever really dies on the moor, and after a time one gets to believe it'.

Sherlock Holmes has some fine original dialogue too. When he is discussing the ingenious use of a hound as a means of murder, he observes: 'That's why so many murders remain unsolved, Watson. People will stick to the facts, even though they prove nothing. Now if we go beyond facts and use our imagination as the criminal does, imagine what might have happened, act upon it as I've been trying to do in this case, we usually find ourselves justified.'

Holmes' deductions are pertinent and credible and he does not have to resort to his seven per cent solution of cocaine

'That dark knife blade-face and snapping mouth,' an eager face 'wearing an expression of high-strung energy' — Graham Greene on Basil Rathbone as Sherlock Holmes.

moment, when it is brought in for Holmes to shoot. In this version, we are constantly aware of its evil presence, and that perhaps, the brilliant and infallible detective may at last have met his match, out on the moor.

When Sir Henry receives his first glimpse of Dartmoor — a vast and impressive interior set — Dr Mortimer says, 'See over there... beyond that hill... those dark spots. That's the great Grimpen Mire. As treacherous a morass as exists anywhere. Thousands of lives have been sucked down into its bottomless depth. The moor is a

during the action. The first and last mention of his addiction comes in the final line of the film. Leaving the Baskerville Hall drawing room for his own chamber, after announcing that he is fatigued by his exertions, Holmes calls back to his associate: 'Quick, Watson, the needle.' Considering Hollywood's strict Production Code at the time, the line was rather a bold inclusion, and on the film's initial release it was removed from the soundtrack. This reference to the detective's drug habit was one reason why this movie wasn't shown on

British television until the 1970s.

Because of the scarcity of potential suspects in the original story, Doctor Mortimer is presented as a sinister figure with pebble glasses and a black beard, giving Lionel Atwill a marvellous red-herring role, much favoured with low key close-ups. Beryl, Stapleton's wife in the novel, becomes his sister in order to make her a more respectable romantic partner for Sir Henry Baskerville, played by a very young Richard Greene in an early Hollywood role. Incidentally, Greene received star billing above Rathbone and Bruce, making this the first time an actor starring as Holmes was not headlining a movie.

Others in the impressive, largely British, cast include Mary Gordon, who played Mrs Hudson (a role she would repeat in future years) with a soft Scottish burr, and John Carradine as Barryman, the butler (the name was changed from Barrymore because it was thought it might be confused with the famous acting family). The American Carradine was not too happy about playing the role of the butler: 'They made me wear a beard to look sinister. Of course no English butler ever wore a beard. But it was for the audience to say 'He did it! He did it!' as soon as they saw me. But I didn't: I was only the red herring. Movies sometime use me just for that purpose.' Of course, the character of Barrymore in the novel does in fact have a large black beard, which is crucial to one of Holmes' deductions.

Morton Lowry, an English actor based in Hollywood, played the villain Stapleton with a smooth, almost effeminate charm. It is a

Above left: The cosy Baker Street rooms. A posed shot with Watson (Nigel Bruce) examining a stick a visitor has left behind, observed by Holmes (Basil Rathbone) and Mrs Hudson (Mary Gordon).
Above right: Beryl Stapleton (Wendy Barrie).
Left: Holmes is introduced to the new Baskerville heir (Richard Greene) by Dr Mortimer (Lionel Atwill).

difficult role to play because for the most part the character has to seem appealing while also being fairly insignificant. This was Lowry's most important role and his career faded after this film. He later appeared in a bit part in one of the Universal Holmes pictures, *Pursuit to Algiers*.

The hound itself is shown without any kind of 'spectral' phosphorous adornment and the emphasis is placed on the fact that it is a real, ferocious dog — which it is: a gigantic 140 pound Great Dane called Chief was used, and is genuinely frightening on screen.

The movie's most surprising aspect is the lack of background music, which would have added to the atmosphere and tension, such as the scene near the climax, where Holmes is tracking down the murderer. The detective moves silently across the spookily gothic mist-enshrouded expanses of the Devonshire moorland, an image enhanced by the use of barely perceptible gauzes over the camera lens.

The moorland set was quite amazing, stretching 300 feet by 200 feet, strewn with boulders and dotted with weird skeletal trees. Smoke machines provided the rolling layers of ever-present fog. In fact, the set was so big that Richard Greene once got lost on it! Frank Nugent, writing in the *New York Times*, felt 'the technicians have whipped up a moor at least as desolate as any ghost-story moor has need to be, the mist swirls steadily, the savage howl of the Baskerville hound is heard at all the melodramatically appropriate intervals... '

Rathbone was never better as Holmes. He kept his interpretation under firm control. There was a total lack of smugness, which marred Brook's and Wontner's portrayals and, indeed, later his own. Even when he appears in disguise as the old pedlar, trying to sell Watson 'a whistle to call your sheepdog', he holds the characterisation within the bounds of reality. This Holmes was an alert, energetic, capricious and sardonic animal, played by the great Rathbone with consummate flair and authority. The actor noted in his autobiography that, 'Of all the 'adventures' *The Hound* is my favourite story, and it was in this picture that I had the stimulating experience of creating, within my own limited framework, a character that has intrigued me as much as any I have ever played.' Hearst newspaper critic, Rose Pelwick, wrote of Rathbone: 'Smoking the traditional pipe and playing the violin, but otherwise making the character credible rather than eccentric, Mr Rathbone is vastly superior to the previous screen impersonators of the Baker Street genius.'

And it was good to see Sherlock Holmes in a deerstalker once again, after the series of trilbys and fedoras worn by the other Holmes of the thirties. It is not given to every actor to be able to wear a deerstalker with style, but Rathbone looked as though he'd just been sketched by Sidney Paget.

Nigel Bruce as Watson hadn't yet succumbed to the excesses he later demonstrated while playing the role. With his hair and moustache darkened to good effect, he looks like a contemporary of Holmes and appears to be a reasonably believable companion for his brilliant detective friend. While never the Watson of Doyle's conception, he played the part with great charm, raising the profile of the cinematic Watson in the process.

The film was an immediate success. 'The Americans have done right by Conan Doyle', was one British critic's view, while *Kinematograph Weekly* commented: 'It's a grand Sherlock Holmes.' What seemed to please and impress was that the authenticity of the movie was a refreshing change after Brook's and Wontner's

modern Holmes. Graham Greene wrote in *The Spectator*: 'In this new film Holmes is undoubtedly Holmes, and he hasn't to compete desperately with telephones and high speed cars and 1939. The atmosphere of unmechanical Edwardian flurry is well caught: the villain bowls recklessly along Baker Street in a hansom and our hero discusses plans for action in a four wheeler.'

Frank Nugent in the *New York Times* was similarly effulgent: 'the film succeeds rather well in reproducing Sir Arthur's macabre detective story along forthright cinema lines.'

It is amusing to relate how *Motion Picture Herald* saw the film's selling points: 'The obvious exploitation cue is for a strong campaign addressed to the millions who have read the book and such others who have not got round to reading it, but have meant to for some time, and now under the circumstances needn't.'

For whatever motive the millions had for going to see *The Hound of the Baskervilles*, see it they did, making it one of the most successful films released in the first half of 1939.

Previous page (above right): Holmes and Watson discover the body of Selden (Nigel DeBrulier), the escaped convict.
Previous page (below left): Holmes in disguise as an old limping pedlar.
Above left: Holmes and butler Barryman (John Carradine) stand by as Mrs Barryman (Eily Malyon) confesses to Sir Henry that Selden is her brother.
Left: The Hound attacks! The 140 pound Great Dane Chief was truly frightening on screen.

BASIL RATHBONE

THE IDEAL HOLMES

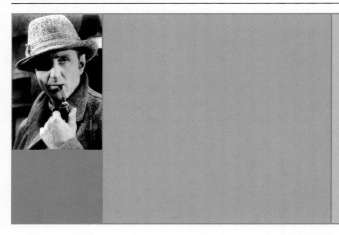

'Ever since I was a boy and first got acquainted with the Great Detective I wanted to be like him... To play such a character means as much to me as ten Hamlets!' — Basil Rathbone.

ONCE DESCRIBED BY DOROTHY PARKER AS 'TWO profiles pasted together', Basil Rathbone not only became *the* Sherlock Holmes of his generation, but for several generations after. Indeed, for many, he remains the ideal Sherlock Holmes.

Rathbone was born in Johannesburg, South Africa, in 1892, but was educated in England at Repton College. At the age of eighteen, he began work as an insurance agent, but his desire to become an actor led him to join Sir Frank Benson's touring company in 1911. He made his stage début at Ipswich playing Hortensio in *The Taming of the Shrew*. However, the First World War interrupted his career, and as an officer in the Liverpool-Scottish Regiment he was awarded the Military Cross.

His screen début came in 1921, in the British film *Innocent*, directed by Maurice Elvey, who worked on most of Eille Norwood's Holmes two-reelers at around the same time. In the mid-twenties Rathbone journeyed to America, where he settled and spent the rest of his life. Although he worked sporadically in silent pictures, it wasn't until the arrival of the talkies, which utilised his beautiful crisp speaking voice, that he really made his mark.

During the thirties he appeared in supporting roles in some of the great films of the decade: *Anna Karenina* (1935), *David Copperfield* (1935), *Captain Blood* (1935), an Oscar-nominated Tybalt in *Romeo and Juliet* (1936) and *The Adventures of Robin Hood* (1938). And then in 1939 he was chosen to play the famous Baker Street detective — a casting that would leave an indelible mark on cinema history. Allegedly, it all started at a Hollywood party: Darryl Zanuck (production executive), Gregory Ratoff (director) and Gene Markey (screenwriter) were discussing various new properties, when one said, 'Somebody should do these damned Sherlock Holmes stories.' Another asked: 'Whom would you get to play Holmes?' 'Whom else, but Basil Rathbone.' None of the trio was quite sure who made the fateful utterance, but within months of the conversation Rathbone was introduced to both moviegoers and radio listeners as Sherlock Holmes.

The casting cannot be considered as anything less than inspired. Rathbone presented an ideal image of Holmes: he was tall — carrying himself with an erect guardsman-like bearing — with an extraordinary angular face, a long aquiline nose and a defiant jawline. His voice was sharp and incisive, yet dark with a majestic quality that betrayed his stage training. This was a Holmes who was not only alert and intellectually superior, but a daring man of action also. These two halves of the character had never before been so evenly balanced on screen. The Rathbone Holmes found immediate acceptance with the public and critics.

The success of the first Fox feature, *The Hound of the Baskervilles* in 1939, led to *The Adventures of Sherlock Holmes* later the same year, but strangely Fox then dropped the character. However, Rathbone continued playing the role on radio, and then in 1942, returned to the screen as a modern Holmes in the Universal series. Despite the charm of these movies — a charm that increases as time passes — they were nevertheless B pictures, churned out at a rate of approximately two a year, and by 1946 Rathbone was tiring of the role. Rather like Arthur Conan Doyle before him, he wanted to be rid of the character in order to concentrate on what he considered more important work. In his autobiography Rathbone explained his frustration: 'the continuous repetition [of the role] left me virtually repeating myself every time in a character I had already conceived and developed. The stories varied but I was always the same character merely repeating myself... in due course, and not unreasonably I think, these endless repetitions forced me into a critical analysis of Holmes that was often disturbing and sometimes destructive. For instance, towards the end of my life with him I came to the conclusion... that there was nothing

Above: *Rathbone and Bruce at their most authentic in* The Adventures of Sherlock Holmes. **Left:** *Rathbone and Bruce, friends in real life, discuss one of their scripts.*

loveable about Holmes. He himself seemed capable of transcending the weakness of mere mortals like myself... understanding us perhaps, accepting us and even pitying us, but only and purely objectively. It would be impossible for such a man to know loneliness or love or sorrow because he was completely sufficient unto himself.'

So it was, when the time came to renew his contract with Universal in 1946 for further Holmes films, Rathbone opted not to continue the series. This decision stunned the studio, and for a time created a rift between Rathbone and his friend Nigel Bruce, who loved playing Watson and was keen to do more movies. In fact Bruce continued the radio series, which Rathbone also dropped, with Tom Conway

playing the lead. Although Rathbone turned his back on Holmes in 1946, he was destined never to lose the Sherlock tag. In 1953 he made a one-off television appearance as the detective, and later that year, at the age of sixty-one, he opened at the Century Theatre on Broadway in a new play, *Sherlock Holmes*, written by his wife Ouida. Nigel Bruce had suffered a heart attack and was unavailable for the Watson part and so Jack Raine played the good Doctor. Unfortunately, the show was a creaky mish-mash lacking dramatic verve, and closed after just three performances. Later, in the fifties, Rathbone recorded some of the original Doyle tales for Caedmon on long playing records, but these versions are flawed to some extent by

Rathbone having to assume the role of Watson, the storyteller, and not that of Holmes.

At the time of his death in 1967, Basil Rathbone was considering returning to the role that had dominated his career in a series of radio plays. Sadly, having been given the all clear at a check-up with his physician, he returned home, placed a new record he had just purchased on the gramophone and then suffered a heart attack. The greatest Holmes had made his last bow.

THE ADVENTURES OF SHERLOCK HOLMES

FIRST SCREENING August 1939
PRODUCTION COMPANY Twentieth Century Fox
DURATION 85 minutes
Black and white
DIRECTOR Alfred Werker

Sherlock Holmes (Basil Rathbone) arrives at the courtroom with vital new evidence against Professor Moriarty (George Zucco), who is being tried for murder, but he is too late to prevent his arch enemy from being acquitted. Now Moriarty determines to commit the crime of the century right under the detective's nose. His plan calls for diverting Holmes' attention by presenting him with two cases, knowing that he will choose the more intriguing one. The Professor concocts a complicated murder threat involving Ann Brandon (Ida Lupino) and her family, in order to mask the real crime — the theft of the Crown Jewels. Ann's brother Lloyd is murdered and, while Holmes is deeply involved in this investigation, he sends Watson (Nigel Bruce) to guard the Crown Jewels at the Tower of London. Unknown to Watson, his police escort is in reality Moriarty and his gang in disguise. Holmes manages to save Ann, capture her would-be murderer and arrive at the Tower in time to shoot it out with Moriarty, who falls from the battlements, presumably to his death.

IT IS CLEAR FROM THE SPEED WITH WHICH THIS impressive feature followed on the heels of Rathbone's first Holmes film, that it was planned and conceived during the filming of *The Hound of the Baskervilles* (1939). This time there was no doubt about the billing: Rathbone and Bruce came top. In many ways this is a better film than *The Hound*; the mystery is more complicated, we see more of Holmes' detective work and we have a striking villain played with creepy menace by George Zucco. The screenplay by Edwin Blum and William Drake was supposedly based on the Gillette play, but the final product bears little resemblance to it. The plot, with its complicated

convolutions, moves at a brisk pace, leaving little time to consider the various anomalies or inexplicable elements within the script — how, for example, did Moriarty know the exact Inca dirge that Ann Brandon had heard before her father's death, and how did he learn of the cryptic significance of the albatross? Also, one perceptive American critic made the observation that even the English climate seldom has thick fogs in May.

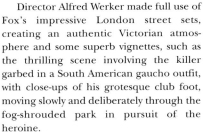

Director Alfred Werker made full use of Fox's impressive London street sets, creating an authentic Victorian atmosphere and some superb vignettes, such as the thrilling scene involving the killer garbed in a South American gaucho outfit, with close-ups of his grotesque club foot, moving slowly and deliberately through the fog-shrouded park in pursuit of the heroine.

George Zucco, who played Moriarty, was one of Hollywood's resident smooth villains. His career was based on menacing heroes of all hues; indeed he was to pit his wits against Rathbone's Holmes on a later occasion in *Sherlock Holmes in Washington*. The ultimate purpose of Zucco's cold and cruelly malevolent Moriarty in stealing the Crown Jewels was not the wealth that they could bring, but the destruction of Sherlock Holmes' reputation. As he replies to one of his minions' queries, 'Holmes again?': 'Always Holmes until the end.'

When the two antagonists appear on screen together — which is all too seldom — the dialogue bristles. As, for instance, at the opening of the film when Moriarty has been found innocent of a murder charge and he encounters Holmes outside the

court. 'You've a magnificent brain, Moriarty,' says Holmes, 'I admire it. I admire it so much, I'd like to present it pickled in alcohol to the London Medical Society.' 'It would make an impressive exhibit,' admits the Professor.

The reason that Moriarty escapes the gallows at the film's opening, for the murder of a man called Lariat, is never explained, nor is the nature of the incriminating evidence gathered by Holmes that it is too late to present to the court. Explanatory scenes had been filmed, but unfortunately they ended up on the cutting room floor. Apparently, Moriarty's alibi for the time of the murder was that he was lecturing at the Royal Society to an audience of more than 300 members. There was an official clock in view the whole time. Holmes brilliantly breaks this alibi by explaining that, when the lecture was taking place, the master clock motor at Greenwich Observatory — the clock that controlled all the standard chronometers in every part of the United Kingdom — had been tampered with. Moriarty had succeeded in accomplishing a time fluctuation by concentrating a counter-magnetic field of such intensity that it

affected the motor of the Observatory clock. No doubt the decision to cut this sequence was because, no matter how brilliantly clever the deduction seems, it is a little slow, complicated and perhaps far-fetched for a cinema audience to digest at the start of the film, and would certainly hold up the action.

Nigel Bruce's portrayal of Watson took another step further away from Conan Doyle's conception in this movie. He was not, as one critic observed, 'reserved in his silly-ass mannerisms.' Encouraged by the script, which has Watson being jealous of Billy the Page (Terry Kilburn), Bruce's character becomes that of an irritating buffoon.

However, Basil Rathbone was superb once again. His timing and phrasing echoed the Holmes of Doyle's stories, while he cut a figure reminiscent of the Paget drawings. As *Variety* observed: 'The Holmes character seems tailored for Rathbone.' It was in *The Adventures* that he gave us one of his finest disguises — that of a music hall singer. Dressed in a striped blazer and wearing a boater tilted jauntily on the side of his head, Rathbone renders 'Oh I Do Like to Be Beside the Seaside' with great aplomb.

Sadly, this was Rathbone's final appearance as Holmes on film in period, the last time he was seen striding through the fog in his Inverness cape and deerstalker. Nevertheless, Rathbone's career as the Great Detective on screen had only just begun.

Previous page (right): *A lobby card, featuring Rathbone, Ida Lupino and Bruce.*
Above left: *Moriarty (Lionel Atwill) charms the unsuspecting Jerrold Hunter (Alan Marshal).*
Above right: *A Spanish poster for the film.*
Left: *Watson (Nigel Bruce) in trouble at the Tower of London.*

SHERLOCK HOLMES AND THE VOICE OF TERROR

FIRST SCREENING September 1942
PRODUCTION COMPANY Universal Pictures
DURATION 65 minutes
Black and white
DIRECTOR John Rawlins

The Second World War is raging and Holmes (Basil Rathbone) is engaged by the British Inner Council to find the German who has been passing information to The Voice of Terror — a Nazi propaganda radio broadcaster who announces various acts of sabotage as they are happening. One of Holmes' agents is murdered, uttering the word 'Christopher' with his last gasp. Holmes enlists the help of the dead man's girlfriend, Kitty (Evelyn Ankers), who learns that the dying words refer to the abandoned Christopher Dock. At the derelict wharf, Holmes and Watson (Nigel Bruce) discover a gang of German spies led by Meade (Thomas Gomez), a known Nazi agent. With the help of Kitty's friends, the gang is arrested, but Meade escapes. The Voice of Terror announces a German air strike on the north coast. Holmes suspects this is a diversionary tactic and persuades the Prime Minister to divert the defences to the south coast. Holmes unmasks Sir Evan Barham (Reginald Denny), the spy in the Council's midst. He then rushes to the south coast to capture Meade and the other agents, but fails to save Kitty from being shot by Meade.

FOX'S *THE ADVENTURES OF SHERLOCK HOLMES* (1939) was every bit as successful as the studio's first Holmes movie, *The Hound of the Baskervilles* (1939), but they didn't follow it up with a third film. By the end of 1939 the Second World War had broken out, and foreign agents and spies were more typical and topical than the criminal activities of Moriarty and his like. It was probably the uncertainty of the box-office appeal of a Victorian sleuth at this time, combined with the difficulty of maintaining the same level of high-budget production, that caused Fox to drop Sherlock Holmes from their schedules. Nevertheless, Rathbone and Bruce continued to play their roles on radio, endearing themselves to millions of listeners.

In 1942 Universal Pictures acquired the screen rights to Sherlock Holmes from the Conan Doyle Estate and immediately put Rathbone and Bruce under contract for a proposed series of films, commencing with *Sherlock Holmes Saves London,* a title which was changed during production to *Sherlock Holmes and the Voice of Terror.*

The Universal Holmes was presented as a contemporary figure, allowing him to be placed in stories involving the Second World War. The updating also eliminated any budget problems concerning period sets and costumes. To explain or excuse this modernisation of Sherlock, the first few films in the series carried this message following the opening credits:

'Sherlock Holmes, the immortal character of fiction, created by Sir Arthur Conan Doyle, is ageless, invincible and unchanging. In solving the significant problems of the present day he remains — as ever — the supreme master of deductive reasoning'.

Somehow it does not seem so very strange to see Rathbone's Holmes riding in a car or using the radio. After all, Norwood, Brook and Wontner had done so before. And although it was now a world of sandbags, blackout curtains and ARP wardens, the cosy rooms at Baker Street

seemed quite untouched by time. Some of the traditional props remained — the dressing gown, the pipes, and the violin for instance — but the trademark fore and aft deerstalker was dispensed with. In *The Voice of Terror*, Holmes is about to don this anachronistic headgear when Watson rebukes him with, 'Holmes, you promised.' 'Oh, very well,' replies the sleuth, putting on a fedora instead.

While the move from one studio to another had not changed the brilliance of Rathbone's performance, something had happened to his hair! It was arranged, or rather disarranged, in a peculiarly wind-swept manner, so that it fell about his temples in an untidy fashion. These came to be known as 'locks of Sherlock'. One can only assume the coiffure was to give the detective an arty bohemian look, at odds with the staid haircuts of the war years. However, this affected style was dispensed with after the third movie in the series,

Sherlock Holmes in Washington, following which Rathbone appeared with his hair sleeked back to emphasise his finely chiselled intellectual features.

Bruce's appearance had also changed. His hair and moustache were no longer dyed, making Watson look considerably older than his lithe companion, which was ironic because Nigel Bruce was, at forty-seven, three years younger than Rathbone.

Mary Gordon, who had played Mrs Hudson in the Fox movies and moved with Rathbone and Bruce to radio, also joined the Universal series. She never did very much, but her presence was always reassuring, and she had a nice line in gentle putdowns. In this movie, the Doctor assures her that Holmes is 'on the greatest case of his... er, our career'. 'Oh, mercy,' replies Mrs Hudson, 'he *always* is.'

Scripted by Lynn Riggs and John Bright, *The Voice of Terror* was directed by John Rawlins — his only entry in the series — and supposedly based on Doyle's 'His Last Bow'. The link is tenuous but the master spy in the film, Sir Evan Barham, turns out to be Heinrich Von Bork, the villain of the original story.

One bold aspect of the production is its portrayal of Kitty who, it is implied, is a prostitute and, indeed, lives with Meade the German spy in order to obtain information from him. The cinema's contemporary code of morals could not allow such a woman to live, but at least she is given a noble death.

The film ends with Holmes and Watson standing in a bombed church watching the dawn come up over the English Channel, with Holmes reciting a patriotic little homily; a device that was to become a feature in most of the series. In this instance the dialogue is pure Doyle, lifted from 'His Last Bow'. 'There's an East wind coming, Watson... '

The reviews were mixed. While *Variety* stated that 'Rathbone carries the Sherlock Holmes role in great style, getting able assistance from the flustery Bruce as Dr Watson', several critics were upset by the updating, including Bosley Crowther in the *New York Times*, who ranted: 'It is surprising that Universal should take such cheap advantage of the current crisis to exploit an old, respected fiction character.'

SHERLOCK HOLMES AND THE SECRET WEAPON

First screening December 1942
Production company Universal Pictures
Duration 68 minutes
Black and white
Director Roy William Neill

With the aid of Sherlock Holmes (Basil Rathbone), Dr Franz Tobel (William Post Jr), inventor of a secret bombsight, escapes from Nazi agents in Switzerland. Arriving in England, Tobel refuses to turn over his invention to the authorities. Instead, he divides the bombsight into four sections — each useless without the others — and sends them to four Swiss scientists living in London for safekeeping. None of the four know who the other three are, but Tobel keeps a record of their identity in a secret code comprising of stick figures. Moriarty (Lionel Atwill), hired by the Nazis to obtain the bombsight, kidnaps Tobel and learns of his ruse. Holmes breaks the code and then races to reach the scientists before Moriarty, but he fails in three cases. The Professor kidnaps the fourth Swiss scientist and takes him to his stronghold, only to find that his captive is Sherlock Holmes in disguise. Holmes plays for time until Watson (Nigel Bruce), Lestrade (Dennis Hoey) and the police come to the rescue. Attempting to escape, Moriarty falls down a secret trap door to his death.

THIS ENTRY, ORIGINALLY TITLED *Sherlock Holmes Fights Back*, saw the arrival of director Roy William Neill, who contributed greatly to the success of the Universal series. Neill, an Englishman, went on to direct the remaining ten films in the series, producing nine of them, and even contributing to the screenplay of *The Scarlet Claw*. Neill became completely immersed in the crafting of the films, and so keen was he to maintain a fidelity to the character of Sherlock Holmes that for his earlier films he brought in Thomas McKnight, a 'technical expert' on Conan Doyle. Although these movies were prod-

uced as B mystery programme fillers, Neill and his crew of writers and technicians infused them with a quality that far exceeded their humble resources. Neill's Holmes adventures were filled with suspenseful Gothic overtones and moody lighting, and they stood head and shoulders above any other contemporary detective or thriller series.

This film introduced Inspector Lestrade of Scotland Yard, a thick-skulled but somehow likeable policeman played by Dennis Hoey. Arrogant, ignorant, bad-tempered and always arresting the innocent party, he was a comic foil for

Holmes and, at times, Watson. Lestrade became a regular in the series, appearing in six of the films. Interestingly, Hoey reprised the character in Neill's *Frankenstein Meets the Wolf Man* (1943). Hoey's police inspector in this film is called Owen, but for all practical purposes it was Lestrade himself, complete with familiar bowler, long raincoat and a brazen personality.

Professor Moriarty returned in *Secret Weapon* to assist the Nazis, and in doing so the screenwriters made a subtle gesture to continuity when reference was made to the Professor's known whereabouts — the bottom of the Thames — which was his watery destination after battling with Holmes in the Fox movie *The Adventures of Sherlock Holmes* (1939). At the close of the new film, the master criminal once more ends up plunging into the river to his death, although as Joseph Pihodna in the *New York Herald Tribune* observed: 'There is, however, considerable doubt as to Moriarty's death. The chances are that Universal will see fit to bring him back.' Pihodna was prophetic, as Moriarty did return three films later, albeit played by a different actor.

The movie's macabre climax finds Holmes playing for time as Moriarty attempts an operation to systematically drain him of all his blood. 'Each second a few more drops leave your desiccated body,' taunts the Professor, in a scene that must rate as one of the most vicious encounters between the detective and the Napoleon of Crime.

Moriarty was played with suave menace by the ubiquitous Universal heavy, Lionel Atwill, who had previously encountered Rathbone's Holmes as Doctor Mortimer in *The Hound of the Baskervilles* (1939).

The screenplay was by Edward T. Lowe, W. Scott Darling and Edmund L. Hartmann, who wove elements from Doyle —

the stick men from 'The Adventure of the Dancing Men' and the false-bottomed chest from 'The Disappearance of Lady Frances Carfax' — into the plot, also utilising Holmes' propensity for disguise. During the course of the film Rathbone appears as a Swiss inventor, a criminal Lascar and a geriatric German bookseller — 'I have some works of an old German writer… Wilhelm Shakespeare.' Unlike in

some other Sherlock Holmes movies, Rathbone's disguises in the Universal series were never meant to fool the audience, only the other characters in the film.

Once more Holmes was given a flag-waving, morale boosting homily at the end. This time the words were borrowed from an old English writer, William Shakespeare. 'Things are looking up, Holmes,' says Watson, 'This little island's still on the

map.' 'Yes,' the detective replies. 'This fortress — built by Nature for herself. This blessed plot, this Earth, this realm, this England.'

The film received reasonable reviews, with more praise for Rathbone's portrayal of the Great Detective. *The Hollywood Reporter* stated: 'Basil Rathbone assumes the part of Sherlock Holmes with the suavity that is his stock in trade.'

Above left: 'Things are looking up, Holmes…'
Far left: Holmes (Basil Rathbone), disguised as a Lascar, is captured by Moriarty (Lionel Atwill).
Left: Atwill had previously appeared with Rathbone in The Hound of the Baskervilles (1939).

SHERLOCK HOLMES IN WASHINGTON

FIRST SCREENING April 1943
PRODUCTION COMPANY Universal Pictures
DURATION 71 minutes
Black and white
DIRECTOR Roy William Neill

Sherlock Holmes (Basil Rathbone) is trying to recover a microfilm containing government secrets which has been hidden in a match folder by Grayson (Gerald Hamer), a British agent travelling to the United States. Grayson is killed, but not before he has passed on the match folder to an unsuspecting young woman, Nancy Partridge (Marjorie Lord). Holmes and Watson (Nigel Bruce) travel to Washington on the trail of the match folder. Nazi spies are also after the microfilm, and kidnap the girl. Examining the blanket in which Grayson's body was found, Holmes deduces that it had seen service in an antique shop, so he and Watson make the rounds of such establishments. Their investigations lead to a bogus antique shop and, posing as an eccentric collector, Holmes encounters the shop's proprietor, Richard Stanley (George Zucco), who is really Herr Heinrich Hinkle, 'the head of the most insidious spy ring'. Holmes is captured, but is rescued by Watson and the police just in time. Eventually the detective catches up with Hinkle who, not realising that it contains the microfilm, has the elusive match folder in his pocket.

SHERLOCK HOLMES IN WASHINGTON, ONE OF the least distinguished entries in the Universal series, is the first not to use a Doyle story for inspiration. The screenplay by Bertram Millhauser and Lynn Riggs plucks Holmes and Watson from their cosy Baker Street nest and transports them to wartime America, which no doubt seemed the ultimate step in modernising the characters. Apart from the deductions, there are no familiar elements left. Watson chews gum and becomes interested in baseball, and Holmes uses modern equipment in the FBI laboratory in his investigations. There had been speculation at Universal about building further adventures for the detective in America; quite logical in one sense, for having modernised the character, why not go the full distance and relocate the mysteries in the New World? In practical terms it would also have meant a reduction in the studio's budget, as there would be no further need to dress up old sets to resemble Britain. But it seemed that Universal had taken their

premise too far, because it soon became apparent that much of the charm and appeal of the first two movies had been lost by using an American setting. In fact, after this feature, Universal returned Holmes to his usual stamping ground, and no longer pitted him against enemy agents. Indeed, after the next entry in the series, *Sherlock Holmes Faces Death*, the wartime theme was eliminated completely.

In this film the match folder containing the important microfilm is merely a 'MacGuffin' (a term coined by Alfred Hitchcock for an item around which the plot revolves, even though its real importance and value is never

fully explained to the audience, because in essence it doesn't matter — its sole purpose is to be the object of desire for both sides). Cameraman Lester White had to concentrate continually on the match folder as it passed from person to person, each one unaware of its secret. This procedure leads to several pleasing moments of dramatic irony. When Holmes confronts the villain Richard Stanley, he teasingly suggests that the documents he seeks might be reduced in size for easy transportation, while at the same time Stanley lights a cigarette using a match from the very folder which conceals the microfilm. 'The man who has the documents doesn't know it,' observes Holmes with a wry grin.

George Zucco, Universal's all-purpose creepy villain, who had appeared as

Moriarty in *The Adventures of Sherlock Holmes* (1939), plays a Nazi agent in very much the same manner as he did the evil professor. Luckily, Zucco's malignant screen presence manages to overcome the rather risible nature of the real name of his character, Heinrich Hinkle, which is, unfortunately, reminiscent of Charlie Chaplin's Adenoid Hynkel — his satirical portrait of Hitler in the then-recent *The Great Dictator* (1940).

Henry Daniell, who had appeared in the previous two films, is seen in this feature as the sinister spy, William Easter; but Daniell's great day was yet to come, when he would play Moriarty to Rathbone's Holmes in *The Woman in Green*.

A welcome addition to the Universal repertory company was the versatile character actor Gerald Hamer, making an uncredited début in the series, as the doomed agent Grayson. He appeared in five of the Rathbone movies in all, particularly excelling as the murderer in *The Scarlet Claw*.

At the close of this film, Holmes and Watson drive past back-projected views of Washington while Holmes muses: 'This is a great country, Watson. Look up ahead — the Capitol: the very heart of this democracy. It's not given to us to peer into the mysteries of the future, but in the days to come, the British and American people will, for their own safety and good of all, walk together in majesty, justice and peace.' 'That's magnificent, I quite agree with you,' says Watson. 'Not with me,' answers Holmes, 'with Winston Churchill. I was quoting from a speech he made in that very building.' The triumphant music swells and heralds: 'The End'.

One of the great commentators on Sherlockian films, Michael Pointer, observed that this sentiment appears to have been the sole motive for making *Sherlock Holmes in Washington*.

While the film attracted only lukewarm reviews — 'plodding fare' was one opinion — Rathbone again received pleasing comment. *The New York Post* was positively ecstatic: 'What a public thinker, that Rathbone is! You can practically see the mighty muscles of his mind tense, grab, and get to the heart of the toughest mystery.'

Previous page (right): *Posed shot of the villain Richard Stanley, alias Heinrich Hinkle (George Zucco), the heroine, Nancy Partridge (Marjorie Lord), and the detective hero, Sherlock Holmes (Basil Rathbone).*
Above left: *Two great screen villains and two screen Moriartys in one scene: George Zucco (far left) and Henry Daniell (with the gun).*
Above right: *Holmes on the trail of the missing microfilm.*
Left: *Holmes looks for clues in a railway compartment while Watson (Nigel Bruce) and the attendant look on with amazement.*

SHERLOCK HOLMES FACES DEATH

First screening September 1943
Production company Universal Pictures
Duration 68 minutes
Black and white
Director Roy William Neill

Watson (Nigel Bruce) has returned to medical practice and is in charge of an army officers' convalescent home, Musgrave Manor, in Northumberland. He requests Holmes' (Basil Rathbone) aid after his assistant, Doctor Sexton (Arthur Margetson), is attacked. Shortly after the detective's arrival, Phillip and Geoffrey Musgrave are murdered, their deaths preceded by the tower clock striking thirteen. Following their deaths, the sole remaining heir to the Musgrave estate, Sally (Hillary Brooke), has to carry out the customary reading of the ceremonial 'Musgrave Ritual', which Holmes believes contains the motives for the crimes. After Sally mysteriously disappears, Holmes uses the Manor's black and white checked hall floor as a giant chessboard and, interpreting the Ritual as a set of chess moves, discovers a hidden cellar and a long-forgotten land grant. Holmes tricks the guilty party, Doctor Sexton, into a confession that is overheard by Watson and Lestrade (Dennis Hoey). Sexton's plan was to eliminate all the Musgrave heirs, apart from Sally, whom he believed he could marry and, with the land grant, would therefore inherit a vast amount of property.

REGARDED BY *AFICIONADOS* AS ONE OF THE BEST of the Universal/Rathbone features, *Sherlock Holmes Faces Death* brings Holmes back to the world of creepy old houses, wild windy nights and mysterious unsolved murders. The mood is Victorian Gothic but the presence of the Second World War is still in evidence, for Musgrave Manor, the scene of the action, is being used as a home for convalescent officers. The screenplay by Bertram Millhauser was supposedly based on Doyle's 'The Musgrave Ritual' but, as with all films in this series, only the smallest germ of an idea was plucked from the literary source and placed in an elaborate new setting. Millhauser was an old hand at writing Holmes — he had scripted Clive Brook's *Sherlock Holmes* in 1932. His inventions in this movie were inspired, not least the use of the Ritual as an allusive chess problem, solved by using the great back and white stone floor of Musgrave Manor as a large chessboard, with the inhabitants taking the place of chess pieces. There were some superb dramatic moments: the discovery of a dead body in the boot of a car, the trapping of the murderer in the ancient crypt beneath the Manor and, above all, the forked lightning crashing through the stained glass window and striking the suit of armour during the reading of the Ritual — one of the greatest Gothic moments from all the Rathbone movies.

Suddenly the series was in its stride. Neill now had full control — he was producing as well directing — and he returned Holmes and Watson to the kind of complex problem and rich atmosphere that make Doyle's tales so satisfying. A happy side effect of this revitalisation was the demise of Rathbone's 'windswept' hairstyle, leaving his sharp, refined features properly emphasised and Paget-like once again.

Rather unrealistically, Inspector Lestrade was on hand to muddy the waters, with no explanation given as to why a Scotland Yard official should be investigating a murder at an isolated Northumberland mansion apart from, of course, to join forces with Watson to provide some comic business.

The romantic lead in the film was Milburn Stone, who played Hillary Brooke's American boyfriend. Stone, who was later to gain fame as 'Doc' in the television series *Gunsmoke*, was a short man — a fact that the producers failed to consider when they cast him. Stone recalled that: 'Everybody in the picture was taller than me. There was this shot where Basil and I had to walk across the room together. He walked on the floor, but they built a special platform for me, so I'd look taller. I had a love scene with Hillary Brooke which was even worse. We were sitting on the sofa and I looked almost like a midget next to her. The property man supplied me with some pillows to prop me up.'

The village used in *Sherlock Holmes Faces Death* was originally constructed on the Universal lot in the thirties for their *Frankenstein* productions. Its quaintness and 'mittel-European' architecture added to the sense of being far removed from a time of international conflict.

The homily at the end is original and one of the most stirring. The case completed, Holmes and Watson are riding through the countryside in an open car on their way back to Baker Street, when the detective is provoked into philosophical thought: 'There's a new spirit abroad in the

land. The old days of grab and greed are on their way out; we're beginning to think what we owe the other fellow, not what we're compelled to give him. The time's coming, Watson, when we shan't be able to kneel and thank God for blessings before our shining altars, while men anywhere are kneeling in either physical or spiritual subjection. And, God willing, we'll live to see that day'.

In the dark days of the war, emotions must have run high on hearing this potent humanitarian speech, beautifully delivered by Rathbone. One American critic picked up on the lines in his review: 'The days of grab and greed are over, remarks that remarkable man, Mr Holmes. It gives one new confidence that he should think so.'

The film was well received, with the *New York Times* particularly fulsome: 'what is admirable about the film is the wonderful sense of atmosphere, of mystery, of sepulchral gloom that oozes like fog throughout the melodrama. No government spy work for Sherlock this time; despite his being contemporised by the studio right up to the minute, this adventure was, paradoxically, a return to all the shadowy Victorian trappings of the richly old-fashioned mystery. This is due in no small measure to the talents of Roy Neill.'

Previous page (below): The film's Spanish poster.
Above left: Holmes and Mrs Hudson (Mary Gordon).
Above right: Inspector Lestrade (Dennis Hoey), about to accuse Captain Vickery (Milburn Stone) of murder.
Below left: Holmes and Watson with Sally Musgrave (Hillary Brooke).
Below right: Discovering the hidden cellar.

SPIDER WOMAN

First screening January 1944
Production company Universal Pictures
Duration 62 minutes
Black and white
Director Roy William Neill

A rash of 'pyjama suicides' is plaguing London, and Holmes (Basil Rathbone) fakes his own death on a fishing trip in Scotland so that he can investigate them undercover. Disguised as a Hindu, he meets Adrea Spedding (Gale Sondergaard), who lends money on insurance policies, making her accomplices the beneficiaries before having the policyholder killed. The murders are ingenious: the victim is bitten by a spider whose venom drives him to suicide. A pygmy carries the deadly spider along the ventilation shaft in the victim's hotel and releases it into the bedroom through the air grill. Spedding discovers that her Hindu acquaintance is really Sherlock Holmes, and an attempt is made on his life using the poisonous spiders. It fails, as does a poison gas attack on Holmes and Watson in their sitting room. Realising that a pygmy is involved in the crimes, Holmes sets off for the fairground, but is captured there by the Spider Woman and her gang. The detective is tied behind a target in a shooting gallery, where he is fired at unknowingly by Watson (Nigel Bruce). Holmes escapes in time and the gang is successfully rounded up.

AFTER HIS SUCCESS WITH *SHERLOCK HOLMES Faces Death*, screenwriter Bertram Millhauser was retained for the next Holmes vehicle. Again, in a brilliant fashion, he was able to blend his own interesting ideas with those adapted from Doyle. The use of the pygmy is taken from *The Sign of Four*; the introduction of a deadly creature into the bedroom of the sleeping victim through a ventilator is from 'The Adventure of the Speckled Band'; Holmes' fall to his apparent death in the swirling waters of a mountain river recalls the Reichenbach incident in 'The Final Problem'; and the poisonous fumes that almost overcome Holmes and Watson is reminiscent of a scene in 'The Adventure of the Devil's Foot'. The cocktail is fresh and exciting and, as *Variety* noted, 'the series is becoming more and more Doyle-ish with each successive edition.'

The script also gave Rathbone the chance to use disguises again, appearing this time as an obnoxious cockney postman and the distinguished Indian officer Rahjni Singh.

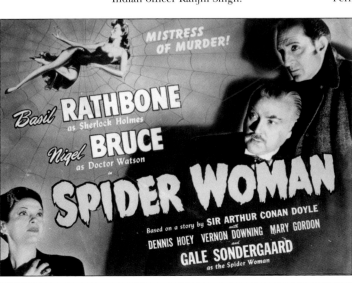

This was the first film in the series to drop Sherlock Holmes from the title. Perhaps after five films, Universal believed that the names of Basil Rathbone and Nigel Bruce alone would tell any film-goer what to expect. But more pertinently, the title *Spider Woman* emphasised the horror element in the movie. At the time Universal were cashing in on their reputation as horror film-makers, turning out a series of cheap money spinners such as *The Ghost of Frankenstein* (1942), *Frankenstein Meets the Wolf Man* (1943; also directed by Neill) and *House of Frankenstein* (1944). The Holmes series was now seen as an adjunct to these movies.

It was also the first time that Rathbone's detective was faced with a woman as his antagonist — 'a female Moriarty... audacious and as deadly as any of her spiders' — and Universal were lucky to engage the services of the Academy Award-winning actress Gale Sondergaard as the eponymous Spider Woman. She returned to the role (though strictly, it was as a new character, Zenobia Dollard) two years later in the non-Holmes film *The Spider Woman Strikes Back*.

Nigel Bruce came the closest he ever did to serious acting in this film. He is touching when recounting the death of Holmes to a subdued Lestrade, but alas it is not long before he returns to his usual bumbling imbecility.

The only reference to the war in this movie — and the last one in the whole series — was the image of Hitler in the shooting gallery, behind which the trussed up Holmes struggles to free himself while Watson, ignorant of his friend's plight, tries to shoot the Führer. There was no patriotic homily this time; instead there was an interestingly dramatic moment which

CRAZY HOUSE

Before the release of *Spider Woman*, Rathbone and Bruce had appeared briefly in the 1943 Ole Olsen and Chic Johnson comedy *Crazy House*, a follow-up to *Hellzapoppin'*, which had featured a guest appearance by the Frankenstein Monster, a talking bear and jokes about *Citizen Kane* and *Here Comes Mr Jordan*. Many Universal contract players were pressed into service for guest scenes to show panic at the news that Olsen and Johnson were arriving at Universal. In a brief scene shot on the set of *Spider Woman*, Watson bursts into the room to find Holmes holding a curved pipe and a magnifying glass. He asks his friend why there is excitement at the studio and why 'everyone's running for the air raid shelter.' Holmes informs him that it is because Olsen and Johnson have arrived. Watson wonders how he knows this and the detective replies: 'I am Sherlock Holmes. I know everything.' Although this scene is meant to be a light-hearted skit on the Holmes character, it does reflect a flaw in Universal's interpretation of the detective: his superhuman omniscience. He is never wrong, and in some cases he is aware of facts which could be gleaned only by committing the crimes himself, or by having a close relationship with the screenwriter!

could have come from an Alfred Hitchcock movie.

Holmes and Watson are crushed in a crowd at the fairground and Holmes observes that this is the ideal place for murder: 'In an isolated place a cry for help or a single shot might well arouse the curiosity of at least one casual witness, but in an arcade, like this, people are bent only on pleasure and will instinctively disregard any deviation from the normal that doesn't immediately involve them. Yes, it's the most logical spot in the world to commit my murder... in the middle of a crowd.' As Holmes is saying this, he and Watson are gradually swallowed up by the throng.

Spider Woman received some of the best reviews of all the Rathbone films. *Variety* commented that while it carried the imprint of past successes, it had 'chiller action all its own, to elevate this meller as topper of the series so far. Roy William Neill must be singled out for outstandingly good piece of endeavor. Neill builds up to strong climax, never allowing action or interest to falter, with a result the picture marks signal triumph for him.'

Previous page (right):
Holmes (Basil Rathbone), in disguise as an Indian officer, tries to fool Adrea Spedding, the Spider Woman (Gale Sondergaard).
Above left: Rathbone and Bruce are joined by Gale Sondergaard for a publicity shot.
Far left: Holmes and Watson (Nigel Bruce) discover another victim of the Spider Woman.
Left: Adrea Spedding gloats with satisfaction as she believes she is sending Holmes, trussed up behind an image of Adolf Hitler in a shooting gallery, to his death.

THE SCARLET CLAW

FIRST SCREENING June 1944
PRODUCTION COMPANY Universal Pictures
DURATION 74 minutes
Black and white
DIRECTOR Roy William Neill

Holmes (Basil Rathbone) is in Canada to attend a conference on the Occult when he is summoned to the village of La Morte Rouge by Lady Penrose, who fears for her life. He arrives too late: she is discovered with her throat torn out. The villagers believe this is the work of a phantom monster who has been glimpsed like a will o' the wisp, an *ignis fatuus*, on the marshes at night. Another death follows and Holmes deduces that these killings are the work of Alistair Ransom (Gerald Hamer), an actor who was jailed for murder but has escaped and is seeking revenge on those individuals he believes responsible for his imprisonment. His instrument of murder is a sharply honed five-pronged garden weeder — the scarlet claw. The problem for Holmes is that Ransom has adopted several disguises to aid him in his revenge, including that of a well known villager, whom everyone trusts. Finally, Holmes sets himself up as a decoy on the marshes and flushes the killer out, who is then killed by the father of one of his victims.

'THERE IS BLOOD ON THE MOON TONIGHT,' exclaimed one poster advertising *The Scarlet Claw*, while another announced that 'The Red Death Strikes...' *The Scarlet Claw* is probably the best of the Rathbone series, brilliantly living up to the eerie credits, which ran through the whole Universal series, showing the serious-faced Holmes and Watson moving slowly through the fog to the accompaniment of the rousing theme music.

With elements of *The Hound of the Baskervilles* — isolated foggy marshes, a phantom killer — *The Scarlet Claw* is a horror story with detective elements. One trade journal described it as 'proceeding on established Hollywood lines of ably suggested horror', and indeed the marshland setting, with stunted trees like grasping hands emerging from the thick fog, looks very similar to that used in *The Wolf Man*, made by the same studio only a few years earlier in 1941. Despite the supernatural elements introduced into the story, Holmes, as in *The Hound*, quite rightly dismisses the locals' belief that the brutal murders are the work of a phantom, assuring Watson that the clever murderer

preceding theirs is 'McKnight'.

Thanks to Neill's expert evocation of mood, aided by the photography of George Robinson, and the startling glowing phantom — 'a ball of spitting flame' — created by special effects expert John P.

'*The Scarlet Claw*... proved that the Sherlock Holmes series could, on occasion, produce a really class thriller' — *Universal Horrors*.

has recreated the monster as a screen for his activities.

The screenplay was an amalgam of talents: the original story by Paul Gangelin and Brenda Weisberg was fashioned into a taut script by Edmund L. Hartmann and producer/director Roy William Neill. Thomas McKnight, who acted as consultant on the first three Universal films and produced at least one Holmes radio series for Rathbone and Bruce, also had a hand in writing the screenplay. His contribution was not credited, but when Holmes and Watson sign the hotel register in the movie, the name immediately

Fulton, who worked on Universal's Invisible Man films, *The Scarlet Claw* overflows with atmosphere. Although set in Canada, the action could easily have taken place in any bleak and isolated backwater in Britain, and so the 'foreign' setting does not intrude as it did in *Sherlock Holmes in Washington*. Apart from Journet (Arthur Hohl), the innkeeper, and his daughter, Marie (Kay Harding), who have gentle French lilts, all the other inhabitants of the grimly named La Morte Rouge speak with English accents.

Gerald Hamer, a familiar actor in the series, had his greatest challenge in this

entry as the murderer, the actor Alistair Ransom, who assumes three different characters.

There are some wonderfully chilling moments, including the scene where Judge Brisson (Miles Mander), the man who sentenced Ransom to prison, terrified for his life, awaits the arrival of Sherlock Holmes. He watches his housekeeper methodically drawing each blind in his room and then, horrifyingly, she turns on him, raising a sharp knife, ready to attack. It is only then that we realise Nora is the mad actor in disguise. When Holmes

arrives minutes later, the judge is dead. Another powerful moment occurs when Ransom, in his disguise as Potts the village postman, goes to murder Marie with 'the scarlet claw', his vicious five-pronged garden weeder. We see him enter her room, assured of his purpose, and then the camera pans to the caged bird the girl loved so much.

After its absence from *Spider Woman*, Holmes' trademark patriotic homily returned. This time the detective is in an open-topped car on the way to the airport when he philosophises: 'Canada, the

lynchpin of the English-speaking world, whose relations with the United States on the one hand, and the British Commonwealth and the Motherland on the other. Canada, the link that joins together these great branches of the human family.' 'Churchill say that?' 'Yes, Watson. Winston Churchill.'

As with *Sherlock Holmes in Washington* and its closing words about the American people, one wonders if the sentiments expressed in this speech were the governing influence to set the story in Canada.

Paul Landres, the picture's editor, recalled that 'everybody involved was very excited about this film because we all knew it was far superior to anything else in the series.' And indeed it was, but strangely the reviews at the time were far from sanguine. For Howard Barnes in the *New York Herald Tribune*, 'Basil Rathbone plays Holmes with rather a tired approach to solving several murders in a village near Quebec. Nigel Bruce, whose fine talents are rapidly buried under the weight of this assignment, does nothing to enliven the proceedings'; while Bosley Crowther of *The Times* called the production 'merely adequate' and sneered that 'our old friend Sherlock Holmes is snooping around misty marshes again.' It is strange to read these carping reviews today when considering that *The Scarlet Claw* is the most successful artistically, and most fondly remembered, of all the Universal series.

Previous page (below left): *A Spanish poster for the film.*
Previous page (right): *Lord Penrose (Paul Cavanagh) threatens Holmes (Basil Rathbone).*
Above left: *Alistair Ransom (Gerald Hamer) in the guise of the postman Potts.*
Above right: *A disguised Holmes tackles Ransom wielding 'the scarlet claw', a five-pronged garden weeder.*
Left: *Sergeant Thompson (David Clyde) and Holmes with Emile Journet (Arthur Hohl), who has just avenged his daughter's murder.*

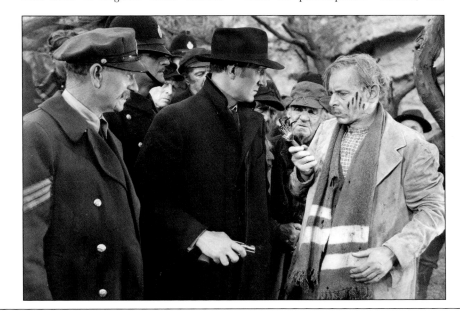

THE PEARL OF DEATH

FIRST SCREENING August 1944
PRODUCTION COMPANY Universal Pictures
DURATION 67 minutes
Black and white
DIRECTOR Roy William Neill

Sherlock Holmes (Basil Rathbone) prevents the theft of The Borgia Pearl by Naomi Drake (Evelyn Ankers), an accomplice of Giles Conover (Miles Mander), a master criminal. The detective returns the precious trinket to the Royal Regent Museum where it is stolen by Conover, who is almost immediately apprehended. However, the pearl is not found on his person. After a series of murders in which the victims are found lying in a pile of broken china and plaster ornaments, Holmes deduces that Conover hid the pearl in one of six identical wet plaster busts of Napoleon, and now he and his murdering henchman, the grotesque Creeper (Rondo Hatton), are trying to find the precious bust. The Napoleons have been distributed around London and their purchasers are being killed one by one. Holmes reaches the sixth and last bust owner, and impersonates him when Conover and the Creeper come to call. Cleverly, Holmes convinces the brute that his master has double-crossed him. Conover is killed by the Creeper, who is then shot by the detective.

IN AN ATTEMPT TO AVOID THE CLICHÉ OF resurrecting Professor Moriarty once more to provide an adversary worthy of Sherlock Holmes, Universal created their own master criminal in Giles Conover for this entry in the series. Played in a smooth, slimy fashion by Miles Mander — who had appeared in *The Scarlet Claw* as a frail judge and in Wontner's 1932 Holmes film *The Missing Rembrandt* — Conover had, according to the detective, many of the attributes of Doyle's villainous professor: 'This man pervades Europe like a plague, yet no one has ever heard of him. That's what puts him on the pinnacle in the records of crime. In his whole diabolical career the police have never been able to pin anything on him. Yet give me a crime without motive, robbery without a clue, murder without trace, and I'll show you Giles Conover.' Later the detective admits: 'If I could free society of this sinister creature, I should feel my own career had reached its summit.' Unfortunately, Con-

over hardly matched this grandiose rhetoric, appearing as a rather seedy inhabitant of the criminal fraternity.

The screenplay by Bertram Millhauser was a reworking of Doyle's 'The Adventure of the Six Napoleons', but as usual Millhauser added extra elements which enhanced rather than padded the original tale. His most interesting addition was the

Hoxton Creeper, Conover's gruesome accomplice 'with the chest of a buffalo and the arms of a gorilla'. The Creeper was played by Rondo Hatton, a grotesque looking actor who suffered from acromegaly, a condition which distorts and enlarges the facial features. Director Neill made the most of Hatton's face, filming him in scenes with deep shadows and low key lighting. Hatton, who was known as the

'With the addition of a horror figure [the film] plays very well and is certainly the best in the series' — Leslie Halliwell.

only horror star to play monsters without make-up, was quickly brought back to play the Creeper again in two non-Holmes films, *House of Horrors* (1945) and *The Brute*

Man (1946), before the disease claimed him in 1946 at the age of fifty-one.

Evelyn Ankers, who had been in the first of the Universal series, returned to play Conover's girlfriend. Ankers must have welcomed the role of the cunning Naomi Drake as a change from the fresh-faced heroines she usually played. In this movie she reveals her versatility by adopting various disguises, including a clumsy shop assistant and a matchgirl.

Rathbone, too, uses disguises, and in one scene we see him remove the complex elements of his aged clergyman persona to reveal his own features beneath. Later, not only does he stand in for the doctor who is the Creeper's last victim (a ploy that was used earlier in *Sherlock Holmes and the Secret Weapon*), but he does an expert imitation of Giles Conover's voice over the telephone. Contrary to the practice of the day, Rathbone actually did mimic Miles Mander's voice without any resort to dubbing.

The Pearl of Death is noteworthy in that it really saw the transition of Rathbone and Bruce into the characters they were playing. Universal practically eliminated the names Holmes and Watson from their advertising from this film onwards. Typical blurbs now ran: 'Basil Rathbone and Nigel Bruce Crack the Mystery of *The Pearl of Death*' or 'Rathbone & Bruce — The Masterminds Tackle The Master Crimes'. The names and identities of the actors had become so synonymous with those of the characters they were playing that as far as Universal was concerned — and the public too — using one name was as good as another.

The film was generally well received by the critics and is regarded by Sherlockian film buffs, along with *Sherlock Holmes Faces Death* and *The Scarlet Claw*, as a high point of the series.

Previous page (below left): Holmes (Basil Rathbone) confronts the slimy villain Giles Conover (Miles Mander).

Previous page (right): Gelder (Harry Cording) shows Holmes and Watson (Nigel Bruce) his stock of Napoleon busts.

Above left: Conover is apprehended after the theft of the pearl. Lestrade (Dennis Hoey), Holmes and Watson look on sternly.

Above right: One of Mary Gordon's many other film roles, in The Little Minister *(1934).*

Far left: The Creeper (Rondo Hatton).

Left: Holmes finally retrieves the fatal pearl.

THE HOUSE OF FEAR

First screening March 1945
Production company Universal Pictures
Duration 69 minutes
Black and white
Director Roy William Neill

The Good Comrades Club, a group of seven men without near kin, have all taken out life insurance policies on each other so, as one of them dies, the others benefit. They have retired to a gloomy mansion on the west coast of Scotland, Drearcliffe House, 'where no man goes whole to his grave', looked after by their equally gloomy housekeeper, Mrs Monteith (Sally Shepherd). Two of their number die mysteriously following the receipt of an envelope containing dried orange pips, and Holmes (Basil Rathbone) is engaged by the insurance company to investigate. When he, Watson (Nigel Bruce) and Lestrade (Dennis Hoey) arrive, there has been another murder. Despite Holmes' presence, the number of the Comrades is reduced to one, Alastair (Aubrey Mather), the instigator of the club. All the bodies of the victims have been mutilated in some way. Watson spots an important clue but, before he is able to tell Holmes, he is kidnapped. The detective discovers a secret smugglers' cave beneath the house where all the Good Comrades, apart from Alastair, are hiding, having faked their deaths in order to collect the insurance.

IN ONE SENSE *THE HOUSE OF FEAR* IS THE nearest the series got to an old-fashioned, old dark house whodunnit — very much in keeping with Doyle. A press release at the time confessed that attempts to modernise Holmes 'to solve problems of the current war, in Canada and Washington, did not meet with the expected response from devotees of the Conan Doyle mysteries. Film fans want to see their Holmes and Watson in typical Doyle plots and in English settings where they belong.' It seems that, eight pictures into the series, the studio had taken an awfully long time to realise the obvious.

And so there was a decided change of direction from Universal's first effort, *Sherlock Holmes and the Voice of Terror.* Although, as the budget demanded, we were still in modern times, with telephones and motorcars, there was an attempt to create a kind timeless environment in which Holmes could operate. The setting of a remote Scottish mansion perched on the cliff top, and a nearby

Doyle tale 'The Five Orange Pips' into a screenplay for the series. Ruthlessly, he

'Walls of hate... holding an orgy of murder — as crime's Master Minds crack their weirdest case' — Poster slogan.

fishing village with quaint inhabitants and even quainter buildings — Universal's *Frankenstein* set again, last seen in *Sherlock Holmes Faces Death* — seemed an ideal way to distance proceedings from the twentieth century. Couple this with howling winds and lashing rain, and you have a piquant Victorian Gothic mood. But unfortunately the script was weak and full of holes. What was intended as — and could have been — a classic Sherlock Holmes mystery, turned out to be, as one critic put it, 'slow-moving and dull.'

Roy Chanslor, who later penned such classic western novels as *Johnny Guitar* and *Cat Ballou*, was drafted in to re-work the

excised every feature of the story except the pips themselves and created a new plot to accommodate them. As in the original tale, they were used as a warning of coming death, but in the film this was just a gimmick and their purpose was never explained. The resulting screenplay was not only a bore, but it made the major mistake of presenting the great detective as incompetent. On arriving in Scotland to solve the deaths of two — it rapidly becomes three — of the Good Comrades Club, he fails to prevent the 'murder' of three of the surviving members. And in the end it is Watson who spots the vital clue that helps to solve the mystery. In the last

HORROR Stalking its Halls !

THE HOUSE of FEAR

Starring
BASIL RATHBONE
NIGEL **BRUCE**

with
AUBREY MATHER   GAVIN MUIR   DENNIS HOEY
PAUL CAVANAGH   HOLMES HERBERT

Based on "The Adventures of the Five Orange Pips"
By SIR ARTHUR CONAN DOYLE

Screen Play by ROY CHANSLOR   Produced and Directed by ROY WILLIAM NEILL   A UNIVERSAL PICTURE   44/380

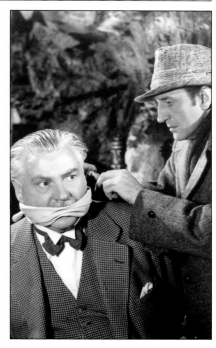

section of the movie, when the plot is crumbling fast, we are presented with a padding sequence featuring the increasingly annoying bumbling Watson blundering around the old mansion in the dark, while the sound effect wind and rain is played at full belt. It is as though the writer has run out of ideas and the script is ten minutes short.

Again Lestrade is on hand to help confuse the investigation, vying with Doctor Watson as to who can come up with the most preposterous theory of the murderer's indentity. By now Hoey's Lestrade had become more than just an incompetent and belligerent policeman, he was a comic turn.

The studio must have felt a little uncertain about this entry, as they delayed its release for over three months. But the problems with *The House of Fear* were not only with the script. It was becoming noticeable that Rathbone was beginning to tire of the role of Sherlock Holmes. After nine features and numerous radio broadcasts, the character was so familiar to him that he felt there was nothing fresh he could bring to the part. The reviewer in the *New York Times* called his performance in this movie 'as pedestrian as a cop on patrol.' Rathbone was aware of this falling off. He admitted in his biography that, 'My first [Holmes] picture was, as it were, a negative from which I merely continued to

produce endless positives of the same photograph.' And for Rathbone, a creative actor, his playing of Holmes at this time in his career must have seemed endless. He was on an exhausting treadmill with a new film every few months – in 1944 alone he and Bruce shot three Holmes movies and recorded fifty-two radio programmes. The crew producing the Holmes films on the Universal lot was the steadiest-working unit at the studio, but now there were fears that the series was beginning to flag. 'Sherlock Holmes has certainly gone to the bow wows', moaned Bosley Crowther in the *Times*, and the *Herald Tribune* cautioned that both the scriptwriting and the direction would have to improve.

Previous page (right): Holmes (Basil Rathbone) asks Sergeant Bleeker (Leslie Denison) about a possible clue. Lestrade (Dennis Hoey) appears to be as mystified as usual.

Above left: The set for the interior of Drearcliffe House was wonderfully atmospheric.

Above right: Holmes comes to Watson's (Nigel Bruce) aid once again.

Far left: Alistair (Aubrey Mather) clings to Holmes as he is about to reveal the terrible secret of The House of Fear.

Left: Holmes and Watson question the dour Mrs Monteith (Sally Shepherd) about the mysterious orange pips.

THE WOMAN IN GREEN

First screening June 1945
Production company Universal Pictures
Duration 68 minutes
Black and white
Director Roy William Neill

Several beautiful women in London have been murdered and their right forefinger amputated after death. Scotland Yard is baffled and Inspector Gregson (Matthew Boulton) calls on Sherlock Holmes (Basil Rathbone) for help. Holmes suspects Moriarty (Henry Daniell) is behind the killings, which are part of an elaborate blackmail racket. Rich victims are chosen and persuaded that they have committed one of the 'Finger Murders'. Initially, Holmes is puzzled as to the method of persuasion used, but after an attempt is made on his life by a sniper who, the detective discovers, is in a trance, he has the answer: hypnotism. At the Mesmer Club, Holmes encounters the lovely hypnotist Lydia (Hillary Brooke), who is in league with Moriarty. Holmes allows her to entice him back to her apartment where she places him in a trance. Moriarty enters and instructs Holmes to step off the parapet to his death, but Watson (Nigel Bruce) and the police arrive to discover that Holmes was never actually hypnotised and was just playing for time. In his attempt to escape, Moriarty falls from the parapet to his death.

Following on from the lurid horror-biased titles of the previous few entries, Universal strangely now came up with the bland and innocuous *The Woman in Green.* One must assume that the lady in question is Lydia Marlowe the hypnotist, but as the colour of her clothes is never referred to and this is a black and white film, the title is pointless and vague. It does not even suggest a murder mystery/detective film, let alone a movie featuring Sherlock Holmes.

With Bertram Millhauser the screenplay was in surer hands than the previous film. As usual, he devised his own intricate plot, but managed to introduce elements from Doyle: in particular the assassination attempt from 'The Adventure of the Empty House' and the icy interview between Holmes and Moriarty at 221B from 'The Final Problem'. There was also an

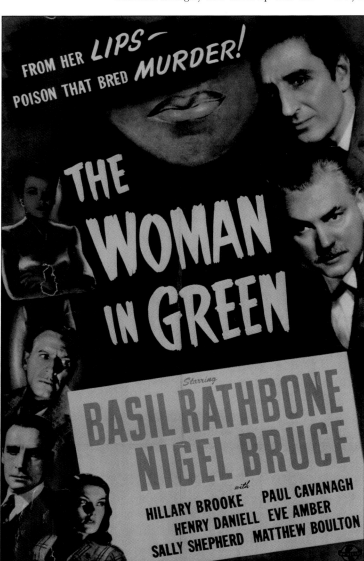

the best Moriarty of them all. In the scene where he and Rathbone cross mental swords he exudes a powerful chilling menace, matching very well Doyle's description of Moriarty's 'soft, precise fashion of speech' leaving 'a conviction of sincerity which a mere bully could not produce.' Indeed, in his autobiography, Rathbone sang the praises of Henry Daniell's masterly Moriarty: 'There were other Moriartys but none so delectably dangerous.' While praising his acting, Rathbone gently intimates that Daniell was not the easiest of actors or warmest of men to work with. In other words, he already had a touch of Moriarty about him. This point was amplified by Hillary Brooke, who played Daniell's accomplice in the movie: 'The only complainer on the set was Henry Daniell… invariably getting upset when things were delayed. He was a great Moriarty though.'

'Once in her arms no man could refuse her love... or his LIFE!' — Poster slogan.

oblique reference to a real-life villain of Doyle's period, in the newspaper headline referring to The Finger Murders as 'the greatest crime wave since Jack the Ripper.'

While the film cannot be rated as the best of the series, it was a notch or two better than *The House of Fear,* and it certainly boasted a great Moriarty in Henry Daniell. Both Rathbone and executive producer Howard S. Benedict thought Daniell to be

By contrast, Brooke had nothing but good things to say about the stars: 'Basil was constantly fooling around on the set. We had a scene in the picture where the two of us were in a cocktail lounge. For some reason, the sequence was taking a long time to shoot, so, to break the monotony, we pretended we were getting drunk… slurring our speech and the like… with the scene ending by both of us sliding under the table and 'passing out'. Willy Bruce was a lot of fun too… always "ho-ho-hoing" and blustering about.' This last comment is evidence enough, if any were needed, that

Nigel Bruce as Watson was virtually playing himself. Indeed, Terry Kilburn, who played Billy the Page in *The Adventures of Sherlock Holmes* (1939), gave this judgement on Bruce: 'He was exactly the way he seemed. He was just the same offstage as he was on.'

However, *The Woman in Green* marked another milestone in the degradation of Watson. The grim nature of the tale and the absence of Lestrade meant there was little comic relief in the picture, except for one scene in The Mesmer Club where Watson, after arrogantly denouncing hypnotists as charlatans, allows himself to

be hypnotised. The fact that Watson makes a fool of himself is one thing, but he also, though indirectly, denigrates Holmes; surely no one of intellectual worth would want to associated with this clown.

Dennis Hoey was unavailable to reprise the role of Inspector Lestrade for this film, so another Doyle policeman was written in: Inspector Gregson, played by Matthew Boulton in a refreshingly realistic and restrained style.

The reviews for *The Woman in Green* were mixed. The *Herald Tribune* thought the film was 'one of the better Sherlock Holmes

mystery thrillers' and that 'Rathbone's performance is always equal to the breadth of the script, which in this case allows him to approach very near to the character of the Sir Arthur Conan Doyle detective.' However, the *New York Times* took a different view: 'A Hollywood scriptwriter named Bertram Millhauser takes full responsibility for what transpires on the screen, and it's just as well, for Sir Arthur never perpetrated such a disappointment as *The Woman in Green*'. Significantly, this was the last Holmes screenplay that Millhauser wrote.

Above left: Watson (Nigel Bruce) examines a corpse with Holmes (Basil Rathbone) and Inspector Gregson (Matthew Boulton).
Above right: Moriarty (Henry Daniell) is caught.
Below right: Apparently hypnotised, Holmes teeters on a ledge, watched by Moriarty and Lydia Marlowe (Hillary Brooke).

PURSUIT TO ALGIERS

First screening October 1945
Production company Universal Pictures
Duration 65 minutes
Black and white
Director Roy William Neill

The King of Rovenia, a small European state, has been assassinated, and Holmes (Basil Rathbone) and Watson (Nigel Bruce) are engaged to escort the heir to the throne from London to his own country. Holmes and the young king, Nikolas (Leslie Vincent), set off by air, while Watson takes passage on the SS Friesland, arranging to meet up with them in Algiers. Watson is distressed to hear a wireless report of a small plane crashing in the Pyrenees — but Holmes and the king are not dead and have been on the boat all the time. For the rest of the journey, the king poses as Watson's nephew. The ship's passengers include several assassins, among them Mirko (Martin Kosleck), a skilful knife thrower. The villains make their final move when the ship anchors in Algiers, subduing Holmes and kidnapping Nikolas. Watson arrives with the Rovenian officials and informs Holmes that the spies have been captured and the young king freed. The detective reveals that Nikolas was in fact a decoy and the real king had been masquerading as a steward for the whole journey.

THIS IS RATHER A SHABBY ENTRY IN THE Universal series. The story, direction, action and production values are all inferior to the preceding films. The screenplay by Leonard Lee, in which Sherlock Holmes is, in essence, reduced to the role of royal bodyguard, lies at the heart of this weakness. The shipboard setting with its enclosed community was ideal for a mystery movie, but unfortunately there is no mystery to unravel and therefore no real suspense. The fact that the villains are captured off-screen at the end is typical of the second rate treatment this project received. Bosley Crowther put his finger on it when he observed in the

New York Times: '[the] unerring accuracy of Holmes — Basil Rathbone that is — has now become so dependable that his pictures have virtually no suspense. All that's left is to sit there and chuckle at Dr Watson's wretched jokes and sniff at the upstart presumptions of the sleuth's transient enemies.'

In this instance the enemies are a motley crew: the jovial Gregor (Rex Evans), the mute giant Gubec (Wee Willie Davis) and Mirko (Martin Kosleck), the expert knife-thrower, none of who exerted an air of genuine threat or menace to the great detective. The pairing of Evans and Kosleck (Davis is a mere silent presence in the

background) was probably meant to recall the classic partnership of Sydney Greenstreet and Peter Lorre in *The Maltese Falcon* (1941): the large, seemingly affable charmer with a heart of stone and the weasel-like foreigner with the killing instinct. In fact Kosleck had lost the role of Joel Cairo in John Huston's film to Lorre. Sadly, the imitation does not work. The writing is flat and the chemistry is just not there. Interestingly, director Roy William Neill did end up working with Peter Lorre in 1946, on *Black Angel*, the director's last film before his death later that year.

Morton Lowry, who was the villainous Stapleton in Rathbone's very first Holmes movie (*The Hound of the Baskervilles* [1939]), appears in *Pursuit to Algiers* in a bit part — as Sanford, the steward who finally turns out to be the new King of Rovenia travelling in disguise.

Nigel Bruce as Watson has more screen time than usual in this movie and is paired for comic scenes with Rosalind Ivan, playing Agatha Dunham, a formidable spinster who carries a gun in her handbag. Ivan had scored a great success as Charles Laughton's nagging wife the previous year in *The Suspect*, and in *Pursuit to Algiers* she easily steals the scenes she has with Bruce. There is also time in this flimsy script to allow Bruce to give a rendition of 'Loch Lomond' and for one of the passengers (Marjorie Riordan) to sing 'Flow Gently, Sweet Afton' which, according to screenwriter Leonard Lee, is Watson's favourite song.

In another scene we have Watson turning into the club bore as he attempts to recount the tale of the Giant Rat of Sumatra using a salt cellar to depict himself and a stick of celery for Holmes. As noted Sherlockian scholar Roger Johnson observed in an essay about the movie: 'This old mumbler could never have written those thrilling accounts for *The Strand*, not in a

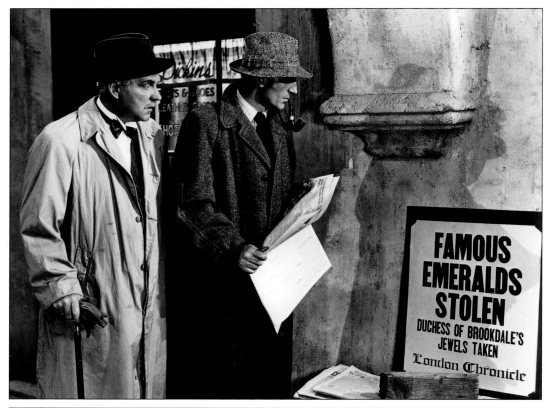

FAMOUS EMERALDS STOLEN
DUCHESS OF BROOKDALE'S JEWELS TAKEN
London Chronicle

million years'. When Bruce is performing his various comic routines, we see Rathbone standing in the background, with a strange distracted half-smile fixed on his lips.

This was the third Holmes film in a row without a break for Rathbone on the Universal conveyor belt. His last non-Holmes role had been *Frenchman's Creek* (1944, also with Nigel Bruce) at Paramount before *The House of Fear*, and the script for the next Universal entry, *Terror by Night*, was already in his hands before he had finished *Pursuit to Algiers*. He must have felt at the time that he was trapped forever playing

Sherlock Holmes, and indeed he only made one other non-Holmes film, a supporting role in *Heartbeat* (1946), before he gave up on Hollywood. He did not return until 1954, when he appeared in the Bob Hope comedy *Casanova's Big Night*. The pressure of being Holmes — and being referred to as Holmes rather than Rathbone — affected his performance, which in *Pursuit to Algiers* is close to sleepwalking.

The reviewer in the *New York Herald Tribune* made this perceptive assessment: 'These twentieth century adventures favour

melodrama rather than keen mental conflict. Holmes himself seems to sense this deterioration from time to time in the excellent Rathbone characterisation, and one of the lines in *Pursuit to Algiers* allows him to be positively nostalgic. He is explaining to Watson that musical talent is not necessarily an indication of good character. With a longing for the gaslit era in Baker Street evident in his eyes, he searches the past for an illustration of his point — then finds it. "The late Professor Moriarty," remarks Holmes, "was a virtuoso of the bassoon."'

Previous page (below): Pursuit to Algiers *is far from Rathbone and Bruce's finest hour.*
Above left: *Holmes (Basil Rathbone), with his fake nephew (Leslie Vincent) and Watson (Nigel Bruce), meets the villainous Gubec (Wee Willie Davis), Gregor (Rex Evans) and Mirko (Martin Kosleck).*
Above right: *A Rovenian official asks for help.*
Far left: *Holmes and Watson order fish and chips while following up a clue.*
Left: *Holmes, his 'nephew' and Watson play deck games with Mirko and Gregor.*

HOLMES ON RADIO

SOUNDS LIKE SHERLOCK

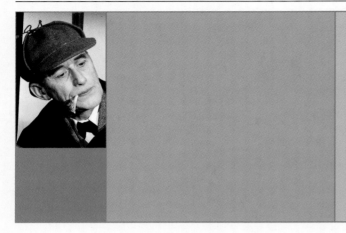

In many ways radio is the ideal medium for Sherlock Holmes. The sets and costumes are cheap, and the actors do not have to look like the characters they are playing. All one has to consider are the voices and the sound effects: the listeners' imagination does the rest.

ALONGSIDE HIS APPEARANCES IN BOOKS, PLAYS and films, Sherlock Holmes is an undisputed star of radio. He was first heard on American airwaves on 20 October 1930 in a version of 'The Adventure of the Speckled Band'. The show, sponsored by G. Washington Coffee, was broadcast before an invited audience at New York's Amsterdam Theatre. For this premier programme in the series *The Adventures of Sherlock Holmes*, William Gillette was chosen to star. At seventy-seven, he was delighted to be able to bring his interpretation of the character to a new medium.

This broadcast, and indeed the whole series, was the idea and work of Edith Meiser, who almost single-handedly brought Sherlock Holmes to American radio and developed his sound career for the next twenty years, adapting all the Doyle stories and creating new mysteries. Later in life, she recalled how it all started: 'I wrote a couple of [Holmes] scripts, but there was no interest at all. Finally G. Washington Coffee, whose executives had been brought up on Sherlock Holmes, agreed to sponsor the programme.' It was Meiser who insisted on using Gillette for the first programme, but then Richard Gordon took over for the rest of the series which ran until 1933. The part of Doctor Watson was given to an English actor, Leigh Lovell. In 1931, Gordon summed up the success of the series and perhaps the magic of all Holmes radio productions: 'Skill in producing a bit of sound over the microphone can set a complete stage in the mind's eye almost instantly. A quick flash and that scene is shifted like a wink for another. How simple and yet how effective, for each listener dresses the stage according to his own fancy.'

The pattern set by this series was followed by all subsequent American radio programmes up to the early fifties. The show's announcer would visit Watson at home, there would be some banter concerning the sponsor's product, and then the good doctor would recount the night's adventure.

Meiser admitted that she fell in love with the character of Watson, and took pains to 'flesh him out into a rather cosy, warm gentleman with a sense of humour, and I began to be aware that [the character] was getting more fan mail than Sherlock Holmes, and we always had to keep that a secret from the detective.'

In 1933, Richard Gordon grew tired of live repeat broadcasts and left. The series returned in November 1934 with a new Holmes, Louis Hector, who later had the distinction of being the first actor to play the detective on television in the 1937 adaptation of 'The Adventure of the Three Garridebs'. Hector, an Englishman, adopted a creaky, nasal delivery with mid-Atlantic tones that was similar to both Gillette's and Gordon's voices. Strangely, before 1939, none of Meiser's Holmes impersonators sounded remotely British.

By the 1934 season, Edith Meiser had run out of Doyle's Holmes tales to adapt. She approached the problem in a very imaginative way: 'I had the idea that I could put Holmes into other Doyle mysteries... I decided to start with 'The Jewish Breast Plate' and managed to get that and 'The Lost Special' on the air, before the estate made me stop adding Holmes to any other Doyle story and promise never to do it again.' In 1935, Meiser adapted the stage play *Sherlock Holmes* for radio. William Gillette played Holmes to Reginald Mason's Watson.

Richard Gordon returned to the role in 1936 for the Mutual Broadcasting System. 'Dick really thought he was Sherlock Holmes and lived the part,' recalled Meiser.

But there was a young lion waiting in the wings to seize the deerstalker, if only briefly — the brilliant Orson Welles. In 1938, at

the age of twenty-three, he adapted the Gillette play as a starring vehicle for himself in his groundbreaking Mercury Theatre of the Air series on CBS. Welles gave Holmes a light, quirky, urbane confident delivery and it is a pity he never returned to the role.

In Britain, the great detective was a comparative latecomer to radio. His first airing was in a 1938 dramatisation of 'Silver Blaze'. The honour of being the BBC's first Holmes and Watson fell to Frank Wyndham Goldie and Hugh Harben. Goldie, then aged forty-one, was 'an actor more of quiet

detachment than of emotional power' according to his obituary in *The Times*. The programme no longer exists, but this description of the actor suggests that his interpretation fell in line with the reserved, laconic and dreamy version of the detective as epitomised by Arthur Wontner in the films of the thirties. In fact, Wontner played Holmes on BBC radio five years later in 1943, in a fifty-minute adaptation of 'The Boscombe Valley Mystery'. His Watson on this occasion was Carleton Hobbs, who later became the British radio voice of Sherlock

Holmes in the fifties and sixties.

Meanwhile, back in the States, thanks to the great success of the two Fox Holmes films in 1939, Basil Rathbone and Nigel Bruce were gracing the airwaves with their version of the Baker Street duo: 'NBC and the makers of Groves Bromo Quinine Tablets bring you *The Adventures of Sherlock Holmes*'. The scripts were by Edith Meiser and initially she returned to Doyle's originals — the first tale broadcast was 'The Sussex Vampire' — but by the time the series was into its third season, Holmes was

Previous page (above): *Carleton Hobbs, the Sherlock Holmes for a generation of BBC radio listeners.*

Previous page (below): *A rare publicity still of Leigh Lovell, promoted as 'a Shakesperian [sic] actor from the English stage', who played Watson in the 1930s American series* The Adventures of Sherlock Holmes.

Above left: *A young Orson Welles appeared in his own adaptation of Gillette's* Sherlock Holmes.

Above right: *Edith Meiser.*

Far left: *Richard Gordon, famous for his on-air role as Holmes, in a shot from the short film* The Radio Murder Mystery.

Left: *Rathbone and Bruce looking as though they've had a glass too many of Petri Wine.*

the Mutual Broadcasting System — and a new sponsor: Petri Wine. Here Meiser again started with Doyle's stories, but gradually her 'free adaptations', as she called them, crept in, and soon Holmes was involved with such mysteries as 'Murder in the Waxworks' and 'The Dying Rosebush'.

By the summer of 1944 Meiser's connection with the Holmes series was severed. During the next two years Dennis Green, Bruce Taylor (aka Leslie Charteris, creator of The Saint) and Anthony Boucher scripted Holmes' exploits. This lively trio maintained the *outré* nature of some of Meiser's wilder scripts, producing titles like 'The Dentist Who Used Wolfbane' and 'The Man Who Drowned in Paddington Station'.

Across the Atlantic, John Dickson Carr, an American crime writer resident in Britain, scripted a version of 'The Adventure of the Speckled Band' for the BBC in 1945. Holmes was

investigating such non-canonical cases as 'The Haunted Bagpipes' and 'The Walking Corpse'.

On occasion Rathbone would moonlight and make guest appearances on

other NBC shows in his Holmes persona. He even helped scatterbrained Gracie Allen solve a mystery on the *Burns and Allen Show* in January 1942. In 1943, Rathbone, Bruce and Meiser moved with the series to

played by Cedric Hardwicke, whose son, Edward, would decades later score such a great success as Watson to Jeremy Brett's Holmes. Cedric Hardwicke's portrayal was restrained, reasonable and quietly spoken. This was a middle class gentleman whose hobby was crime, rather than the dynamic crusader with a quixotic bohemian nature.

When Rathbone decided to cut himself free of Holmes in 1946, the series continued as *The New Adventures of Sherlock Holmes*, written by Boucher and Green with Nigel Bruce as Watson and Tom Conway, the brother of George Sanders, playing Holmes.

In 1947 the production of the shows switched to the East Coast, and so both Bruce and Conway, actors earning their living in the Hollywood studios, dropped out. The show was recast with virtual unknowns — John Stanley as Holmes and Alfred Shirley as Watson — who might be described as worthy, but dull. Edith Meiser was once more back in harness, reworking some of her old scripts and introducing new titles like 'The Laughing Lemur of Hightower Heath'. This series was short lived. The programme's producers decided the shows needed a more modern feel; 'They wanted me to put violence into the 'free adaptations' I was writing,' recalled Meiser. 'I refused and was dropped.'

In 1949 the detective took a final trip to

the West Coast for the last American network season on ABC. Dennis Green as writer, Ben Wright as Holmes and Eric Snowden as Watson brought the golden era of American Sherlockian radio shows to a close. However, in Britain, the great days of the sound Sherlock had yet to begin.

The casting of Carleton Hobbs as Sherlock Holmes and Norman Shelley as Watson was either wonderfully inspired or a remarkably lucky accident. Hobbs, with his high, reedy, alien tones, and Shelley, with his dark, plum pudding of a voice, were the vocal representations of the Paget drawings. These actors starred as Holmes and Watson on radio from 15 October 1952 ('The Naval Treaty') to 10 July 1969 ('His Last Bow'). Most of the scripts were written by Michael Hardwick and were all based on the original tales — with one exception. On 3 January 1953, Hobbs and Shelley were heard in a version of the Gillette play, adapted by Raymond Raikes, on the BBC's Home Service *Saturday Night Theatre*. On the day of the broadcast, ex-Chief Inspector Fabian of Scotland Yard unveiled a plaque outside the Criterion Restaurant, Piccadilly Circus, commemorating the meeting there of Dr Watson and Stamford that led to the first encounter between Holmes and Watson. Hobbs, dressed as the detective, arrived in a hansom cab to attend the ceremony.

Perhaps the most illustrious of all radio Holmes and Watsons were Sir John Gielgud and Sir Ralph Richardson, who appeared in a series of canonical adaptations independently produced by Harry Alan Towers. Directed in part by John's brother Val and scripted by John Keir Cross, these programmes were originally broadcast on the BBC Light Programme in 1954 and later picked up by NBC for American listeners. The two stars never quite managed to submerge their own formidable personalities into their roles, but they made a jolly pairing, presenting a friendship that one could believe in. Orson Welles appeared as Moriarty in the last episode, 'The Final Problem'.

Once the Hobbs and Shelley series disappeared from the airwaves in 1969, the BBC occasionally presented Holmes plays, including *A Study in Scarlet* (1974) with Robert Powell and Dinsdale Landen, *Sherlock Holmes vs Dracula* (1980) with John Moffat (who went on to portray Poirot on radio) and Timothy West, and *The Valley of Fear* (1986) with Tim Pigott-Smith and Andrew Hilton. There was also a series of thirteen half-hour adaptations recorded in Stereo Binaural Sound starring Barry Foster and David Buck in 1978.

Then, after the success of *The Hound of the Baskervilles* in 1988 with Roger Rees and Crawford Logan, and urged on by the adapter, Bert Coules, the BBC considered the idea of presenting all the Holmes stories in the order in which they were published, starring the same actors as the Baker Street duo. (Remarkably, although the Sherlockian career of Hobbs and Shelley had been a long one, there were some of the sixty stories that they had not recorded.) Eventually, the project received the green light and Clive Merrison and Michael Williams were chosen to star. Merrison presented a rather cold but nonetheless brilliant Holmes, whereas Williams carried out a difficult balancing act, revealing Watson's humanity and warmth while at the same time assuring us of his intelligence and independence of thought.

The programmes featuring the short stories were all forty-five minutes long. While other adapters were brought in, Bert Coules remained the principal writer, and had the distinction of penning the first instalment — 'A Study in Scarlet' — and the last — a re-working of *The Hound of the Baskervilles*. By August 1998 the whole Doyle Holmes canon had been recorded and broadcast. All the programmes are brilliantly preserved on CD for posterity.

Such was the popularity of the series that the BBC commissioned Coules to script a new series featuring his own stories based on throwaway references in the original tales. By the time *The Further Adventures of Sherlock Holmes* was broadcast in 2002, Michael Williams had died and Andrew Sachs (best known for his role as Manuel in *Fawlty Towers*) took on the role of Watson, but he did not quite capture the depth of characterisation of Williams. A second series was broadcast in 2004.

Meanwhile in the States, the Seattle-based radio production company Imagination Theatre began a series of original Holmes plays in 1998 with John Patrick Lowrie as Holmes and Lawrence 'Larry' Albert as Watson. To date, the series is still running.

TERROR BY NIGHT

First screening February 1946
Production company Universal Pictures
Duration 60 minutes
Black and white
Director Roy William Neill

Holmes (Basil Rathbone) and Watson (Nigel Bruce) are hired to safeguard the Star of Rhodesia diamond while en route from London to Edinburgh by the overnight express train. Inspector Lestrade (Dennis Hoey), pretending to be on a fishing trip, is also present. Following the theft of the gem and the murder of its owner, Holmes interrogates the train's passengers and begins to suspect that the crime is the handiwork of Colonel Sebastian Moran. Holmes discovers that the killer, Sands (Skelton Knaggs), was smuggled onto the train in the false bottom of a coffin. Sands, using an air gun that fires poison darts, commits two more murders before being shot by Moran himself (Alan Mowbray), who has boarded the train in the guise of Major Duncan Bleek, an old army friend of Watson's. After narrowly escaping death by being pushed from the train, Holmes exposes Bleek's true identity and, with some sleight of hand in the darkened railway carriage, manages to retrieve the stolen diamond. Moran is arrested by Lestrade as he leaves the train.

Aafter the very disappointing *Pursuit to Algiers*, *Terror by Night* is a pleasant surprise, showing the series returning to something like its old form. As in the previous film, Holmes is once more a glorified courier and we have a closed community — this time on a train — but Frank Gruber's tightly plotted screenplay is suspenseful and exciting. Gruber was a prolific writer, mostly of thrillers and Westerns. Of his many film scripts, the best is probably his adaptation of Eric Ambler's classic *The Mask of Dimitrios* (1944). While to some extent influenced by Hitchcock's *The Lady Vanishes* (1938), Gruber's screenplay for *Terror by Night* brings in elements from the Doyle stories in much the same way Bertram Millhauser's work did. There is, for example, the priceless diamond, the Star of Rhodesia — 'all who possessed it came to sudden and violent deaths' — a similar attribute was given to the Countess of Morcar's precious stone which was swallowed by a goose in 'The Adventure of the Blue Carbuncle'. Indeed, in the film

journey, Holmes asks to examine the famous Star of Rhodesia diamond and, later, when the theft has taken place, the detective produces the gem from his breast pocket, stating that the stolen jewel is a fake substituted by him when he was examining

'Obviously Hitchcock's *The Lady Vanishes* inspired the author of the script, but that's not a bad inspiration... told in tight continuity with flavorsome atmosphere' — *New York Times*.

Watson refers to the Star of Rhodesia as being as 'large as a duck's egg'. Then we have the character of Colonel Moran, and the very special air gun, which come from 'The Adventure of the Empty House'; the coffin with the concealed compartment from 'The Disappearance of Lady Frances Carfax'; and deadly poisoned darts, similar to Tonga's weapons in *The Sign of Four*.

One of the pleasing aspects of this movie is the way in which 'fair play' is observed in the displaying of clues, on one occasion at least. At the beginning of the

the original. A close examination of the earlier scene does in fact reveal Rathbone exhibiting a dextrous sleight of hand and slipping the jewel into his breast pocket, while palming another one — the fake — into the diamond case. The use of a decoy is similar to the ruse Holmes employed in the previous film, *Pursuit to Algiers*.

Like the train, the plot rattles along at such a pace that one isn't afforded the leisure to spot or at least dwell on the various loopholes in it. We know that Bruce's Watson is dumb, but surely even he

can tell the difference between an old army friend and Colonel Moran, one of Holmes' deadly enemies?

Universal ran through a good deal of stock train footage to punctuate the action and we are shown several scenes of the 'Scotch Express' racing through the countryside. While these shots are artificially darkened to simulate the nighttime, this does not hide the fact that the engine and carriages differ wildly from shot to shot. However, to compensate for this anomaly, a fairly accurate British

Railways train interior was used throughout the film.

Dennis Hoey made his last appearance as Inspector Lestrade in this entry, belligerent and baffled by events to the end. Alan Mowbray, who played the duplicitous Major Duncan Bleek, had himself played Lestrade in the 1933 production of *A Study in Scarlet*. Another series regular, Gerald Hamer, whose versatility had proved a valuable asset to these films, also made his final appearance, as Alfred Shallcross, a timid

small-time crook.

Terror by Night was shot in the closing months of 1945. By the time it was in the can and the script for the next feature, *Dressed to Kill*, was ready, Basil Rathbone had made the momentous decision to say goodbye to Holmes. He had been handcuffed to the character because of long term contracts with MGM — who loaned him to Universal for the Holmes films — and the Music Corporation of America, with whom he had signed years earlier for the Sherlock Holmes radio series. But in 1946 both his contracts with MGM and MCA were due to expire and Rathbone had decided that he was not going to renew them, seeing this as the perfect opportunity to lose his shackles for good. He still had one more film and another radio season to complete, but then he would be free. Seeing the light of artistic freedom at the end of the Sherlockian tunnel may explain why Rathbone's playing in *Terror by Night* is sprightlier than in the previous two entries. One reviewer called him 'silky smooth'. And indeed the film was generally well received. The *Motion Picture Independent* stated: 'There's plenty of suspense and action, enough to hold any audience's attention. Sherlock Holmes fans will be especially pleased...'

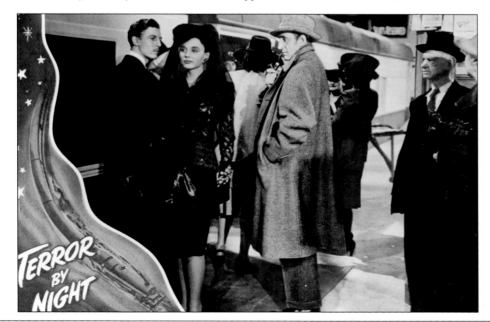

Previous page (right): *Boarding the overnight express.*
Above left: *Holmes (Basil Rathbone) examines Lady Margaret's (Mary Forbes) precious diamond, in the company of her son, Ronald (Geoffrey Steele), who is soon to be murdered.*
Above right: *Holmes discusses events with Watson (Nigel Bruce) and his supposed old school friend Major Duncan Bleek (Alan Mowbray).*
Left: *The glamorous widow, Vivian Vedder (Renee Godfrey), catches the attention of the Great Detective.*

DRESSED TO KILL

UK TITLE Sherlock Holmes and the Secret Code
FIRST SCREENING May 1946
PRODUCTION COMPANY Universal Pictures
DURATION 72 minutes
Black and white
DIRECTOR Roy William Neill

Sherlock Holmes (Basil Rathbone) is on the trail of stolen Bank of England printing plates. The key to their secret hiding place is concealed in the different coded tunes of three musical boxes manufactured by a thief serving a term in Dartmoor prison. The detective's protagonist is the glamorous femme fatale Hilda Courtney (Patricia Morison). She and her gang are in a race with Holmes to obtain all the musical boxes in order to possess the whole of the message. Courtney lures Holmes into a trap and he is trussed up and left to die by suffocation from the poisonous fumes of a car exhaust. Meanwhile, Courtney visits Baker Street and tricks Watson (Nigel Bruce) into revealing the whereabouts of the one musical box that she lacks to complete the code. Fortunately, Holmes manages to escape death and, with some incidental help from Watson, deduces that the plates have been hidden in the museum home of Doctor Samuel Johnson. With Inspector Hopkins (Carl Harbord) in tow, Holmes thwarts Courtney and her gang when they attempt to retrieve them.

DRESSED TO KILL, THE LAST OF THE UNIVERSAL series, has divided critics since its release. Michael B. Druxman, the author of *Basil Rathbone His Life and His Films*, called it 'a lemon', adding that it was 'a dismal conclusion to an often exceptional picture series.' And yet, Joe Pihonda in the *New York Herald Tribune* raved that, 'For a change the modernisation of Sherlock Holmes and Doctor Watson is bearing fruit on screen… *Dressed to Kill* stands out like a drum major. Recommended highly to mystery fans'.

One thing did seem to unite the critics — a dislike of the meaningless title. The *New York Times* declared that 'mystery is added by the fact that the title has nothing to do with the story and remains inexplicable to the end'. In Britain, the film was given a serviceable, but rather uninspired new name: *Sherlock Holmes and the Secret Code*.

The plot, fashioned by Frank Gruber and scripted by Leonard Lee, purported to be based on a Conan Doyle story, but you will look in vain for such a tale in the Holmes canon. However, there are elements from 'A Scandal in Bohemia' in the movie. Hilda Courtney uses the ruse of the smoke bomb to discover the hiding place of a precious object, in the same way Holmes did with Irene Adler in the Doyle story. Indeed, Holmes is as respectful of the lady as he was of Ms Adler, observing that Courtney was 'a brilliant antagonist. It is a pity her talents were misdirected.'

However, the rest of the script has a catchpenny feel to it — Gruber was a pulp fiction writer — and relies too heavily on the formula used in *Sherlock Holmes and the Secret Weapon* and *The Pearl of Death*, where Holmes and the criminals are in a race with each other — in this case for the stolen Bank of England plates. And, again, it seems that Holmes succeeds in the end through luck rather than deductive prowess.

By the time this movie was in production, Rathbone knew it would be his last as Holmes, and his total lack of interest in the project is evident. As one critic observed: 'Rathbone's mediocre performance brought the series to a close with a whimper rather than a bang'.

However, there were flashes of the old brilliance, such as when Watson observes that his childhood music teacher aided his tuition by numbering the keys. Holmes leans forward, his eyes flashing with excitement as that incisive, dark voice lashes out: 'Numbering the keys, Watson! The nineteenth key of the keyboard is the nineteenth letter of the alphabet. You've solved it!'

A press release for *Dressed to Kill* provides an interesting insight into the whole series: 'Basil Rathbone holds a record which no other screen player can approach. He's worn the same basic wardrobe in his twelve Sherlock Holmes films at Universal.' (This included a green tweed sack suit, tweed overcoat, modified fedora hat and black woollen dressing gown.) 'Authenticity, rather than economy, demands the same clothes in every Holmes film. Sherlock was so dressed that way in fiction, somewhat on the untidy side, and that's the way his millions of fans expect to see him on screen.' Many of his fans who knew their Doyle will remember references to Holmes' cat-like neatness and precise habits, rather than appearing 'somewhat on the untidy side'.

Posing in his standard attire for a full

'A price on her lovely head, a dare on her luscious lips, danger in her icy heart…' — Poster slogan.

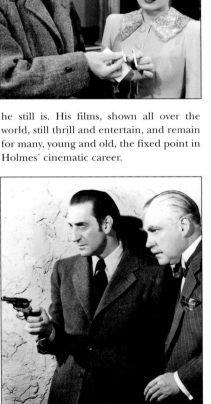

page magazine advertisement for Liggett and Myers Tobacco Company in 1946, in which *Dressed to Kill* also gained a plug, Rathbone made his final bow as the Universal version of Sherlock Holmes. Interestingly, he had grown his pencil moustache back by the time the picture was taken. It seemed throughout the forties and after, whenever he wasn't playing the clean-shaven Holmes, he would grow the moustache back. It was as though the actor was desperate to reassert his own persona.

Rathbone left Hollywood and fled to New York to resume his stage career, but he carried the Holmes tag with him for the rest of his life. In 1953 he appeared on television as the detective in an adaptation of 'The Adventure of the Black Baronet', a pastiche by Adrian Conan Doyle and John Dickson Carr, and then starred in the ill-fated stage production of *Sherlock Holmes*, a new drama written by his wife Ouida.

Sadly, Basil Rathbone, the greatest Sherlock Holmes, was naïve enough to believe that he really could escape from the all-embracing shadow of the Great Detective. Just as Conan Doyle had failed, so did Rathbone. With so many films and radio shows to his credit, he *was* Sherlock Holmes, and, of course, for countless fans

he still is. His films, shown all over the world, still thrill and entertain, and remain for many, young and old, the fixed point in Holmes' cinematic career.

Above left: Basil Rathbone, in his final performance as Holmes for Universal.
Above right: Trouble at Baker Street: a grim Mrs Hudson (Mary Gordon), Watson (Nigel Bruce) and Holmes.
Middle: Holmes demonstrates to Hilda Courtney (Patricia Morison) how he has traced her through her cigarettes.
Far left: Holmes is confronted in this original lobby card.
Left: Rathbone and Bruce, bringing the series to an end with 'a whimper rather than a bang'.

HOLMES IN VIEW
THE EARLY TELEVISION ADVENTURES

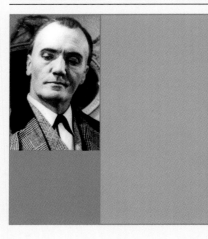

With the advent of the new medium of television in the 1930s, the character of Sherlock Holmes quickly became a popular choice to feature on the small screen.

ALTHOUGH JOHN LOGIE BAIRD GAVE THE FIRST practical demonstration of black and white television in January 1926, it was not until ten years later in November 1936 that the world's first public television service was inaugurated by the BBC at Alexandra Palace in north London. Despite this head start, it was the Americans who first brought the Great Detective to the domestic screen. In 1937 the National Broadcasting Company produced the first Sherlock Holmes 'tele-play', choosing a

Doyle story in which an American played a central role, 'The Adventure of the Three Garridebs'. It was scripted by veteran radio writer Thomas H. Hutchinson after NBC gained permission from Lady Jean Conan Doyle. Sherlock Holmes was portrayed by Louis Hector, who had already played the character on radio, and William Podmore was Watson. On 27 November 1937, the sage of Baker Street appeared on television for the first time. The drama was performed live, with several brief filmed

inserts of London scenes which gave the actors time to move from one set to another, or alter their costume as necessary. There were three sets: Holmes' flat in Baker Street, Nathan Garrideb's study and the office of Inspector Lestrade. The *New York Times* reported on this momentous occasion: 'Sherlock Holmes sleuthed around the television cameras at Radio City during the past week and stalked across the ultra-short wave lengths in the most ambitious experiment in teleshowmanship so far attempted in the air over New York. The shadow reincarnation of Conan Doyle's master detective served to introduce the first full-length presentation of Radio City television showmen. In six performances for members of The Radio Relay League, the ingenious welding of film with studio production offered an interesting glimpse into the future of a new form of dramatic art.

'The Holmes play opened with a film of the London skyline and then shifted to the 'live' studio where Louis Hector, as Holmes, was seen looking out of his Baker Street window. [This observation is at odds with the script, which states that Watson is looking out of the window and Holmes enters wearing a dressing gown and carrying 'a foolscap document'.] The major portion of the Doyle tale was confined to two sets, one representing the detective's apartment and the second the home of Nathan Garrideb, London ornithologist. The action shifted between the two scenes, although a film was used,

and with considerable success, to tie up the two points. This film showed Holmes and Doctor Watson riding in a hansom cab through the streets of London to the home of Garrideb in search of a new clue. Their dismissal of the cab, their entrance into the building and their inspection of the nameplate of Garrideb's door, all tended to link the action.'

The reporter on the *New York Times* thought problems for the camera were created by the cramped conditions on the sets, which 'was not sufficient to show simultaneously the detective as he observed Killer Evans' manipulation of the secret passageway concealed in a bookcase — a treatment that would have heightened the scene's dramatic effect'.

However, Louis Hector was praised for his performance: 'Hector, in traditional cape, peaked cap and double breasted suit, played Holmes in the approved manner and at all times gave the impression that a manhunt was in progress. His determined manner throughout gave the convincing evidence of the ultimate outcome — that the detective would surely "get his man." His demeanour was in marked contrast to the mild-mannered Doctor Watson, as acted by William Podmore. Both actors have had considerable training in broadcast terms and proved equally at home before the television cameras'.

The outbreak of the Second World War placed the development of television broadcasting on hold, and it wasn't until the late forties that Sherlock Holmes eventually returned to the small screen —

once again in America. On 12 March 1948 a whimsical little one-act play called *Tea Time in Baker Street* was aired on Station WWJ in Detroit, Michigan. The writer, Russell McLaughlin, a staunch Sherlockian and founder of the Amateur Mendicant Society, the local branch of the Baker Street Irregulars, claimed to have written the play to mark Holmes' ninety-fourth birthday.

Because of copyright restrictions, Holmes and Watson were absent from the drama, and the crime was solved by Mrs Hudson, her cockney chum Mrs Wiggins and Mrs Watson. McLaughlin stated that these ladies 'had developed, probably by contagion, something of the enterprise and deductive skill of the Great Detective himself.' Irene Adler also put in an appearance, as did Professor Moriarty, who was captured and tied up by the ladies for 'him — the man upstairs' to deal with. As the play came to an end, an announcer, with tongue firmly in cheek, told the audience that, 'All the characters in *Tea Time in Baker Street* are real persons and any resemblance to any fictitious character is purely coincidental. WWJ-TV regrets that it is unable to place Mr Holmes himself before you this evening, but he is much occupied at present with his bee-farm on the Sussex Downs, besides being rather crippled with rheumatism.'

If the tone of *Tea Time in Baker Street* was gently humorous, the next television project to feature Holmes was broad farce. On 5 April 1949 NBC's *Texaco Star Theatre* starred Milton Berle in the hour-long

production, 'Sherlock Holmes in the Mystery of the Sen Sen Murder or Who Was the Louse Who Shot the Grouse?' Berle, one of the first comedians to make the new medium of television his very own, starred as Holmes, with Victor Moore as Watson and the British singer Gracie Fields as Mrs Vanderpool. Basil Rathbone made a guest appearance — as 'Rathbone of Scotland Yard'.

The same year, NBC's series *Story Theatre* presented a ZIV production of 'The Adventure of the Speckled Band'. Reports on this twenty-five minute programme, which featured Alan Napier as Holmes and Melville Cooper as Watson, are confusing. Some sources state that it was universally panned by the reviewers, while other say it was 'a decent show.' The bulk of the criticism was aimed at the miscasting of Napier. It has been suggested that this actor, who specialised in playing members of the British aristocracy and butlers — he went on to play Batman's manservant Alfred in the Adam West series in the sixties — gave a wooden, stilted performance.

The first British attempt to put Sherlock Holmes on television was an unmitigated disaster. A pilot film, *The Man With the Twisted Lip* (aka *The Man Who Disappeared*), was produced by Rudolph Cartier in 1950. It starred John Longden as Holmes and Campbell Singer as Watson. In October, an advertisement was

Previous page (below): A smug Holmes (John Longden) interviews Doreen St Clair (Beryl Baxter) in the dire The Man With the Twisted Lip (1950).
Above left: John Longden as Holmes.
Above right: Holmes (John Longden) and Watson (Campbell Singer) gaze out of the window to see if there is any way out of this dreadful film.
Below: Louis Hector, the first actor to play Holmes on television.

rather shoddy manner; the plot development moves at some points at the most startling speed.'

Sherlock Holmes' first appearance on British television was in July 1951. The BBC produced a thirty-minute version of 'The Adventure of the Mazarin Stone', scripted by Alan Harmer, who also used Doyle's play, *The Crown Diamond* (which was the source for 'The Mazarin Stone'), as the main frame-work. Holmes was played by Andrew Osborn, with Philip King as Watson. It is most likely that this programme was used to test the waters for a projected series of Holmes adventures based on the Doyle canon. The BBC were evidently unhappy with the result and gave the project a complete revamp with new stars, a new producer, Ian Atkins, and a new writer, Miss C. A. Lejeune, a distinguished film critic on *The Observer*. The series of six thirty-minute shows — 'The Empty House', 'A Scandal in Bohemia', 'The Dying Detective', 'The Reigate Squires', 'The Red-Headed League' and 'The Second Stain' — began transmission in October of the same year, under the title *Sherlock Holmes*.

Alan Wheatley, who later found fame as The Sheriff of Nottingham in the television series *The Adventures of Robin Hood* (1955-

59) starring Richard Greene, was engaged to play Sherlock Holmes; and Raymond Francis, who later appeared as Detective Chief Inspector Lockhart in the crime series *No Hiding Place* (1959-67), was the new Watson. *The Times* noted that Wheatley's performance 'was done in a proper spirit of seriousness' but added that the actor was 'rather younger and fuller in face than the Holmes of his opponents' nightmares, yet catches the essential character. He is a figure, not merely of wonder or of fun, but of romantic possibility.'

However, the scripts for the shows were

placed in *Variety* encouraging potential advertisers to book advertising spots: 'A new series of half-hour weekly adventures of the greatest detective of them all is now being filmed in England.' This was far from the truth: only one film was being made as a try out, and by any standards this pilot was awful: continuity was awry, performances were amateurish, sets were cramped and unconvincing, and the script lacked coherence and tension. It never reached the television screens and wound up being released as a B movie short, receiving damning reviews. *Kinematograph* thought that 'the uninspired direction frequently causes the film to border on the burlesque', while the *Monthly Film Bulletin* stated that it was 'directed and acted in a

Rathbone agreed to play the part of Holmes in CBS's *Suspense* mystery series, as he believed it would give a publicity boost for his play, *Sherlock Holmes*, which was due to open later that year. Nigel Bruce was too ill to play Watson and so Martyn Green stepped into his shoes. CBS had decided to use a new story, 'The Adventure of the Black Baronet', penned by mystery writer John Dickson Carr and Adrian Conan Doyle, son of Sir Arthur. Rathbone believed at the time that if this episode was successful, a whole series would be commissioned, but the public and press reaction put paid to any such idea. The *New York Times* was fulsome in its dismay: 'Something was amiss. Holmes and Watson who have proved durable characters did not seem too happy in the cathode glare. On the printed page, Mr Doyle and Mr Carr have kept faith with Baker Street, but the television adaptation by Michael Dyne appeared to have come by way of Hollywood and Vine. The deerstalker, pipe and comfortable tweeds were all present

Previous page (above left): A nicely detailed Baker Street set with Holmes (Alan Wheatley) and Watson (Raymond Francis).
Previous page (above right): Wheatley and Francis pose for a publicity shot.
Previous page (below right): 'The Reigate Squires'.
Left: Wheatley 'catches the essential character' stated The Times.
Below: 'The Reigate Squires'. Left to right: Holmes, Alec Cunningham (Thomas Heathcote), Watson, Mr Cunningham (Beckett Bould) and Colonel Hayter (H. G. Stoker).

wordy, with Lejeune lifting a great deal of the dialogue straight from Doyle's texts. Alan Wheatley found this problematic, as he later observed: 'I must say I found it the most difficult thing to speak that I've ever done in my career. [Lejeune] also did some things that again really she shouldn't have fallen into — technical things like not allowing anything like enough time for changes. Of course, television was all live in those days, and in one particular scene, which I'll never forget, she finished up one scene with a sentence from me and opened the next scene with a sentence from me, *in heavy disguise*, with no time at all, and they could not think of a way of altering this.

The only thing we could do was for me to play the previous scene out of camera while I was making up in the corner of the set… But it created quite a lot of comment because people thought — how on earth was that done? At the time it certainly was a successful series, and it had an enormous amount of publicity.' Despite its success, the BBC failed to commission a further set of episodes, and it was over ten years before they gave Sherlock Holmes another thought.

In 1953 Basil Rathbone returned to the role that he had shunned since the mid-forties. This time he was back in the Victorian period and on television.

and accounted for, but the intellectual brilliance and personality of Sherlock was largely mislaid for the half-hour. In compressing *The Adventure of the Black Baronet* into a thirty-minute period, most of the traditional characterisation was left out and only the remnants of the straight narrative were seen.' Surprisingly, the strongest criticism was reserved for Basil Rathbone: 'Mr Rathbone did not seem happy with the part with which he never really could come to grips.'

Rumours have circulated for years that somewhere a copy of this television show exists but, as yet, it has failed to come to light.

SHERLOCK HOLMES

FIRST SCREENING 1953-54
PRODUCTION COMPANY Guild Films
DURATION thirty-nine 30 minute episodes
Black and white
REGULAR CAST
Ronald Howard (Sherlock Holmes),
Howard Marion Crawford (Doctor Watson),
Archie Duncan (Inspector Lestrade)

In the early fifties, television screens were awash with detective series and one canny American entrepreneur thought it was time for the man from Baker Street to join them.

IN 1953, AMERICAN PRODUCER SHELDON Reynolds, a life-long fan of Sherlock Holmes, decided to get a piece of the television action by producing a Holmes series in Europe, where the costs were cheaper. Having done a deal with Sir Arthur's son, Adrian, who was keen to make money out of his literary inheritance, Reynolds came to England to look for his star. He realised the time was ripe to bring a fresh new Holmes to the screen. In *A Study in Scarlet*, when Holmes and Watson first meet, the two men are in their twenties, and yet Holmes is almost always portrayed on screen as being middle-aged, with Watson racing toward senility. Conscious of the youth market, Reynolds wanted to reverse the trend. When he interviewed the thirty-five year-old Ronald Howard, he knew he had his man. He was the son of Leslie Howard, the Hollywood star who had died tragically when his plane was shot down by the Germans during the war. Ronald always suffered from the stigma of being a great

'Reynolds has avoided the customary clichés that seem inevitable in any treatment of the Sir Arthur Conan Doyle stories and instead has concentrated on straight detection work' — *Variety*.

actor's son. At first he had rejected the idea of acting as a career and began work as a journalist, but after his father's death there was a sudden interest in him. Could Ronald possibly take his father's place? Attempts were made to persuade him to change his name to Leslie Howard Junior, but he refused. However, he did take up acting and in 1946, after a spell in repertory theatre, Howard entered films. He was a competent actor but he lacked his father's charisma and in 1953, when he met Sheldon Reynolds, his career was in the doldrums. However, on meeting him, the producer signed him up straight away. Sadly, he cast Howard Marion Crawford as his Watson. Crawford was only four years senior to Howard but looked, and played, much older; his Watson was in the same 'hail fellow, well met' school of per-

formance as Nigel Bruce.

Reynolds produced thirty-nine half-hour shows between 1953 and 1954 on a shoestring budget. The series was set in period and filmed in Paris because it was cheaper than either America or Britain. There was a week's location shooting in England to provide a range of exterior shots for the whole series, but it rained heavily for seven days and many of the shots were unusable. A small number of British actors took the leading roles, while the rest were French. Archie Duncan, who later played Little John to Richard Greene's Robin Hood in another television series, was a dour Scottish Inspector Lestrade.

Actor Harry Towb (then billed as Harris Towb) appeared in several of the episodes and remembered the experience fondly:

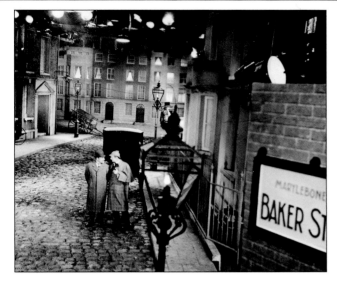

'They used to pay in francs — 50,000 francs for four days which was £50. They paid your fare, but you had to pay your own expenses, so you didn't make much from it... but I must say they were super to work for. They shot them very quickly. It wasn't really quality stuff. Shelly Reynolds was clever though, because to shoot twenty-seven minutes in four days was some going. They were great fun, but they were really an excuse to go to Paris.'

The Baker Street set was built inside the Post Parisien Studios, and very cramped and strangely Gallic it looked. In watching several episodes, it is amusing to note that the lamp-post on the set has a life of its own, and moves up and down Baker Street, appearing in different locations. In one

episode, 'The Texas Cowgirl', it disappears altogether to allow for a covered wagon to roll down the cobbled street.

In the main, the plots were new, but now and then there were borrowings from the Conan Doyle stories. The pilot of the series, 'The Case of the Cunningham Heritage', written by Sheldon Reynolds, contains the only filmed version of the meeting between Holmes and Watson at St Bartholomew's Hospital, lifted from the opening of *A Study in Scarlet*. Reynolds cunningly protected himself against the pilot not blossoming into a full series by making certain that the next two scripts, 'Lady Beryl' and 'The Winthrop Legend', contained elements that would allow all three episodes to be edited together into

one feature-length film. But the television pilot did sell, and the cobbled together theatrical film never materialised.

Howard must have expected great things from the series, but his optimism was quickly doused. The scripts, written either by Reynolds himself, or a group of expatriate Hollywood writers living in France after suffering persecution during the Communist witchhunts, were poor and often embarrassingly whimsical. Titles such as 'The Baker Street Nursemaids' and 'The Mother Hubbard Case' give an indication of their level. In the aforementioned 'The Texas Cowgirl', a wigwam was erected in Holmes' sitting room.

The four day shooting schedules placed a great strain on the actors, particularly Howard who, as Holmes, inevitably shouldered the bulk of the dialogue. He was trapped in France for nearly a year making the series which, ironically, was not shown in Britain until several years later and then in a sporadic fashion by regional ITV companies at off peak times. When he finally returned, Howard found that he had been forgotten by agents, management and audiences alike. This was a great shame for, despite the poor quality of the series in many departments, Howard gave a refreshing and appealing performance. Certainly he was a lightweight Holmes, his actions bordering on the frivolous at times (repeatedly trying card tricks out on Watson, and failing, in the episode 'The Split Ticket', for example), but there was an essential Doylean fidelity to his portrayal. And he looked good in a deerstalker and cape.

While most British viewers missed Howard's Holmes series, it was syndicated for years on US television. However, now it's available on DVD on both sides of the pond.

Previous page (below left): Holmes (Ronald Howard) and Watson (Howard Marion Crawford) meet for the first time in the opening episode, 'The Case of the Cunningham Heritage'.
Previous page (right): Location shooting in wet and windy London.
Above left: The cramped Baker Street studio set.
Above right: Behind the scenes of 'The Mother Hubbard Case'.
Left: Holmes and Watson soak their feet while Inspector Lestrade (Archie Duncan) enjoys a cigar.

THE HOUND OF THE BASKERVILLES

First screening 4 May 1959
Production company Hammer Films
Duration 87 minutes
Colour
Director Terence Fisher

The legend of the Hound of the Baskervilles relates how the wicked Sir Hugo Baskerville (David Oxley) fell victim to 'a hound from hell' on Dartmoor after murdering an innocent servant girl, and how this beast has haunted the Baskerville family ever since. Doctor Mortimer (Francis De Wolff) visits Sherlock Holmes (Peter Cushing) to tell him of the recent death of Sir Charles Baskerville, who died of fright out on the moor. He enlists Holmes to protect the new heir to the estate, Sir Henry (Christopher Lee), who narrowly escapes death in a London hotel when he discovers a deadly tarantula placed inside his boot. Holmes and Watson (André Morell) travel with the baronet down to Devonshire, where they learn of the escaped convict Selden (Michael Mulcaster), who is at large on the moor. They also encounter Barrymore (John Le Mesurier) and his wife (Helen Goss), servants at Baskerville Hall. Holmes discovers that Sir Henry's neighbours, Stapleton (Ewen Solon) and his beautiful daughter Cecile (Marla Landi), are behind the killings. Despite being injured while trapped down an old tin mine, Holmes manages to save Sir Henry from the Hound.

AFTER THE INTERNATIONAL SUCCESS OF THEIR colour treatments of *Frankenstein* and *Dracula*, Hammer Films began trawling through the list of horror classics and turned their attention to Conan Doyle's timeless chiller. Having secured the rights to the novel, Hammer began filming in September 1958. It was envisaged that this would be the first in a series of Hammer Holmes adventures in colour.

Peter Cushing, the studio's main star at the time, was chosen to play Sherlock. Being a Holmes enthusiast and owning a collection of *The Strand Magazine* featuring the original stories, he was delighted at the prospect. He admitted that he had been fascinated by the character since child-

hood: 'I remember an uncle of mine telling of a friend who had been accused of molesting a lady in a train. As a child, I remember my uncle saying he proved the lady was telling a lie "rather like Sherlock Holmes". This man called the guard along and said, "This lady has accused me of molesting her and it's impossible. Look at my cigar." And it had about an inch of ash on it. And I thought, what an extraordinary man Sherlock Holmes must be.'

Perhaps Cushing was slightly concerned when he learned that executive producer Michael Carreras had presold his incarnation of the Great Detective as a 'sexy Sherlock'. Nevertheless, he approached the part in a scholarly fashion, even

changing some dialogue to make it more appropriate for the character. A case in point is Holmes' reply to Doctor Mortimer's boast concerning his generosity in the matter of fees. Cushing recalled: 'They had some line which was absolutely wrong, so I asked, "Why can't we use one that Holmes actually said?" And so we used a line from the story 'The Problem of Thor Bridge': 'My professional charges are upon a fixed scale. I do not vary them, save when I remit them altogether.''

Similarly, Cushing asked for parts of the Baker Street sitting room set to be modified: 'Holmes had the habit of keeping correspondence fixed to the mantelpiece with his jack-knife... As fate would have it, the mantelpiece was made of marble because it was one they had in stock, so I asked them to put a piece of balsa wood on top of it.'

Watson was played by another Hammer stalwart, André Morell, who gave what was generally regarded as the most realistic and sensible portrayal of the Doctor on film to date. He said: 'It was agreed not to do Watson as a comic character. Conan Doyle, after all, felt that Watson was a

doctor and not an idiot as he was often made out to be.'

Writer Peter Bryan took certain liberties with his adaptation of the novel to add more drama and horror-tinged incidents, in keeping with the Hammer approach. Christopher Lee had to endure a tarantula spider crawling up his arm; Stapleton's innocent sister is turned into his vengeful daughter while he, no longer the urbane entomologist, is a disgruntled farmer with a webbed hand; and Holmes is trapped down an old tin mine, narrowly escaping death

when the mineshaft supports give way.

As with all Hammer productions, the sets and costumes were of the highest quality, although there are no scenes of London exteriors, as in the 1939 version, to give a real sense of period and location. The moorland exteriors were filmed at Frensham Ponds, although brief shots of both Dartmoor and Holyport are seen in the film.

Hammer was keen to make the actual Hound as frightening as possible in order to obtain an X certificate for the film,

which they felt sure would increase their box office takings, but this proved problematic. Cushing remembered that they dressed two little boys in the same suits as Holmes and Baskerville, and built a set the size of these children and put a dog in it so that it appeared huge: 'And that's what it looked like — two small children dressed up, a big dog and a small set… It looked ludicrous'. Matters were not helped by the benevolent nature of the dog. Director Terence Fisher said: 'The dog was the kindest and loveliest dog around. In fact for a lot of the close cutting work we used an artifical head and kept pushing it into various actors' faces'.

In the end the movie was given an A certificate and received a poor response from both critics and cinema audiences. *Picturegoer* thought it 'less of a thriller than a flamboyant period caricature, acted out in eye-popping Sweeney Todd style'. To *Films and Filming*, Cushing appeared 'wildly athletic', presenting an 'impish, waspish Wilde-ian Holmes'; while *Variety* was more positive, stating 'it is difficult to fault the performance of Peter Cushing.'

Opinion of this film has changed over the years and it is now generally regarded as one of the best versions of *The Hound*. However, low box office returns upon release ensured that this was Hammer's last foray into the realms of Sherlock Holmes.

Previous page (right): The wicked Sir Hugo Baskerville (David Oxley) with the innocent servant girl (Judi Moyens).
Above left: Humphrey Morton and Stanley MacKenzie, two members of the Sherlock Holmes Society of London, meet Cushing and Morell on set.
Above right: Peter Cushing and André Morell: a memorable Holmes and Watson.
Left: The clue is in the portrait: Holmes explains to Watson.

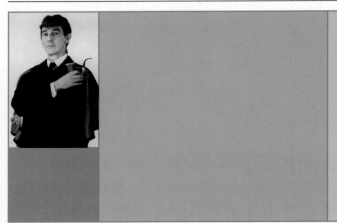

'I can never resist a touch of the dramatic.' Sherlock Holmes in 'The Naval Treaty'.

'You would have made an actor, and a rare one.' Inspector Athelney Jones to Holmes in *The Sign of Four*.

FOUR YEARS AFTER ARTHUR CONAN DOYLE had consigned his hero to a watery death at the bottom of the Reichenbach Falls in the story 'The Final Problem', his desire to write a really successful play for the theatre prompted the author to create a vehicle for his detective character. However, he soon lost interest and the project eventually ended up with the American actor William Gillette who, according to Doyle, turned his original draft 'into a fine play'. The

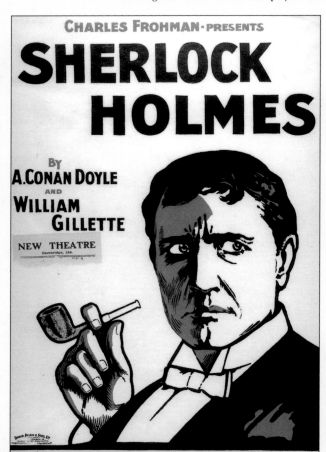

drama, *Sherlock Holmes* (first performed in 1899), which also involved Professor Moriarty, was described as a hitherto unpublished case in the career of the Great Detective, relating his connection with 'the strange case of Miss Faulkner'. However, the plot relied heavily on two of Doyle's short stories, 'A Scandal in Bohemia' and 'The Final Problem'.

The most striking innovation in the play was Holmes' romance. Hitherto, the detective had always been seen as a confirmed bachelor with misogynist tendencies. 'I should never marry lest I bias my judgement,' he observed in *The Sign of Four*. Now here he was on stage telling the heroine that he loved her.

After the success of this 'absurd, preposterous and thoroughly delightful melodrama' in New York, Gillette toured with it, eventually bringing the play to London in 1901, where the young Charlie Chaplin played Billy the pageboy.

Gillette revived *Sherlock Holmes* in 1923 and then retired; but in 1929, at the age of seventy-six, he began an astonishing Farewell Tour of the United States with the play. So overwhelming was the response to this tour that it wasn't until three years later, in May 1932, that it was finally completed. The play was again revived, with great success, by the Royal Shakespeare Company in 1974, featuring John Wood in the title role, a production that later transferred to Broadway, where such actors as John Neville and Leonard Nimoy played Holmes.

Conan Doyle made two further attempts to write a Holmes play. Late in 1909 the author took a lease on the Adelphi Theatre in London and invested a great deal of money in his own play, *The House of Temperley*, a boxing drama. It

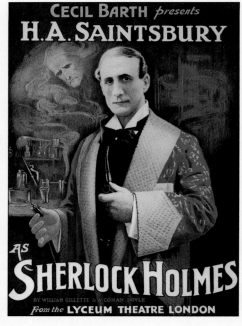

floundered at the box office and closed early. Conan Doyle was left with an empty theatre and a tremendous deficit on his hands. Once more he turned to Sherlock Holmes. A month after the curtain fell for the last time on *The House of Temperley*, it rose again on *The Speckled Band*, a dramatised version of one of the best Holmes stories. The production successfully paid off Doyle's theatrical debts. Holmes was played by H. A. Saintsbury, who in 1903 had taken over from Gillette in *Sherlock Holmes* at the Lyceum Theatre.

Conan Doyle wrote one other Holmes drama, *The Crown Diamond*, billed as 'An Evening with Sherlock Holmes', which appeared at the Coliseum in 1921. Dennis Nelson-Terry played the detective. Doyle later fashioned the play into a story, 'The Adventure of the Mazarin Stone', which featured in *The Casebook of Sherlock Holmes*.

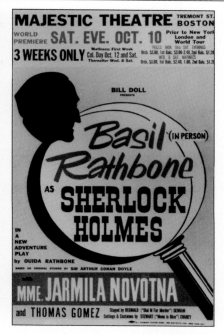

1923 saw the great screen Holmes of the day, Eille Norwood, tread the boards in *The Return of Sherlock Holmes* by J. E. Terry and L. Arthur Rose, which was another amalgam of Doyle stories. The play was revised by L. Arthur Rose and Ernest Dudley after the war, and as recently as 1997 it toured Britain, with Michael Cashman in the title role.

In 1933, Felix Aylmer appeared as an elderly, retired Holmes in Basil Michael's *The Holmeses of Baker Street*, attempting to cope with a brilliant daughter named Shirley, who wishes to employ the deductive powers she has inherited to investigate the mystery of the theft of the Black Pearl. Holmes tries to prevent her, explaining that his detective work had

been the cause of an unhappy marriage which culminated in the premature death of his wife. Nevertheless, Shirley does investigate and, with some help from her father, manages to solve the case. *The Daily Telegraph* called the play 'thundering good entertainment.'

The next major Sherlock Holmes play appeared in 1953. One can easily understand how the producers would have considered this venture a box office certainty, for it starred none other than Basil Rathbone. *Sherlock Holmes*, based on several of Doyle's stories, including 'The Final Problem', was written by Rathbone's wife, Ouida. The play was spectacularly mounted, with Professor Moriarty (Thomas Gomez, who had played the villain in Rathbone's first Universal movie, *Sherlock Holmes and the Voice of Terror*) tumbling into the Reichenbach Falls from the balcony of a Swiss villa. But the storyline was cumbersome and lacked real drama. The production ran on Broadway for only three days.

The same year also found Holmes doing pirouettes on stage when Sadler's Wells in London presented *The Great Detective*, a ballet featuring Kenneth MacMillan. Another melodic venture was *Baker Street*, the musical by Jerome Coopersmith, Marian Grudeff and Raymond Jessel. The singing sleuth was played by Fritz Weaver, whose Watson was Peter Sallis. *Baker Street* was a critical success and ran for eight months on Broadway in 1965, but failed to break even financially and never reached Britain. Peter Sallis remembers it as a very lavish production: 'I

cannot tell you the amount of money which was poured into it. The sets were brilliant, and we had these puppets — they dropped a cloth down, and across the cloth was a painted scene of London with all the obvious landmarks, and you saw this little carriage drawn by eight horses with Queen Victoria in it, bowing. This was all done with marionettes! I remember it because I used to have to sit behind it every night, and the cloth would go up and there were Fritz and I — we were the next scene — and there was a roar of applause from the audience when they began to realise what was happening.'

The plot involved Irene Adler falling in love with Holmes, and Moriarty's attempt to steal the crown jewels during Queen Victoria's jubilee celebrations.

Less successful was Leslie Bricusse's *Sherlock Holmes — The Musical*, which originally opened in the late eighties, starring Ron Moody in the lead. In this show, Holmes falls in love with Bella, Professor Moriarty's daughter. The construction and presentation were old-fashioned, and the show was panned by the critics. There was later a revised version, starring Robert Powell, which had an unsuccessful tour of the provinces. The tour was cut short in Blackpool when some scenery crashed down, injuring Powell.

Still in the musical world, in 1997 *Sherlock Holmes and the Case of the Purloined Patience — or The Scandal at the D'Oyle Carte* gathered an array of good reviews when it was performed at the Folger Elizabethan theatre in Washington. The show, written by Nick Olcott, was a clever blending of the

Previous page (above left): John Wood as Holmes in the 1974 revival of William Gillette's play.
Above left: *A scene from the play Sherlock Holmes (1953). Moriarty (Thomas Gomez), Irene Adler (Jarmila Novotna) and Holmes (Basil Rathbone).*
Left: *From the extravagant 1965 musical Baker Street. Holmes (Fritz Weaver) charms Irene Adler (Inga Swenson) while Watson (Peter Sallis) looks on. Sallis was surprised to be chosen for the role, believing that the producers really wanted Peter Sellers and there was a mix-up with the names!*

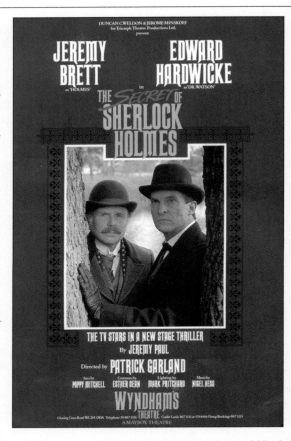

a new interest in Holmes on stage and since the mid-seventies there has been a steady stream of Sherlock plays. One of the most successful has been *The Crucifer of Blood* by Paul Giovanni, which is a reconstructed version of *The Sign of Four*, presenting Mary Morstan as the villain. It was staged both in London and New York. In the Broadway production, Holmes was played by Charlton Heston and Watson by Jeremy Brett who, of course, went on to play the master detective himself, in the excellent series produced by Granada Television.

The Granada series itself spawned a play, *The Secret of Sherlock Holmes*, written by Jeremy Paul, one of the regular writers of the Jeremy Brett episodes. It was a two-hander which paired Brett with his screen Watson, Edward Hardwicke. The premise was that Moriarty was actually a figment of Holmes' imagination. It ran at Wyndham's Theatre in London's West End for a year before touring.

Watson had his own play in *221B*, a one-man drama written by Martin Read. It

worlds of Baker Street and Gilbert and Sullivan. It took an actual incident — the pirated American version of the Gilbert and Sullivan opera *Patience* in 1881 — as its focus, and Holmes is brought in to solve the case.

Olcott's conceit was to take thirty Gilbert and Sullivan songs from a variety of shows and insert them at appropriate places in his detective story. Some of the songs fitted the plot without much tailoring. For example, 'Things Are Seldom What They Seem' (originally from *HMS Pinafore*) is sung by a disguised Holmes to a clueless Watson, while 'He Is an Englishman' (also from *Pinafore*) is sung by the ensemble as a paean of praise to Holmes. In other instances Olcott tinkered with the lyrics in order to fit his plot. 'I Am the Very Model of a Modern Major General' (from *Pirates of Penzance*) became a Sherlock Holmes solo, 'I Am the Very Model of a Crack Victorian Sleuth'.

Of a darker hue was Matthew Lang's *Sherlock's Last Case*. This seventies drama presented an angry Watson (Peter Bayliss) bent on murder, taking revenge on his insufferable detective friend (Julian Glover) after being abused for many years with sarcastic taunts and ridicule.

The success of the Royal Shakespeare Company's revival of Gillette's play created

toured Britain in 1983/4 and starred Nigel Stock, who had played Watson on BBC Television to the Sherlocks of both Douglas Wilmer and Peter Cushing. Shortly before his death in 1986, Stock recorded a shortened version of the play for BBC Radio 4.

Apart from the many adaptations of Holmes stories to appear in British regional theatres in the last fifteen years or so — *The Hound of the Baskervilles* being by far the most popular — there have also been several original dramas. In 1988 Brian Clemens penned *Holmes and the Ripper*, which toured with Francis Matthews and Frank Windsor as Holmes and Watson. Royce Ryton wrote *To Kill a King* (1981), which involved an assassination attempt on Edward VII. Tim Heath's cleverly staged *The Adventure at Sir Arthur Sullivan's* (1996) presented a cocktail party at which Holmes dramatises two of his most famous cases: 'A Scandal in Bohemia' and 'The Adventure of Charles Augustus Milverton'. Even the hilarious comedy duo Maggie

Fox and Sue Ryder, known as Lip Service, sent Holmes up in their ingenious *Move Over Moriarty* (1996). This two-hour romp, in which all the characters are played by Sue and Maggie, sees Holmes investigating the baffling Garibaldi Biscuit Affair. There are surprises along the way, not least when Holmes calls for his needle — not for an injection of cocaine but to continue his French knitting!

The latest stage incarnation of Holmes is found in my own play *Sherlock Holmes — The Last Act!* This is a one-man drama in which Holmes, on returning to his old Baker Street rooms from Watson's funeral in 1916, reflects on all the things he wished he had told his old friend when he was alive. The play not only allows Holmes to consider his past career — thus peopling the stage with his interpretation of characters from his life, including Moriarty — but also to dig deep into his psyche to examine his own character, his childhood and the nature of his relationships. Roger Llewellyn is the actor who has grasped the nettle of this demanding interpretation of Holmes, and has received stunning reviews for his performance. London's *Time Out*

stated that, 'From Basil Rathbone to Jeremy Brett there have been many fine portrayals of Conan Doyle's greatest creation. The name Roger Llewellyn can now be added to the distinguished list.' This publication also referred to the script as 'incisive, elegant and deeply moving.' The play premièred at Salisbury Playhouse in May 1999 and achieved five star reviews at the Edinburgh Festival the same year. The play continues to tour — having spent two months in Canada in 2000.

While *Sherlock Holmes — The Last Act!* can claim to be unique in that it is the first play in which the Great Detective takes centre stage on his own, there can be no doubt that there will be many more theatrical ventures featuring the sleuth from Baker Street in the future.

Previous page (above left): Ron Moody starred in the ill-fated Sherlock Holmes — The Musical.

Previous page (below): The Crucifer of Blood: Charlton Heston as Holmes, Jeremy Brett as Watson and Suzanne Lederer as Irene St Clair.

Above left: Roger Llewellyn in the one-man drama Sherlock Holmes — The Last Act!

Left: Jeremy Brett and Edward Hardwicke in The Secret of Sherlock Holmes.

SHERLOCK HOLMES AND THE DEADLY NECKLACE

GERMAN TITLE Sherlock Holmes und das Halsband des Todes
FIRST SCREENING 1962
PRODUCTION COMPANY Constantin Film Verleih of Berlin
DURATION 86 minutes
Black and white
DIRECTORS Terence Fisher with Frank Winterstein

A dying man arrives at Baker Street just in time to whisper the word 'Hare' and make a curious flowing gesture with his hands before expiring. Holmes (Christopher Lee) deduces that he is referring to a dockland pub known as the Hare and Eagle. With Watson (Thorley Walters), Holmes visits the pub, where he learns that Professor Moriarty (Hans Söhnker) is planning to steal a priceless necklace recently discovered in Cleopatra's tomb. Failing to prevent the theft, Holmes breaks into Moriarty's apartment in disguise and discovers the necklace hidden in a sarcophagus. He hands the precious item over to Inspector Cooper (Hans Nielson), who is to guard it until the auction at which it is to be sold. Certain that Moriarty will attempt to recover his prize, Holmes, again in disguise, joins the Professor's gang and scuppers their attempt to steal it back again. He arrives at the auction room with the necklace just in time for the sale. While most of Moriarty's gang have been rounded up by the police, the Professor himself escapes arrest.

THE FIRST SHERLOCK HOLMES FILM OF THE sixties is one that, until recently, was somewhat obscure, and had been seen by very few. It was made in Germany in 1962, but not shown in the States until 1964, where it went straight to television, while in Britain it eventually gained a limited theatrical run in 1968 before disappearing for many years.

In the planning stages the film looked as though it would be an impressive effort, with Christopher Lee as Holmes and the excellent British character actor Thorley Walters as Watson. Terence Fisher, one of the stellar craftsmen from the Hammer Films stable, was set to direct. The screenplay was written by Curt Siodmak, a fine thriller writer who had created Lawrence Talbot, the Wolf Man for Universal's 1941 horror movie of the same name, and whose other film credits included the classic *The Beast with Five Fingers* (1946). Originally *The Deadly Necklace* was meant to be an adaptation of *The Valley of Fear* but, apart from one incident where a dead man's real identity is deliberately disguised by his mutilated face, the finished film bore no resemblance to the Doyle novel. The final version, savagely rewritten by the production team, lacked

the German producers, which ruined it. Even the music was ludicrous. [It is a highly inappropriate modern jazz score]. My portrayal of Holmes is, I think, one of the best things I've ever done because I tried to play him really as he was written, as a very intolerant, argumentative, difficult man, and I looked extraordinarily like him with the make-up. Everyone who's seen it said I was as like Holmes as any actor they've ever seen both in appearance and interpretation. I can claim to have come close to Conan Doyle's conception of Holmes, both physically and professionally.'

EUROPRODIS
présente

Christophe **LEE**
Santa **BERGER**
Yvan **DESNY**
dans
Une réalisation
TERENCE FISHER

Sherlock Holmes
et le COLLIER de la MORT

'This is the Teutonic Holmes, perpetrated in Berlin, dubbed in American... I have read the synopsis — ouch!' — *Sherlock Holmes Journal*.

cohesion and logical development, and one can only suspect that there were too many cooks with their spoons stirring this particular broth. The movie was a German/Italian/British/French co-production, and with all those nationalities involved it is perhaps no wonder that there was a breakdown of communication along the way. For English director Fisher it was an experience he wished to forget: 'It's a film well worth left alone'.

The star Christopher Lee was of the same opinion: '[It] was a badly edited hodge podge of nonsense.' He went on to express regret at the missed opportunities that the film presented: 'I think it was a pity, this film, in more ways than one. We should never have made it in Germany with German actors, although we had a British art director and British director. It was a hodge podge of stories mixed together by

Christopher Lee was a natural choice to play Holmes, and one might suppose if Peter Cushing had not been available for Hammer's *Hound* (1959), Lee would have been an ideal substitute: he is tall and authoritative with a thin, aquiline nose, which was enhanced by make-up for this production. Unfortunately, one cannot judge Lee's portrayal in *Sherlock Holmes and the Deadly Necklace* fully, because on all available copies he has been overdubbed by an unidentified American actor. Certainly he looks good, even when he is wearing a rather garish Inverness Cape with large squares more fitted to a pantomime Holmes, but the rather expressionless nasal voice which he has inherited in the dubbing process virtually kills the performance. Sadly, a similar fate befell Thorley Walters as Watson, who appeared as a paler version of Nigel Bruce's good Doctor. However, Walters, like Lee with Holmes, would have further stabs at the role in the future.

Visually the film was eccentric also, for while the set of the Baker Street rooms was impressive and Victorian, the costumes were a strange mixture of periods, so that the setting could be either the 1880s or 1920s. Indeed, some of the ladies' outfits, with their calf-length skirts, had a look of the 1950s about them. Certainly, with Professor Moriarty, presented almost as a Godfather figure, driving around in a Rolls Royce, one supposes that we are well into the twentieth century. Both Holmes and Watson are also seen driving cars and seem completely *au fait* with the internal combustion engine.

Understandably, the few reviews the film received were far from sanguine. The *Monthly Film Bulletin* noted that, 'The photography has an occasional grainy look, rather reminiscent of an early German silent film; and apart from some startling anachronisms the period detail (on the whole) is nicely done (in particular the snake motif of Moriarty's apartment). But the film itself, feebly directed by Terence Fisher, is plodding and colourless.' The fact that Moriarty walks scot free at the end indicates that there was perhaps a sequel in the offing. If there was, thankfully, the film was never made.

Previous page (below left): *The striking French poster for the film.*
Previous page (right): *Mrs Hudson (Edith Schultze-Westrum) is given a shock by Holmes' knife practice.*
Above: *Professor Moriarty (second from left, Hans Söhnker) offers Inspector Cooper (right, Hans Nielson) a drink from his flask-concealing cane, as Holmes (Christopher Lee) and Watson (Thorley Walters) look on in the film's puzzling climax.*
Left: *Lee, who returned to role of the Great Detective decades later in* Sherlock Holmes: The Golden Years.

DETECTIVE/SHERLOCK HOLMES

FIRST SCREENING 1964-1965
PRODUCTION COMPANY BBC
DURATION 13 x 50 minute episodes
Black and white
REGULAR CAST
Douglas Wilmer (Sherlock Holmes),
Nigel Stock (Doctor Watson),
Enid Lindsey (Mrs Hudson),
Peter Madden (Inspector Lestrade)

In the sixties, when BBC Television contemplated bringing Sherlock Holmes back to the small screen, they first gave him a trial outing in the 1964 BBC series *Detective*, which presented a set of fifty-minute dramas, each featuring a different literary sleuth.

AMONG OTHERS, THERE WERE CASES FOR G. K. Chesterton's Father Brown (Mervyn Johns), Ngaio Marsh's Inspector Alleyn (Geoffrey Keen) and Margery Allingham's Campion (Brian Smith). And of course there was Sherlock Holmes, played by Douglas Wilmer. In essence, this series was

a collection of pilot shows used to test the public's reaction to dramatised adventures of the various detectives. After eighteen episodes, only two characters emerged from the experiment with a series of their own: Gil North's dour Yorkshire policeman Cluff, played by Leslie Sands, and Sherlock Holmes.

The BBC had played safe in choosing 'The Adventure of the Speckled Band', one of the most popular tales, for the pilot episode. It was adapted by Giles Cooper and directed by Robin Midgley, and it worked a treat. Wilmer, looking not unlike a younger (and shorter) Basil Rathbone, appeared to great effect with Nigel Stock as Watson. The press and viewer response was positive and so a series was planned. This, according to Wilmer, was when the trouble started: 'I was let down by the BBC from the word go. I agreed to do a series of twelve episodes based on the Doyle stories

wrong!" For example, the script of 'The Red-Headed League' bore no relation to the original story. I said, "That's going in the wastepaper basket. I won't do it." This, of course, made me unpopular but I felt so

'[The *Sherlock Holmes* series] promises to combine nostalgia with well-mannered excitement in a pleasing mixture' — *Variety*.

on the understanding that the director of 'The Speckled Band' would direct most of them. He didn't do one of them. Not one.' An exacting perfectionist, Wilmer soon lost his temper with producer David Goddard concerning the relaxed approach to the series: 'The powers that be only saw it as just another television show and weren't concerned enough to get the details right. Even then, I felt the shadow of the Sherlock Holmes Society looming over me like a great black bat. I used to say, "They'll tear you apart if you get these details

strongly about it. So they said, "Well, what are we going to do? We start in ten days." So I said, "Get the book, take a cake slice, fish out all the dialogue, and get that so-called script editor to knit it together. We don't need fourteen extraneous characters with names like Harry the horse and other Runyonesque names who are not in the original." One of the most interesting aspects of the story is the villain Clay who has aristocratic blood in him — the illegitimate son of a royal duke — well there was no mention of that in the

original script. He was reduced to being a common-or-garden barrow boy!'

The series commenced on Saturday 20 February 1965 with 'The Illustrious Client', adapted by Giles Cooper and featuring Peter Wyngarde giving a memorable performance as the cold-hearted Baron Gruner. *Variety* commented: 'convincing sets from Roy Oxley showed admirable fidelity to Conan Doyle's original descriptions of background and character and the scripting by Giles Cooper also captured the true flavor…' Wilmer too received praise: '[he] struck the right note of cool and probing composure.' Stock's Watson was described as 'a loyal slower witted help mate to the 'tec but dodging the peril of seeming too stupid.' In essence, while Wilmer's interpretation of Holmes remained constant throughout the series, Stock's portrayal of Watson vacillated somewhat depending on the script, sometimes causing him to replicate Nigel Bruce's approach to the part.

Meanwhile, back on the studio floor, there were still problems. Wilmer, dismayed at the quality of the scripts, would burn the midnight oil in rewriting them to his own

satisfaction: 'I took on the series on the understanding I would receive my script three weeks in advance of shooting. This never happened; it was always a last minute job. 'The Devil's Foot', would you believe it, when I received the script, was only twenty minutes long? Giles Cooper who wrote it, poor man, was in the throes a nervous breakdown, but nevertheless this twenty-minute script was presented to us by the producer at the read through as though it was all right! No eyebrows were raised. And we had a fifty-minute show! So in the end, I wrote the thing myself'.

Whatever problems there were behind the scenes, they didn't really show on screen, but nevertheless the series did not make many ripples and viewing figures were only average. Wilmer blamed this on the scheduling of the show on Saturday nights: 'I begged them not to put the shows out then. I said that no one will see them on Saturdays. In those days people went out to the pub, or dancing or whatever. They didn't stay in to watch television. As a result the series excited very little notice. Then about a year later [the BBC] thought, well, we need something in this slot, so they dug

out the series and showed it on a Monday night after *Panorama* [the BBC's flagship political programme]. Immediately it got into the top ten. Immediately, they thought, what was the name of that chap who played Holmes…? We must get him back. I was in Hong Kong when I got the phone call asking me if I'd do another series. I told them they could stuff it!'

So, while Stock stayed on as Watson, the BBC began the search for another Holmes. Wilmer was in Hong Kong because he was working on the Fu Manchu film series produced by Harry Alan Towers. He appeared in the second and third films, *The Brides of Fu Manchu* (1966) and *The Vengeance of Fu Manchu* (1967), in the very Sherlockian role of Nayland Smith, sworn enemy of the evil Oriental (played by Christopher Lee). Alongside Smith as his 'Watson' was Doctor Petrie, played by Howard Marion Crawford, who had appeared as Doyle's good Doctor in the fifties Holmes television series starring Ronald Howard.

Previous page (below left): Douglas Wilmer and Nigel Stock as Holmes and Watson in 'The Speckled Band'. *Previous page (right):* Peter Wyngarde as the unscrupulous Baron Gruner in 'The Illustrious Client'. **Above left:** Holmes ponders the mystery of 'The Man With the Twisted Lip'. **Above right:** Wilmer and Stock pose for a 'pub'-licity shot. **Below:** Holmes experiments in 'The Red-Headed League', as Watson and Inspector Hopkins (John Barcroft) look on.

A STUDY IN TERROR

First screening November 1965
Production company Compton/Sir Nigel Films
Duration 95 minutes
Colour
Director James Hill

It is 1888, and Jack the Ripper is terrorising London's East End. Sherlock Holmes (John Neville) receives a mysterious package, postmarked Whitechapel, containing a case of surgical instruments, complete except for the post-mortem knife. Concealed on the lid is a coat of arms, which leads Holmes and Watson (Donald Houston) to the home of the Osbournes, where the Duke of Shires (Barry Jones) recognises the case of instruments as belonging to his eldest son, Michael, whom he has disowned because he married a prostitute. Holmes later discovers that the instruments were pawned by a woman calling herself Angela Osbourne, whose given address was an East End hostel which is financed by the Duke's younger son, Lord Carfax (John Fraser). Meanwhile, on behalf of the government, Mycroft Holmes (Robert Morley) engages his brother to catch the Ripper. Holmes traces Angela (Adrienne Corri) to a pub owned by Max Steiner (Peter Carsten), who has been blackmailing Lord Carfax about his brother's marriage. Angela's face was badly scarred by acid thrown at her in a fight between Osbourne and Steiner. That night the Ripper attempts to murder her but Holmes prevents him, exposing the killer as Lord Carfax.

Sir Nigel Films, a company formed by the Sir Arthur Conan Doyle Estate to bring his works to the screen, was the moving force behind *A Study in Terror*. The premise of the movie was inspired — that of pitting the world's greatest detective against the world's most fiendish killer, Jack the Ripper. Herman Cohen, the executive producer, was keen to capture the youth market, presenting Holmes as a kind of

Victorian James Bond, and even employing such phrases in the film's advertising campaign as 'Sherlock Holmes — the Original Caped Crusader', to cash in on the success of the contemporary Batman television series. One publicity statement announced: 'No longer is Holmes the old fuddy-duddy which the public tended to classify him as in the past, he is now way out and with it.' Cohen wanted to call the film *Fog*, because he thought any picture with the word 'study' in the title would put off the teen punters. However, the film did achieve an X certificate, awarded for sexual elements implicit in the movie rather than its horror content.

Doyle's son, Adrian, became involved in the project, contributing to the financing of the film as trustee of his father's estate and, it has been claimed, adding ideas to

Even when he accepted the role in *A Study in Terror*, the logistics of playing the part were somewhat complicated. Neville made the film while at the same time appearing each night on stage in *Volpone*. He flew from Nottingham to the studios in London first thing in the morning and flew back at night after a day's filming, just in time to put on his make-up, don his costume and enter stage right. As Neville said at the time, 'everyone bent over backwards to allow me to do it.' Of his approach to playing Holmes, he commented: 'I'd always felt, having seen Sherlock Holmes in my childhood, that he was perhaps rather more stiff-backed, stuffy, arrogant and conceited than he need be. I was worried about his relationship with Watson. I felt that he'd often been treated as an old duffer. I think

'Donald and Derek Ford have created an intelligent and exciting vehicle for the return of Sherlock Holmes' — *Motion Picture Herald*.

the script, which was written by Donald and Derek Ford. In general, the dialogue is convincing, but the music, attitudes and make-up are redolent of the 1960s rather than the 1890s.

Noted stage actor John Neville was cast as Sherlock Holmes. Producer Henry E. Lester had been trying to entice Neville into playing the character for a least a year before he agreed to appear in the film. Originally, Lester had wanted him to play the lead in the musical *Baker Street* in America in 1964, but Neville had been too busy working as both actor and manager at the Nottingham Playhouse.

there's a warm relationship between them, even though Holmes teases Watson. This was something that Donald Houston and I worked on, so that this relationship had a sort of fun about it and warmth, rather than Holmes just being arrogant and condescending to Watson.'

Sadly, the relationship with Watson (played by Houston as a young duffer) is never really established as Neville wished. This was despite Houston's claim that he had no intention of playing Watson as an idiot and Adrian Conan Doyle's view that the actor 'was so completely right for the part'. This opinion was not reflected in the

reviews. One American critic stated that Houston 'has spiced the role with a blushing bashfulness reminiscent of the great Oliver Hardy'. While the *Daily Mail* said that 'Houston is at once dog-like and bovine, trotting meekly at his master's heels and perpetually gasping at his deductive powers.'

Neville fared a little better. He is neither a great Holmes nor a poor one. As *The Times* observed: 'Not perhaps everyone's idea of Holmes... but the casting will serve.' Others thought he was 'too handsome', 'faintly camp' and had 'stilted

charm'. Most critics, with some reluctance it would seem, thought *A Study in Terror* was a jolly romp but nothing more. 'The entire cast, directors and writers, play their roles well enough to make wholesale slaughter a pleasant diversion', was the *New York Times*' verdict. The film did poor business, and ideas of producing more horror-tinged Holmes adventures were shelved.

The real hit of the production is Robert Morley as Mycroft. Morley's rotund appearance and sharp features fit exactly Doyle's concept of the character, as outlined in 'The Greek Interpreter': 'His

body was absolutely corpulent, but his face, though massive, had preserved something of the sharpness of expression which was so remarkable in that of his brother.' As the reviewer in *The Sunday Telegraph* noted: 'I knew that [Mycroft] had been Robert Morley from the beginning of time'.

Interestingly, two actors who appeared in *A Study in Terror* — Anthony Quayle as Dr Murray and Frank Finlay as a suitably rat-faced Inspector Lestrade — also turned up in the 1978 Holmes/Ripper feature, *Murder by Decree*; Finlay even played the same part.

Above left: *Holmes (John Neville) fiddles while brother Mycroft (Robert Morley) burns with indignation.*
Above right: *Watson (Donald Houston) and Holmes examine the contents of a strange parcel that has arrived at Baker Street.*
Far left: *Behind the scenes at 221B.*
Left: *Face to face with the Ripper?*

SIR ARTHUR CONAN DOYLE'S SHERLOCK HOLMES

First screening 1968
Production company BBC
Duration 16 x 50 minute episodes
Colour
Regular cast
Peter Cushing (Sherlock Holmes),
Nigel Stock (Doctor Watson),
Grace Arnold (Mrs Hudson)

The BBC was caught on the hop by the late success of *Sherlock Holmes* starring Douglas Wilmer, and when they tried to set up a further series with Wilmer he turned the offer down.

WILMER HAD BEEN THOROUGHLY DISMAYED BY the broken promises and sloppy production standards of the first series, and when the BBC could not agree to his demand for a fourteen day schedule per episode for a new series, he bowed out. While Nigel Stock was happy to remain as Watson, there was now a frantic search for a new Sherlock Holmes. Both John Neville and Eric Porter (who later played Moriarty to Jeremy Brett's Holmes) were offered the part, but for various reasons turned it down. Then the BBC approached Peter Cushing, who had been a huge television star in the fifties before he moved into films, and had of course played Holmes before in Hammer's *The Hound of the Baskervilles* (1959). In the late sixties Cushing's movie career was somewhat in the doldrums — he was forever busy but the standard of the films he made was rather poor — and so he jumped at the chance of a return to the small screen in what he believed would be a quality product. Cushing was no doubt encouraged by the plans to feature major guest stars such as Peter Ustinov, Sean Connery, George Sanders and Orson Welles, but sadly those ambitions were never realised.

The pre-publicity blurb was titillating rather than exciting: 'What is new in this series is the basic approach — a daring realisation of the lurking horror and callous savagery of Victorian crime, especially sexual crime. Here is the recreation of the Victorian half world of brutal males and the furtive innocents they dominate; of evil hearted servants scheming and embracing below stairs; of murder, mayhem and the macabre as the hansom cab once again sets out with Doctor Watson and his debonair, eccentric and uncannily observant friend — Mr Sherlock Holmes.'

Once this Holmes series (the first to be made in colour) was underway, Cushing found himself in a similar situation to that experienced by Wilmer: 'We had been promised ten days to do each one of those sixteen episodes. Now that's enough so long as you have the scripts beforehand. We got the scripts all right, but for each of the sixteen episodes there were filmed inserts and the BBC had not made allowances for the English weather. By the time we got half way through the series, the series was already being shown, so we had to catch up and in the end we were doing them in *three* days. Whenever I see some of these, they upset me terribly, because it wasn't Peter Cushing doing his best as Sherlock Holmes, it was Peter Cushing looking relieved that he had remembered what to say and said it.'

The first story was a two-part

adaptation of *The Hound of the Baskervilles*, which had some scenes filmed on Dartmoor, near Newton Abbott in Devon, using a vintage steam engine on the Dart Valley Railway. But here again the BBC ran into trouble. The Grimpen Mire sequence proved to be unusable and had to be remounted at Ealing. By the time filming of 'The Hound' was completed, the series had already gone over budget by £30,000.

There were more problems when the shows were transmitted. On 24 September 1968, an unfinished edit of 'The Dancing Men' went out, which included rehearsal shots. The next day the *Daily Mail* took umbrage at this calamity: 'I was disgusted by the generally low aim of 'The Dancing Men' which stretched itself to fill its time by blowing up the character of the

housekeeper into a figure of mysteriously unexplained menace by the crude device of dressing her in black and photographing her outside doors looking fierce. But it made no attempt to visualise Holmes' ingenious solution to the cipher which was the whole point of the story.'

Despite all these mishaps, Cushing's portrayal of Holmes was praised, and indeed his devotion to the character and attention to detail were invaluable to this jinxed series. His preparation was meticulous: 'I re-read all the stories in detail. There are so many facets of Holmes that you have to be careful that Doyle had not contradicted himself. For example his attitude to the country. On one occasion Holmes hates the country because nothing happens there; then he absolutely contradicts himself and says far

worse things happen in the country.' The actor found dialogue phrases in the scripts that were too modern for the Victorian era and asked for them to be changed. He also made sure that Holmes never uttered the deathless words 'Elementary, my dear Watson', 'because it's not true — he never said the two together.'

Cushing requested that the costumes for the series replicated those shown in the Paget illustrations. The BBC agreed, and in doing so exploded the myth of Holmes' Inverness cape: 'It's not an Inverness cape in the drawings, it's a long overcoat with a hood.' It was this policy of following Paget that lead Cushing to wear a trilby hat rather than a deerstalker when he finally confronts the Hound on the moor.

The colour of Holmes' dressing gowns as stated in the stories was also copied: the purple, the grey and the famous 'mouse-coloured' one. Charatars in Jermyn Street, London was engaged to provide all Cushing's pipes: '[They] are all well described and the reason Holmes smokes them: his favourite was the dirty old black clay pipe that ponged the study out; that was his great one for thinking. Then he had a long cherrywood one for tranquillity. I never had a Meerschaum. That's not in the canon. William Gillette introduced that because it was big enough for him to rest on his shoulder when he was on stage.'

Despite the background troubles, the series was popular and received awards in Italy and Hong Kong, but later Peter Cushing admitted that 'I would rather sweep Bombay station with a broom than go through that experience again'.

Previous page (below): *Peter Cushing as Holmes and Nigel Stock as Watson.*
Above left: *Holmes and Watson are joined by Inspector Hopkins (James Kenny) in 'Black Peter'.*
Above right: *Cushing (with canonically correct pipe) in 'A Study in Scarlet'.*
Left: *Holmes and Watson investigate 'The Boscombe Valley Mystery'.*

DOCTOR WATSON

THE ONE FIXED POINT IN A CHANGING AGE

Doctor Watson was far more than just the biographer of Sherlock Holmes. He was a brave, loyal friend, an ex-army doctor and a writer of great skill. Our knowledge of Sherlock Holmes comes to us from the pen of John H. Watson — he is the filter through which the genius of the Great Detective is presented to us.

CONAN DOYLE, IN A FILMED INTERVIEW HE gave to Movietone late in life, referred to Watson as Holmes' 'rather stupid friend'. Not only is this grossly unfair but it is inaccurate. If we have to categorise Watson at all, he is the reader, the man in the street

— he is us! Who would not appear somewhat slow in comparison with the genius of Sherlock Holmes?

Watson is the narrator of the stories and Holmes' sounding board, so when it came for the character to be taken from the page and dramatised, it's perhaps not surprising that other writers had problems knowing what to do with him. In the stories Watson is always at the centre of the action with Holmes, although he may do little but react to events. In drama you cannot have such a figure, and that is why for many years film-makers sidelined the role, and often made Watson a comic character to bring some light to the shade of the drama. It was only when Nigel Bruce came to play the character that Watson received equal billing with the actor playing Holmes. Of course, Bruce was still a comic foil to Basil Rathbone's Holmes, but at least he was part of the team. Since Bruce there have been many other 'comic' Watsons, but gradually the trend has shifted towards a more realistic and truthful rendition of the character. In particular, André Morell, in Hammer's *The Hound of the Baskervilles* (1959), and both Jeremy Brett's Watsons — David Burke and Edward Hardwicke — have done much to redress the balance.

When we first meet Doctor Watson in Doyle's *A Study in Scarlet*, he has just been invalided out of the army having been wounded in the bloody battle of Maiwand in Afghanistan. Without 'kith or kin in England', he is at a very low ebb, living on a meagre army pension of eleven shillings and sixpence a day in London, 'that great cesspool into which all loungers and idlers of the Empire are irresistibly drained'. He is desperate to find cheaper lodgings, and a chance meeting with an old medical colleague leads to an introduction to Sherlock Holmes, who is looking for someone to go halves on the rent of a suite of rooms in Baker Street.

The pair set up lodgings together, but it is only gradually that Watson learns of Holmes' profession — that of consulting detective. When he accompanies his new friend in the investigation of an unidentified corpse in a derelict house in the Brixton Road — the mystery at the heart of *A Study in Scarlet* — he is both fascinated and impressed by Holmes' detective prowess. At the end of the investigation Watson is appalled to learn that Holmes will receive no credit for solving the case — that honour will go to the official police — and he decides to right this injustice: '"Never mind," I answered; "I have all the facts in my journal, and the public shall know of them."' And so the good Doctor assumed the role of Holmes' biographer — his 'Boswell'.

In the second published account of Holmes' detective work, *The Sign of Four*, Watson falls in love with the heroine of the piece, Mary Morstan, and announces at the end of the adventure that 'Miss Morstan has done me the honour to accept me as a husband in prospective.' Holmes emits a dismal groan.

Nevertheless, despite the attractions of domestic bliss, Watson often leaves his cosy fireside to accompany his friend on one of his baffling investigations.

Sherlock Holmes admits that apart from Watson he has no real friends and, certainly, the Doctor is a great aid to the detective, helping to point him in the right direction. At the opening of *The Hound of the Baskervilles*, Holmes passes Watson a walking stick which an unknown visitor has left behind in their rooms and asks him to 'reconstruct' the owner by examining the stick. Watson makes a series of sensible and intelligent suggestions, only to be told by Holmes that his deductions are 'erroneous'. However, the detective does add: 'I am bound to say that in all the accounts which you have been so good as to give of

my own small achievements, you have habitually underrated your own abilities. It may be that you are not yourself a conductor of light. Some people without possessing genius have a remarkable power of stimulating it.'

Watson is astute enough to understand his role in their relationship. In the story 'The Adventure of the Creeping Man', he explains: '[Holmes] was a man of habits, narrow and concentrated habits, and I had become one of them. As an institution I was like the violin, the shag tobacco, the old black pipe, the index books, and others perhaps less excusable. When it was a case of active work and a comrade was needed upon whose nerve he could place some reliance, my role was obvious. But apart from this I had my uses. I was a whetstone for his mind. I stimulated him. He liked to think aloud in my presence. His remarks could hardly be said to be made to me — but none the less, having formed the habit, it had become in some way helpful that I should register and interject. If I irritated him by a certain methodical slowness in my mentality, that irritation served only to make his own flame-like intuitions and impressions flash up more vividly and swiftly. Such was my humble role in our alliance.'

That was Watson: brave, loyal, modest, perceptive, articulate and invaluable. Without him, maybe Sherlock Holmes would never have become the Great Detective. As Holmes observed on many occasions: 'Good old Watson.'

Previous page (above): Colin Blakely played the good Doctor in The Private Life of Sherlock Holmes.

Previous page (below): André Morell, one of the best post-War screen Watsons.

Above left: David Burke, Jeremy Brett's first Watson.

Above right: Brett's second Watson, Edward Hardwicke, who brought a gentle gravitas to the role.

Far left: Paget's Holmes and Watson.

Left: Nigel Bruce's Watson has blundered again, prompting an angry reaction from a fellow passenger in Terror by Night.

THE PRIVATE LIFE OF SHERLOCK HOLMES

First screening 28 October 1970
Production company Mirisch Production Co/
United Artists Phalanx/Sir Nigel
Duration 125 minutes
Colour
Director Billy Wilder

Holmes (Robert Stephens) is summoned to the Russian ballet where it transpires the leading dancer wishes to have a child by the detective, assuming it would have her beauty and his brains. Holmes extricates himself from the delicate situation by suggesting, much to Watson's (Colin Blakely) fury, that women are not his 'glass of tea'. Holmes then becomes involved with Gabrielle Valladon (Genevieve Page), who wishes him to find her engineer husband. Mycroft (Christopher Lee) warns his brother to abandon the case, but Holmes persists. The trail leads to Scotland, where he discovers that Gabrielle's husband died during secret experimental trials of a submarine at Loch Ness. Mycroft reveals that Madame Valladon is in fact Ilse Von Hoffmannsthal, a spy for the Kaiser. Holmes conspires with his brother to reveal the location of the submarine to Von Hoffmannsthal's accomplices, who die in their attempt to steal it. Von Hoffmannsthal is then taken away to be exchanged for an imprisoned British agent, and later Holmes learns that she has been executed in Japan for spying. She had been using the name that she and Holmes had used in Scotland when they posed as man and wife. The detective is much affected by her death.

THIS IS ONE OF THE MOST INTRIGUING OF all Holmes films, and carries several mysteries of its own. *The Private Life of Sherlock Holmes* was the brainchild of celebrated film-maker Billy Wilder, the director and co-writer of such masterpieces as *Sunset Boulevard* (1950), *Some Like It Hot* (1959) and *The Apartment* (1960). Each of these movies, however dramatic or comedic, explores the eccentricities of human nature — its failings and its glories. And these elements also find their way into *The Private Life*.

Wilder became interested in a Holmes project in 1954 when he negotiated with Adrian Conan Doyle, Sir Arthur's son, to use the Sherlockian characters, but at this time the concept was for a musical. However, Wilder's trusted co-writer I. A. L. (Izzy) Diamond was committed to another writing task, and so the project was put on hold. The idea of turning the whole thing into a movie came about in the early sixties, and Wilder and Diamond worked on the script intermittently between other films. Things

Mrs Hudson was played by the veteran comic actress Irene Handl who, according to Robert Stephens, had difficulty with her lines: 'She was used to improvising and paraphrasing which was an anathema to Billy. So one day he told her that the script had been laboured on over many years, and honed, and she must speak the words exactly as written'.

Wilder began filming *The Private Life of Sherlock Holmes* in May 1969, his intention being 'to fill in what Conan Doyle had left

'If Wilder came to scoff at Sherlock Holmes, he remains to pray at the shrine' — *The Times*.

seemed to be coming together in the mid-sixties and Wilder planned on casting Peter O'Toole as Holmes and Peter Sellers as Watson, but it was not to be. Rex Harrison, adrift without a part to call his own after *My Fair Lady* (1964), was desperate to play Holmes but his offer was turned down.

However, Wilder was determined that the famous duo be played by British actors. He finally settled on Robert Stephens as Holmes and Colin Blakely as Watson. According to Stephens, Wilder was most impressed with Blakely because as he left the audition interview he turned, smiled brightly at the director and said, 'God bless you.' 'Very British,' thought the director, 'and very Watson.'

In an inspired piece of casting, Christopher Lee was given the part of Mycroft, Holmes' brother. While looking nothing like Doyle's conception of the character, Lee gives a strong and charismatic performance that prompted one reviewer to observe: 'It should be the end of [his] shoddy Draculas'.

out.' He added, 'We could have filmed one of the existing stories but that wasn't enough of a challenge. We want to explore the characters and fill in the gaps.'

It seemed to serious Sherlockians at the time that 'filling in the gaps' meant sending Holmes and Watson up, but Wilder professed otherwise: 'We're approaching the characters and the Baker Street atmosphere in a straightforward manner, with warmheartedness and good humour. I love the stories, and the last thing I would want is to guy them in any way. We hope to treat Holmes and Watson with respect but not reverence. There is a certain amount of natural humour but the stories in our picture essentially show the relationships and friendship between the two men'

With a budget of $10,000,000, this was Wilder's most extravagant production yet, involving a nineteen-week schedule at Pinewood Studios and six weeks' shooting around Inverness in Scotland. During the location filming, the Scottish Tourist Board trade index increased by about 200 per cent,

and many happy visitors went away hugging pictures they had taken of the Loch Ness monster, little realising that it was one built especially for the film.

Production designer Alexander Trauner's *pièce de résistance* for the film was one of the most impressive sets ever erected at Pinewood — 150 yards of Baker Street, with fully built-up fronts and smaller buildings receding in false perspective. Many of the houses actually had cellars with drainage systems, and the street was laid with real cobblestones, taken from a village in the north of England and ferried down to Pinewood in a fleet of lorries. Sadly, despite its visual magnificence, the exterior set was little used in the film.

The Baker Street living room was also incredibly detailed, thanks not only to Trauner's expertise but also Wilder's meticulous attention to detail. Adrian Conan Doyle, who visited the set shortly before his death, commented: 'If Sherlock Holmes were to visit this room he would immediately feel right at home — everything is exactly in its place. It's a brilliant recreation'. Equally lavish was the set of the Diogenes Club, which featured 500 yards of books and a specially commissioned marble bust of Queen Victoria.

The screenplay credit goes to Wilder and Diamond, but other pens had added the odd sentence or idea along the way, including American writer George Axelrod and Rumpole of the Bailey creator, John Mortimer.

One of the puzzles connected with the film concerns the script. Surely a practised film-maker like Wilder realised that he had an unwieldy three-hours' worth of material in his final shooting script? When the film was finished and shown to studio executives, they forced Wilder to cut it. Nearly an hour of material went, leaving behind a slimmer,

Previous page (below): Filming on the set of the Baker Street sitting room.
Above left: Colin Blakely and Robert Stephens.
Above right: Christopher Lee as a slender but imperious Mycroft Holmes.
Left: A scene, replicating a Paget drawing, which was excised from the final film.

but also oddly disjointed and uneven version lasting two hours and five minutes. It was not the film the director had conceived, and it remains Wilder's greatest disappointment.

Originally there were to be four untold adventures of Sherlock Holmes in *The Private Life* — cases which Watson had previously withheld because of their 'delicate and sometimes scandalous nature': 'The Curious Case of the Upside Down Room', 'The Dreadful Business of the Naked Honeymooners', 'The Singular Affair of the Russian Ballerina' and 'The Adventure of the Dumbfounded Detective'. In the end, it was only the last two that survived, though all four were filmed.

In the first of these — the 'Upside Down Room' mystery — we find Holmes indulging in cocaine again as there are no interesting cases to hand. Then, out of the blue, Inspector Lestrade (George Benson) calls to tell him of a strange mystery: a dead Chinese sailor has been found down by the docks in a room in which all the furniture is upside down — fixed to the ceiling. There is also a strange collection of objects in the room, including a meat cleaver, a child's toy, a stuffed parrot and a playing card — the seven of diamonds.

It does not take Holmes long to deduce that this 'mystery' has been set up by Watson

in an attempt to keep his friend's mind occupied and prevent his hands from straying towards the cocaine bottle. These disparate items with no connection to each other were placed there to confound the detective.

Returning to Baker Street, Holmes points out that, in the same road as the building housing the topsy-turvy room, he observed a series of shops where he

makes a mess of it. He goes to Cabin A on B deck and discovers two honeymooners in bed. Unfortunately, he doesn't realise they are not dead — just exhausted!

As well as these two major sequences, there were also some individual scenes and short sections that did not make it into the final print. To explain Holmes' lack of trust of women there was a flashback sequence to the detective's days at university. Wilder

'[It] was a wonderful picture, [but] too long... It was the most elegant picture I ever shot' — Billy Wilder.

deduced Watson purchased the various items used as tantalising clues: a taxidermist (stuffed parrot), an iron mongers (meat cleaver) and a toy shop. At this point Mrs Hudson enters, somewhat frustrated because she is unable to complete her game of patience. 'This is what you need,' says Holmes, handing her the seven of diamonds.

'The Naked Honeymooners' is even more bizarre. Holmes and Watson are on an ocean liner. Watson remarks: 'I've studied your methods for so long, Holmes, I would like to have a chance to solve a case.' Conveniently, at this moment the captain approaches with the news that two naked corpses have been found in Cabin B on A deck. 'Now's your chance, Watson,' grins Holmes. 'You solve the mystery.' Watson agrees, on the understanding that Holmes does not try to help him. Of course, Watson

plumped for Oxford as Holmes' *alma mater* — probably because it was conveniently near to Pinewood Studios, where the main filming took place. This sequence centred on the Oxford and Cambridge boat race, and showed the youthful Holmes (played by Stephens) in a doomed romantic relationship with a girl who jilts him after the race. This sequence took a week to shoot, involved the building of two rowing boats to replicate those used in the Victorian period and employed 3,000 extras.

Originally, the film's opening showed Watson's Canadian grandson visiting the vaults of the Cox & Co bank to retrieve the battered old tin box which contains, amongst other items, papers documenting these previously stifled accounts. The sequence was heavily truncated and the grandson was never seen.

Despite the thought and care which went

into the movie, the huge budget which had been lavished upon it and the considerable talent involved in the venture, *The Private Life of Sherlock Holmes* was a flop at the box office. Even disregarding the uneven narrative — a penalty of the forced editing — Robert Stephens disappointed as Holmes. He presented an almost effeminate version of the character, with languid movements, a nasal drawl and wavy hair. Anthony Howlett, writing in the *Sherlock Holmes Journal*, stated that: 'Stephens' appearance is tolerably acceptable but [he] effects a namby-pamby petulance of voice that is wholly and irritatingly wrong'. *Variety* was of the same opinion: 'Stephens plays Sherlock in rather gay fashion under Wilder's tongue in cheek direction'. Strangely and sadly, Blakely's fine comic performance as Watson was largely ignored by contemporary critics.

The film as a whole received mixed

reviews. Real enthusiasm was also missing from the cinemagoers, who gave the movie the cold shoulder. As late as 1980, ten years after its release, it had only made back a tenth of its production budget.

The picture played at New York's Radio City Music Hall in October 1970, where its gross was disappointing. *The Motion Picture Exhibitor* reported: 'It was the first time a pre-Xmas booking in RCMH history was yanked prior to Thanksgiving Day.'

For years the greatest mystery concerning this film was the whereabouts of

the missing sequences. Miraculously the Region 1 DVD release in 2003 gave the salivating Holmes fans a chance to see versions of the deleted sections. With some slender footage, supplemented by stills and script extracts and snatches of soundtrack dialogue we are given a wonderful insight into these self-contained gems: 'The Case of The Upside Down Room', 'The Dumbfounded Detective' and 'The Naked Honeymooners', along with the original prologue. The search continues for the missing elements.

THEY MIGHT BE GIANTS

First screening 9 March 1971
Production company Universal Pictures
Duration 88 minutes
(expanded to 98 minutes for TV)
Colour
Director Anthony Harvey

Since his wife's death, Justin Playfair (George C. Scott) has withdrawn into a private fantasy in which he believes he is Sherlock Holmes. His brother, Blevins (Lester Rawlins), who is being blackmailed, hopes to have Justin committed to an asylum so that he can gain control of his money. Taken to a clinic for analysis, Justin encounters Doctor Mildred Watson (Joanne Woodward). He fascinates her, but she is disconcerted by his accurate description of her own mental state. Justin believes that at last fate has provided him with his long awaited Watson and persuades her to join him in his pursuit of Moriarty. Their quest leads them across New York looking for clues, and Watson sees how Justin is completely accepted as Sherlock Holmes by a group of unhappy urbanites. Meanwhile, he is being trailed by the blackmailers, who are intent on killing him, so that Blevins can inherit his fortune. A romance blossoms between Justin and Mildred, as their search finally ends in Central Park, where they wait for Moriarty in the darkness. A bright light engulfs them as though something immense is coming to them out of the night.

Below left: Mildred Watson (Joanne Woodward) is bemused as Justin Playfair (George C. Scott) is mistaken for Basil Rathbone by a New York cop.
Below right: Watson and Playfair search for Moriarty.

James Goldman's *They Might Be Giants* began its life as a play and was first performed at the Theatre Royal, Stratford East, London, in June 1961. Starring Harry H. Corbett as Justin Playfair and Avis Bunnage as Doctor Mildred Watson, it was intended as a pre-Broadway tryout, but the production flopped. The play handles a fascinating idea, exploring the heroic qualities embodied in the character of Sherlock Holmes, qualities that engender a strong desire in those who seek a purpose in life or maybe a role model; to believe in him not only as a real person but also as a genuine force for good in an immoral world.

Unfortunately, despite Goldman opening up his play and developing the action, the basic premise behind the story is perhaps too fanciful, too fragile for a major movie. Maybe it was the success of *The Lion in Winter* (1968), another adaptation of a Goldman play, also directed by Anthony Harvey, that encouraged Universal Pictures to finance this project. On its release, however, Universal had so little faith in the final product that they excised its denouement — a scene of comic mayhem in a supermarket. Justin causes a near riot with the aid of his eccentric cohorts when he announces give-away prices over the tannoy system. The resulting mêlée allows Justin and Watson to escape the clutches of both the police and the bad guys and enter Central Park to rendezvous with 'Moriarty', who is in essence a metaphorical symbol for all the social evils in the city. Universal thought the supermarket scene gave a too-raucous note to the film. And yet on its release to television, the missing footage was replaced in order to fill the two-hour slot.

There is a charming moment in the movie, when Justin and Watson are on the run and bump into a police officer who, seeing the deerstalker and cape, grasps Justin's hand, exclaiming 'Oh, Mr Rathbone, this is an honour, sir.'

Despite engaging performances from Woodward and Scott, the film slipped quickly from sight.

THE HOUND OF THE BASKERVILLES

TV movie
FIRST SCREENING 22 February 1972
PRODUCTION COMPANY
Universal Pictures/ABC Television
DURATION 73 minutes
Colour
DIRECTOR Barry Crane

In a flashback narrated by Watson (Bernard Fox), we learn of the legend of the phantom hound that haunts the Baskerville family. Doctor Mortimer (Anthony Zerbe) believes the Hound was responsible for the recent death of Sir Charles Baskerville and enlists the help of Sherlock Holmes (Stewart Granger) to protect the new heir, Sir Henry (Ian Ireland). Holmes and Watson travel down to Baskerville Hall with Sir Henry to investigate. Holmes visits Black Tor, the scene of Sir Charles' death, and becomes convinced that he had been waiting to meet someone there when he was attacked by the Hound. Holmes pretends to return to London, but remains on the moor disguised as an old beggar in order to spy on the various suspects, including Laura Lyons (Sally Anne Howes), Stapleton (William Shatner) and his sister Beryl (Jane Merrow). Holmes instructs Sir Henry to return from the Stapletons' farm across the moor at night, knowing that Stapleton will release the Hound. Grappling with the beast, Holmes manages to kill it, while Stapleton perishes in the Grimpen Mire.

Below: Universal's seventies version of the Baker Street sitting room with Watson (Bernard Fox) and the white-haired Holmes (Stewart Granger).
Right: Fox and Granger failed to convince, and viewing figures were low.

THIS TELEVISION VERSION OF *THE HOUND OF the Baskervilles* was actually the pilot for an ABC *Mystery* series designed to feature several detectives. In the end only two shows were actually filmed: *Nick Carter* with Robert Conquest, which was well received, and the Sherlock Holmes movie, which was not. Speedily made on a slim budget, this first Hollywood colour version of *The Hound* was shot on Universal's sound stages and extensive, rather familiar backlot, with the old ramparts of Dracula's castle substituting for parts of the gothic Baskerville Hall. However, the great sweep of Dartmoor was merely a cramped, sparsely decorated and unconvincing studio set. One American reviewer wrote that the moor sets seemed to have been borrowed from a childrens' show: 'the stars were so obviously tramping through plastic.'

The atmospheric, panoramic view of London in the opening sequence (actually glass shot artwork provided under the

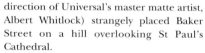

direction of Universal's master matte artist, Albert Whitlock) strangely placed Baker Street on a hill overlooking St Paul's Cathedral.

Stewart Granger made a reasonable stab at playing Holmes, but he failed to convince. Like Rathbone, he had a reputation on the screen as a cad and expert swordsman, but he lacked Rathbone's quixotic, dynamic delivery. Also, his white hair and uncanonical string tie — which made him look like a Mississippi gambler — seemed at odds with the accepted image of Holmes. Bernard Fox's portrayal of Watson fell between two stools: neither completely straight nor a total buffoon, his performance was, as *Variety* noted, 'dull'.

Regrettably, the entire mystery is given away by the fact that William Shatner, who plays the villain Stapleton, is very recognisable as the wicked Sir Hugo in the opening flashback sequence.

Audience figures were poor for this *Hound*, as was the press reception, which can be summed up by *Variety*: 'The plot did suggest that there might be some mileage left to the Holmes mystique with tighter scripting and more attention paid to Holmes' cerebral machinations as an audience challenge.'

A DIFFERENT SLANT

SHERLOCK IN THE SEVENTIES

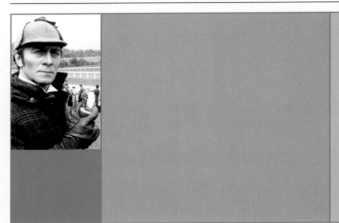

The 1970s was a time when the Great Detective became a focus of experimentation for writers and performers. It seemed more interesting to present the character from a different and unusual angle.

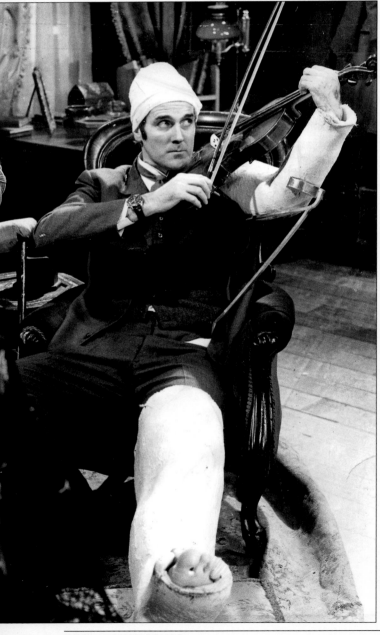

IT WAS AS THOUGH FILM- AND PROGRAMME-makers had decided collectively that too much reverential homage had been paid to the sage of Baker Street, and now was the time to take him down a peg or two. On television in Britain, a less than sensible Sherlock Holmes starred in a 1973 episode of the BBC series *Comedy Playhouse*, 'Elementary, My Dear Watson', which featured John Cleese as the detective and Willie Rushton as Watson. The bizarre script was by N. F. Simpson — a playwright whose comedies of the absurd include *Rhinoceros* and *One-Way Pendulum* — and involved a family curse, five dead solicitors, a television panel game and Fu Manchu. It was the pilot for a series that never materialised, but John Cleese returned to the role in 1977 with Arthur Lowe (of *Dad's Army* fame) as his Watson. They starred in *The Strange Case of the End of Civilisation as We Know It*, a fifty-five minute burlesque written for ITV by Joe McGrath. This was an updated comedy about Arthur Sherlock Holmes and his partly bionic companion, Watson. While Holmes was portrayed as a bumbling idiot, Watson was 'an absolute moron, the worst doctor ever qualified.' In fact, Watson accidentally and unknowingly causes the murder which Holmes investigates. In the course of the incredibly whimsical plot, Holmes and Watson attempt to lure the descendant of Professor Moriarty to a detectives' convention, where they encounter other famous sleuths, including Sam Spade, Columbo, McCloud, Ironside and Hercule Poirot. Allen Eyles in *Sherlock Holmes — A Centenary Celebration* considered this show 'an hour of turgid slapstick.'

On a more serious level, 1974's *Dr Watson and The Darkwater Hall Mystery*, a seventy-minute production for the BBC written by the comic novelist Kingsley Amis, eliminated the character of Sherlock Holmes from the proceedings altogether, allowing Watson (Edward Fox) to move to centre stage, taking on a case in the country while the detective is away. Using his friend's methods, even to the extent of donning a deerstalker and, at one point in the plot, adopting a disguise, he attempts to solve the mystery. The play's main point of interest lay in Watson becoming amorously involved with a pretty Spanish maid.

A darker manifestation of Watson was found in Matthew Lang's stage play, *Sherlock's Last Case*, staged on the London fringe in 1974. In this drama the Doctor, angered by Holmes' cruel treatment of him over the years, captures and torments him, before pouring acid over his face.

Two series of *The Rivals of Sherlock Holmes* ran on ITV in the mid-seventies. Although, as the title suggests, these hour-long plays concerned detectives other than Holmes,

they did feature several actors who had played the Great Detective in the past: John Neville appeared as Austin Freeman's Dr John Thorndyke, Douglas Wilmer played Jacques Futrelle's The Thinking Machine and Robert Stephens was Ernest Bramah's Max Carrados.

Leonard Nimoy, who appeared in the American tour of the Royal Shakespeare Company's production of Gillette's *Sherlock Holmes* (1975/6), made a strange little film for Kentucky Educational Television in which he featured as the detective. Only fifteen minutes long, *The Interior Motive* (1975), which co-starred Burt Blackwell as Watson, involved Holmes trying to deduce the contents of a large-sized globe of the world without opening it.

Before he donned a large Stetson and assumed the character of J. R. in *Dallas* (1978-91), Larry Hagman slipped on the deerstalker to star in a seventy-eight-minute

TV movie, *The Return of the World's Greatest Detective* (1976). This comedy was created, written and produced by Roland Kibbee and Dean Hargrove and directed by Hargrove. Hagman played an incompetent police officer who idolised Sherlock Holmes, constantly re-reading the Holmes stories for inspiration. One day he is involved in a motorcycle accident, suffers concussion and, of course, when he revives believes that he *is* Sherlock Holmes. With echoes of *They Might Be Giants*, the officer is attended by a psychiatric social worker called Dr Joan Watson (Jenny O'Hara). He even has a housekeeper called Mrs Hudson, and, inevitably, goes on to solve a baffling case. It was generally well received by viewers but, though NBC did have hopes of turning the concept into a regular series, they never followed up on the pilot show.

For the real Sherlock amongst all these challenging variations we have to look to Harlech Television's production of *Silver Blaze*. This rather rushed version — it only lasts twenty-five minutes — starred Christopher Plummer as Holmes and Thorley Walters having another stab at Watson. Despite its brevity, the film does justice to the story, following the plot faithfully; and it is beautifully played, especially by Plummer who looks wonderfully gaunt in his deerstalker and Ulster. One can only imagine that it was his performance in *Silver Blaze* that secured him the lead in *Murder by Decree* a few years later. The real mystery behind this film is quite why it was ever made in the first place. Certainly it was not planned as a

pilot for a series, and when it was televised on 27 November 1977 it was simply as an episode in the series of dramas *Classic, Dark and Dangerous*. It has never been shown on British television again. It seems it was just a very rare Sherlock one-off.

Basil Rathbone was given his shining half-hour by the *That's Hollywood* programme in 1976. Narrated with affection by Tom Bosley, the show paid homage to the Rathbone/Holmes oeuvre by showing a brilliant selection of cleverly edited scenes from the fourteen movies.

Even the *Saturday Night Live* team had a crack at getting laughs out of Sherlock in the seventies, in a skit called 'The Case of the Scarlet Membrane', which aired on 8 April 1978. The most remarkable aspect of this spoof was the stellar nature of the cast: Michael Palin as Holmes, Dan Aykroyd as Watson, Bill Murray as Inspector La Trad and John Belushi as a Bobby.

Previous page (above): Christopher Plummer's first crack at Holmes in Silver Blaze (1977).
Previous page (below left): John Cleese as a plastered Holmes in 'Elementary, My Dear Watson' (1973).
Previous page (below right): A furtive Watson (Edward Fox) tackling the mystery at Darkwater Hall.
Above left: Holmes (Cleese again) and Watson (Arthur Lowe) in The Strange Case of the End of Civilisation as We Know It (1977).
Above right: Sherman Holmes (Larry Hagman) in The Return of the World's Greatest Detective (1976).
Middle: Holmes (Plummer) and Watson (Thorley Walters) in Silver Blaze.
Left: Robert Hardy, who played Holmes in eight stories recorded on four LPs. His Watson was Nigel Stock.

THE ADVENTURE OF SHERLOCK HOLMES' SMARTER BROTHER

FIRST SCREENING 14 December 1975
PRODUCTION COMPANY A Roth/Jouer Production
DURATION 91 minutes
Colour
DIRECTOR Gene Wilder

Sherlock Holmes (Douglas Wilmer) delegates the 'Bessie Bellwood' case to younger brother Sigerson (Gene Wilder) in order to work undercover on a related case of missing state documents. 'Bessie', a soubrette named Jenny Hill (Madeline Kahn), is being blackmailed by opera singer Gambetti (Dom DeLuise) over some indiscreet letters. Jenny is engaged to Lord Redcliff (John Le Mesurier) and the price of the letters is the state documents in his keeping. Jenny begs Sigerson to retrieve them. Moriarty (Leo McKern) is also after the documents and tries to kill Jenny. With Sergeant Orville Sacker (Marty Feldman), Sigerson attempts to break into Gambetti's safe but they are caught. Escaping, they later interrupt a performance at the opera during which Gambetti was to hand over the documents to Moriarty's messenger. Sigerson poses as the messenger and engages Moriarty in a duel over a set of fake documents, until the Professor is toppled into the Thames and Sacker appears with the genuine papers. Sherlock Holmes emerges from the shadows — he has been following events throughout — and retrieves the precious documents. Next day Jenny and Sigerson are reunited and realise they are in love.

In 1974 MEL BROOKS AND GENE WILDER collaborated on the screenplay of the horror movie spoof *Young Frankenstein*, which was directed by Brooks and starred Wilder. It was a tremendous success, brilliantly mixing elements of farcical comedy with a respectful homage to the old Universal chillers. Wilder attempted to repeat this formula with the Holmes saga, but he did not bring Mel Brooks along with him. The resultant project missed Brooks' steadying hand and suffered to some extent from self-indulgence. Wilder directed, starred and created the screenplay for *The Adventure of Sherlock Holmes' Smarter Brother*, which was shot in England, on location in London and at Shepperton Studios. Douglas Wilmer appeared in the movie as the 'real' Sherlock Holmes and hated the experience: 'Wilder had no real feeling for the character of Holmes. In fact the part I played as written merely ridiculed the man. And Wilder's sense of humour was far too lavatorial for my taste.'

acter' in a comedy where one would find 'romance, intrigue, adventure... and an undercurrent of seriousness and a little melancholy'. This all-embracing mixture was designed to give Wilder the opportunity to play comedy, a dashing romantic lead, and to sing and dance. A tall order even for the real Holmes.

Of course, the name Sigerson was a nod to the Doyle canon, because this is the *nom de plume* Sherlock Holmes used when he was travelling around Europe and beyond during the period following his supposed death at Reichenbach. Similarly, Wilder's Watson character, named Orville Sacker, played by googly-eyed comedian Marty Feldman, is similar to Ormond Sacker, the name that Doyle originally gave to John H. Watson. Thorley Walters was cast again as the real Watson, but both he and Wilmer

'Unlike Billy Wilder's affectionate pastiche, this Sherlock Holmes has little to do with the original' — *Films and Filming*.

In a press statement released at the time of the shooting, Wilder admitted to being a life-long Holmes fan, and that he had cherished the idea of doing a Holmes comedy for some years, but had been worried that 'Sherlock Holmes was much too revered a figure to make fun of.' However, in conversation with his producer friend Richard Roth, Wilder hit upon the idea of how he might approach the subject. 'I'm not doing a spoof on Sherlock Holmes,' he stated. 'I have created a new character: Sherlock Holmes' insanely jealous brother Sigerson', who refers to his elder sibling as 'Sheer-luck'. Wilder claimed to have created 'a real and a many-sided char-

were encouraged to 'overact.'

Smarter Brother was a lavish production, and production designer Terry Marsh created a series of impressive sets, such as the mammoth throne room at Buckingham Palace, the Tivoli Music Hall (which was based on the old Wilton Music Hall in Mile End Road), the interior of an opera house, a huge outdoor set — which was used effectively in the hansom cab chase sequence — and, of course, the rooms at 221B Baker Street.

As well as surrounding himself with many members of the Mel Brooks repertory company, including Madeline Kahn, Marty Feldman and Dom DeLuise (the first two having appeared in *Young*

Frankenstein), Wilder employed some of the best British comedy actors, including Leo McKern as a deranged, Irish Professor Moriarty, John Le Mesurier, who had played Barrymore in the 1958 Hammer version of *The Hound*, and Roy Kinnear.

Unlike Wilmer, McKern enjoyed the experience of appearing with Wilder: 'Although I'm often cast as the 'heavy', I think I'm a better comedian than a straight actor. But when I'm allowed to combine the two as in this film, then I really can take

off. I've never had a part like this... it's a part an actor prays for.' Relish the part he did, for McKern gives us one of the most remarkably manic, face-twitching Moriartys of all time, a villain who admits 'I must do something absolutely rotten every twenty-four minutes.'

Released for the Christmas holidays in America, the movie was a great success at the box office, and the critics in general were enthusiastic. In *Saturday Review* Judith Crist referred to the film as 'the fastest escape from the blahs Hollywood is offering this season'. A more detailed, insightful comment came from Vincent Canby in the *New York Times*: 'a charming slapstick comedy that honours Sir Arthur Conan Doyle's original creation as much by what it doesn't do as by what it does. The film is a marvellously lowbrow caper but it makes no attempt to parody the great Sherlock himself, who is treated with cheerful if distant respect, measured entirely in terms of Sigerson's ineptitude.' Wilder's treatment 'is full of affection and generous feelings for the genre it's having fun with.'

Since its original release the movie has been rather neglected, falling under the shadow of the more subtle, and indeed funnier, *Young Frankenstein*. However, the long overdue DVD release of *Smarter Brother* gives Wilder's movie a new lease of life.

Previous page (below): Finney (Roy Kinnear), one of Moriarty's assistants, attempts to hail a cab.
Above left: Sigi (Gene Wilder) and Orville (Marty Feldman) are discovered eavesdropping by Moriarty (Leo McKern) and Gambetti (Dom DeLuise).
Above right: Orville does the 'Bunny Hop', one of the musical numbers from the film.
Left: Watson (Thorley Walters) and Holmes (Douglas Wilmer) find the film a drag.

THE SEVEN-PER-CENT SOLUTION

First screening 24 October 1976
Production company Universal Pictures
Duration 113 minutes
Colour
Director Herbert Ross

Sherlock Holmes (Nicol Williamson) is suffering from cocaine addiction and ranting about being persecuted by his old mathematics tutor, Professor Moriarty (Laurence Olivier), who is now a feeble old man. Watson (Robert Duvall) and Mycroft (Charles Gray) conspire to take the deranged Holmes to Vienna — on the pretext of following Moriarty — where he can be treated by Sigmund Freud (Alan Arkin). While recovering, the detective assists Freud in trying to track down one of his old patients, the red-headed beauty Lola Deveraux (Vanessa Redgrave). Holmes deduces that she has been kidnapped. Lola's abductor is Baron Von Leinsdorf (Jeremy Kemp), who is working for Amin Pasha (Gertan Klauber), head of the Ottoman Empire and a collector of red-heads. Holmes, Watson and Freud hire a special train to chase the Pasha, who is heading for Istanbul. They rescue the girl and Holmes impales the Baron on his sword. Later, under hypnosis, Holmes reveals that, as a child, he saw his father shoot his mother after he caught her in bed with Moriarty. Freud tells him the memory will vanish. Holmes insists on a holiday, and Watson returns to London to fabricate the reason for his friend's absence.

In 1974, the publication of Nicholas Meyer's Holmes pastiche novel, *The Seven-Per-Cent Solution*, along with the Royal Shakespeare Company's revival of the Gillette play, brought about what Sherlockians regard as 'The Great Revival'. Certainly, Meyer's novel created a new wave

of interest in Holmes, Watson and the Baker Street world. The book presented a clever re-interpretation of events surrounding the supposed death of Holmes featured in Doyle's 'The Final Problem' and the reason for his disappearance from London for three years. It is one of the great mysteries of the publishing world why this particular pastiche above all others should have captured the imagination of the general public as well as the fans. But it did, and it triggered off the fashion for 'discovering' old, hitherto unpublished accounts of the adventures of Mr Sherlock Holmes. The book was a bestseller on both sides of the Atlantic and thus caught the attention of Hollywood, and very soon a film project was set up. The screenplay was written by Meyer who remained reasonably faithful to

Powell, who played the detective in *Sherlock Holmes — The Musical* in the late 1980s, regard the script alone as the sole source of all the information required to play the part. Nicol Williamson was of the latter persuasion. In accepting the role, he stated — or rather boasted — that he had never ever seen a Holmes movie, 'nor read any of Conan Doyle's stories' and that he did not intend to do so. In a press interview during the course of shooting, Williamson admitted: 'Everyone has had a go at playing Sherlock Holmes, but my Holmes is different, a man in the grip of a terrible affliction, a man in a state of collapse. Serious, but with spice and dash and humour. Above all, a living man to whom things are happening, not just a hat and a pipe'. He also confessed that playing Holmes was 'a responsibility — but it's okay

'Herbert Ross' direction is strikingly inadequate... Holmes' fever-induced nightmare becomes the audience's nightmare too...' — *Films and Filming*.

the plot of his novel, apart from the inclusion of the suggested romance between Holmes and the new character Lola.

Nicol Williamson, who had been considered and rejected for the lead in Billy Wilder's *The Private Life of Sherlock Holmes*, was cast as the detective — the first blond-haired Sherlock. It seems that actors approach this difficult part in one of two ways. There are those, like Peter Cushing and Jeremy Brett, who regard the Holmes canon as their bible, devouring every word and using it as a research tool to aid their characterisation. Other actors, like Robert

when you have a director like Herb Ross. He works intensely and inventively and, best of all, economically, so that you don't waste time.'

Unlike Billy Wilder, who was determined that his Holmes and Watson would be British, that quintessential American film actor, Robert Duvall, was cast as the stalwart quintessential British icon, Doctor Watson. Director Herbert Ross explained this choice: 'I wanted an original for the part of Watson. An English actor who could surprise us by doing a Watson who didn't bumble in the traditional way. Then one day this

unsolicited tape was sent in. I listened to it without knowing who the actor was, and I was enchanted. When I was told it was Bob Duvall, I was amazed…Vanessa Redgrave thought the man [on the tape] was South African. Others pinpointed the voice as coming from one remote part of England or another. One man guessed Canadian, which brought him closest, but nobody said American.' It's worth noting that nobody said 'a clear English voice' either…

Duvall himself claimed that he always did have 'a mimic ear. In any case, I've fooled around with languages for years. And I've always wanted to play English. The first time I tried Watson I was winging it, but I knew right away I could do it.' This was not the opinion of the reviewer in *Films and Filming*, who wrote that Duvall's 'English vowel sounds seem to have been prepared by some badly programmed computer.'

The authentically English actor Charles Gray made an impressive Mycroft, a role he was to assume again years later, opposite Jeremy Brett in the Granada television series.

In general the press were disappointed in the movie. *The Guardian* stated that Williamson and Duval were 'an ill-matched pair'. *The Daily Express* referred to Williamson's Holmes as 'chattering like a demented typewriter', while *Films and Filming* stated that 'Williamson rants and raves with wavering effectiveness'.

Critics commented on the uneasy structure of the movie, which starts out as a psychological study of the Great Detective and then switches gear and becomes an old-fashioned chase thriller. *Films and Filming* thought that Herbert Ross's direction was 'strikingly inadequate' and 'even mundane items like the climactic train chase fail to come off.'

As a result of his novel's success, Nicholas Meyer turned out another pastiche — a more slender and less sensational volume — *The West End Horror*, which also sold well. Even before *The Seven-Per-Cent Solution* was released, Universal had plans to film the second book with Williamson and Duvall, but these were ditched when the movie flopped at the box office.

Previous page (below): *The timid and persecuted Moriarty (Laurence Olivier).*
Above left: *Holmes (Nicol Williamson) and Watson (Robert Duvall) arrive in Vienna.*
Above right: *Freud (Alan Arkin), Holmes and Watson.*
Left: *Watched by a stern-faced Watson, Freud attempts to hypnotise Holmes in order to discover the source of his neurosis.*

SHERLOCK HOLMES IN NEW YORK

TV movie
FIRST SCREENING 18 October 1976
PRODUCTION COMPANY Twentieth Century Fox
DURATION 100 minutes
Colour
DIRECTOR Boris Sagal

Professor Moriarty (John Huston) plots the humiliating downfall of Sherlock Holmes (Roger Moore). His scheme involves threatening the world's gold supply by gradually emptying New York's International Gold Exchange of its contents. Holmes and Watson (Patrick Macnee) set off for New York to investigate the matter. Once there the detective is contacted by Irene Adler (Charlotte Rampling), his long-time love who is appearing at the Empire Theatre. She confesses that their romantic liaison ten years ago in Montevideo produced a son, who up to now she has kept a secret from the detective. The boy, Scott (Geoffrey Moore), has been kidnapped by Moriarty, who sends a message to Holmes warning him not to interfere with the theft of the gold, or he will never see his son again. Donning several disguises, Holmes manages to outwit Moriarty, recover the gold and rescue Scott. But the Professor snatches the boy again and Holmes races to Moriarty's secret New York headquarters for a showdown. Although beaten this time, Moriarty manages to elude capture by escaping through a secret passage.

Below left: The cast. Front row left to right: Moriarty (John Huston), Irene Adler (Charlotte Rampling), Scott Adler (Geoffrey Moore), Sherlock Holmes (Roger Moore). Back row left to right: Watson (Patrick Macnee), Mortimer McGraw (Gig Young), Inspector Lafferty (David Hudleston).
Right: The tie-in novel.

FAMOUS FOR PLAYING *THE SAINT* ON TELEVISION and James Bond on the big screen, Roger Moore added a further character to his pantheon of heroes in the mid seventies: Sherlock Holmes. At first he had not been interested in playing the detective but, after reading Alvin Sapinsky's screenplay, changed his mind: 'It's funny and original and there is more dialogue in this script than I ever had in 120 *Saint* episodes and two Bond films. Holmes comes to life in the script. I wear a number of disguises which appeals to me. And most important, I do my own interpretation and don't copy any previous actors who have done the role.' Another joy for him with this movie was the chance to act with his own son, Geoffrey, who played Scott, his on-screen offspring.

Moore made a sexually attractive Holmes, which was in keeping with the idea that he and Irene Adler had been lovers and had produced a son. (This was not an original notion, incidentally. It had first been suggested in William S. Baring Gould's 1962 'biography' *Sherlock Holmes of Baker Street*.) Judith Crist, reviewing the film for *TV Guide*, noted that Moore's Holmes 'has a dash of the debonair and the

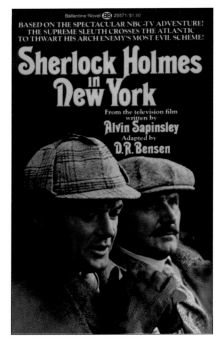

worldly.' However, critic Allen Eyles was of the opinion that '[Moore] has a lightweight, flippant manner that is at odds with the essence of Conan Doyle's character as well as the requirements of this particular story… the actor has little gift for registering Holmes' emotional distress when his son is kidnapped by Moriarty.'

Patrick Macnee lowered and hoarsened his voice to replicate Nigel Bruce's bumbling delivery and gave an embarrassing Wode-housian 'silly ass' portrayal as Watson, even down to the missing g's at the end of words: 'Amazin' Holmes.'

The film had been conceived in order to make further use of the extensive 'period New York' sets that had originally been built for *Hello, Dolly!* (1969) on the Fox backlot. Although planned as a TV movie, it was released to cinemas in parts of Europe.

THE HOUND OF THE BASKERVILLES

First screening 5 November 1978
Production company Michael White Ltd
Duration 85 minutes
Colour
Director Paul Morrissey

Sherlock Holmes (Peter Cook), the dissipated detective, despatches Doctor Watson (Dudley Moore) to investigate the suspicious death of Sir Charles Baskerville. Lodged at Baskerville Hall with the new owner, Sir Henry (Kenneth Williams), Watson is woken on the first night by the carousing of the housekeepers, Mr and Mrs Barrymore (Max Wall and Irene Handl). Holmes is summoned for the auction of the contents of the Hall — left to the Barrymores in lieu of unpaid wages — and purchases a portrait which verifies the existence of the Hound. That evening Selden is murdered, having been mistaken for Sir Henry. Later the Stapletons, the Franklands and Sir Charles' executor, Dr Mortimer (Terry-Thomas), are interrupted at dinner by Holmes, Watson and Mrs Holmes (Dudley Moore), who has arrived to ensure Watson's safety. In the ensuing mêlée the Hound materialises, and a moorland chase ends with the unmasking of Mortimer, the architect of a scheme to murder both Sir Henry and Sir Charles' favourite dog, his genuine legatee. On the dog's death, Mortimer would inherit the Baskerville fortune. Later, as Mrs Holmes predicted, the hall is blown up by a volcano.

Below left: Dr Mortimer (Terry-Thomas), the aged Sir Henry (Kenneth Williams), Watson (Dudley Moore) and Holmes (Peter Cook).
Below right: The Jewish Holmes and Welsh Watson.

IT PROBABLY SEEMED A GOOD IDEA AT THE time. The plan was to create a kind of *Carry On Sherlock* with a whole array of British comedy stars and feature Cook and Moore as a comic Jewish Holmes and Welsh Watson in a lively parody of *The Hound*. What resulted was, as *Films and Filming* pointed out, a 'dismally uninspired, desperately jumbled picture.' The publicity for this movie claimed that it brought a fresh comedic slant to the classic Conan Doyle story which would 'appeal to devotees of Mel Brooks, Woody Allen, and *Monty Python*.' Those are strange bedfellows for a start: the neurotic Jewish New York angst of Allen and his preoccupations with

relationships, art and sex seems a world away from the sharp burlesque style of Brooks and the anarchic lunacy of the *Monty Python* team. In reality, director Paul Morrissey (who shared the screenplay credits with Cook and Moore) was a great fan of the *Carry On* films and wanted to create a similar vehicle. He was particularly pleased when Kenneth Williams, a stalwart of that series, agreed to play the sixty-five year old Sir Henry. However, Morrissey had never directed comedy before; he was well known for his graphic sex and horror movies with Andy Warhol: *Flesh* (1968), *Trash* (1970), *Heat* (1972), *Flesh for Frankenstein* (1974) and *Blood for Dracula*

(1974). This does not seem the sort of pedigree suitable for someone attempting to emulate the seaside postcard sauciness of the *Carry On* farces. Cook and Moore did not help matters by inserting some of their old tried and tested comic routines into the script — whether they fitted the story or not.

The film was met by a hostile reception from the critics and received a very low-key cinematic release. The reason can be summed up by the verdict given by *Films and Filming*: 'Morrissey misses out all along the line… the jokes are, almost without exception, neither funny, surprising nor witty.'

MURDER BY DECREE

First screening 2 February 1979
Production company Ambassador Films/Famous Players, Ltd/Avco Embassy Pictures
Duration 120 mins
Colour
Director Bob Clark

Holmes (Christopher Plummer) and Watson (James Mason) become involved in the search for Jack the Ripper. Holmes traces the elusive Mary Kelly (Susan Clark), whom he believes holds the key to the mystery, but is knocked down by a cab and Mary is abducted. Holmes and Watson visit Mary's 'dumb' friend Annie Crook (Genevieve Bujold) at an asylum. Here the detective learns that Annie has been incarcerated and blackmailed into silence about her baby and secret marriage to Eddy, Duke of Clarence, the heir to the throne. Scouring the East End, Holmes surprises the two murderers eviscerating Mary in her room. After a duel with Holmes, one of the villains is killed. Summoned by the Prime Minister (John Gielgud), Sir Charles Warren (Anthony Quayle) and the Home Secretary (Geoffrey Russell), who are all Freemasons, Holmes accuses them of shielding Eddy, and being involved in the plot to eliminate all Annie's friends who knew of the marriage. The murders were committed by Sir Thomas Spivey, the royal physician, now mad, and William Slade, whom Holmes dispatched. Holmes reluctantly agrees to keep silent providing Annie's child, who is now being raised in a convent, remains unharmed.

THIS ANGLO-CANADIAN PRODUCTION ONCE more has Holmes investigating the Jack the Ripper murders, but it is a far darker movie than *A Study in Terror*. The script by John Hopkins was based on a theory presented in *The Ripper File* (1973), a BBC drama documentary television series written by John Lloyd and Elwyn Jones, in which two modern detectives attempted to establish the real identity of Jack the Ripper.

Christopher Plummer, who is a cousin of Nigel Bruce, portrays Sherlock Holmes. He had appeared as the character in a 1977 television adaptation of *Silver Blaze*, but 'was not wholly satisfied' with his performance. While filming on location in London in the autumn of 1978, Plummer explained why he was keen to return to the part: 'In this script John Hopkins has brought out a lot of unforeseen passion in Holmes. *Murder by Decree* gives Holmes the opportunity to be human. It's easy to play him as supercilious and rather snobbish but that's not what I intend to do. I'm trying very hard not to be influenced by other actors' performances. I'm trying to be myself. I think I can trust myself to look like him. I had my hair

character that he was playing: 'I see Watson as someone, who in the Army, would have passed for an intelligent man. In civilian life, he would be accepted as a good sort as well as an indomitable friend. He was not a buffoon. Holmes on the other hand was rather weird. Watson needed sterling qualities to be with him. Holmes' daily behavioural pattern was that of a rather strange individual and, of course, he was a misogynist. Watson was the reverse.'

It is the warm and believable relationship between the detective and his friend that has made this movie a favourite with Holmes fans, rather than the controversial nature of the plot. This is partly due to John Hopkins' careful scripting. In an interview in *Films Illustrated* in October 1978, Hopkins explained his approach: 'Although a tacit nod is made in

'1888... Jack the Ripper stalks the streets of London... Conspiracy the corridors of power...' — Poster slogan.

streaked to make him warmer, more human. In the original Sidney Paget drawings in the *Strand Magazine*, Holmes had slicked down hair, which looked very sinister.'

Another aspect of the film to please Plummer was 'that the two characters of Holmes and Watson are equally written. One isn't towering above the other in the script. Obviously the chemistry between them is very important.'

Interestingly, Plummer had first been considered for the part of Watson, but it went eventually to James Mason who, although eighteen years older than Plummer, made an excellent partner for this humanistic Holmes. Mason also had strong, definite opinions about the

every Sherlock Holmes film to the relationship between Holmes and Watson, I think there is a great deal more. The more you look at Basil Rathbone and Nigel Bruce in the old films, and the more you read the stories, the deeper is the relationship. It's slightly masked because of the kind of writer Conan Doyle was. There is that British tradition of male friendship which Billy Wilder made such happy fun of in *The Private Life of Sherlock Holmes* where he, I think, suggested that the relationship might be homosexual. But I feel that the relationship was much deeper than that. I wanted to go through the traditional reserve of Holmes. It's only an image; it's not the real thing. You look at Rathbone,

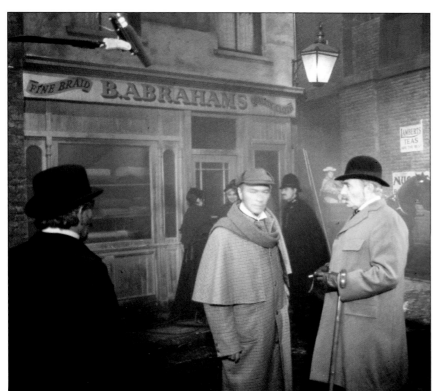

an extraordinary actor, and you look for a response to Bruce. You find in the two-shots and the medium shots that he often looks across at Bruce with affection, or at least that is how I see it. So when I started work on *Murder by Decree*, the relationship between the two men appealed to me deeply. I wanted to make my interpretation both passionate and caring'.

The warmth and closeness between Holmes and Watson in the film is beautifully encapsulated in the scene where Watson very noisily tries to trap the last pea on his dinner plate with his fork. Holmes obligingly whips the fork from his friend's hand and squashes the pea between its prongs. 'You've squashed my pea,' observes Watson with chagrin. 'Now you've got it cornered,' replies Holmes. This simple solution does not please Watson. 'But squashing a fellow's pea. I didn't want it squashed. I like it whole so you can feel it pop when you bite down on it.' This amusing, inconsequential ex-change underlines with brilliant economy both the comfortable friendship and the different natures of the two men.

Sadly, the film was viewed with in-difference by the critics, who saw it as just another Holmes movie. *Films and Filming* stated that despite 'a cast heavy with top 'names' the film is pure hokum'. However, respect for the film has grown over the years. Allen Eyles, writing of the movie almost a decade after its release, stated that it was 'a powerful work.'

Jeremy Brett had great respect for Plummer's interpretation of Holmes and even suggested that he play the part in a proposed American tour of the play *The Secret of Sherlock Holmes*.

Previous page (below): Watson (James Mason) and Holmes (Christopher Plummer). **Above left and left:** Filming on one of the Whitechapel sets. **Top right:** Watson, Inspector Lestrade (Frank Finlay) and Holmes visit the scene of one of the Ripper's crimes. **Above right:** Inspector Foxborough (David Hemmings) threatens Holmes.

THE GUESTING SLEUTH

SHERLOCK IN THE EIGHTIES

With the arrival of the 1980s, the great revival of interest in Sherlock Holmes really kicked in, with two lavish television movies starring Ian Richardson and the great Granada series with Jeremy Brett. But the man in the deerstalker also popped up in other diverting projects.

WITH HIS SHARP NOSE FOR A COMMERCIAL venture, Sheldon Reynolds, who had been behind the Sherlock Holmes series with Ronald Howard in the fifties, saw that the famous detective was in vogue again and decided that the time was ripe for another production. This new venture, *Sherlock Holmes and Dr. Watson*, filmed in 1979-80, has an air of *déjà vu* about it. Like his first series, it was shot in Europe for reasons of economy. Veteran film-maker Roy Ward

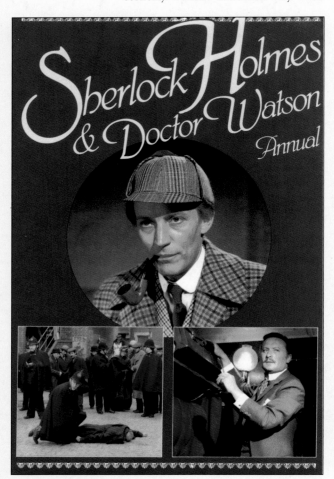

Baker, who directed several of the episodes, explained how the series came about: 'Sheldon had got the bug to do another Sherlock series and he set it up with the state-run Polish Television — the equivalent of the BBC. Apparently Holmes is very popular in Poland. They built a huge exterior set for Baker Street — probably bigger than the one they built at Pinewood for the Billy Wilder movie. They were half hour shows — twenty-five minutes of film actually — which I found a little restricting. The characterisation, atmosphere and plotting were sketchy at best. Geoffrey Whitehead played Holmes and Donald Pickering was Watson. They were both fairly young men then and their relationship was perhaps a little more playful than is usual. Patrick Newell, who I directed in *The Avengers* when he was Mother, played Inspector Lestrade and Kay Walsh was Mrs Hudson.'

Apart from the occasional British guest star such as Bernard Bresslaw, Derek Bond and Derren Nesbitt, the rest of the cast and crew were Polish.

Reynolds had difficulty in finding writers to come up with Holmes stories to fit into the tight time slot, so he dusted off the old scripts that he had used in the fifties. One day Pickering came up to Baker clutching a script and shaking his head: 'They're recycling the scripts!' he moaned. A glance at the list of the twenty-four episodes from this series confirms this sad state of affairs. Titles such as 'The Case of the Deadly Prophecy', 'The Case of the Baker Street Nursemaids', 'The Case of the Luckless Gambler' and 'The Case of Harry Croker' are identical to those used in the earlier series. Roy Ward Baker added, 'I got

on with Reynolds very well, but he was hardly ever at the studio. He was always off around Europe trying to scoop up dollops of money to keep the whole thing going.'

The series never made it to Britain and was only shown on regional stations in the States. Eventually eleven of the films were shown on West German television, and some episodes are now available on video.

In the eighties several American television series utilised the character of Holmes for novelty episodes. 'Save Sherlock Holmes' was the title of a *Fantasy Island* (1978-84) show in which Ron Ely played a store detective whose fantasy is to work with the Great Detective. Donald O'Connor appeared as Watson, his bumbling assistant. Together they set off to the Dartmoor Sanatorium to find Holmes (Peter Lawford), who has been imprisoned there by Moriarty (Mel Ferrer). Lawford has very little to do but mumble a few lines, and the whole show was far too whimsical

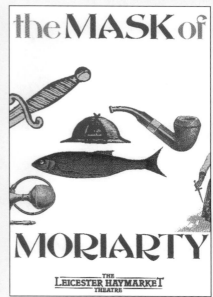

to be amusing. *Magnum P.I.* (1980-88) got in on the Sherlock act with the episode 'Holmes is Where the Heart Is', in which Higgins (John Hillerman) receives a visit from an old friend (Patrick Macnee) who believes that he *is* Sherlock Holmes. The popular series *Murder, She Wrote* (1984-96) featuring Angela Lansbury trod the same path with an episode called 'Who Killed Sherlock Holmes?', in which a murder is committed at a fancy dress party, and a body wearing a deerstalker and cape is found floating in the swimming pool. In these shows the connection with Conan Doyle's Holmes is tentative to say the least, but his use in this fashion underlines the continuing potency and appeal of the character and his image.

One television show which gave more

substance to Holmes when they squeezed him into their format was *Star Trek: The Next Generation* (1987-94). In the first season episode 'Lonely Among Us' (1987) there is something sabotaging the *Enterprise*'s main computer, and Captain Picard (Patrick Stewart) begins to act like a private detective, making clever deductions as he investigates the mystery. Picard notes that the fictional sleuth Sherlock Holmes would have an interesting view on their problem. Commander Data (Brent Spiner), an android, is intrigued by these observations and studies the Holmes canon. Soon he begins to assume the Holmes persona, smoking a meerschaum pipe and uttering Sherlockian aphorisms. Data's obsession with Holmes takes a leap forward in the second season's 'Elementary, Dear Data'

(1988), when he takes on the guise of the detective in a mystery set in the *Enterprise*'s holodeck, as the crew battle a powerful Professor Moriarty hologram (Daniel Davis) who materialises and cannot be returned to the computer memory.

The genuine Sherlock Holmes was to be found on the premium cable channel Home Box Office, impersonated by Frank Langella in a production of Gillette's play produced at the Williamstown Theater Festival in 1981. The videotape of the show was shown at least seven times from 15 November 1981.

In 1985 the Gate Theatre in Dublin produced *The Mask of Moriarty*, a Holmes comedy by Hugh Leonard, who had worked as a writer on the Peter Cushing television series in the sixties. The play presented another case from the suppressed papers of Doctor Watson. Apparently this one had been kept from the public because the good Doctor had been under the influence of Holmes' drugs! The plot involved an 'impossible' murder on Waterloo bridge, Dr Jekyll and Mr Hyde, plastic surgery (Moriarty is given Holmes' face), the identity of Jack the Ripper and Moriarty's role in making a rare bird extinct. Holmes was played with relish by Tom Baker and the production was enthusiastically received, but a hoped-for London run never materialised. It had a short revival at the Haymarket Theatre in Leicester in 1987, with Geoffrey Palmer as Holmes.

YOUNG SHERLOCK

TV serial
FIRST SCREENING October-December 1982
PRODUCTION COMPANY Granada Television
DURATION 8 episodes: 1 x 50 minutes;
7 x 30 minutes
Colour
DIRECTOR Nicholas Ferguson

Seventeen year-old Sherlock Holmes (Guy Henry) returns from school to his home in the north of England for the Christmas vacation only to discover that his mother and father have sold the house and fled to France because of debt. There are now new people at the Manor House, and Sherlock is forced to accept accommodation at the home of his Aunt Rachel (Heather Chasen). He is suspicious of the Turnbulls, the new family at the hall, and when a tramp is discovered in the woods, murdered by a poisoned thorn, he decides to investigate. Taking tea at the Manor with his aunt, Sherlock meets Jasper Moran (Christopher Villiers), who is being educated by a Professor Moriarty. Holmes discovers that Mrs Turnbull (June Barry) is in fact an actress, and with the assistance of the local doctor's son, John Whitney (Tim Brierly), he manages to uncover a plot to abduct Queen Victoria. She was to be held, in a drugged state, while Mrs Turnbull impersonated her in order to steal the Koh-I-Noor diamond for the villains, headed by Professor Moriarty.

This page: Guy Henry as the young Sherlock Holmes.

GRANADA TELEVISION PRODUCED *YOUNG Sherlock*, an eight-episode serial (with a double length first episode) for the Sunday teatime family viewing slot. The story, 'The Mystery of the Manor House', starring Guy Henry as the teenage Holmes, was devised and written by Gerald Frow. It is an account of one of the young detective's adventures which had been left on a series of dictaphone cylinders to be listened to by Watson after Holmes' death. The voice of an older (and uncredited) Holmes informs us: 'I have assiduously devoted my retirement to recording details of certain events

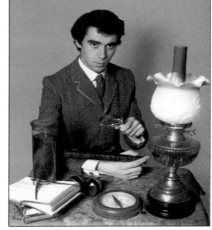

that took place during my youth; adventures that took place some years before you and I met, and of which I have hitherto apprised no one.'

Guy Henry had been chosen for the role after a nation-wide search by producer Pieter Rogers for a young actor who matched the conception of what Holmes probably looked like as a teenager. Guy was spotted at RADA and, although he was twenty-two, made a very convincing seventeen year-old.

There are many instances in Frow's script where we can see the moulding of Holmes' character and habits. For example, at one point he discards the battered old billycock he has been wearing and accepts the present of a hat from Scotland — a deerstalker — and pronounces it 'excellent.' At the conclusion of

the story he says goodbye to Mrs Cunliffe, his aunt's servant of whom he is particularly fond, only to discover that she is marrying a man called Hudson, and moving to London — to an address in Baker Street.

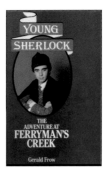

'The Mystery of the Manor House' was an intriguing tale, but stretched over eight weeks and four and a half hours of television it failed to grip or create tension. Frow had more adventures for *Young Sherlock* in the pipeline, but Granada lost interest. A second story that never made it to the screen and which featured a young Mycroft — 'The Adventure at Ferryman's Creek' — was novelised, as was 'The Mystery of the Manor House'.

THE HOUND OF THE BASKERVILLES

TV serial
FIRST SCREENING October 1982
PRODUCTION COMPANY BBC Television
DURATION 4 x 30 minutes
Colour
DIRECTOR Peter Duguid

Doctor Mortimer (Will Knightley) consults Sherlock Holmes (Tom Baker) regarding the legend of the phantom Hound of the Baskervilles and the recent death of Sir Charles Baskerville, by whose body he discovered the footprints of a gigantic dog. Mortimer is worried about the safety of the heir, Sir Henry (Nicholas Wodeson), and so Watson (Terence Rigby) is despatched to Baskerville Hall on Dartmoor to keep an eye on him. Here he meets the naturalist Stapleton (Christopher Ravenscroft) and his sister Beryl (Kay Ashead) who, thinking he is Sir Henry, tries to persuade him to return to London. Watson discovers that the wife of Barrymore (Morris Perry), the butler at the Hall, is the sister of Selden (Michael Goldie), an escaped murderer roaming the moor. During a bid to apprehend Selden, Watson and Sir Henry hear the cry of a hound and catch a glimpse of a stranger watching them. Watson tracks down the stranger to discover that it is Sherlock Holmes, who has been on the moor all the time. The detective now sets his trap for the murderer, Stapleton, who, after the Hound is shot, sinks to his death in Grimpen Mire.

Below: Tom Baker, an underrated Holmes, with Terence Rigby as Watson.
Right: Baker and Rigby wait for a take on location.

THE 'CLASSIC SERIAL' DRAMAS RAN FOR MANY years on BBC Television in the Sunday teatime family viewing slot. The purpose of these serials was to present, as faithfully as possible, adaptations of popular works of literature. For example, other titles in the eighties included *The Prisoner of Zenda* and *A Tale of Two Cities*. The adapters were given the brief that no major changes or additions should be made to the original stories and, therefore, we have in this four-part adaptation of *The Hound of the Baskervilles* by Alexander Baron the most faithful version of the novel that has ever

been seen on the screen. Not only are almost every one of Doyle's plot points incorporated into the script, but there are also great chunks of dialogue which have been lifted straight from the page. Adaptors will tell you that this slavish approach does not work. Bert Coules, who contributed many of the scripts for the BBC's Holmes radio series in the eighties and nineties, explains it thus: 'Dramatisations have to be dramatic, and what is dramatic in a book is not necessarily dramatic on screen or radio. Each medium has its own rules and structures. Dialogue in a drama needs to be

pithier and sharper than it is in a book.' However, having said that, Baron's *Hound* does work very well, aided no doubt by the original novel's linear plotting and natural dramatic rhythm.

When Tom Baker came to the end of his time in *Doctor Who*, the BBC asked him what he wanted to do next and he, having wanted to play the Great Detective for some time, said simply 'Sherlock Holmes'. And so the whole project of *The Hound* was set up especially for him. He was an underrated Holmes who, with the script's assistance, played the role with Doylean fidelity. Unfortunately, he was lumbered with a blimpish, charmless Watson and the shortest Sir Henry ever. Protecting a five-foot baronet from a glowing Hound tended to introduce a note of unintentional humour to the proceedings.

IAN RICHARDSON
THE CASE OF THE SHORT-LIVED SHERLOCK

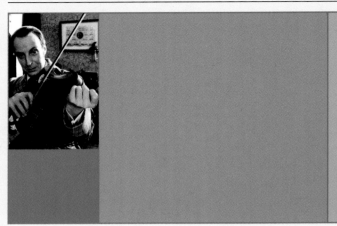

After more than a decade without any serious attempt to bring Holmes to the screen in Doyle's stories, two television productions lit upon the idea at the same time. The first to reach the screen starred Ian Richardson.

AMERICAN PRODUCER SY WEINTRAUB HAD BEEN successfully producing Tarzan adventures for television in the seventies, but as that decade grew to a close he began a search for a new character to turn into a television star. He chose Sherlock Holmes. Unfortunately, Weintraub was unaware that the copyright on the Holmes stories was about to expire in England, and he went through a great deal of unnecessary legal wrangling with the Conan Doyle estate in order to gain permission to use them. He was also unaware of Granada Television's plans to film a Sherlock series once the stories came into public domain at the end of 1980 — fifty years after Doyle's death. Blissfully ignorant of this threat to his venture, Weintraub came to England to look for his Holmes. He engaged a producer named Otto Plaschkes, who by chance happened to see Ian Richardson on television. The actor said that he was appearing in 'a terrible little detective thing that I did called *The Cotswold Murder*, playing a police inspector who in the course of his duty attempted to emulate the methods of Sherlock Holmes.' Plaschkes turned to his wife and said, 'That's our Holmes.'

Richardson explained what happened next: 'I went along to be interviewed for the part, and they were slightly dismayed that I was only five foot ten. I explained that in *The Cotswold Murder* I had worn lifts! Anyway, Weintraub liked me and he signed me up for six films.'

In preparation for the series, Richardson read all the stories, annotating them in order to create a detailed file on all aspects of the detective's life: his habits, moods, sayings, clothes, etc. 'It was my Holmes bible and I became a walking encyclopaedia of Sherlock.'

The first film to be shot was *The Sign of Four*, in the late summer of 1982, followed by *The Hound of the Baskervilles*. Halfway through the shooting of the second feature,

the news broke that Granada was 'going to do all the Sherlock Holmes stories with Jeremy Brett,' Richardson recalled. 'Weintraub was furious because he'd paid a lot of money to obtain permission from the Doyle estate', and here was Granada waltzing in to steal his thunder.

Weintraub took them to court. According to Richardson, the producer had a very good case, but eventually there was an out of court settlement for 'an extraordinary sum of money, which was enough for Weintraub to cover his costs on both *The Sign* and *The Hound* and make a profit too.' And so the producer took the money and wrapped up his Holmes project after just two movies.

Richardson had mixed feelings about the early termination of his Holmes career: 'In an odd sort of way, I heaved a sigh of relief. That was because I didn't want to get too associated with Sherlock Holmes. I felt that Jeremy [Brett] — such a nice man — towards the end rather regretted it. And I lost out on playing the emperor in the film *Amadeus* [1984; Jeffrey Jones got the part] because Weintraub wouldn't let me go while the court case was pending. This upset me terribly.' There was another reason for Richardson's relief at not making more of the movies: 'I had to battle all the time to keep things true to the character and the books. The writer was Charles Pogue. Very

American. And the writing was very American: there were phrases and actions in the films that no English writer worth his salt would have countenanced. I spent a great deal of time Anglicising my text to make it sound like Conan Doyle, and I was also able to put them right on a few inaccuracies. However, I couldn't, unfortunately, budge them and prevent them spending £10,000 on top of the budget to build a separate bedroom to show that Watson actually occupied a separate room from Holmes' bedroom to avoid any suggestion… [A wave of the hand]. I said to them, "What are you worried about?"'

Similarly, Weintraub and Plaschkes had puritanical views on Holmes' cocaine habit: 'I wanted to do more of the drug thing, but they wouldn't have it. I thought this was important because, in a curious way, this one area of human weakness humanises an otherwise inhuman-computer type of man. They did allow me to smoke a lot, but I had

to bow to the American request to smoke a Meerschaum. Weintraub said, "This is the image of Sherlock Holmes." But I pointed out that he smoked all sorts of pipes — briars, clays — but not a monstrosity like a meerschaum. Sy just hooded his eyes and said, "You will smoke a meerschaum." It was all part of the attitude on the set — a kind of, "What does it matter? Who will notice?" attitude.'

Ian Richardson died quietly in his sleep in February of 2007. He had a distinguished stage and television career, but he has a special affection in the hearts of many Holmes fans for his very attractive portrayal of the Great Detective.

Previous page (right): Beryl Stapleton (Glynis Barber), Holmes and Watson (Donald Churchill).

Above left: *Richardson with director Douglas Hickox.*

Above right: *The indoor set for the Grimpen Mire.*

Left: *Watson, Dr Mortimer (Denholm Elliott) and Sir Henry (Martin Shaw) remain silent as Holmes questions Beryl.*

THE SIGN OF FOUR

TV movie
First screening 13 May 1983
Production company Mapleton Films
Duration 90 minutes
Colour
Director Desmond Davis

On his death bed, Major Sholto (Thorley Walters) reveals to his two sons the existence of the Agra treasure hidden in their home, Pondicherry Lodge. He and Captain Morstan stole the treasure in India some years before. They cheated their co-conspirators, one of whom, the Englishman Jonathan Small (Joe Melia), has returned home seeking the treasure and revenge. Meanwhile, Mary Morstan (Cherie Lunghi) has received a precious diamond from an anonymous source and been summoned to a house in South London. She consults Holmes (Ian Richardson) and Watson (David Healy), and together they encounter Thaddeus Sholto (Richard Heffren), who sent the diamond — the Great Moghul — regarding Mary as part-owner of the treasure. At Pondicherry Lodge, Bartholomew Sholto (Clive Merrison) is discovered murdered and the treasure gone. Using Toby the dog, Holmes is able to track the intruders down to the river where they escaped by boat. Small, discovering that the Great Moghul is missing, kills Thaddeus. Finally, Holmes traces Small and his murderous companion, the pygmy Tonga (John Pendric), and a river chase ensues. On capture, Small pretends to have thrown the treasure overboard but Holmes reveals its hiding place in the villain's wooden leg.

Below: Ian Richardson as Sherlock Holmes.
Right: Holmes asks Mary Morstan (Cherie Lunghi) how she came to possess such a valuable gem, part of the Agra treasure.

THIS IS THE FIRST OF WHAT WAS INTENDED TO be a series of six feature-length films starring Ian Richardson as Sherlock Holmes. Although only two films were made, there was a script for a third — *The Napoleon of Crime* written by Charles Pogue — which was later revamped and made as *Hands of a Murderer* with Edward Woodward in the deerstalker and cape.

The Sign of Four featured the better of Richardson's Watsons, David Healy. 'He made you feel that Holmes and Watson were friends,' said Richardson. 'Here is an insight into how this worked: When I was starring at the Royal Shakespeare Company, David Healy joined us as an understudy to Brewster Mason as Falstaff. One day Mason was off ill, and David had

to play. Now some of Falstaff's biggest scenes are with Ford [the role Richardson was playing] and I had to help him through the performance. The point of me telling the story is that from then on, he hero-worshipped me. The sun shone from my nether regions as far as David was concerned. And he brought this hero-worship thing, still extant all these years later, with him to the studio when he was playing Watson.'

Clive Merrison, who later played Sherlock Holmes on BBC Radio, recording all sixty of the Holmes stories, appears briefly as Bartholomew Sholto.

The Sign of Four and *The Hound of the Baskervilles* were first screened at the Cannes Film Festival in 1983 and created no excitement whatsoever. As Allen Eyles noted: 'Ian Richardson was more than competent, but [the films] have a fatally perfunctory feel about them. They did little to suggest that the stories had modern appeal'. However, after a recent reissue on video, Roger Johnson, editor of *The District Newsletter*, a publication of The Sherlock Holmes Society of London, commented: 'Ian Richardson is always worth watching and makes a splendid Holmes. Not a classic film but good fun.'

THE HOUND OF THE BASKERVILLES

	TV movie
First screening	13 May 1983
Production company	Mapleton Films
Duration	99 minutes
	Colour
Director	Douglas Hickox

Believing that the death of his friend Sir Charles Baskervilles is linked to the curse of the Hound of the Baskervilles, Doctor Mortimer (Denholm Elliott) consults Sherlock Holmes (Ian Richardson) about the safety of Sir Henry (Martin Shaw), the new heir. However, Sir Henry has no intention of going to Baskerville Hall, and plans to return to America once legal matters are settled. But when he is shot at in the street, his curiosity is aroused. Watson (Donald Churchill) travels with him to Baskerville Hall on Dartmoor. Among Sir Henry's neighbours are Laura Lyons (Connie Booth), her drunken artist husband (Brian Blessed), the naturalist Stapleton (Nicholas Clay) and his sister Beryl (Glynis Barber), with whom Sir Henry falls in love. Watson discovers that Mrs Barrymore (Eleanor Bron), the butler's wife, is the sister of the escaped convict, Selden. On the moor at night, Watson and Sir Charles hear the cry of a hound and catch a glimpse of a stranger watching them. Watson tracks the stranger only to discover that it is Sherlock Holmes. Following the murder of Laura Lyons, Holmes is convinced of Stapleton's guilt and sets a trap for him and the Hound.

Below: Holmes examines the walking stick.
***Right:** Richardson in his gypsy pedlar disguise with director Douglas Hickox.*

THE MAIN WEAKNESSES OF THIS FILM ARE THE additions and infelicities introduced into the plot by the scriptwriter, Charles Pogue. The greatest of these is the creation of a new character, Geoffrey Lyons, the drunken artist played without subtlety by Brian Blessed. The character was created to add to the meagre number of suspects, but his irrational and overly dramatic behaviour are embarrassing rather than intriguing. The 'new' murder — of Laura Lyons — is at odds with the whole idea of the original story, in which the villain uses an ingenious means to kill — a phantom Hound. Allowing Stapleton to behave like a common thug and simply strangle his

victim diminishes the sense we have of him as a criminal genius and a suitable foe for Sherlock Holmes.

Similarly, Watson and Lestrade (Ronald Lacey) are crudely drawn. On one occasion Watson tells the Inspector to 'bugger off', which no doubt would have had Doyle, to whose mind such language was abhorrent, spinning in his grave.

For the most part the actual Hound is impressive, a black silhouette created by computer graphics, which shocks with the suddenness and speed of its appearance.

Richardson, an excellent Holmes, found the shoot an enjoyable one: 'For one scene I was disguised as a gypsy [a plot idea taken from the 1939 Rathbone *Hound*]. The first time I got into the gypsy outfit nobody, only the make-up man and the director, had seen me. I was sitting in my caravan waiting to be summoned and wondered if there was anywhere I could get a cup of tea. So I stepped outside and nearby was a minibus full of gypsy extras all waiting to be bussed up to the location. With them was an assistant who, on seeing me in my outfit, cried out: "Ere! You! Get in this effing bus. We've been bleeding well waiting for you." I was so stunned I began to obey. As it happened, another assistant saw this and rushed forward: "Don't talk to our star like that," he cried. "This is Mr Richardson. He's Sherlock Holmes, for Christ's sake!"'

THE BAKER STREET BOYS

FIRST SCREENING March-April 1983
PRODUCTION COMPANY BBC Television
DURATION 8 x 30 minutes
Colour
REGULAR CAST
Jay Simpson (Wiggins),
Damion Napier (Beaver),
Adam Woodyatt (Shiner),
David Garlick (Sparrow),
Debbie Norris (Queenie),
Suzi Ross (Rosie),
Hubert Rees (Doctor Watson),
Roger Ostime (Sherlock Holmes),
Stanley Lebor (Inspector Lestrade)

'The mere sight of an official person seals men's lips. These youngsters, however, go everywhere and hear everything.' Sherlock Holmes in *A Study in Scarlet*.

Below: Cover to the now-deleted video release of the series.

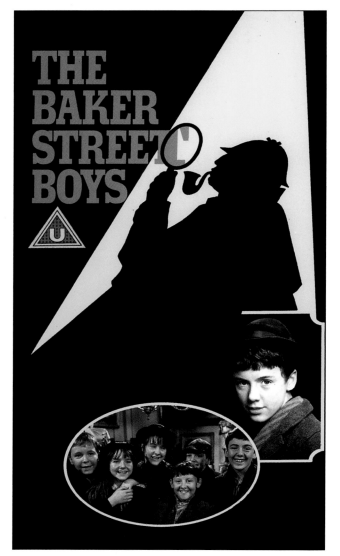

THE BAKER STREET IRREGULARS WERE A GROUP of 'street Arabs' whom Sherlock Holmes employed as 'the Baker Street division of the detective police force.' They were 'as sharp as needles' observed the detective.

The Irregulars found a murdered man's cab in *A Study in Scarlet* and the elusive steam launch *Aurora* in *The Sign of Four*. Holmes paid them each a shilling a day, with a guinea bonus to the Irregular would found the object of the search. Their leader was a lanky lad called Wiggins.

The idea of a group of youths working for the world's greatest detective was taken up in 1983 by writer Anthony Read, and shaped into a series of adventures for BBC Television, for the weekday teatime slot devoted to children's viewing. The stories were in two parts, one episode being shown on the Tuesday and the concluding one on Friday.

The Baker Street Boys were, in essence, The Baker Street Irregulars reduced down from around a dozen to six. However, rather than working for the detective, The

presence was felt in every story, as viewers would catch a glimpse of his silhouette or his shadow and hear his voice — that of actor Roger Ostime. However, Watson played a significant role in each of the programmes, in particular 'The Adventure of the Winged Scarab' in which Sherlock Holmes is kidnapped by Professor Moriarty. Watson joins forces with the Boys to seek out the Professor's lair, and this leads to a dramatic confrontation between the Doctor and the master criminal. Moriarty was portrayed with chilling authority by Colin Jeavons, who would later take up the mantle of Inspector Lestrade in the Granada series starring Jeremy Brett. Hubert Rees played Watson and — surprisingly for a children's programme in which one might expect a bumbling, comic version of the Doctor — his portrayal was sensible and realistic.

'There's more work to be got out of one of those little beggars than out of a dozen of the force' — Sherlock Holmes in *A Study in Scarlet*.

Baker Street Boys had, as the *Radio Times* explained, 'learned the art of detection by helping Sherlock Holmes on his most illustrious cases and now they embark upon some adventures of their own.'

Despite the programme's title, *The Baker Street Boys* comprised of four boys — Arnold Wiggins (Jay Simpson), Beaver (Damion Napier), Shiner (Adam Woodyatt, who went on to appear in the popular soap opera *EastEnders*) and Sparrow (David Garlick) — and two girls — Queenie (Debbie Norris) and Rosie (Suzi Ross). Even though they were independent of the Great Detective and investigating their own cases, Holmes'

Incidentally, Rees had been Inspector Lestrade to Tom Baker's Holmes in the BBC's *The Hound of the Baskervilles* serial the year before.

There were four two-part adventures in all, written by either Anthony Read or Richard Carpenter. Between them they created challenging stories that appealed as much to the adult Holmes fans as to the target teenage audience. The stories were: 'The Adventure of the Disappearing Dispatch Case' (Read), 'The Ghost of Julian Midwinter' (Carpenter), 'The Adventure of the Winged Scarab' (Carpenter) and 'The Case of the Captive Clairvoyant' (Read).

SHERLOCK HOLMES

FIRST SCREENING 1984
PRODUCTION COMPANY Pacific Arts
DURATION 3 x 48 minutes,
1 x 70m (The Baskerville Curse)
Colour
REGULAR CAST
Peter O'Toole (voice of Sherlock Holmes),
Earle Cross (voice of Doctor Watson)

In one sense it is quite surprising that Peter O'Toole has never appeared on screen as Sherlock Holmes. Given his tall, gaunt appearance and acting talents, he would seem to be an ideal big-name choice to portray the sleuth of Baker Street.

Below: Watson, as depicted in the animated adaptation of The Valley of Fear.

Of course he was on Billy Wilder's list of possible Sherlocks for his movie *The Private Life of Sherlock Holmes*, but when the director couldn't get his dream team of O'Toole and Peter Sellers together, he moved on to the next set of names on his list.

However, Peter O'Toole did appear briefly on stage as the Great Detective in a comedy play, *Dead Eyed Dicks* by Peter King, which toured the British provinces in 1976 but never made it into the West End. The action in the play takes place at Bogmore Manor where a murder has been committed. Each act is set in a different decade — the 1920s, the 1940s and the

then-futuristic 1990s — with O'Toole playing a different detective in each act. In the forties he appeared in a long raincoat and broad-brimmed trilby as a kind of Philip Marlowe/Sam Spade clone, while in the twenties he was Sherlock Holmes, dressed in broadly checked Inverness cape and deerstalker.

In 1984 Peter O'Toole played Sherlock Holmes again. But this time he was only heard and not seen. He voiced the character for a series of four cartoons for television, based on the Holmes novels *The Hound of the Baskervilles* (the cartoon was called *Sherlock Holmes and the*

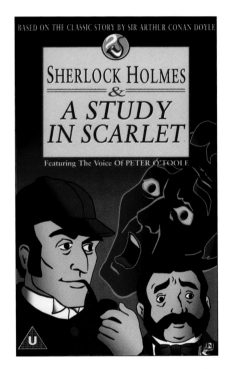

'Perhaps these pedestrian cartoon films featuring the dreary voiced Peter O'Toole should be re-titled *The Somnambulist Adventures of Sleepy Holmes*' — Sherlock Holmes — The Detective Magazine.

Baskerville Curse), *The Sign of Four, A Study in Scarlet* and *The Valley of Fear*. His Watson was Earle Cross.

The films were produced by Eddy Graham for Pacific Arts in Australia. In general the adaptations remained faithful to the novels, but the flashback sequences in which Holmes does not appear — and which feature in all the stories except *The Hound* — were streamlined and dealt with briefly, so that the detective was never removed from centre stage. The programmes were aimed at introducing great literature to young school children, and as such were 'Recommended by the National Education Association' in America.

The most surprising aspect of these

somewhat tame and insipid cartoons is the performance of the star: even when the drawn image moves and gestures in a dramatic fashion, O'Toole's rather somnambulistic tones do not vary their pitch or rhythm. It has been suggested that the actor recorded the dialogue for all four films in one day; whatever the reason, Peter O'Toole failed to impress as the voice of the Great Detective.

Another disappointment with this series was the missed opportunity in *A Study in Scarlet* to show the scene where Holmes and Watson meet. This episode, one of the highlights from the novel, was cut from the cartoon's script altogether, probably because Watson, yet again, was presented as a fat and much older man than his detective friend and not the young doctor he was in Doyle's original.

PETER CUSHING

THE METICULOUS HOLMES

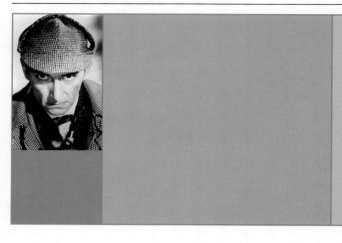

No other actor who played Sherlock Holmes approached the part with quite the same painstaking attention to detail, aiming above all to bring Conan Doyle's version of the detective to life. Peter Cushing would always stress the importance of going 'back to the source'.

Above: *Cushing in the Hammer* Hound.
Below: *With Nigel Stock.*
Right: *On Dartmoor for the BBC* Hound.

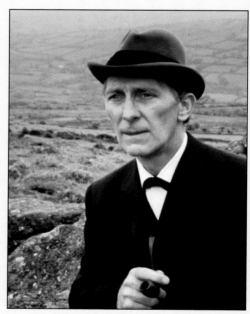

CUSHING WAS A FAN OF SHERLOCK HOLMES from his childhood: 'I love all the stories. It's the atmosphere I love so much, and they've all got that. I love the way they start: it is always foggy and there were those equinoctial gales.' It was, therefore, not surprising that when he was approached to play the part in Hammer's *The Hound of the Baskervilles* (1959) he accepted immediately: 'I was absolutely thrilled. It's a marvellous opportunity when you've got so much detail to base your character on.'

Cushing shared many qualities with the Great Detective, including a steely gaze, gaunt features and a preciseness of speech, although he did lack height. This might have mattered less if the casting director at Hammer had not chosen two of the tallest actors from their 'repertory company', Christopher Lee and Francis De Wolff, to play opposite him.

Cushing's interpretation of Holmes is decidedly prickly in the Hammer *Hound*, but when he resumed the part for the BBC series in 1968 he presented a softer, more humane version of the Baker Street sleuth. I asked Cushing the reason for this and he just smiled and said, 'Let's say that Holmes got up from a different side of the bed that day.' The actor set up his own keep-fit regime to prepare himself for the gruelling process of filming a long television series, explaining that, 'I wanted to be a hale and hearty Holmes.' Each morning he would run on the beach near his home in Whitstable before breakfast to help build up his stamina.

However, the BBC series was not a happy experience, and one might have thought that Cushing would not want to play the character again. Nevertheless, he was coaxed out of semi-retirement in 1984 by Kevin Francis of Tyburn Films to star as an old Holmes in *The Masks of Death*. It was to be Cushing's last leading role, and was perhaps his best interpretation of the detective. His co-star John Mills said of Cushing, 'he is a most dedicated actor and one always had a feeling of great security, because Peter turned up on the first day of shooting absolutely word and letter perfect. I have never known an actor more popular on the set.'

The success of *The Masks of Death* prompted Francis to commission another script, *The Abbot's Cry*, but by now Cushing felt that it really was time to hang up the deerstalker. Ian Richardson was approached to take on the role of Holmes with John Mills still in place as Watson. Richardson even met Cushing to discuss the possibility but nothing ever came of the venture, although the script is still on the shelf at Tyburn.

Peter Cushing continued to retain a keen interest in Holmes right up until his death in 1994. In the late eighties he became the first Honorary Member of The Northern Musgraves Sherlock Holmes Society, and provided them with a sketch of Holmes which the society adopted as their logo.

THE MASKS OF DEATH

US TITLE Sherlock Holmes and the Masks of Death
TV movie
FIRST SCREENING 23 December 1984
PRODUCTION COMPANY Tyburn Films
DURATION 90 minutes
Colour
DIRECTOR Roy Ward Baker

In 1913, Sherlock Holmes (Peter Cushing) is persuaded to take on a case by Inspector MacDonald (Gordon Jackson). Three corpses have been found in the Thames bearing looks of terror on their faces but displaying no visible cause of death. Holmes is diverted from this investigation by the Home Secretary (Ray Milland), who requests him to find a missing German envoy. The trail leads to the country home of Von Felseck (Anton Diffring), a German diplomat with whom Irene Adler (Anne Baxter) happens to be staying. While investigating at night, Holmes and Watson (John Mills) narrowly escape a plot to kill them. This convinces Holmes that the 'abduction' of the envoy is a ploy to lure him away from his other case. Returning to the East End he discovers a secret laboratory beneath a derelict public house. It is part of a plot to gas a large part of London's population on the outbreak of war. The corpses in the river had been killed by the gas, each of them terrified by the last thing they saw: the gas-masked Germans. Holmes's discovery foils the plan and, in recognition of his actions, the King summons him to Windsor Castle.

Right: Sketches by Peter Cushing.
Below: Cushing came out of semi-retirement for the film.

AT THE AGE OF SEVENTY-ONE, PETER CUSHING played Sherlock Holmes for the last time in 1984 in the TV movie *The Masks of Death*. It was with some reluctance that the actor returned to face the camera. 'I didn't have the old energy y'know and I didn't want to let anyone down.' Filming schedules were, to a large extent, arranged to give Cushing maximum rest between the takes. The story was set in 1913 when Holmes — or at least Doyle's Holmes — was approaching sixty, and so in essence it is a kind of geriatric adventure. However, with his 'toupee nailed in place' (his own words) and effective make-up, Cushing made a fine figure of a senior citizen Holmes. To accompany him was Sir John Mills — who was seventy-six — as Doctor Watson.

Director Roy Ward Baker expressed the opinion that Mills was the best Watson he had ever seen: 'He had intelligence, humanity and dogged loyalty; and the relationship between the two men was totally believable.'

The Masks of Death, while not a great Holmes film, is thoroughly enjoyable and Cushing gives a wonderful performance. *The Times* noted that he was 'a vigorous survivor' and 'that age cannot wither him; he was a Prospero rather than a Hamlet, but none the worse for that.'

Kevin Francis collected a tremendous cast of old troupers to appear along side Cushing, including Oscar-winner Anne Baxter, who made a charming Irene Adler, effectively suggesting a beguiling mixture of brains and beauty. She obviously enjoyed making the movie. She told *The Sunday Times*: 'I drive in a 1910 Mercedes Benz with great big headlights like aquariums. It was fun. Damn it!'

Ray Milland was sad casting as the Home Secretary. The effect of a recent stroke can be clearly seen from his halting performance. Originally Sir John Gielgud had been given the role, but another filming project overran and Milland was brought in at the last minute.

THE ADVENTURES OF
SHERLOCK HOLMES

FIRST SCREENING April-June 1984;
August-September 1985
PRODUCTION COMPANY Granada Television
DURATION 13 x 50 minutes
Colour
REGULAR CAST
Jeremy Brett (Sherlock Holmes),
David Burke (Doctor Watson),
Rosalie Williams (Mrs Hudson)

It was Michael Cox, a drama producer at Granada Television, who had the idea of bringing the authentic Doylean Sherlock Holmes to independent television in a series of lavish one-hour productions.

At FIRST COX HAD TO BATTLE WITH THE WAVES of indifference from the men in suits in order to get the project off the ground. They just sighed and moaned, 'Not corny old Sherlock Holmes again.' But that was the whole point. It wasn't 'corny old Sherlock Holmes again'; this time it was to be the exciting genuine article.

The dream began in 1980. Michael had finally persuaded Granada to set up the Sherlock Holmes series. They wanted a well-known actor in the lead and suggested both Anthony Andrews and Jeremy Irons, but Cox wanted Jeremy Brett. And he got his way. At first Brett was unsure whether he wanted to play the character, and then he went away to Barbados to research locations for a film of *The Tempest* that he was hoping to make: 'It was there that I became fascinated with Doyle's tales. I thought, "Oh yes, there are things I can do with this fellow!" I learned it wasn't all pipes and deerstalkers... Best of all, there was a dark and mysterious character to explore.'

Television veteran John Hawkesworth was brought in as senior scriptwriter, and he helped shape the format of the series. Both he and Cox were determined to set the record straight on Watson, and show him as 'a reasonable man, quite a dashing fellow with moderate intelligence and a definite sense of humour.' Cox had his eye on an actor he had worked with before: David Burke. Fortunately for all concerned, playing Watson took Burke's fancy and he agreed, becoming a splendid foil for Brett's Holmes. The Baker Street trio was completed by Rosalie Williams as Mrs Hudson.

The project was halted for two years while Granada became involved in a court case with Sy Weintraub and his company, who had already commenced filming their series with Ian Richardson. The matter was settled out of court, and Weintraub and co handed over the baton to Granada. So it was not until 1983 that the Brett series went into production.

In the meantime, Michael Cox had not only been commissioning scripts but had also supervised the construction of Baker Street itself. This was the huge outdoor set which features in the opening credits of the series. In essence, it was just a façade of the street hanging on a very stout girder structure, and Cox was told that if the Sherlock Holmes series didn't last long, the façade could easily be ripped off and replaced by some other exterior set. It was built at Granada's Manchester studios, within a hundred yards of the company's other famous thoroughfare, the main set for the soap opera *Coronation Street*.

It had been agreed from the outset that the series would begin with 'A Scandal in Bohemia' — the first short story — and conclude with 'The Final Problem' and the supposed death of Holmes.

By the time the series was about to go into production, both producer and star were steeped in Sherlockian lore. However, Cox realised that it was essential that their knowledge and understanding of the Holmes canon should be passed on to all the creative artists working on the series: 'I thought sympathetically of designers, make-up artists, costume designers, cameramen, property buyers, set dressers — and I thought to myself, I can't expect them to know that Holmes kept his tobacco in the toe of a Persian slipper, or that he kept his unanswered correspondence nailed to the mantelpiece with a dagger. So I decided that we needed a reference manual which could be referred to quickly and easily. The sort of thing you could look up that would tell you what Holmes would wear if he went out to buy a newspaper — whether it was spats or a top hat or whatever'.

So Cox, associate producer Stuart Doughty and programme researcher Nicky Cooney trawled through all the stories lifting out any piece of information that could be useful for the series. The end result was *The Baker Street File: A Guide to the Appearance and Habits of Sherlock Holmes and Dr Watson*. It was a card-covered stapled booklet containing nearly 1,200 listings.

Viewers in Britain got their first sight of this new Sherlock Holmes one mild spring evening in 1984, in an adaptation of 'A Scandal in Bohemia'. However, it was not the first episode to be filmed. Cox considered this a very important story, not just because it introduced Brett and Burke to the television audience, but it also dealt with the strange ambivalent relationship — redolent with repressed sexuality — the detective has with the American adventuress, Irene Adler, played by Gayle Hunnicutt. Irene Adler is the only woman in the stories to whom Holmes expresses a personal warmth that goes beyond mere pleasantry. Watson wrote that to Holmes, 'she predominates and eclipses the whole of her sex.' Cox wanted to make sure both Brett and Burke were comfortable with

their roles before attempting this episode, and so it was the third to be filmed.

The great joy for Jeremy Brett on this particular story was his use of disguise. His remarkable appearance as the 'drunken-looking' groom was a triumph. He even fooled the producer, who turned up on location and asked where Brett was, only to be informed he was standing a few feet away from him.

Both the Holmes fans and the press were unanimous in their praise for the first episode, and for Jeremy Brett's portrayal. Nancy Banks-Smith in *The Guardian*

Previous page (below): An early publicity still for the Granada series.
Above left: *Burke and Brett emulating a Paget drawing.*
Above right: *The Baker Street triumvirate: Holmes (Jeremy Brett), Mrs Hudson (Rosalie Williams) and Watson (David Burke).*
Far left: *Granada's impressive Baker Street set.*
Left: *Jeremy Brett and producer Michael Cox on location for 'The Naval Treaty'.*

enthused, 'I recommend this series as a luxurious, even luscious way of passing the time... *The Adventures of Sherlock Holmes...* is a very posh job indeed'. Philip French in *The Sunday Times* went further: 'Jeremy Brett and David Burke are the best Holmes and Watson I've ever seen. For once we can see why Holmes' only passion is detection. The first hint of an assignment galvanises him into a fury of excitement. He takes an inordinate pleasure in dressing up as a labourer and an aged clergyman in order to spy on Irene Adler, and he takes mischievous delight in the little deductive feats to astound Watson.'

'The Solitary Cyclist' was actually the first programme to be filmed. It was probably the most problematic of the whole series, as the director who had been assigned to the show was offered the chance to make a cinema movie, and left with hardly any warning. Paul Annett stepped in at the last minute and was, according to Michael Cox, 'a godsend. He

did all the hard work on how Jeremy and David were going to play their parts: what they looked like, what sort of clothes they'd wear and what sort of relationship there would be between them. Jeremy was always in danger of playing as some kind of grotesque if he wasn't directed properly. I remember Paul saying to him one day, "Jeremy, isn't there going to be anything of you in this portrayal?" Brett responded well, replying, "What a good thought. You've pulled me up short and made me realise that I could be going too much into the area of a bizarre character." Paul agreed, noting, "Don't, because there is a place in this for things of your own, Jeremy — your magnetism, your ability to charm people, to deal with people — use those in playing Holmes. Don't put them aside. Don't think this man is a wierdo because he's not."'

Fidelity to Doyle was always at the forefront of Cox's and Brett's minds. At the start of the project, both men agreed to use the Sidney Paget drawings as 'their image', and in the early shows at least one shot was set up to mirror a Paget illustration. 'The Naval Treaty', which contains the famous rose speech — 'What a lovely thing a rose is' — is a case in point. The passage and the Paget drawing present Holmes as a dreamer and philosopher, and Brett reproduces the pose very effectively.

The Adventures was shown in two series. The first series featured seven stories,

beginning with 'A Scandal in Bohemia' on 24 April 1984, and running through to 'The Blue Carbuncle' on 5 June. The growing number of devotees had to wait over a year for the second series, but for the production team there was no such gap. The second series began on 25 August 1985 with 'The Copper Beeches', coming to a climax with 'The Final Problem' on 29 September.

The second show in this series, 'The Greek Interpreter', was especially interesting for two reasons. Firstly, it introduced Holmes' brother, Mycroft, portrayed by Charles Gray, who had first played the character in *The Seven-Per-Cent Solution*. His bulk and demeanour were exactly as Doyle had described Mycroft. For their opening scene together, Brett devised a clever shot in which Sherlock is at first hidden by his brother's frame and then emerges from behind him, creating the impression of the younger sibling escaping from his big brother's shadow. This was also the first film in which major changes were made to the original story. Cox explained the need for the alterations: 'It's a super story up to the last few paragraphs... where it ends somewhat abruptly. We wanted a grandstand finale.' And so the Granada version has an exciting train sequence in which the Holmes brothers pursue the malefactors. One of the villains, Kemp, was played by George Costigan, with pebble glasses, a chilling grin and a high sing-song voice, deliberately reminiscent of Peter Lorre as

Joel Cairo in *The Maltese Falcon* (1941). 'So,' said Cox, 'we ended up with a Sherlock Holmes film containing an echo of one of my all-time favourite films.' The successful new ending of 'The Greek Interpreter' paved the way for future scripts to be doctored and 'improved', with varying degrees of success.

As the series neared the last episode, in which Holmes locks horns with his arch enemy, Professor Moriarty, on the path overlooking the Reichenbach Falls, Cox decided he wanted to bring Moriarty into

the penultimate show, 'The Red-Headed League': 'He was too fascinating a character to be relegated to one appearance and we thought it would be more effective to introduce Holmes' nemesis in an earlier episode, so that the dramatic events of 'The Final Problem' could be seen in a more detailed context.'

Eric Porter was chosen to play Moriarty and he was delighted: 'I'm collecting English villains. I've notched up Soames Forsythe and Fagin — I couldn't resist this monster.' He played the part brilliantly, even emulating Doyle's description of the Professor moving his head in a 'strange reptilian fashion.'

The climax of 'The Final Problem' was actually filmed at the Reichenbach Falls in Switzerland. Michael Cox was determined to show Holmes and Moriarty's plunge over the edge into the watery depths below. Stuntmen Marc Boyle (Holmes) and Alf Joint (Moriarty) were each suspended by lengths of thin steel cable fixed to harnesses under their costumes and run from a specially constructed platform, hidden from view, at the top of the falls. When the cry for action came they were dropped into the foaming spray at a speed of a little over thirty miles per hour. Alf

Joint said, 'It took about twenty-five seconds to make the fall. We fell about 375 feet until we were stopped by the wires.' Byron Rogers wrote in *The Times* that 'it was the best fall ever filmed, much better than Butch Cassidy and Sundance'.

'The Final Problem' was a spectacular end to a series that had been a critical and commercial success. Nancy Banks-Smith stated in *The Guardian* that the series was 'so polished that, if you rub your hand over it, you would leave greasy finger marks, so don't'.

Previous page (above): Holmes, Violet Smith (Barbara Wilshire) and Carruthers (John Castle) — in disguise. A candid picture taken on location for the first film to be made: 'The Solitary Cyclist'.
Previous page (below): Holmes and Moriarty (Eric Porter) on the brink of the Reichenbach Falls.
Above left: Stuntmen Alf Joint (left) and Marc Boyle dressed as Holmes and Moriarty in readiness for their plunge down the Reichenbach Falls.
Above right: Burke and Brett received unanimous praise for their performances.
Far left: Filming for 'The Final Problem' on Oakworth Station in Yorkshire — doubling for Canterbury.
Left: 'What a lovely thing a rose is.' Another Paget pose, from 'The Naval Treaty'.

JEREMY BRETT

DANCING IN THE MOONLIGHT

'What Brett offers is a combination of fidelity and audacity. Everything he does can ultimately be justified by chapter and line from Conan Doyle's stories, but he has taken liberties with the myth so confidently that he has... taken possession of it and displaced the literary Holmes' — Kevin Jackson in *The Independent*.

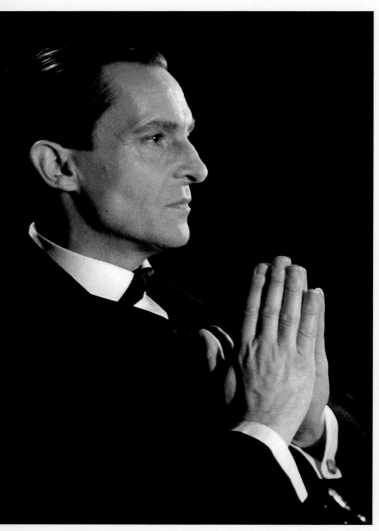

I ONCE ASKED THE PRODUCER MICHAEL COX why he had chosen Jeremy Brett to play Sherlock Holmes. 'What was right for Holmes was the classical actor's Hamlet factor, if you like,' he said. 'The fact that he could play the role; that he had the voice and the actor's intelligence, the presence, the physique, the ability to jump over the furniture, handle the horses, do the disguises and whatever may be. To me he had the best combination of all those.'

The casting of Jeremy Brett as Holmes was more than inspired: it was a magical yoking of star to vehicle — a combination that enriched each element and, ultimately, elevated and illuminated both. Brett became Sherlock Holmes to millions of fans all over the world. Because of his magnetic performance, in the minds of the fans there was no dividing line between actor and character: they were as one. And yet, in the early days, he was very uncertain about his interpretation. Michael Cox said, 'I honestly think that Jeremy didn't understand the part when he started. He'd no idea what kind of pull we would have with the viewing public. He didn't realise he would be playing a kind of intellectual superman who was also an approachable helper. And that came to him during the time he played the character when he began to realise that he was playing one of the saviours of the twentieth century'.

The controlled eccentricities and mannered delivery which mesmerised viewers was partly a result of Brett's dark secret: he was a manic depressive, an affliction that can send a person's emotions racing for the moon or scrabbling down to hell. It was an instability that he was able to channel most effectively into his greatest performance — as Sherlock Holmes. As an actor — and a flamboyant one — he was able to cover up his manic depression for years. He once told me that if he'd been a bank manager or a greengrocer, he would have been found out straight away, but 'it's easy to disguise the demon when you're a fellow that struts about the stage ranting and raving every night'.

The death of his wife in 1985 exacerbated the condition, as did his recurring heart problem. The drugs he took for both these ailments fought with each other, weakening his constitution and

causing water retention that bloated his body. Slowly, the lithe young fellow who gazed down on Baker Street in the opening credits of the Granada shows faded away to be replaced by a large, puffy-faced individual. By the time he filmed *The Hound of the Baskervilles* in 1988 the change was beginning to show. He hated his appearance in the later shows, knowing that he no longer resembled the ideal image of Holmes he had once been.

Playing Sherlock Holmes was never just a job for Brett. He researched the character and the stories thoroughly and became a champion for Conan Doyle. It was a crusade that occasionally led him into disputes with the writers and producer. For example, David Burke remembered Brett being upset with aspects of the script of 'The Crooked Man'. In this story, when the two lovers meet after many years — she now married to a bully of an army officer, he a crippled wreck — they do so in the lonely, darkened thoroughfare under a

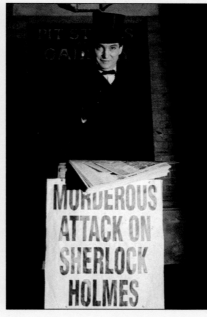

street lamp. For practical purposes, in the Granada version the meeting was transposed to a crowded Salvation Army-style bazaar, which to Brett's mind destroyed all the poignancy of the moment and the isolation of these two figures. 'There was a big row over that,' said Burke. 'Jeremy was very angry with the change. Blood was almost spilt and tears were shed, but he lost the battle.'

Despite his efforts to stay true to Doyle, he hated wearing a deerstalker, even when the Paget illustrations indicated that it was appropriate. Sue Milton, who was his make-up artist, said that, 'Jeremy was most comfortable wearing the big black Homberg.'

In the autumn of 1988 he starred in the stage play *The Secret of Sherlock Holmes* with Edward Hardwicke. It ran for a year at Wyndham's Theatre in the West End before touring the provinces. At the start of the run Brett was in fine form but, sadly, the mental stress of playing this very demanding role took its toll on his health and his performance. He began to ad lib outrageously and when Hardwicke commented on this Brett exploded with anger, only to beg forgiveness the next day.

There were two more series and three feature-length Holmes films which followed on from the play, but Brett never quite achieved the greatness of the early programmes. In the nineties he was very bulky and began to wear black all the time to help disguise his size. He told me, 'I was blowing up like a balloon with all these drugs — retaining water, you see. In the last few films I actually waddled.'

Brett died of heart failure in September 1995. Shortly before his death, he expressed his thoughts to me about playing Sherlock Holmes: 'I never actually saw him, y'know — he was always a few steps ahead and I never caught up with him. To be Sherlock is difficult because he is such an elusive pimpernel. Maybe I got one or two things right. But Sherlock is evergreen. He is one of the most elusive intellectual geniuses who has ever been written about. Men find him fascinating because he is so self-contained and totally in control, while women see him as a challenge: they want to break that icy demeanour and reveal the real emotion beneath. Of course SH has a feminine side too — the intuitive quality that is part of his magic. Bless his heart, he's streets ahead of us. But I've had a fascinating time playing him. I said to Dame Jean [Conan Doyle] that I've danced in the moonlight with your father for ten years. The moonlight, not the sunlight — Holmes is a very dark character.'

SHERLOCK'S RIVALS

THE COMPETING SLEUTHS

As soon as Sherlock Holmes became the star of *The Strand Magazine*, other writers rushed to create similarly dynamic sleuths, attempting to rival the success of the Great Detective of Baker Street.

WITH SHERLOCK HOLMES, ARTHUR CONAN Doyle laid down the basic guidelines of detective fiction which almost immediately initiated an explosion of Sherlockian copycats. However, Doyle had based his crime-solver on an earlier sleuth, Chevalier Auguste Dupin, created by Edgar Allan Poe. Dupin appeared in three stories published in the first half of the nineteenth century, 'The Murders in the Rue Morgue',

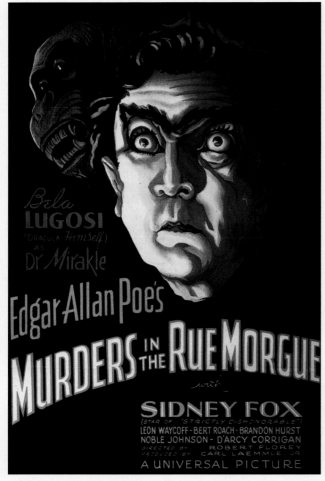

'The Purloined Letter' and 'The Mystery of Marie Roget'. Dupin's activities are recorded by an unnamed chronicler, an admiring and somewhat slow-witted fellow — the Watson character. Dupin is not only brilliant and disdainful of the official police, but also eccentric, shunning daylight and only venturing from his rooms at night. He is given to astounding his companion by reading his thought processes. Doyle thought Poe 'the master of all'. Dorothy L. Sayers, the creator of Lord Peter Wimsey, believed that, "The Murders in the Rue Morgue' constitutes in itself almost a complete manual of detective theory and practice.' Not a complete manual, perhaps, for while Poe's stories were clever puzzles they lacked excitement, pace and a really charismatic central character. It was Doyle who, in refining Poe's rudiments, excited the reading public with his detective hero. Dupin has appeared in movies, but usually the character is significantly changed from the one conceived by Poe. In two versions of 'The Murders in the Rue Morgue' (*Murders in the Rue Morgue* [1932] and *Phantom of the Rue Morgue* [1954]) Dupin is presented as a young medical student, while 1971's *Murders in the Rue Morgue* eliminates him altogether from the plot. In the 1942 adaptation of 'The Mystery of Marie Roget', Dupin's first name becomes Paul and he is chief medical officer of Paris.

Following the success of the Holmes stories, there was a rash of brilliant detectives who had one particular idiosyncratic trait. The most notable was Ernest Bramah's Max Carrados, the blind detective, who could make the most incredible deductions through the senses of smell, touch and hearing. He could even read the newspaper by letting his sensitive fingers run across the print. Other eccentric investigators of this period included Jacques Futrelle's Professor S. F.

X. Van Deusen — The Thinking Machine, Clifford Ashdown's Romney Pringle and Arthur Morrison's Martin Hewitt (the latter's stories, like those of Holmes, appeared in *The Strand* illustrated by Sidney Paget).

The most obvious Holmes copycat was Sexton Blake. He was known as 'the office boy's Sherlock Holmes' because there was an air of comic book heroics about his

investigations. Created by Harry Blyth, he made his first appearance during 1893 in a boys' weekly paper, the *Halfpenny Marvel*, in the story 'The Missing Millionaire'. Since then over a hundred known authors, as well as countless anonymous ones, have created exploits for Sexton Blake, all penned in the third person. Like Holmes, Blake lives in Baker Street with a housekeeper, Mrs Bardell, who has a tendency to exclaim 'Lawks a mercy' at moments of crisis. He also has a young assistant called Tinker who is under the sleuth's tutelage.

Sexton Blake appeared in several silent movies with titles such as *Sexton Blake v Baron Kettler* (1912) and *The Further Exploits of Sexton Blake: The Mystery of the SS Olympic* (1919). In the thirties, George Curzon appeared in three B movies as Blake in *Sexton Blake and the Bearded Doctor* (1935), *Sexton Blake and the Mademoiselle* (1935) and

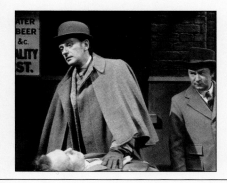

Sexton Blake and the Hooded Terror (1938). In the forties the role was taken over by David Farrar who featured in two poverty row productions: Meet Sexton Blake (1944) and The Echo Murders (1945).

Sexton Blake was an ITV series that ran from 1967 to 1971, starring Laurence Payne. The setting was the late twenties and there were sixty-four twenty-five minute episodes in all. This detective was last seen

on screen in 1978, when Jeremy Clyde starred in the six-part BBC serial Sexton Blake and The Demon God.

Perhaps the most serious attempt to reproduce the Holmes stories was made by R. Austin Freeman with his 'scientific detective', Dr Thorndyke. Freeman certainly created baffling mysteries to challenge Thorndyke, but the detective was rather a cold fish, with no depth or charisma, and so has largely been ignored as a dramatic character. He did feature in one episode of BBC's Detective series in 1964, played by Peter Copley, and in one episode of the ITV series The Rivals of Sherlock Holmes, played by an ex-Sherlock, John Neville.

Dorothy L. Sayers took the Holmes format up an aristocratic notch when she created her detective, Lord Peter Wimsey, who resided in Piccadilly at number 110A, which is approximately half of 221B! His 'Watson' was his manservant Bunter, and

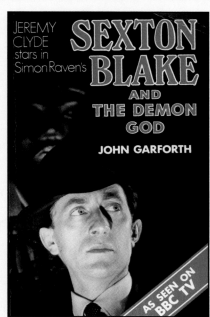

JEREMY CLYDE stars in Simon Raven's **SEXTON BLAKE AND THE DEMON GOD**

JOHN GARFORTH

AS SEEN ON BBC TV

Previous page (above left): The 'office boy's Holmes', Sexton Blake.
Previous page (below left): Poe's Auguste Dupin was an important precursor of Holmes.
Previous page (right): Dupin (Edward Woodward, right), with Charles Kay as Poe, in an episode of Detective (1968).
Above: Max Carrados (Robert Stephens, left) with Inspector Beedel (George A. Cooper) in The Rivals of Sherlock Holmes.
Far left: Another episode of The Rivals... featured Barrie Ingham (left) as Thorndyke.

his Lestrade was his brother-in-law, Inspector Parker, a sensible if shortsighted Scotland Yard man whom Lord Peter referred to, with affection, as 'old Parker Bird'. If there was a strong touch of the Wodehousean 'silly ass' qualities to Wimsey in the early stories, he still maintained the shrewdness and deductive brilliance of Holmes. He also voiced many Sherlockian type aphorisms such as, 'In solvin' a problem you should take the probable impossible rather than the impossible probable.'

Wimsey has only appeared in two movies: *The Silent Passenger* (1935) — played by Peter Haddon — which was based on a 'theme' provided by Sayers, and *Busman's Honeymoon* (1940; aka *Haunted Honeymoon*) — played by Robert Montgomery — a version of Sayers' play. The foppish sleuth has been better served by television. In the seventies, Ian Carmichael played Wimsey in

five BBC television adaptations of Sayers' novels: *Clouds of Witness* (1972), *The Unpleasantness of the Bellona Club* (1973), *Murder Must Advertise* (1973), *The Nine Tailors* (1974) and *Five Red Herrings* (1975). Carmichael threw himself into the role with great gusto. He said, 'I like Wimsey so much... because I identify with him. In fact to be absolutely truthful I wish I had been him. He is such a bloody fine character.'

Carmichael's adaptations were all from the early Wimsey books, before he met and fell in love with Harriet Vane and developed into a deeper, more sober character. These later novels were eventually dramatised in 1987 in the series *A Dorothy L. Sayers Mystery*, with Edward Petherbridge taking on the role of Wimsey and Harriet Walter as Harriet Vane, whom the detective saves from the gallows in the first story, 'Strong Poison'. The other stories in the series were 'Have His Carcase' and 'Gaudy Night'.

Sayers' stories contained numerous references to Holmes, as did the early work of Agatha Christie, whose Belgian sleuth Hercule Poirot had many of the qualities of the great Sherlock, despite the difference in his appearance and nationality. Robert Barnard, in his review of Christie's work, *A Talent to Deceive*, observes: 'It is easy to forget that the young Christie and the elderly Doyle were writing detection simultaneously and that Poirot first appeared in the shadow of the incomparable Sherlock Holmes... Like many other young writers, Agatha Christie's

reaction to success was to copy it.'

After the success of her first Poirot novel, *The Mysterious Affair at Styles* in 1920, Christie featured her detective in a series of short stories, eleven of which were brought together in a 1924 volume called *Poirot Investigates*. One only has to dip into this collection to see how the form and structure of the stories echo those of the Holmes tales; and how the relationships between Poirot, his friend and chronicler, Hastings, and Inspector Japp mirrors those between Holmes, Watson and Lestrade.

Hercule Poirot has had a healthy screen career. He featured in three movies in the thirties, portrayed by Austin Trevor: *Alibi* (1931), *Black Coffee* (1931) and *Lord Edgeware Dies* (1934). In 1966 Tony Randall appeared as Poirot and Robert Morley as Hastings in *The ABC Murders*. Albert Finney, with plastered-down hair, became the Belgian sleuth solving the *Murder on the Orient Express* in 1974. The film was such an international success that another big-budget Poirot mystery followed, *Death on the Nile* (1978), but Finney was not interested in reprising the role and so Peter Ustinov stepped in. He went on to make two more cinema Poirots, *Evil Under the Sun* (1982) and *Appointment with Death* (1988), and several TV movies.

In 1989, London Weekend Television produced the first of their long-running series *Agatha Christie's Poirot* with David Suchet giving a universally acclaimed portrayal. Suchet has continued with the role and it is his wish to film all the Poirot

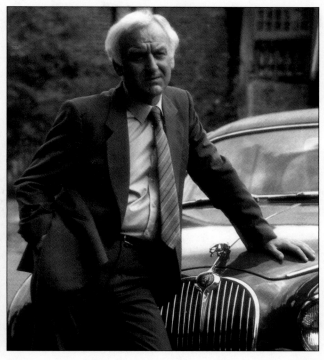

novels.

One of the most inscrutable of Holmes' rivals is the oriental detective Charlie Chan, famous for his razor-sharp intelligence and shrewd detective work, usually accompanied by one of his enigmatic sayings, such as, 'He who rides a tiger cannot dismount' or, 'Bad alibi is like dead fish. Cannot stand test of time.' Created by Earl Derr Biggers, Charlie Chan of the Honolulu Police Department first appeared in print in *The House Without a Key* in 1925. It wasn't long before the character was snapped up by Hollywood, and through the thirties and forties he appeared in a string of B movies featuring first Warner Oland and then, from 1938, Sidney Toler. Chan was a well-travelled detective as well as a clever one, as many of the titles of his movies bore witness, such as *Charlie Chan in London* (1934), *Charlie Chan in Paris* (1935), *Charlie Chan in Egypt* (1935), *Charlie Chan in Shanghai* (1935), *Charlie Chan in Reno* (1939) and *Charlie Chan in Rio* (1941).

In 1957, J. Carrol Naish starred in a dull television series, *The New Adventures of Charlie Chan*, which was filmed in England. Peter Ustinov switched from a Belgian to an oriental accent to appear in the woeful *Charlie Chan and the Curse of the Dragon Queen* (1981.

It is true to say that every detective who has a sharp mind, spots *the* vital clue and is something of a loner has a debt of gratitude to Sherlock Holmes. That goes for the Father Browns, the Philip Marlowes,

the Campions, the Dr Fells et al. There is a strong line of heredity linking all these sleuths, right up to the modern practitioners. If Sherlock Holmes was the father, then Inspector Endeavour Morse is surely the great grandson. In reviewing one of the Inspector Morse television programmes, a *Daily Mail* critic referred to the detective and his assistant, Sergeant Lewis, as 'a latterday Holmes and Watson.' Certainly this is not far from the mark: Morse and Holmes are very much their own men, often insensitive to the feelings of others, passionate about disparate interests — both love music, for example — and while Holmes craves cryptograms, Morse has his crosswords. And they both have partners on whom they depend. Watson and Lewis, on the other hand, are both good-natured 'ordinary' fellows with a heightened sense of loyalty and tolerance.

Inspector Morse was created by Colin Dexter and had a respectable literary career but it was with the television series which began in 1987 that the character achieved the kind of success that Holmes did in his day. Starring the charismatic John Thaw, *Inspector Morse* became one of the greatest detective series on television. The final film, 'The Remorseful Day', in which Morse dies, was shown on 16 November 2000 and attracted fourteen million moist-eyed viewers in Britain. Nothing so sensational had happened in the world of crime fiction since the Great Detective tumbled into the Reichenbach Falls. To Lewis, Morse was 'the best and

wisest man' he had ever known, which surely makes this illustrious inspector the greatest rival of Sherlock Holmes. However, unlike Holmes, Morse was not to return.

The idea of death and rebirth of a detective character, which is such a major part of the Sherlock Holmes legend, was examined in the cunning surrealistic TV film *Reichenbach Falls* (2007), which featured a police officer, a clone of Ian Rankin's character, Inspector Rebus, working in modern day Edinburgh. He is visited by the spirit of Conan Doyle (Richard Wilson) who informs him that he, like Holmes, is a fictional creation and that his author is about to kill him off too, as Doyle had with Sherlock over the Reichenbach Falls.

Previous page (above left): Lord Peter Wimsey (Ian Carmichael) with Rev Venables (Donald Eccles) in The Nine Tailors *(1974).*

Previous page (above right): David Suchet, star of London Weekend Television's Agatha Christie's Poirot.

Previous page (below left): Another Poirot, Albert Finney, with fellow passenger Lauren Bacall in Murder on the Orient Express *(1974).*

Above left: Warner Oland is Charlie Chan in Shanghai *(1935).*

Above right: A latter day Holmes? John Thaw as Chief Inspector Endeavour Morse.

Left: A tie-in comic book to the 1957 TV series starring J. Carrol Naish as Charlie Chan.

YOUNG SHERLOCK HOLMES

UK TITLE Young Sherlock Holmes and the Pyramid of Fear	
FIRST SCREENING 4 December 1985	
PRODUCTION COMPANY Amblin Entertainment for Paramount	
DURATION 109 minutes	
Colour	
DIRECTOR Barry Levinson	

In 1870, Sherlock Holmes (Nicholas Rowe) meets John Watson (Alan Cox) at college and falls in love with Elizabeth (Sophie Ward). She is the daughter of Professor Waxflatter (Nigel Stock) who, struck by a tiny dart, suffers a frightening hallucination and stabs himself to death. Elizabeth's pet dog attacks a sinister hooded figure and tears off a piece of cloth that leads the three sleuths to a textile warehouse in Wapping, which houses a huge pyramid and a sacrificial temple. Escaping, they are each struck by a dart and suffer hallucinations. Holmes learns that some years before, a group of old boys of the college planned to build a luxury hotel in Egypt until the discovery of a sacred tomb on the site. In quashing the protests of the locals, the British army razed a village to the ground. An Anglo-Egyptian youth swore revenge. Holmes now realises that this enemy is Rathe (Anthony Higgins), the college fencing master, who has kidnapped Elizabeth. Holmes fights Rathe in a duel on a deserted wharf and the villain falls through the ice. Holmes is reunited with Elizabeth, but she dies in his arms. Rathe, meanwhile, has survived: we see him signing in to a Swiss hotel under the name 'Moriarty'.

YOUNG SHERLOCK HOLMES DESCRIBED ITSELF AS an 'affectionate speculation' and offered an alternative version of Watson's first introduction to Holmes when he joins the same public school. Following the opening credits, there is a message on screen which tells us that 'The following story is original and is not specifically based on the exploits of Sherlock Holmes as described in the works of Sir Arthur Conan Doyle.' Of course, readers of the Holmes stories know

that John met Sherlock in a laboratory at St Bart's Hospital, but big movies are not made for readers. Nevertheless, the prospect of two adolescents called Holmes and Watson meeting up for 'the adventure of a lifetime' is really appealing.

Sadly, the film does not live up to this entertaining premise. The main problem lies in the attempt to introduce too many disparate elements and fantasy sequences into a Holmes mystery. The hallucinatory episodes are brilliantly carried, but they almost seemed designed to be a showcase for George Lucas's Industrial Light & Magic special effects factory rather than making a significant contribution to the plot. Allen Eyles believed that 'some of the effects are... nasty, and it is difficult to

weak point. Alan Eyles commented that scriptwriter Chris Columbus's 'attempt to explain the detective's aloofness towards women is weak; the ending, though painful to Holmes, is not psychologically hurtful enough to explain his later attitude, and the suggestion that he will spend the rest of his life being true to his first great love, looking forward to their reunion in the next world, certainly gives him Conan Doyle's belief in the afterlife... but it is hard to accord with the rational figure of 221B Baker Street.' Also, the romance, not helped by a vacuous performance by Sophie Ward, serves only to distract attention from the developing relationship between Holmes and Watson which should have been at the heart of the film.

'On his first case, a brilliant schoolboy is swept into a perilous adventure' — Advertising slogan.

distinguish between the hallucinations and the real action.'

Another episode which fits uncomfortably into the movie is the sequence when Holmes soars skywards on Waxflatter's flying machine, which resembles a bike with large flapping wings. Holmes is seen pedalling for all he is worth, silhouetted, E.T.-like, against the moon. *Films and Filming* observed that 'the introduction of the flying machine is a historical anomaly which takes liberties with both the chronology of invention and the film's consistency of tone. This Disneyesque interpolation only serves to compound the problem of the film's polyglot style.'

However, the majority of reviewers focussed on the insipid romance between Holmes and Elizabeth as the film's real

One of the real bonuses is the performance of eighteen year-old Nicholas Rowe as the embryonic detective. As he matures through the course of the action, acquiring a curly pipe and a deerstalker hat along the way, he presents the very image of a teenage Sherlock. He was chosen from ten thousand hopefuls to play the part, and after filming he resumed his university studies. Fourteen year-old Alan Cox was a rather surly and unadventurous Watson, while Michael Hordern provided the narrative voiceover for the older Doctor, suggesting by his delivery that the youth we see on screen developed into a somewhat stately and staid old man.

There were some interesting Sherlockian connections in the casting. The first academic to die was played by Patrick

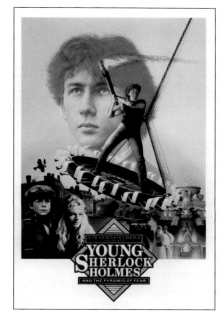

Newell, who was Lestrade in the early eighties Polish television series and Blessington in the Granada version of 'The Resident Patient'. Nigel Stock (Professor Waxflatter) played Watson to both Douglas Wilmer and Peter Cushing, and on stage in the one-man play *221B*. Anthony Higgins, who played the Moriarty character, went on to portray Holmes in the TV movie *1994 Baker Street: Sherlock Holmes Returns*.

The movie was shot at Shepperton Studios in England and on location in East London, Eton College, Belvoir Castle and Oxford. It was while the crew were in Oxford that they upset the residents, as the *Oxford Times* reported in June 1985: 'Bringing snow to an Oxford square may have been elementary to makers of a film about Sherlock Holmes but there was a sting in the tale. For the artificial snow used by Stephen [sic] Spielberg's Amblin Entertainment company to recreate winter in Radcliffe Square for the film *Young Sherlock* has killed a large area of grass

behind the historic Radcliffe Camera building. Contractors have been called in to relay the turf'.

The film did badly at the box office, indicating that the name Sherlock Holmes no longer ensured success. Critics were of the opinion that Holmes' image was too dated to appeal to young, modern audiences on the scale necessary to support a major and expensive production. The poor reception the film received in America prompted the retitling to *Young Sherlock Holmes and the Pyramid of Fear* when it was released a few months later in Britain. The producers hoped that the new title, along with the 'Presented by Steven Spielberg' tag, would make people think they were in for a rollercoaster Indiana Jones-type movie. The punters weren't fooled.

Previous page (below): *Young school friends Holmes (Nicholas Rowe) and Watson (Alan Cox).*
Above left: *Holmes and Watson experimenting with the uncanonical meerschaum pipe.*
Above right: *Holmes, Watson and Elizabeth (Sophie Ward) in Professor Waxflatter's workshop.*
Left: *Holmes escapes from the Pyramid of Fear.*

WORLDWIDE HOLMES

HAVE DEERSTALKER – WILL TRAVEL

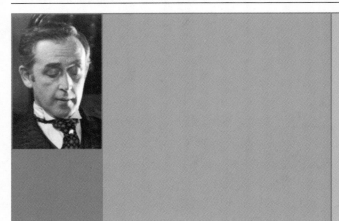

The lean man with the hooked nose, the curly pipe, the Inverness cape and the ability to solve the most baffling of crimes is known, loved and revered all over the world.

ONE OF THE REMARKABLE QUALITIES OF THE character of Sherlock Holmes is his international appeal. Copies of the Holmes stories can be obtained in most languages, including Yiddish. There are even Pitman shorthand editions available. Not only that, but Holmes societies and fan clubs have sprung up in many countries around the world. It is impossible to say exactly why this Victorian detective has been taken to the hearts of, amongst others, the Japanese, the Spanish and the Russians — whose cultures and social mores are so very different from that eccentric and resolutely British Baker Street world. Possibly it is because Holmes is seen to represent the image of true, rather than man-made, justice. Or maybe it's just that everyone loves a mystery and a man who can solve it.

As is evident from the plethora of silent movies and the European vogue for Holmes films in the thirties, the detective has graced the international screen from the beginning of his film career. So desperate for a screen Holmes were the Germans immediately after the Second World War that they spliced together two of the Rathbone/Bruce movies from the Universal series, *The Scarlet Claw* and *Spider Woman*, somehow managing to merge the two plots into one and adding a dubbed German soundtrack. The result was *Sherlock Holmes Sieht Dem Tod Ins Gesicht*. This was so successful that the formula was repeated with *Sherlock Holmes Faces Death* and *The Pearl of Death*, which became *Sherlock Holmes Jagt Den Teufel Von Soho*.

Germany produced a six-episode television series of Holmes stories in 1967 starring Erich Schellow, a respected stage actor, as Holmes. It was actually based on the scripts written for the BBC TV productions starring Douglas Wilmer. Talking about the series in 1992, Schellow said, 'The director, Peter May, wanted Holmes to present a contrast to the other,

action-orientated heroes of the 1960s. He was to be shown as a highly intelligent but a clean character. I wanted to show him as a little bit neglected and drug addicted but director May rejected this. I was allowed to show the brilliance of Holmes but not the maniacal side, which is part of his real genius. My Sherlock is cool: he never loses his temper.'

However, Schellow believed that he was able to compensate for these strictures by revealing Holmes' arrogance towards lesser minds and demonstrating the quality of his friendship with Watson (Paul Edwin Roth). He believed that any close working relationship is based on humour: 'I hoped we showed mutual respect but were also able to send each other up in a good-natured way.'

One of Schellow's favourite scenes was in 'Die Bruce-Partington Plane' when Holmes tells Watson that his brother Mycroft 'occasionally… is the British Government'. Watson looks momentarily surprised and then replies wryly, 'Oh, the poor man.'

Schellow remembered that the series was made under difficult conditions: 'At the same time I was playing [on stage] in Berlin. That meant every morning I took the first flyer to Cologne, where the series was being made; each evening I was playing Posa in *Don Carlos* or doing *Hamlet*. Cologne was very exhausting because we filmed in an old air-raid shelter which I found very depressing.' The series was originally televised between 1 October 1967 and 17 March 1968. It was repeated in 1991, and gained Schellow a new generation of German fans. He died in 1995 at the age of eighty.

Other countries were also busy bringing the Great Detective to the screen. In Italy, *The Hound of the Baskervilles* and *The Valley of Fear* were adapted for Italian television in 1968. *L'ultimo dei Baskerville* and *La valle della*

paur starred Nando Gazzolo as Holmes.

In 1971, the gentle comedy film *Touha Sherlocka Holmese* ('The Longing of Sherlock Holmes') was made in Czechoslovakia with Radovan Lukavsky as Holmes, Vaclav Voska as Watson and Josef Patocka as Sir Arthur Conan Doyle. The plot concerns Doyle's revelation of Holmes' lifelong ambition to pit his wits against the police by perpetrating the perfect crime. The realisation of this dream is thwarted only by Watson's conventional common sense.

A German television film based on *The Sign of Four* called *Das Zeichen der Vier* was made in 1974 with Rolf Becker as Holmes and Roger Lumont as Watson. More humour was provided by the 1975 Dutch comedy film *De dwaze lotgevallen van Sherlock*

Jones ('The Crazy Adventures of Sherlock Jones'), starring Piet Bambergen and a basset hound.

Between 1979 and 1983 Soviet television screened a series of Holmes films, each based on a Doyle original. Produced by Lenfilm, all the episodes featured Vasily Livanov as Holmes and Vitaly Solomin as Watson. The leading actors were chosen for the Englishness of their appearance and for their compatibility with the Paget drawings. Similarly, the adaptations, which included *The Hound of the Baskervilles* and 'The Speckled Band', remained very close to the original plots. In 1991, Czech television filmed a half-hour version of 'The Adventure of the Creeping Man' with Viktor Priess as Holmes and Josef Somr as Watson.

The bizarre Venezuelan production *Sherlock Holmes in Caracas* appeared in 1992. This low-budget comedy, shot in English, starred Jean Manuel Montesinos as Holmes and Gilbert Dacournan as Watson, and is actually a very loose adaptation of 'The Adventure of the Sussex Vampire', albeit with slapstick jokes.

Then there was the weird *Sherlock Holmes and the Chinese Heroine* (China, 1994) in which Holmes becomes involved in the 1900 Boxer rebellion. This comic concoction presents us with a Kung Fu Sherlock who uses his violin as a weapon to defeat his enemies.

It is probable that Conan Doyle never envisaged Holmes visiting Brazil, but that is what he does in *O Xango Baker Street* (2001), a fascinating amalgam of humour, mystery and elegiac story-telling with a comic

Holmes (Joaquim de Almeida) who is not only a glutton but also incredibly clumsy. His Watson (Anthony O'Donnell) is portrayed at the typical Englishman abroad at odds with local customs. Sarah Bernhardt also puts in an appearance. Set in Rio de Janeiro, the plot, based on a novel by Jo Soares, involves murder and the theft of a precious Stradivarius violin.

Previous page (above): Vasily Livanov as Holmes.
Previous page (below) and bottom far left: Radovan Lukavsky as Holmes with Vaclav Voska as Watson in Touha Sherlocka Holmese (1971).
Top far left: Erich Schellow as Holmes and Paul Edwin Roth as Watson in the underground, attempting to solve the mystery of the Bruce-Partington plans.
Top: Piet Bambergen in the Dutch comedy De dwaze lotgevallon van Sherlock Jones (1975).
Middle: 'Violence does, in truth, recoil upon the violent.' The demise of Grimesby Roylott in the Russian version of 'The Speckled Band'.
Bottom: Erich Schellow in a nicely detailed Baker Street sitting room set, complete with letters speared to the mantelpiece with a knife.

THE RETURN OF SHERLOCK HOLMES

FIRST SCREENING July-August 1986; April 1988
PRODUCTION COMPANY Granada Television
DURATION 11 x 50 minutes
Colour
REGULAR CAST
Jeremy Brett (Sherlock Holmes),
Edward Hardwicke (Doctor Watson),
Rosalie Williams (Mrs Hudson)

Despite his brilliance as a detective, on his return 'from the dead' three years after Reichenbach, Sherlock Holmes failed to notice that he had a new Watson...

WHILE TELEVISION AUDIENCES WATCHED David Burke as Watson mourning the loss of his friend in 'The Final Problem', the last episode of *The Adventures of Sherlock Holmes* (1984-85), shooting was already underway on the third Granada series, *The Return of Sherlock Holmes*. But things were not quite the same as before. Michael Cox, pleased with the way the first two series had

gone, felt relaxed enough about the future of Sherlock Holmes to take one step back to become executive producer, handing over the producer's chair to June Wyndham Davies. Cox still vetted the scripts and was involved with casting decisions but the day-to-day business of the series was left to Wyndham Davies. This turned out to be far from ideal, as Cox explained in his memoirs of the series, *A Study in Celluloid*: 'June Wyndham Davies... remained based in London. This was fine for the preparatory stages of production but not so convenient for the filming — most of which still took place in the north — or editing. Of course, June made regular visits to Manchester but, inevitably, there were details which one or the other of us overlooked. It is also true to say that she and I approached the series from different angles. I was the Holmes enthusiast,

'Despite his grief at the loss of his wife Joan, Jeremy was determined to carry on as Holmes when the call came' — Michael Cox.

concerned to retain the underlying spirit of the original stories, whereas June was more interested in the highly polished surface. I doubt if this is an assignment she would have chosen for herself'.

There was also the problem of the new Watson. The real reason for David Burke's departure is fogged by a series of different stories. One version was that he was desperate to spend more time with his wife and young son in Kent, and had been offered a role with the Royal Shakespeare Company. However, on one occasion Burke confessed to me that he would have stayed

with the series had not Brett, while in one of his bleak moods, said that he 'wasn't going to do any more Sherlocks'.

Ironically, it was Burke who suggested his replacement, Edward Hardwicke. The new casting gained Jeremy's blessing, and Granada soon followed with a contract. Wisely, Hardwicke made no attempt to imitate Burke. Cox said that 'he gave us his own Watson: an older, more serious man, saddened by the tragedy at the Reichenbach Falls and the three drab years which followed. It was entirely believable that this was the character which David

Burke's Watson might have become.'

Jeremy Brett was far from well when he commenced shooting *The Return of Sherlock Holmes* in the summer of 1985. He had lost his wife to cancer a few months earlier, a blow which had stirred the demon of manic depression within him once again. Initially there were no obvious signs of his illness, but to those who knew him well there were subtle differences in demeanour — differences that would become more manifest as the series progressed.

In the same way that 'A Scandal in Bohemia', the first important story in *The Adventures*, had not been the first to go before the cameras in order for the leading players to feel comfortable with their roles, so it was with 'The Empty House'. This story tells of Holmes' return to London, to Baker Street, to detective work and to Watson. Cox wanted Hardwicke to be fully relaxed with his character before tackling the emotional scenes in this episode, and so it was the fourth to be filmed.

Granada was less fulsome with its budget for this series. Economies were now being made. The scenes of the struggle between Holmes and Moriarty from 'The Final Problem' were re-used in 'The Empty House', but the long shots of the new Watson discovering his loss and Holmes' escape were filmed in Wales rather than Switzerland.

As Watson bellows out Holmes' name over the roar of the falls, we see the detective clinging to the hillside some distance away, watching his friend. At one moment it almost seems as though he is about to respond with a cry of 'Watson', but he stops himself. Brett explained: 'That was deliberate. It wasn't in the script, but I just wanted to show that Holmes had affection for Watson and for a fleeting second his emotions almost get the better of his practical mind.'

The first episode to be shot was 'The Abbey Grange', in which Hardwicke had little to do. This was a deliberate ploy by the producers to help ease the actor into his part and the series. By contrast, one can observe from this episode the burden Brett carried in fronting the series. He has a great number of lines and long, intricate, analytical speeches; as a result he is carrying the bulk of the script and therefore the flow and punch of the narrative. Any healthy man might crack under such pressure and Brett was not a healthy man. Nevertheless, none of the stress shows on screen; or if it does, it is in the sharp edge that Brett gives to his characterisation.

Brett's ease with and closeness to Edward Hardwicke was reflected in the warm touches he brought to their scenes in this series. One telling moment is found in

'The Priory School', when Holmes and Watson are out on the moor following the cycle tracks which they hope will lead to where the kidnapped boy, Lord Saltire, is being kept. They rest on a rock and while Holmes remains silent, peering at the landscape, sensing and hearing nothing but his interior consciousness juggling with various possibilities, Watson is consulting a map to work out where they can head for lunch. Watson notes the location of a nearby inn. Holmes apparently takes no

Previous page (below left): 'The Priory School'. Brett with Chatsworth House in the background, doubling as Holdernesse Hall.
Previous page (right): Jeremy Brett emulating a Paget pose.
Above left: 'The Priory School'. Dr Huxtable (Christopher Benjamin) with Holmes and Watson.
Above right and left: Publicity shots introducing Brett's new Watson, Edward Hardwicke.

notice of his companion's utterances and so, with a sigh of exasperation, Watson rises. 'Well, that's where I'm going to try my luck,' he says. 'I'm hungry.' Breaking from his trance, Holmes looks up to his friend and cries, 'Lunch! My dear fellow you must be starving. Observe that map, you'll see there is a hostelry three miles in this direction.' Watson nods wearily and follows his companion, who is already streaking ahead of him. The scene is instructive, paradoxically revealing both the separateness and the closeness of the two men. The performances are splendid because they are understated and tinged with humour — and yet significant points are made. 'The Priory School' is in fact Edward Hardwicke's favourite episode: 'For my money that is the best film we ever made.'

The first series of *The Return* contained seven episodes and some of Brett's best

work. However, shortly after finishing the last episode, 'The Six Napoleons', the actor was admitted to Maudsley Hospital in South London, well known for the treatment of mental disorders. Hardwicke described the place as 'grim and depressing'. Gradually, over the ten weeks Brett spent in this hospital, with the aid of drugs, the doctors managed to bring him down and help to eliminate the manic element of his illness. Hardwicke remembers seeing Brett in the hospital: 'He told me one day that he was really frightened and I asked him why. He

help me play the character.' Sadly, the reason for the change had more to do with Brett's mental health than any ploy to humanise Holmes. Around this time he was reported in *The Mail on Sunday* as saying, 'I never liked the devil [Sherlock Holmes] from the start. I can't find anything of me in him. I must learn to live again.' Hardwicke told me that Brett had attacked his own hair with a pair of scissors in some kind of symbolic act, trying to shake off the dark shadow of Holmes.

It is strange how many times the second

'Jeremy Paul's adaptation of 'The Musgrave Ritual' deservedly won him the Edgar Allan Poe Award' — Michael Cox.

said, "Because by balancing me and subduing me, I may have lost it — lost the ability to act."'

As a result of Brett's illness there was a delay in the filming of Granada's first two-hour special, *The Sign of Four* (1987; see pages 140-1), but shortly after it was completed, he had a relapse and suffered another severe bout of manic depression. It was during this period that Brett cut his hair very short. He explained the reason for the change thus: 'Before, my hair was long and it had to be combed back and plastered down to keep it in place. Now it's short, I can play with my hair, run my fingers through it, ruffle it, which I just couldn't do before. It's something else to

series of *The Return*, and in particular Holmes' demeanour, reflected the real life of Jeremy Brett. The first episode was 'The Devil's Foot', a tale in which the detective is suffering from exhaustion and depression, and is forced to take a holiday in Cornwall. At this time Brett was feeling 'up' and would entertain members of the cast by singing to them at the dinner table in the evening. Edward Hardwicke confessed, 'I always used to exit before the cabaret began. It always rather embarrassed me.'

Brett gained permission from Dame Jean Conan Doyle, Sir Arthur's daughter, to film a scene in which Holmes rejects the drug cocaine which had kept him in its thrall for years. We see him throw down the

hypodermic syringe onto the sand and squash it under foot. Brett told me, 'I did it mainly for the young people. I wanted to show them Holmes didn't rely on drugs.'

It was also Brett's idea to call out Watson's first name, 'John', when he emerged from his near-fatal experiment in the story. Brett worked with the director Ken Hannam to devise the sequence featuring Holmes' drug-induced dream. It was strange and Freudian, consisting of contorted images of the detective's struggle with Moriarty, Holmes rubbing his eyes as dark red blood oozed from his clenched hands, and staggering in slow motion amongst the strange monoliths on the Cornish peninsula. Michael Cox, back up in Manchester, had no control over these uncanonical self-indulgences.

There were only four instead of six hour-long episodes in the second series of *The Return* because the other two hours were devoted to a feature-length version of *The Hound of the Baskervilles* (1988), which was filmed at the same time but shown later.

For Michael Cox, conscious of the restricted budget, the second show in the second series, 'Silver Blaze', was a real problem. For this episode, the Granada unit went on location to Bangor racecourse with a string of horses and a crowd of extras which cost far more than the allotted budget for the show. As a result, more cuts were needed for the other shows in the series and by the time they came to film *The Hound*, the purse was very light indeed.

The final case in *The Return* is 'The Bruce-Partington Plans' which once again co-starred Charles Gray as Mycroft Holmes.

Both he and Brett were stouter than they had been in their first association together in 'The Greek Interpreter'. In Gray's case it was his natural build, but Brett's weight gain was the result of the conflicting medications for his mental illness and his heart condition. He put a brave face on the problem, but it was painful to him. Brett was well aware that he had been just under twelve stone (168 pounds) when he began playing the part and by this time he was moving towards sixteen stone (224 pounds). In the revised 1994 edition of Peter Haining's book on the Granada series, *The Television Sherlock Holmes*, Brett apologised for 'not being as lean as I should have been in the last twenty films. This is due to what has only recently been diagnosed as heart failure. I am now living on foxgloves and water pills and I'm told that in the not too distant future I will be lean once more.' This note highlights the growing unease with which Jeremy Brett carried on playing the character of Sherlock Holmes — a character noted for

his leanness and finely chiselled features. Sadly Brett, despite his hopes, was never to return to his natural slim self again.

THE GREAT MOUSE DETECTIVE

AKA The Adventures of the Great Mouse Detective
UK TITLE Basil, The Great Mouse Detective
FIRST SCREENING 2 July 1986
PRODUCTION COMPANY Walt Disney in association with Silver Screen Partners II
DURATION 74 minutes
Colour
DIRECTOR John Musker, Ron Clements, Dave Michener, Burny Mattinson

London, 1897. When toymaker Flaversham (voiced by Alan Young) is kidnapped by a peg-legged bat, his daughter Olivia (voiced by Susanna Pollatschek) seeks the help of Basil, the Great Mouse Detective (voiced by Barrie Ingham), who lives beneath the floorboards of 221B Baker Street with his friend Doctor David Q. Dawson (voiced by Val Bettin). Basil deduces that the bat is Fidget (voiced by Candy Candido), henchman of his arch-enemy, Professor Ratigan (voiced by Vincent Price). Assisted by tracker-dog Toby from upstairs, they trace Fidget to a toy store where he is stealing mechanical parts for an invention Ratigan is working on, with Flaversham's enforced help. Fidget escapes with Olivia but drops his shopping list. Analysing the paper leads Basil and Dawson to a waterfront dive. Here they spot Fidget and chase him through the sewers to Ratigan's lair, where the Professor is waiting for them. Basil and Dawson are left tied to a lethal trap while Ratigan leaves for the palace with his invention. He plans to replace the Queen with a mechanical dummy and seize the reins of power. Basil escapes from the trap and, pursuing Ratigan's getaway balloon, puts paid to the villain after a duel atop Big Ben.

Below: The cover to the original edition of a book from the Basil of Baker Street series by Eve Titus, illustrated by Paul Galdone.

THE FILM WAS BASED ON THE SERIES OF children's books by Eve Titus featuring Basil of Baker Street, who was named after Rathbone. Production notes for *The Great Mouse Detective* claim that four years were spent in pre-production and story development and only one year in actual animation, half the time that was usually required during this period for such a project. It was the early use of computer graphics which helped to speed up the process. The technical skill by which the 125 animators and four directors handled this new process was generally applauded. *Films and Filming* stated that the animation in '*The Great Mouse Detective* is in many ways the best Disney has done in years.' However, this reviewer, along with others, was less happy with the plot and the over emphasis on action set pieces. Roy E. Disney, son of Walt's brother, Roy O. Disney, explained that they had attempted in animation something that couldn't already be done in the special-effects extravaganzas of Spielberg and Lucas. Bearing this in mind, it is interesting that *The Great Mouse Detective* and *Young Sherlock Holmes* (in which Spielberg and Lucas were involved) both feature a chase around Big Ben in a flying machine.

The strong focus on wham-bang action — too violent for the Norwegian censors who banned children under the age of twelve from seeing it — tends to diminish the gentle parody implicit in the idea of a rodent Holmes. *Films and Filming* observed: 'The approach to the mousehole at 221B Baker Street, which duplicates life in the famous apartments upstairs with Doctor Dawson explaining his recent history and service in Afghanistan to the bereft Olivia Flaversham, is more affecting than... set pieces disproportionately filled with gloating violence.'

British actor Barrie Ingham provided a sprightly and youthful sounding hero. In one scene the real Holmes and Watson are heard talking and, fittingly, Rathbone's voice was used for the detective, although Watson was voiced by Laurie Main rather than Nigel Bruce.

Basil AND THE PYGMY CATS

A BASIL OF BAKER STREET MYSTERY

BY EVE TITUS

ILLUSTRATED BY PAUL GALDONE

THE RETURN OF SHERLOCK HOLMES

	TV movie
FIRST SCREENING	10 January 1987
PRODUCTION COMPANY	CBS Entertainment
DURATION	100 minutes
	Colour
DIRECTOR	Kevin Connor

Jane Watson (Margaret Colin), a Boston private eye, inherits an old house in England, in the cellar of which she discovers the cryogenically frozen body of Sherlock Holmes (Michael Pennington). Moriarty's brother infected Holmes with a plague virus for which there was no cure, so the detective had himself frozen until one could be found. Once Miss Watson has restored the sleuth to full health with an injection of antibiotics, he decides it is time to begin detective work again. Miss Watson persuades him to fly to Boston with her, to help solve a mystery she is investigating involving four crooked FBI agents who have stolen a stash of counterfeit money and then exchanged it for the real thing. They buried the money until the heat died down, but the thieves are now being murdered by a mysterious killer. It is Holmes' task to track the survivors and recover the money. Eventually, he and Watson corner the villain, who turns out to be one of the gang, Carter Morstan (Barry Morse), who faked his own death to avoid suspicion.

Below: Holmes (Michael Pennington) with his saviour Miss Jane Watson (Margaret Colin).

THE IDEA OF BRINGING SHERLOCK HOLMES back from the dead to fight crime in the modern age is appealing, but a difficult trick to get right, and this movie fails. The plot is convoluted and lacking in excitement. The humour, which mainly relies on the Victorian detective coming to terms with a society which is alien to him, is also strained. For example, Holmes asks for a 'Whisky tidy' rather than 'neat' and when the barman says, 'Mud in your eye', the detective rubs his eye. The most successful joke in the

movie occurs when, fully resuscitated, Holmes insists on returning to Baker Street only to find, to his horror, that 221B is now a branch of MacDonald's. The closing credits offer 'apologies to the late Sir Arthur Conan Doyle.'

The mystery at the heart of the screenplay presents a modern reworking of Doyle's *The Sign of Four*, and the writer peppers his script with a number of Sherlockian references and in-jokes. Many of his characters have names taken from

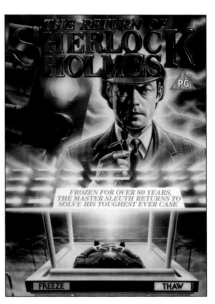

the Sherlockian canon, including the mysterious Miss Morstan (Connie Booth).

Despite most of the action supposedly taking place in America — Boston, Seattle and Arizona — the film was mainly shot at Shepperton Studios and the pseudo-American sets look phoney. However, there was one sequence, filmed in Arizona, where Holmes is alone and lost in the desert. Delirious, he stumbles on London Bridge at Lake Havasu and believes he has died and 'gone to heaven.' Actor Michael Pennington, on the other hand, said that the American location shooting in the desert was 'hell'. When he learned that the movie, which had been made as a possible pilot for a series, had not been 'picked up', Pennington was relieved. He made a passable Holmes but, as *Sherlock Holmes — The Detective Magazine* reported, 'he lacked the charisma of the real thing.' Pennington later played Moriarty in 'The Final Problem' to Clive Merrison's Holmes for BBC radio.

THE SIGN OF FOUR

TV movie	
FIRST SCREENING 29 December 1987	
PRODUCTION COMPANY Granada Television	
DURATION 100 minutes	
Colour	
DIRECTOR Peter Hammond	

On the same date for the past six years, Mary Morstan (Jenny Seagrove) has been sent a large pearl by an anonymous source. Now she has received a summons from her unknown benefactor. She consults Sherlock Holmes (Jeremy Brett) and Doctor Watson (Edward Hardwicke), who agree to accompany her. Their journey ends at Pondicherry Lodge, where the Sholto brothers have been digging up the grounds in search of hidden treasure, which their dying father admitted to having stolen while in India. However, Thaddeus Sholto has been killed by a poison dart and the treasure stolen. With the aid of Toby, Holmes and Watson are able to track the villains as far as the river, but there the trail ends. Disguised as an old sailor, Holmes reconnoitres the area and learns that Jonathan Small (John Thaw) and his murderous companion Tonga (Kiran Shah) plan to escape by river launch. Holmes and Watson chase after them in a police boat. Tonga is shot and falls overboard but Small is apprehended. He explains the plot to steal the treasure, how he was betrayed and why the Sholtos felt that Mary should share their riches. Before he was captured he threw the treasure into the river.

IT HAD BEEN GRANADA'S INTENTION TO FILM *The Sign of Four* as a special, longer introductory episode to the first series, *The Adventures of Sherlock Holmes*, but in 1983 the two-hour TV movie format was not in demand. So, although the project was placed on the back burner, the opening sequence concerning Holmes' drug taking was lifted from the story and interpolated into 'A Scandal in Bohemia'. As a result, Granada could not use this again when they came to film *The Sign of Four* in 1987.

For their first feature-length Sherlock Holmes production, Granada Television really pushed the boat out and filmed in 35mm. It is true to say that both producers,

Michael Cox and June Wyndham Davies, had their own particular favourites in writers, directors and actors, and it would seem that with *The Sign of Four* a compromise was reached between them. John Hawkesworth, a veteran of the Granada series and a Cox handpicked man, wrote the screenplay, while Peter Hammond, a favourite of Wyndham Davies, directed.

Hawkesworth was particularly pleased to be working on *The Sign of Four*. 'Doyle is a splendid writer and I've always liked [this novel] personally — because it has enormous quality.' The main problem with

in Doctor Watson's life. At the end of the original story, Holmes' client, the charming Miss Morstan, becomes engaged to the good Doctor — much to Holmes' disgust. However, the whole Granada concept had been built around the notion that Holmes and Watson were two bachelors sharing rooms. At the outset Michael Cox said: 'We're not doing the marriage. In our version Miss Morstan walks out of Watson's life at the end. However, I do feel sorry for Doctor Watson particularly. There's a lovely actress playing Mary — Jenny Seagrove — and one could well see why Watson would fall in love with

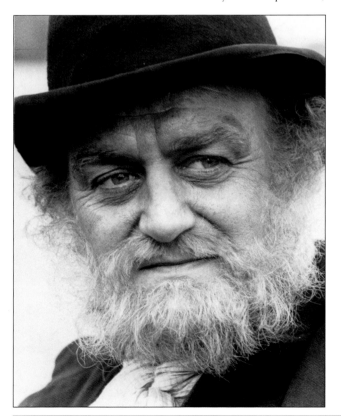

'Granada has recreated the nearest I think I'll ever get to experiencing the thrill of reading this novel for the first time' — *Sherlock Holmes Journal*.

adapting this story for the screen is that there are, in fact, *two* stories to present and, although the events of one touch up on the other, the resulting whole is somewhat unbalanced. What is acceptable to the reader can appear disjointed and unwieldy in dramatic form. In this adaptation, Jonathan Small's story, one of theft, deceit and betrayal — following, as it does, an exciting river chase — becomes something of an anti-climax. Holmes has got his man, none of his deductions have to be explained and, while there are some questions to be answered, for the most part our curiosity has been satisfied. John Hawkesworth could have turned the story round, presenting events in chronological order, but he decided not to play around with the dramatic flow of the original.

In the Doyle version, this tale is pivotal

her. On the other hand, I think that the great strength of all the stories is that the relationship between Holmes and Watson is simply one of the greatest friendships in literature. And it doesn't quite work if there's a wife around the corner. My theory is that Doyle rather regretted marrying Watson off.'

Brett agreed: 'She would have got in the way. Watson was more in love with Holmes — in a pure sense — than he could have been with a woman. He wouldn't want to give up the excitement, the danger. As for Holmes, if Watson had gone off and left him for a woman he wouldn't know what to do. He'd be stoned out of his mind every night.'

Brett accompanied the crew when they travelled to Malta to film the flashback sequences for Jonathan Small's story.

Although the actor played no part in these scenes, it was hoped that this brief holiday would help to restore his mental equilibrium.

The cast was a strong one. Apart from Jenny Seagrove, there was John Thaw, fresh from the successful first series of *Inspector Morse*, as the villainous Jonathan Small and Ronald Lacey as both Thaddeus and Bartholomew Sholto.

Peter Hammond, whose obsession with mirrors and reflective surfaces was reasonably restrained on this occasion, directed with great flair, and it was he who chose the locations along the Thames for the river chase. As Michael Cox observed: 'He filmed these locations so cleverly that the 1980s are indistinguishable from the 1880s'. The review in the *Sherlock Holmes Journal* was fulsome in its praise for this sequence: 'Towards the end of the river chase when darkness has descended, the camera pulled well back from Holmes' launch to reveal, high on the river bank, a group of men standing in silhouette round a brazier, The shot lasted a brief moment but added greatly to the evocation of the time, place and period.'

However, there was not always such close attention to detail throughout the filming. In the scene where Holmes is on the roof of Pondicherry Lodge following the trail of the intruder, a television aerial is clearly visible.

Nevertheless, 'The Sign of Four' was well received, not only by the press, but also by members of the Sherlock Holmes Society of London, who attended a special pre-transmission showing at Granada Studios, organised by Michael Cox.

Previous page (below): Jonathan Small (John Thaw).
***Above left:** Holmes (Jeremy Brett) at the start of the river chase.*
***Above right:** Jonathan Small with his deadly associate Tonga (Kiran Shah).*
***Left:** Mary Morstan (Jenny Seagrove).*
***Below:** Tracking the murderer, with the help of Toby the dog.*

THE HOUND OF THE BASKERVILLES

TV movie
First screening 31 August 1988
Production company Granada Television
Duration 105 minutes
Colour
Director Brian Mills

Doctor Mortimer (Neil Duncan) consults Sherlock Holmes (Jeremy Brett) concerning the safety of Sir Henry Baskerville (Kristoffer Tabori), the new heir to the Baskerville estate whose uncle Sir Charles died in mysterious circumstances. Mortimer connects his death with the legend of the phantom Hound which supposedly haunts the family. Holmes is aware that while in London Sir Henry is being followed and, believing him to be in danger, he despatches Doctor Watson (Edward Hardwicke) down to Dartmoor to look after the young Baronet. Watson discovers that the butler Barrymore (Ronald Pickup) is signalling to a man on the moor. This turns out to be Mrs Barrymore's brother, an escaped convict. Sir Henry falls in love with Beryl Stapleton (Fiona Gillies), whose brother (James Faulkner) initially objects to the relationship. Watson discovers that Holmes has been living in an old stone hut on the moor, watching events from afar, and after the death of the convict Selden (William Ilkley), the detective sets his trap for the killer, Stapleton. With the help of Mortimer, Holmes and Watson wait on the moor as the villain sets the Hound loose on Sir Henry. They kill the Hound and Stapleton sinks into the Grimpen Mire.

In a conversation I had with Jeremy Brett in the spring of 1995 (the year of his death) I asked him if he could have a final crack at one of the unfilmed Holmes stories, which would it be? Without hesitation he replied: 'I'd like to do *The Hound* again. I think we can do much better than that. I was terribly unwell making the film. It was under-conceived. The script drifted — which is fatal. Holmes was away too long.'

If it was under-conceived, that was partially due to it being under-funded. There was no money, for example, to include Inspector Lestrade, who enters the story in the last act to help Holmes tackle the Hound and the villain. He was written out of the script. Granada was also unable to secure the services of the first-choice director. Trevor Bowen, who wrote the screenplay, observed: 'I wrote 'The Priory

School' for Jeremy and that was a tremendous experience. I was extra-ordinarily lucky that John Madden directed it. He was wonderful. I realised we'd got a film director here and he could actually think film.' Edward Hardwicke also believed John Madden was the ideal director for this project, but ultimately the job went to Brian Mills.

The lack of finance made Bowen angry: 'There is nothing more ludicrous than a television company groping through one of its periodic fits of parsimony. They've got this marvellous product with a huge following and they've got *the* classic Holmes story — and they mess it up by not allowing us to do it properly.'

The measure by which the purse strings had been tightened can be gauged by the fact that while 'The Devil's Foot' had been

this version of the story is the strong sense of the supernatural which at any moment can overwhelm Holmes' rational certainties. However, Brett deliberately tried to show that his Holmes, unlike the character in the novel, is not sure whether there is a scientific explanation to the mystery. The actor believed that it was important to let the audience think that perhaps Holmes does believe in the existence of a supernatural Hound. 'Now as a man of logic, that's an enormous jump, but he is so disturbed by how disturbed Mortimer is — a doctor and a man of science — that he considers there may be something... ' This may have worked well if a mood of Gothic fear had been imbued into the film, but there is no sense of the dark shadow of the Hound cast over the events.

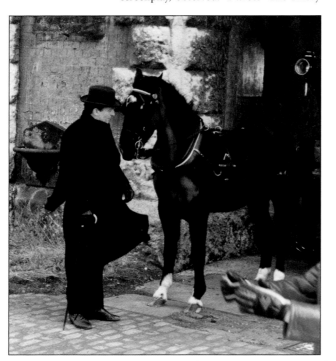

'The definitive version of *The Hound* is a sort of Sherlockian Holy Grail. Granada's production is one of the best — but it is far from definitive' — *The Ritual*.

filmed in Cornwall and 'Silver Blaze' involved some location filming in Ireland, by the time the showcase production of *The Hound of the Baskervilles* came to be made, the film crew had to make do with Brimham Rocks in Yorkshire, a few hours' drive from Granada's Manchester base. It is an area that doubles reasonably well for Devonshire, but nonetheless it isn't Dart-moor. For some night scenes on the moor, Granada used a large studio set evocative of, but much smaller than, the one created by Twentieth Century Fox for their 1939 version of *The Hound*.

One important element missing from

When the Hound finally made its appearance, it was a great disappointment. Unfortunately, the dog, a large eleven-stone Great Dane named Kahn, was very friendly and, despite being treated with a green phosphorous effect on screen, was far from frightening. A ferocious robot head with flashing teeth and fiery eyes was devised for close-ups, but this was hardly seen in the final cut.

The reception in the popular press was critical and sneering. With the heading 'The Disappearing Fizz', the review in *Today* referred to the film's lacklustre appeal. *The Guardian* also used the term,

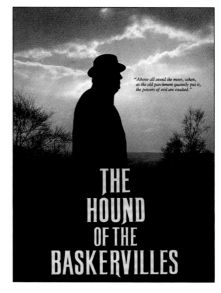

THE
HOUND
OF THE
BASKERVILLES

"Above all avoid the moor, when,
as the old parchment quaintly put it,
the powers of evil are exalted."

adding that the adaptation moved at a leaden pace. The normally charitable *The Stage* made some perceptive and some unjust comments: 'Like a child who likes to read the same Pooh story time and time again, it's not so much the narrative that you love as the manner of its telling. For most of its two hours, this latest *Hound* is predictable and plodding, relieved only by some ravishing camerawork and Jeremy Brett's outrageously mannered performance, alive with tics and grimaces. He is aided by Edward Hardwicke, an actor born to play dear, dependable, dense Watson, ever the panting dog to his master's voice. [The production] fails to impress as a mystery or thriller... the biggest let down is the hound which looks more silly than menacing with its luminous outline.'

This production, and the seriously hostile reviews it received, were the turning point in the fortunes of the Granada series of Holmes films. They never again received the acclaim of the early days. And with a much-reduced budget, an ailing leading actor and the best stories already filmed, the only path open to them led downwards.

Previous page (below) and below: *On location in Liverpool.*
Above left: *Brett and Hardwicke pose for an atmospheric publicity shot on the studio moor set.*
Above right: *The cover of a promotional brochure for the film.*
Left: *Sir Henry (Kristoffer Tabori) and Holmes, with Baskerville Hall in the background.*

WITHOUT A CLUE

First screening 21 February 1988
Production company ITC/An Eberhardt Stirdivant production
Duration 107 minutes
Colour
Director Thom Eberhardt

Sherlock Holmes, the famous detective, is actually Reginald Kincaid (Michael Caine), a failed actor hired by John Watson (Ben Kingsley), the real genius behind the sleuth's success. Infuriated by Kincaid's boastful stupidity and drunkenness, Watson kicks him out of Baker Street and tries to set up on his own as 'The Crime Doctor'. However, he is forced to ask Kincaid back when Lord Smithwick of the Treasury (Nigel Davenport) insists on consulting 'Holmes' concerning missing banknote printing plates. Kincaid takes a shine to Leslie Giles (Lysette Anthony), daughter of a missing printer at the mint. Watson deduces that Professor Moriarty (Paul Freeman) is attempting to wreck the economy of the Empire, but the Doctor is killed in a dockside skirmish with the Professor. In despair, Kincaid attempts to commit suicide — but fails. He realises that, as Sherlock Holmes, he must solve the case for Watson's sake. A clue leads him to an old abandoned theatre, where Moriarty has his printing press. There, Leslie reveals herself as a member of Moriarty's gang, whilst Watson, who faked his death to work undercover, reappears. Using his stage fencing skills, Kincaid duels successfully with Moriarty, who is killed in an explosion trying to escape.

Below: Another explosive performance as 'Holmes' from actor Kincaid (Michael Caine).

THE PREMISE BEHIND THIS FILM IS AN entertaining one but it lacks sufficient steam to sustain a feature-length production. With a screenplay by Gary Murphy and Larry Strawther, *Without a Clue* is in essence a one-joke movie. Once we move into the mystery at the heart of the film, we find that the plot is negligible and weak. It also lacks certain logic. Why, for example, does Moriarty want to bring about financial ruin to the Empire? Wouldn't this affect his own wealth also?

The main character is a pretend Holmes, a puppet whose strings are pulled by the brighter Doctor Watson, but for this comic role reversal to work, the character impersonating Holmes must put on a convincing performance as the master sleuth, in public at least. This Michael Caine fails to do. *Films and Filming* stated: '[Caine] is so unconvincing in the opening sequence, in which we are supposed to take his Great Detective at face value, that there is very little comic mileage to be gained from his subsequent blundering.'

However, there are some genuinely funny moments in the film and Ben Kingsley turns in a fine comic perfor-

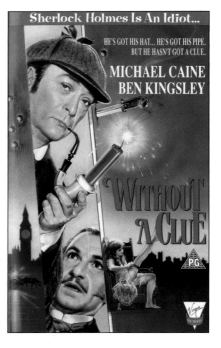

mance as a slightly twitchy Watson. On the other hand, Paul Freeman as Moriarty, with a limited script, gives us a *cliché* comic-book villain.

Critics were very divided in their response to *Without a Clue*. While the *Daily Express* thought it 'a gloriously comic romp', Leslie Halliwell called it 'a witless spoof'. However, the Holmes fans tended to view it as an affectionate send-up. The *Baker Street Journal* claimed 'it was the best Sherlock Holmes movie comedy to date.'

Apparently, at the time the movie was being made, Michael Caine found himself in the same lift as Dame Jean Conan Doyle. She asked the actor what he was doing at the moment. Caine said that he was making a comedy film, but carefully avoided mentioning that he was involved in a movie that ridiculed her father's creation!

HANDS OF A MURDERER

AKA Sherlock Holmes and the Prince of Crime
TV movie
FIRST SCREENING 16 May 1990
PRODUCTION COMPANY Green Pond Productions Inc
and Stoke Enterprises Inc in association with
Yorkshire International Films
DURATION 97 minutes
Colour
DIRECTOR Stuart Orme

Professor Moriarty (Anthony Andrews) escapes from the gallows. Moriarty's lover, Sophy (Kim Thompson), hypnotises Farrington (Harry Audley), a young civil servant, into assisting with the theft of secret state documents. However, the documents are in a numbered code set by Mycroft Holmes (Peter Jeffrey) and so Moriarty also abducts him. Sherlock Holmes (Edward Woodward) believes this to be the work of Moriarty, and has his suspicions confirmed when the Professor visits to warn him not to interfere. Later, Holmes and Watson (John Hillerman) capture one of Moriarty's men, Finch (David Sibley), attempting to rifle their safe, seeking information about the code. By using drugs and hypnosis on Mycroft, Moriarty learns that the solution to the code lies in marrying numbers with pages and words in a certain book. Holmes persuades Lestrade (Terrence Lodge) to allow Finch to escape and lead them to Moriarty's lair. Here Holmes exposes Colonel Booth (Warren Clarke), one of Mycroft's colleagues, as a traitor. Moriarty escapes and Holmes is killed. In disguise, Moriarty attends the detective's funeral, only to have handcuffs snapped on his wrist by a disguised Holmes who had faked his own death. A fight in a runaway carriage results in Moriarty crashing into a lake and drowning.

Right: Holmes (Edward Woodward) and Watson (John Hillerman). When Woodward was first asked to play the part of Holmes, he refused, claiming that he would be better as Watson. But he was prevailed upon to don the deerstalker.

Far right: Moriarty (Anthony Andrews) about to be hanged at the beginning of the film.

WHEN THE SERIES OF IAN RICHARDSON FILMS was cut short, the actor was somewhat relieved. He had been worried about typecasting, and had been very uncertain about the third script, *The Napoleon of Crime* by Charles Edward Pogue, that had been written but was not filmed. Richardson said, 'It began with the public hanging of Professor Moriarty and I said to Chuck Pogue that public hangings no longer existed in Holmes' time, but he simply wouldn't listen. "Who will know, who will notice?" he said.' Pogue hung onto the script and eventually, some eight years later, it was filmed with Pogue as co-producer. It was now called *Hands of a Murderer* and the anachronistic public hanging, set in 1900, remained. Unlike Pogue's other scripts, this is an original story, but it contains elements from several of Doyle's tales (the code idea is from *The Valley of Fear*, for example) and from other movies (Doctor Watson being decoyed away from Baker Street and held while

Moriarty visits Holmes is lifted from Rathbone's *The Woman in Green*).

Perhaps the most interesting and most radical aspect of this movie is the presentation of Moriarty as a sexy lover. He has a passionate girlfriend, Sophy, who at one point sits on his lap while he smothers her with kisses. Anthony Andrews' portrayal is far from the stooping, round-shouldered academic figure of Doyle's imagination.

The unsuitable casting of Edward Woodward as Holmes and John Hillerman as Watson can only be explained by their then-recent appearances in two popular detective television shows: *The Equaliser* (1985-89) and *Magnum P. I.* (1980-88). Woodward — a good actor — is the wrong shape for Holmes. He is far too bulky and not quite tall enough. Hillerman played Watson seriously, but as though he was asleep. The film was rebroadcast on CBS in August 1992 under the new title, *Sherlock Holmes and the Prince of Crime*.

STRANGE SHERLOCKS
THE UNUSUAL GUISES OF THE GREAT DETECTIVE

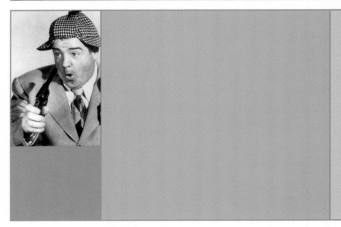

Sherlock Holmes became an easily identifiable icon very quickly and has been presented in many weird and wacky ways over the years, appearing in everything from Victorian stage revues to 1970s X-rated films.

Before Conan Doyle's ink was dry on the first set of Sherlock Holmes stories, comedians were already soliciting laughs by sending up the detective and his methods. The first time Holmes and Watson were impersonated comically was in the revue *Under the Clock* at the Royal Court Theatre in 1893. *Sheerluck Jones or Why D'Gillette Him Off*, an early parody of the Gillette play which ridiculed the actor as much as the detective, was a great success at the Lyceum Theatre in 1902.

There were numerous silent movies that presented Holmes in a humorous guise, such as *A Midget Sherlock Holmes* (1912), which concerned, according to *Motion Picture World*, 'a very small boy with beard and make-up to look like a detective' and *Sherlock Holmes, Junior* (1911), featuring a young boy who solves the mystery of his father's disappearing whisky — the cook is drinking it. There were also the Sherlocko and Watso comedies, based upon a cartoon strip, the first one being *The Robbery at the Railroad Station* (1912), advertised as 'a mystery surrounding the theft of a railroad lantern — A dark deed!'

Mack Sennett, one of the great silent film comedy directors, came up with the *Two Sleuths* series, featuring himself and Fred Mace as two incompetent detectives. Each actor was costumed as Holmes with deerstalker and pipe. There were eleven two-reelers in all between 1911 and 1913 with titles such as *Trailing the Counterfeiters* and *The Sleuths at the Floral Parade*.

Aspiring detectives were often given the Sherlock tag, as in *Sherlock Brown* (1921) starring Bert Lytell and *Sherlock, Jr.* (1924), one of Buster Keaton's most famous comedies. Even Laurel and Hardy got in on the act with *Do Detectives Think?* (1927), in which Ollie appears as Sherlock Pinkham, assisted by Stan as Ferdinand Finkleberry.

With the coming of sound, many comedians donned a deerstalker, grabbed a magnifying glass and pretended to be the Great Detective. Harpo Marx did so in *Duck Soup* (1933); The Three Stooges in *Dizzy Detectives* (1943); both Laurel and Hardy in *The Big Noise* (1944); Huntz Hall in one of

the Bowery Boys movies, *Hard Boiled Mahoney* (1947); and Lou Costello in *Who Done It?* (1942) and *Abbott and Costello Meet the Invisible Man* (1951). For the majority of these comedians the Sherlockian props were merely a shorthand way to denote a brainy and arrogant detective ripe for debunking.

One of the earliest sound oddities was *The Limejuice Mystery or Who Spat in Grandfather's Porridge* (1930) from Associated Sound Film Industries, England. This was a marionette film featuring Herlock Sholmes (based on Clive Brook), who never seems to notice the dead body in the room with him, and Anna Went Wrong (based on the oriental actress Anna May Wong).

Mister Magoo, the famous short-sighted, accident-prone cartoon character voiced by Jim Backus, was first seen on the cinema screen in the fifties and early sixties, before transferring to television in 1964 in the series *The Famous Adventures of Mr Magoo*. In one episode of this series, 'Mister Magoo, Man of Mystery', he adopts the role of a blundering Doctor Watson and 'assists' Sherlock Holmes in investigating a jewel robbery, with the usual confusing results.

An even unlikelier Sherlock is the spinach-swallowing sailor Popeye, but in the cinema cartoon *Private Eye Popeye*, the

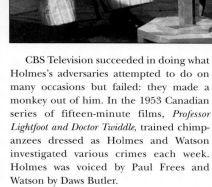

truculent tar runs a detective agency, wearing a deerstalker hat and carrying a magnifying glass. He is called out to find his girlfriend Olive Oyl's jewels. As might be expected in Popeye's case, brawn rather than brains wins the day.

A later manifestation, *Popeye and Son*, a Hanna-Barbera television cartoon series from 1987, featured an episode — 'The Case of the Burger Burglar' — in which Wimpey, Popeye's guzzling glutton friend, and his nephew decide to open a burger stand. At first all goes well, but then burgers start to disappear mysteriously. Wimpey's nephew dons a deerstalker, whips out a magnifying glass, pops a bubble pipe in his mouth and sets out to discover the solution to the mystery. Popeye's son assists, wearing a bowler hat, in the role of Watson. At one point in the programme 'Sherlock' turns to Popeye junior and exclaims, 'Come, Watson, the game is afoot.'

In 1979, the first of several Japanese cartoons featuring Lupin the Masterthief appeared. The second production, based on Maurice Leblanc's original pastiche stories from 1907, was *Lupin vs Holmes* (1981), in which the Great Detective is sent to France track the devilish gentleman thief Arsène Lupin at the instigation of Baron Autrech. However, there are complications when the Baron is murdered and his priceless blue diamond stolen. The cartoon includes a scene from Leblanc's story 'The Jewish Lamp' (1907) — a tense face-off between the two adversaries, as they find themselves on a sinking boat.

Many long-running crime shows on television have brought in a Sherlock Holmes character at some point. Among them was the 1960s *Batman* series starring Adam West. In the episode 'The Lon-

dinium Larcenies' (1967), Batman travels to Londinium to help Ireland Yard's Inspector Watson solve a series of thefts carried out in the fog. The crooks wear deerstalkers and plan to steal the crown jewels. *The Avengers* episode 'The Curious Case of the Countless Clues' (1969) featured Peter Jones as Sir Arthur Doyle, a private investigator. One of the *Father Dowling Mysteries*, 'The Consulting Detective Mystery' (1991), brings Holmes back from the dead to assist Father Dowling (Tom Bosley) in solving a case. Holmes (Rupert Frazer) can only be seen by Dowling, which adds to the confusion and mayhem.

CBS Television succeeded in doing what Holmes's adversaries attempted to do on many occasions but failed: they made a monkey out of him. In the 1953 Canadian series of fifteen-minute films, *Professor Lightfoot and Doctor Twiddle*, trained chimpanzees dressed as Holmes and Watson investigated various crimes each week. Holmes was voiced by Paul Frees and Watson by Daws Butler.

Holmes transformed from monkey to rat in the BBC's *Tales of the Rodent Sherlock Holmes* (1990). The cocky puppet Roland Rat played Holmes to Kevin the Gerbil's Watson in a series of slapstick parodies on Saturday morning children's television.

Previous page (above and below left): Lou plays detective in Abbott and Costello Meet the Invisible Man *(1951), which also featured Adele Jergens.*
Above left: Harpo Marx in Duck Soup *(1933).*
Above right: Laurel and Hardy in The Big Noise *(1944).*
Left: 'Anna Went Wrong' and 'Herlock Sholmes' in the marionette oddity The Limejuice Mystery *or who Spat in Grandfather's Porridge (1930).*

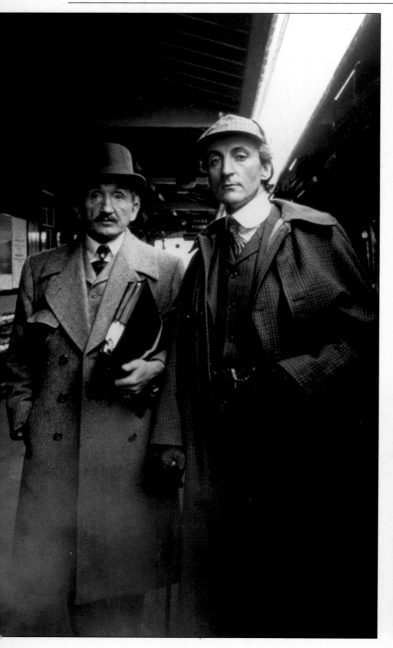

and Ronald Fraser was Watson.

Perhaps the most disturbing of exhibits in this unusual collection of Sherlockian oddities is a short independent movie made in 1987 called *The Loss of a Personal Friend*. Written and directed by N. G. Bristow, the fifteen-minute film presents a nightmare version of the events following the death of Sherlock Holmes. The film opens with Watson (Ian Price) on the edge of the Reichenbach Falls (a scene actually filmed in North Wales), realising the terrible truth that Holmes and Moriarty have perished in the cauldron of foam below. After the credits we move to London, and Watson is writing to George Newnes, owner of the *Strand Magazine*, to tell him of a remarkable incident he has experienced. Apparently, he collided with an old bookseller in the street on the way home and later the fellow turned up at his home to return the cigarette case which he had dropped. Suddenly, the visitor reveals himself as Sherlock Holmes (Peter Harding). So far this scenario more or less replicates the return of the Great Detective

he has ever known is beside him once more, and will never leave him again. The film is chilling, brilliantly acted and thought provoking. Strange and, to some extent, silly it may be, but it has more fidelity to the characters of Holmes and Watson and the idea of the Great Detective than so many so-called straightforward presentations of the canon.

Jim Henson's *Sesame Street*, a puppet series aimed at educating the young in an entertaining and humorous way, presented a set of sequences in the 1990s called 'Mysterious Theater' featuring Sherlock Hemlock and his canine partner Watson. These segments, essentially a parody of PBS's *Mystery Theater* (which showed the Jeremy Brett series in the States) were introduced by a dapper, moustachioed puppet by the name of Vincent Plice.

The 1976 comedy film, *Murder by Death*, presented the conundrum of the disappearing Holmes. Written by Neil Simon, the plot concerns a group of the world's greatest sleuths arriving at a fog-shrouded manor house in northern

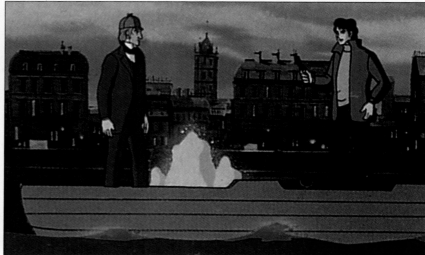

Other regulars in the show were Barbara Windsor as Irene Wilson and Roy Sampson as the Moriarty-like villain McDreadful.

The characters of Holmes and Watson were utilised in a documentary produced by BBC television to investigate the mystery of the Piltdown Man in *Murder on the Bluebell Line* (1987). The *Radio Times* explained that the programme 'takes Holmes and Watson on a voyage of discovery down the Bluebell Line to Piltdown', and on the way they review the evidence and the 'criminal records of the people involved.' Holmes was played by Hugh Fraser, who would later portray Captain Hastings to David Suchet's Poirot,

as recorded in Doyle's 'The Adventure of the Empty House'. But as Holmes explains to Watson how he made his escape from the Reichenbach Falls, the viewer gradually begins to realise that this interpretation of events is based on Watson's own desperate wish fulfilment that his dear friend is not really dead. As he sees Holmes before him by his fireside, the mirror over the fireplace actually reflects the image of the old bookseller. Watson is so entranced with his hallucination of the returned Holmes, that when the bookseller attempts to leave, he determines that his friend should stay with him — forever. Watson kills his visitor, happy now that 'the best and wisest man'

California and being challenged to solve a murder. The detectives included the noted Belgian detective Milo Perrier (a thinly disguised parody of Hercule Poirot, played by James Coco); San Francisco's best gumshoe Sam Diamond (Sam Spade — Peter Falk); Jessica Marbles (Miss Marple — Elsa Lanchester); the inscrutable oriental detective, Sidney Wan (Charlie Chan — Peter Sellers); and the sophisticated sleuths Dick and Dora Charleston (Nick Charles, 'The Thin Man', and his wife Nora — David Niven and Maggie Smith). In the original script, Holmes and Watson arrive late at the house. Holmes solves the murder but

refuses to divulge the solution and leaves. Some of the stars objected that the arrival of the supreme detective dwarfed their presence, and this was exacerbated by the fact that Holmes was being played by an actor who was not famous: Keith McConnell (Richard Peel was Watson). So although Holmes' scenes were shot, in most release prints they were cut out of the film altogether.

The sex industry has also taken a shine to the sleuth from Baker Street, with several pornographic movies using the detective. In the sixties, Playboy Flicks produced *Dressed to Kill — The Case of the Pilfered Panties*, in which excerpts from various Rathbone and Bruce black and white movies are interspersed with colour clips of naked women. The short film parodies Holmes and Watson on a case at a girls' college. This was tame fare compared to *The American Adventures of Surelick Holms* (1975), possibly the first X-rated pornographic film to parody the character. Holms (David Chandler) and Watson (Frank Massey) fly to America to track down Maryarty, a transvestite killer. The plot, involving an all-male cast, is negligible, merely a thread on which to hang a series of gay sexual encounters.

The similarly named *Sherlick Holmes* (1976) stars a heterosexual Holmes (Harry

Reems) and Watson (Zebedy Colt) who travel through time to modern California, where they proceed to take various women to bed. It was a case where, as the advertising blurb had it for this triple X-rated movie, 'The Master Detective Stepped into the Master Bedroom'.

Doyle's Holmes was a confirmed misogynist, who believed that 'women are not to be entirely trusted', and so this presentation of the detective as a raunchy stud is probably the strangest and most perverse manifestation of Sherlock Holmes on screen.

Previous page (left): *Watson (Ronald Fraser) and Holmes (Hugh Fraser) in* Murder on the Bluebell Line *(1987).*

Previous page (right): *The Great Detective faces the Masterthief in* Lupin vs Holmes *(1981).*

Above left: *The all-star cast of* Murder by Death *(1976).*

Above right: *The Doctor (Tom Baker) donned Holmesian garb in the 1977* Doctor Who *story 'Talons of Weng-Chiang'. Baker later played Holmes himself on televsion and on the stage.*

Left: *Steed (Patrick Macnee) meets Sir Arthur Doyle (Peter Jones) in the 1969* Avengers *episode 'The Case of the Countless Clues'.*

THE CASEBOOK OF SHERLOCK HOLMES

FIRST SCREENING February-March 1991
PRODUCTION COMPANY Granada Television
DURATION 6 x 50 minutes
Colour
REGULAR CAST
Jeremy Brett (Sherlock Holmes),
Edward Hardwicke (Doctor Watson),
Rosalie Williams (Mrs Hudson)

By the time *The Casebook of Sherlock Holmes* went before the cameras in 1990, it had been two years since Granada's last Holmes film and, initially, the health of the star threw the whole project into jeopardy.

AFTER THE SOMEWHAT DISAPPOINTING response to the second series of *The Return of Sherlock Holmes* (1988) and *The Hound of the Baskervilles* (1988), Michael Cox was invited back by David Plowright, now the chairman of Granada Television, as free-lance producer for *The Casebook of Sherlock Holmes*. With Cox firmly seated in the producer's chair once again, it was hoped that his steady hand would bring a shine back to the project.

However, it was now a different Granada from the early eighties, when Cox had worked on establishing the series. The drama department, under new management, had moved to London, leaving few familiar faces to greet him along the corridors of the Granada building in Manchester. There were many new employees and most of them, it seemed to Cox, were script editors and accountants. As a freelance producer rather than a company executive, he felt like 'the gamekeeper turned poacher, the film-maker concerned with his own production, who had to be prepared to challenge the company in order to get a favourable

Jeremy Brett and Edward Hardwicke had been away from filming for over eighteen months. They had starred in *The Secret of Sherlock Holmes* at Wyndham's Theatre for a year — the play opened in October 1988 — and then they went on a gruelling provincial tour. During the run of the play, Brett suffered bouts of manic depression that began to affect his

'We chose stories which seemed the best and most dramatic of those left after seven years of filming' — Michael Cox.

deal... I fought my corner there with reasonable success but I never won with the accountants.'

The budget was very tight, especially after the luxuries of the early days. 'Shoestring Holmes' was how Cox now regarded the project. One bitter irony concerned the exterior set of Baker Street, which had been Cox's idea, and was created for the original series. This was now part of the Granada Studios Tour, in essence a separate concern from the television company. As a result, whenever Cox wished to film on Baker Street, he had to find £1,000 a day from his budget to do so.

performance. Edward Hardwicke remembered: '[Jeremy] used to quote a line from *Twelfth Night* and, as the run went on, it got longer and longer and finally he was doing the whole opening speech: "If music be the food of love". Duncan Weldon [one of the producers] came in one night and said, "What the hell's going on?"'

By Christmas 1989, both actors were on their knees. It was time for a break, for they were committed to start filming *The Casebook of Sherlock Holmes* in the spring of 1990. Shortly before rehearsals began for 'The Disappearance of Lady Frances Carfax', the first episode of *The Casebook*, Jeremy Brett had to be brought home from

holiday abroad by his son, and was hospitalised once more. Cox was in a dilemma. Should he go ahead with plans for the series and risk Brett being healthy enough to participate, or should he postpone the production and threaten its future? After discussions with a drug-sedated Brett and his doctors, Cox 'gambled on Jeremy's determination and commitment'. Thankfully, Brett emerged from the clinic on time, but his co-star Edward Hardwicke observed that his friend was not himself: 'I had never seen him as tentative and unsure at he was in that first ten days or so of rehearsal, worrying about lines and how to pitch them. Because his delivery was so like a machine gun he had to be absolutely on top of his words, and it was the only time I saw him struggling. But he was terribly good in the end. Once we started filming he was fine. Subsequently he told me that he had been ill and on a "downer". Some of the filming of 'Carfax' took place in the Lake District, which Jeremy loved. The scenery and the pleasant spring weather did much to raise his spirits.'

I spent a day at Granada Studios watching filming on 'Carfax', and saw at first hand the organised chaos of a television shoot. The morning was spent on

one brief scene that occurs at the beginning of the film. Brett had to knock a small model figure from the mantelpiece in the Baker Street sitting room, and it had to fall on a pile of scattered newspapers in a certain position so as to attract Holmes' attention to a particular news item. There was no dialogue. For all sorts of reasons — faulty sound, wrongly placed shadows, the figure not falling correctly — Brett had to do this scene time, after time, after time. It

took over two hours to obtain this twenty-second sequence. Brett did the repeated takes with humour, good grace and smiling patience.

In the afternoon, filming moved to a graveyard near Manchester in order to shoot the climax of the story. This piecemeal arrangement of shooting scenes in no sequential order must be very difficult for an actor to cope with. Rather like a juggler with several balls in the air, he

This spread:
Casebook's *guest stars included David Langton (previous page), Robin Ellis and Elizabeth Wheeler (above left) and Eric Sykes (above right).*
Below left: *Filming the opening of 'Carfax'.*
Below right: *'Teeth in or out?'.*

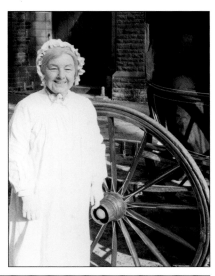

THE CASEBOOK OF SHERLOCK HOLMES

has to see the overall pattern of the flow, while at the same time concentrate on handling one specific ball at a time. One can see that this procedure of moving from one part of the story to the next, without any narrative logic, places an extra strain on the main actors, who have to know their scripts inside out to cope.

One extra, who was playing the corpse found in the coffin with a false bottom, wandered around the graveyard, ashen-faced in a Victorian shroud, while the shot was being set up. When the crew were ready for the take and she settled down in the coffin, she asked the director, John Madden, if he wanted to film her with her teeth in or out!

Michael Cox agreed that with twenty-six of Doyle's stories already filmed, it was becoming very difficult to pick tales that were strong enough to make good television. Two stories in particular that

had been chosen for *The Casebook* had caused problems: 'The Disappearance of Lady Frances Carfax' and 'The Creeping Man'. In Doyle's story, a great deal of 'Carfax' is set in Switzerland. With the current financial restraints, shooting in Switzerland — as they had done on 'The Final Problem' — was now out of the question. And so writer Trevor Bowen re-jigged the plot so that that the 'foreign' location became the Lake District. Cox admitted, 'The result is quite different from the original story although the version meets Doyle's at several key points and is, I hope, true to the spirit if not the letter of the familiar tale.'

It was clear that the original premise, to produce the authentic Doyle Sherlock Holmes stories — true not only to the spirit but also the letter — had to be compromised. No one was really to blame, unless it was the viewing public who

series was firmly back on the rails again and was being as true to Doyle as it was possible to be. He had also passed his 'I hate Sherlock' phase and settled down to playing the character without regret or angst. And gone was the short, spiky haircut so that, although plumper and more haggard than he had been when he started playing Holmes, Brett did look more like his old self than he had done in the second series of *The Return*.

Some years later he confessed to me that he did things in this series that he wished he hadn't. What surprised me was that, after playing the character so long and being recognised as the definitive Sherlock Holmes, Brett still craved direction when playing a scene, direction which, as was sometimes the case, would make him behave in an un-Sherlockian manner. 'My dear boy,' he said, 'I am like Bambi. I lay down and say, "Tell me what to

'While the centre holds in this quality series, the edges are now beginning to fray a little' — *Yorkshire Post*.

clamoured for more of Jeremy Brett's Holmes no matter what, or the executives who wanted to keep the Sherlock bandwagon rolling in order to keep cashing in on its international appeal.

The writers for this series were Cox's favourites: John Hawkesworth, Jeremy Paul, Gary Hopkins, Trevor Bowen and Robin Chapman. Cox had already rejected a script by one writer for 'the difficult' 'The Creeping Man'. And so he called in one of his old favoured writing colleagues, Robin Chapman, to tackle the story. Cox explained the problem: 'We know from the start that there is something odd about Professor Presbury, that he creeps and crawls around his house and menaces his daughter in the middle of the night. There is hardly a mystery for Holmes to solve, only a diagnosis to be made. So Robin has offered him a puzzle about the identity of the creature who terrifies Edith and the theft of primates from British zoos.'

From this dissection we can see that Cox aimed to keep a good balance between the demands of a popular drama series, a restricted budget and a concern for Doylean fidelity. It was a balancing act that Jeremy Brett admired and respected. The presence of Cox about the set was comforting to the actor. He felt that the

do."' This was not the voice of the man who had caused such a fuss regarding the adaptation of 'The Crooked Man' and argued vigorously about the insertion of the rose speech in 'The Naval Treaty' a few years earlier. It was as though his illness had drained all the fight from him.

One example of the strange excesses he found himself committing can be seen in 'The Creeping Man'. It is breakfast time and Holmes, for no apparent reason, stubs his cigarette out in his half-eaten boiled egg — an eccentric but crude action that Brett came to regret as being totally inappropriate to the character of Holmes.

Michael Cox said that he tried to persuade John Hawkesworth to adapt 'The Adventure of the Three Garridebs' for the new series: 'but he side-stepped it on the perfectly reasonable grounds that it is a re-run of 'The Red-Headed League' which he had scripted for *The Adventures*'. Instead, Hawkesworth chose 'The Boscombe Valley Mystery'. This was Hawkesworth's last contribution to the series, his role as script consultant had already been taken from him by those whom Michael Cox called 'the new brooms in Granada's drama department.'

'The Boscombe Valley Mystery' is a strong story but, like many of Doyle's,

154 THE CASEBOOK OF SHERLOCK HOLMES

depends upon a flashback to another time and another place. The place was Australia — a location that presented a headache for the producer: 'We were very lucky to find a lookalike for Gold Rush Australia as near as Manchester as we did. It was an exotic quarry near Bolton. We imported the horses, the covered wagons, the guns, the stunt team and tons of sand — but we were unable to import the weather. And on Tuesday 5 June 1990, the unalterably scheduled day for Black Jack of Ballarat to make his pile, it rained from dawn to dusk. But then it does rain in Australia sometimes, I believe.'

The British press was pleased with the series. *The Mail on Sunday* greeted it with delight: '*The Casebook of Sherlock Holmes* returning to ITV for what are bound to be six glorious weeks... [Jeremy Brett's performance is] still so superlative that no superlatives of mine are adequate to describe it'. *The Daily Mail* was equally effusive, praising the series' continuing high standards and commenting on Brett's 'fruity performance'. *The Stage* stated that Granada had liberated Sherlock Holmes from 'the *Boy's Own* world' he had once inhabited, and noted that Brett's 'gothic demeanour added a char-

isma' which was so often lacking in lesser portrayals of the part.

However, a perceptive note was struck by the reviewer in the *Daily Express*, who regretted that Brett had 'run out of really good material to apply his genius to.' Whether this journalist meant Sherlock Holmes' genius as a detective or Jeremy Brett's genius as an actor is unclear. Perhaps the comment is symptomatic of how actor and character were often viewed as one and the same.

Previous page: Lestrade was played with great panache throughout the Granada series by Colin Jeavons, who humanised and enhanced Doyle's sketchy portrait of the Inspector.
This page: More scenes from The Casebook.

THE CRUCIFER OF BLOOD

TV movie
First screening 4 November 1991
Production company Turner Pictures/Agamemnon Films/British Lion
Duration 131 minutes
Colour
Director Fraser C. Heston

In 1857, officers Ross (Edward Fox) and St Clair (John Castle), and Corporal Small (Clive Wood), steal the Agra Treasure from The Red Fort. They swear an oath to each other, drawing a crucifer with their own blood, but the officers cheat on Small. From guilt, St Clair relinquishes his part of the treasure and Ross takes full control of it. Thirty years later, St Clair's daughter Irene (Susannah Harker) consults Sherlock Holmes (Charlton Heston) after her father has disappeared. Holmes deduces that he has sought help from Ross, who lives at Pondicherry Lodge. Ross is killed by a poison dart and St Clair disappears again. Holmes traces him to an opium den and, disguised as a Chinese opium seller, the detective extracts the truth from St Clair before he is murdered. Meanwhile, Watson (Richard Johnson) has fallen in love with Irene. Holmes learns of Small's plan to escape and a river chase ensues. On capture, Small kills himself with a dagger. Alone with Watson, Irene reveals that she killed her father and only consulted Holmes as a means of locating the treasure for herself. Her attempt to kill Watson fails and Holmes hands her over to Lestrade (Simon Callow).

THE CRUCIFER OF BLOOD STARTED LIFE AS A stage play written by Paul Giovanni. It was first performed in a small theatre in Buffalo in early 1978, where it scored such a success that it moved to Broadway and later London's West End. In a production at the Ahmanson Theatre, Los Angeles (5 December 1980 to 17 Jan 1981), Charlton Heston took on the role of Holmes — with Jeremy Brett playing his Watson. Heston had such a good time playing the character that he suggested a film version of the play to his son, Fraser C. Heston. This eventually came to pass in 1991 when the movie, written, produced and directed by Heston junior, went before the cameras at Pinewood Studios.

The Crucifer of Blood is a radical reworking of Doyle's *The Sign of Four*, with the most significant difference being that the young female client, called Irene St Clair in this version, is actually a bad lot.

The introduction of this twist in the tale interferes with the original focus of Doyle's plot — the revenge of Jonathan Small and the desperate search for his whereabouts. As Allen Eyles noted: 'the new ending does have a belittling effect on Holmes and Watson; it has a cynical mis-anthropic thrust that takes away from Conan Doyle's story its positive aspects... it shatters the nostalgic charm of the stories by imposing a harsher reality.'

It would seem that Giovanni had fun with the characters' names, dragging them in from other Doyle stories. Major Ross borrows his name from the Colonel in 'Silver Blaze'; Birdy Edwards, the butler at Pondicherry Lodge, appears in *The Valley of Fear*; Neville St Clair

is really 'The Man With the Twisted Lip'; and his daughter is named Irene which, especially because of her apparently amorous nature, has resonances with Irene Adler — 'The Woman'.

Charlton Heston makes a perfectly acceptable Holmes. He is tall, lean and, with the aid of prosthetics, has a hawk-like nose. However, the script never gives him moments to really shine. Reviewing the movie, *Scarlet Street* observed that 'Heston acquits himself well, but he's undermined by the Great Detective's almost peripheral

involvement in much of the action... Time and time again [the movie] cuts away from Holmes to indulge in static, plot-filled dialogues between supporting players. The star's best moment, oddly enough, comes not when he's playing Holmes as Holmes, but when he plays Holmes in the guise of an ancient Chinese proprietor of a Soho opium den. Stereotypical though it is, it's one of the best Holmes-in-disguise sequences ever committed to film.'

Indeed, the movie betrays its stage origins all too clearly, with the actors restricted to a limited number of theatrical

'Heston is a better Holmes than might be expected, but he lacks the fire and danger of Brett' — *Sherlock Holmes — The Detective Magazine*.

looking sets, and action often taking place off screen. When Irene is drugged in 'the filthy looking café' above the opium den, we are only told about it, we do not witness this dramatic moment. Even the river chase, which was the spectacular climax of the stage presentation, is dealt with quickly, almost in a desultory fashion. Edward Fox as Ross, James Coyle as Birdy Edwards and Simon Callow presenting a predictably stupid Inspector Lestrade, all overact as though they were in a stage production rather than on a film set.

It is interesting to note that Charlton Heston as Holmes and Richard Johnson as Watson were both well into their sixties when they made the film, and yet no reference is made to their advancing age. However, Johnson's elderly Watson romancing Irene, played by Susannah Harker, an attractive young lady in her twenties, is not only somewhat unrealistic but is far from a comfortable sight. *Scarlet Street* observed that these 'love scenes' were 'not exactly palatable'.

Previous page (below left): *A signed still of Charlton Heston as the Great Detective.*
Previous page (right): *A sketch of Heston in character, taken from the programme for the 1980-81 production at the Ahmanson Theater.*
Above left: *Sherlock Holmes (Heston) and Doctor Watson (Richard Johnson).*
Left: *A bemused-looking Inspector Lestrade (Simon Callow) meets Irene St Clair (Susannah Harker).*

THE RESTING SLEUTH

SHERLOCK IN THE NINETIES

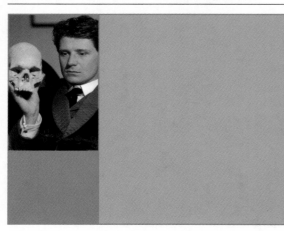

Surprisingly and sadly, the last decade of the twentieth century was the quietest for the screen career of Sherlock Holmes. In fact, he failed to appear in the cinema altogether.

THE PAUCITY OF HOLMES PROJECTS IN THE nineties must be due partly to the potency of Jeremy Brett's Granada Television series. Brett, like Rathbone before him, had made the character his very own, and television companies were loathe to attempt any new Holmes productions while the series was running. Similarly, Holmes was also absent from the cinema screen. It seemed that a Victorian detective could hardly compete with *Reservoir Dogs* (1992), *Pulp Fiction* (1994) and the other high-octane crime thrillers of the period.

On television, *Star Trek: The Next Generation* continued to feature Brent Spiner as Data slipping into the Holmes world. In the fourth season episode 'Data's Day' (1991), Data narrates, Watson-style, the events of his day, including the disappearance of a Vulcan ambassador while being transported to a Romulan ship. Data is charged with determining what went wrong and he works on the problem as Holmes would, quoting the famous maxim: 'Once you have eliminated the impossible, whatever remains, however improbable, must be the truth.' He solves the mystery by eliminating all of the impossible causes of the disappearance.

In the opening prologue of 'Ship in a Bottle' (1993), Data appears dressed in Holmes regalia in the holodeck representation of 221B Baker Street. Subsequently, the holodeck Sherlock Holmes program SH-3a malfunctions, and Professor Moriarty (Daniel Davis) returns, this time with full awareness of what he is — supposedly an impossibility for a computer program. When Captain Picard refuses to free the villain's girlfriend, Moriarty takes control of the *Enterprise*. Data eventually deduces that the crew have merely been trapped in the holodeck, and turns the tables on Moriarty, tricking him into thinking he is escaping, setting forth in a spacecraft to horizons new, when in

reality the holographic Professor is being confined within a computer chip once more.

Also from the world of science fiction came the innovative and imaginative cartoon series *Sherlock Holmes in the 22nd Century*, produced by Scottish Television. There were twenty-six episodes made, but only thirteen were broadcast in the summer of 1999. Holmes is brought out of cold storage to deal with crime in the London of the future, which has more than a passing resemblance to the city featured in Ridley Scott's *Blade Runner* (1982). Watson is a robot and Holmes's close cohort is Beth Lestrade, a feisty female cop. The scripts, while satisfying the craving of the target youth audience for wham-bang action, give numerous sly nods to the original tales. Holmes spouts several of his favourite maxims, such as, 'You see, but you do not observe', and some of the episodes use Doyle's titles, including 'The Resident Patient' and 'The Dancing Men'. In the version of *The Hound of the Baskervilles*, Holmes investigates a creature that is terrorising a lunar base, and discovers that it is a robot created by Moriarty's clone.

Another youth-orientated series was *The Adventures of Shirley Holmes* (1996), filmed in Manitoba, Canada. This featured Meredith Henderson as schoolgirl Shirley, the great, great niece of Sherlock Holmes. She inherits a chest that belonged to the famous detective and can only be opened

by an ingenious mind. Having succeeded, Shirley finds a letter from Holmes inside, in which he expresses the hope that the clever individual who solved the puzzle of the chest will carry on his work in solving crime. 'Any mystery created by mortal minds', he writes, 'can be solved therewith.' The young girl takes up the challenge and with the help of her best friend Bo Sawchuk (John White), her Doctor Watson, she solves many crimes. Like her illustrious ancestor, Shirley, using deductive reasoning, is always one step ahead of the police. The show aired for four seasons from 1996 to 1999 and ran for fifty-two episodes.

In 1992, ITV ran a forty-eight hour Telethon to raise money for various charities. Included as part of the entertainment was a four-part crime story, *The Four Oaks Mystery*, for viewers to solve. Each episode featured a different detective: Taggart (Mark McManus), Van der Valk (Barry Foster), Inspector Wexford (George Baker) and Sherlock Holmes (Jeremy Brett). The Sherlock sequence was the first to be screened and showed Holmes and Watson (Edward Hardwicke) staying with Holmes' godmother, Lady Cordelia (Phyllis Calvert), at Tunlow Hall, when they are called upon to solve a double murder. Holmes is intrigued by the reference made by one of the dying victims to 'four oaks' but, before he is able to make any headway in the matter, he is called away

on another important case which, Watson informs us, would lead to a fatal appointment by a waterfall in Switzerland. The enigma is left for the other three detectives to unravel in turn. The short sequence was shot immediately following the filming of *The Last Vampyre*.

Towards the end of the decade, news emerged from Hollywood that a major, big-budget movie featuring the Great Detective was in the early stages of planning. Writer Michael Valle reportedly secured a fee of $1,000,000 from Columbia Pictures for his first screenplay, *Sherlock Holmes and the Vengeance of Dracula*. Christopher Columbus, who wrote *Young Sherlock Holmes*, was involved from the beginning and it was stated that his production company 1492 Productions would be handling the movie. The plot involves Dracula returning to England to take revenge on Professor Van Helsing and the others who tried to destroy him in Transylvania (as chronicled in Bram Stoker's novel). When one of the group dies of a 'mysterious suicide', the victim's cousin, Constance Bracknell, enlists the help of Sherlock Holmes. This plunges the detective into the nightmare world of the undead, one in which the arch vampire joins forces with

Holmes' nemesis Professor Moriarty to wreak havoc on London. Sherlock Holmes finds not only his rational core of beliefs being shattered but, also, his emotions are unleashed when he falls in love with Constance. However, the whole project was put on hold when Chris Columbus was whisked away to direct the first Harry Potter movie.

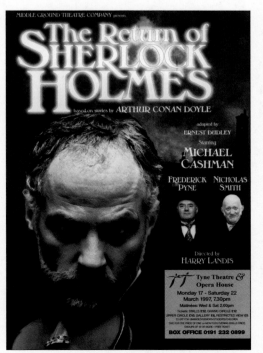

Previous page (above left and right): A youngish Holmes (Reece Dinsdale) as he appeared in Sherlock Holmes and the Case of the Missing Link, *a 1992 science documentary.*
Previous page (below left): Simon Callow starred in the short-lived and underrated radio series The Unopened Casebook of Sherlock Holmes *(1993).*
Above left: A staged publicity shot from the Holmes segment of The Four Oaks Mystery.
Above right: 'The Other Side' (1992). Conan Doyle (Frank Finlay) and Madame Moshel (Cathryn Harrison) examine the body of Sherlock Holmes (Richard E. Grant), who has materialised during a séance.
Left: The 1997 tour of The Return of Sherlock Holmes *starred Michael Cashman as rather a short Holmes.*

THE MASTER BLACKMAILER

TV movie
First screening 2 January 1992
Production company Granada Television
Duration 108 minutes
Colour
Director Peter Hammond

Lady Swinstead's (Norma West) life is blighted by a blackmailer. Twelve years later, the aged Dowager (Gwen Ffrangcon-Davies) entreats Sherlock Holmes (Jeremy Brett) to discover the identity of the man who has ruined her family by means of blackmail. Refusing to buy silence concerning his homosexual past, Captain Dorking sends a note to Holmes with the name of his blackmailer, Charles August Milverton (Robert Hardy), before shooting himself on the eve of his wedding. Holmes disguises himself as a plumber in order to gain entry into Milverton's house. Here he forms a romantic alliance with the maid, Aggie (Sophie Thompson), in order to gain information. Holmes discovers that Lady Swinstead's goddaughter, Lady Eva Blackwell (Serena Gorden), is being blackmailed and agrees to act for her. He summons Milverton to Baker Street but the blackmailer refuses to relinquish Lady Eva's letters. Holmes and Watson (Edward Hardwicke) break in to Milverton's house with the intention of rifling his safe and see Lady Swinstead shoot Milverton, avenging Eva's suffering and her own. Holmes refuses to help the police uncover the murderer.

Ostensibly, Granada's thinking behind extending the showing time from one hour to two was so that the stories were allowed to 'breathe more': the atmosphere of Victorian London could be captured to better effect and the Holmes and Watson relationship could be explored in greater detail. This latter aspect certainly was never realised. There was, of course, a more important reason: money. If Central — the

company who produced Morse — could grab fourteen million viewers with a two-hour Morse, surely Granada could do the same or even better with a two-hour Sherlock? The problem was that the Morse films were based on tightly plotted novels of 200 or so pages: all that Granada had were bottom-of-the-barrel Conan Doyle tales averaging around twenty pages.

This did not seem a problem to June Wyndham Davies who, with Michael Cox having left the scene, was now totally in charge of the Holmes series. She was under instruction from the top to make feature films for television with 'pretty pictures' and 'to cut down on dialogue'. There appeared to be no concerns regarding Sherlockian accuracy or fidelity.

Jeremy Brett was unsure how he felt about making two-hour movies. At the time of shooting he was fairly sanguine, but later he confessed that 'the two hour [films] were a mistake, although I thought *Blackmailer* was good...'

The master blackmailer is Charles Augustus Milverton, from the Doyle story of the same name. It was writer Jeremy Paul's task to convert this slim twelve-page tale into two hours of television. Embedded in the text are tantalising hints of untold tragedies and scenarios that surround the blackmailer, and Paul decided to tell the untold. He teased threads from the original to weave them into a broader tapestry — a tapestry that presents graphically the full effect of this evil genius on the lives of his victims. With these developments, the writer was able to expand Holmes' involvement with the case and to create a mystery for him to solve.

In his research, Paul learned that around the same time as the story was written (1904) there was in London society a morally ambivalent character, a friend of Ruskin, Whistler, Rossetti, Burne-Jones and other artists. His name was Charles Augustus Howell and many believed that he was a blackmailer. It is most probable that Doyle knew of this character and it is possible that he based his 'king of all the

blackmailers' on him. Paul certainly followed this line of reasoning and presented Milverton as an art dealer — an ideal occupation for such a scoundrel — allowing him to move with ease in high society, gaining access to secrets of the wealthy and vulnerable.

Robert Hardy played the part of Milverton and he stole the show. He was the image of the man as Doyle described him: 'a round, plump hairless face, a perpetual frozen smile and two keen grey eyes, which gleamed brightly from behind broad gold-rimmed glasses.'

As an experiment in doubling the length of a Sherlock Holmes episode, *The Master Blackmailer* was deemed a success. However, there are several weaknesses, particularly 'the kissing scene'. In order to inveigle his way into Milverton's house,

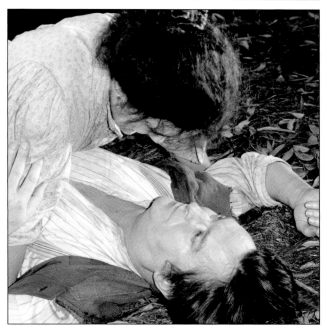

Holmes disguises himself as Escott the plumber on the pretext of 'fixing the pipes'. His real intention is to learn the layout of the establishment and the habits of its inmates. He is aided and abetted by a young housemaid, Aggie, who takes a shine to Sherlock in his workman's disguise. The term 'disguise' must be used loosely here. After the spectacular make-up jobs which Brett applied in earlier series, here he appears merely with uncombed hair, a rather vacant demeanour and a strange rural accent which visits various locations around the British Isles.

The Aggie/Escott relationship is dealt with briefly in the original story. Holmes tells Watson that he is engaged to Milverton's housemaid — because 'I wanted information.' How this unlikely situation actually came about is not divulged. Not so in this film. Unwisely, Granada explored it in some detail. The shy Escott confesses that he does not know how to kiss, and no doubt we are meant to

believe that this is also Holmes' predicament. It is left to Aggie to show him. Once the kiss is over we see Escott — or is it Holmes — emotionally overcome. The whole thing does not work and, later, Brett agreed: 'The kissing business was a mistake. It should have been left to the viewer's imagination. Holmes was inexperienced with women, but he wasn't inexperienced as a detective and he shouldn't have reacted in the way I did. I wish that scene wasn't in the film.'

For the press, Holmes' kiss was the main point of interest. *The Sun* exclaimed: 'Sherlock shows he's no homo! The strait-laced sleuth romps with a busty serving maid in a £1 million TV special being screened by ITV in the New Year. Jeremy Brett, 58, said yesterday: "I was worried about the kissing scene. I took toothpaste and mouthwash on the set. I thought we would be infringing Sherlock's sexuality, given that he is such a private man."'

The critics, by now a little bored with the Sherlock Holmes series, were in the main grudgingly complimentary; although *The Daily Express* summed up what a number of viewers and critics were thinking when it said: 'That is not to say that it did not pass a fairly enjoyable two hours, but there was a definite feeling of things being stretched.' *The Guardian* also pointed out that, 'Jeremy Paul who expanded the story, Chris Truelove who designed it, and Peter Hammond who directed it, beautifully conceal the fact that there is no story there at all.'

There was little actual press comment concerning Brett's performance as Holmes

— or indeed Edward Hardwicke's as Watson. Probably it was felt that it had all been said before — the series had been running eight years. But this sense of omission was indicative of how Jeremy Brett's portrayal was now being marginalised by the critics.

Previous page (below left): Milverton (Robert Hardy), the Master Blackmailer.
Previous page (right): Lady Eva Blackwell (Serena Gordon) asks for help.
Above far left: Holmes (Jeremy Brett) with the Dowager (Gwen Ffrangcon-Davies).
Below far left: Bertrand (Nickolas Grace), one of Milverton's minions.
Top: The infamous kissing scene. Holmes 'playing' Escott, with Aggie (Sophie Thompson).
Middle: Brett, in his Escott guise, between takes.
Bottom: Peter Hammond, the director.

SHERLOCK HOLMES: THE GOLDEN
YEARS SHERLOCK HOLMES AND THE LEADING LADY

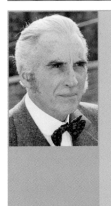

TV movie
FIRST SCREENING August 1992
PRODUCTION COMPANY Harmony Gold and
Banque Caisse, D'epargne De L'etat,
Banque Paribas, Luxembourg in association with
Silvio Berlusconi Communications
DURATION 200 minutes
(originally shown in two parts)
Colour
DIRECTOR Peter Sasdy

Vienna, 1910. A scientist develops a device which detonates explosives by remote control. Before he is able to hand it over to a representative of the British government it is stolen, and Mycroft Holmes (Jerome Willis) persuades his brother Sherlock (Christopher Lee) to travel to Vienna and retrieve it. Holmes encounters the recently widowed Irene Adler (Morgan Fairchild) who proposes marriage to the detective. Reluctantly he refuses. However, Holmes persuades Irene to be hypnotised by Sigmund Freud (John Bennett) because he believes the device has been hidden in the opera house where she is appearing and it is possible that she may have seen the thief. Holmes' trail leads him to Budapest, where he encounters the spy Oberstein who has the blueprint of the mechanism, which is also being sought by Germany and Russia. Holmes destroys the blueprint but one device has been made and is in the hands of a group of anarchists, who plan to assassinate Emperor Franz Joseph on the night he visits the opera. With the help of Watson (Patrick Macnee), he foils the assassination and prevents a world war — for the time being.

*Below left: Watson
(Patrick Macnee),
Holmes (Christopher
Lee) and the leading
lady, Irene Adler
(Morgan Fairchild).*
*Below right: Old school
friends Lee and Macnee.*

'SHERLOCK HOLMES AND THE LEADING LADY' was the first of two long films made as a mini-series under the title of *Sherlock Holmes: The Golden Years*, so called because the actors playing Holmes and Watson, Christopher Lee and Patrick Macnee, were both sixty-nine. The stories were set in 1910. Bob Shayne, who had scripted the disappointing TV movie *The Return of Sherlock Holmes* (1987), was engaged to provide both screenplays for this venture, which was funded mainly by European

money. Early on, Shayne realised that he needed help to craft two very long Sherlock Holmes adventures, and so he contacted British crime writer and Doyle expert H. R. F. Keating, inviting him out to Hollywood to help with the storylines. Keating remembers the experience more as a vacation than a writing project: 'We would walk along the beach at Malibu and discuss the plots. Shayne had no sense of history. I remember him suggesting one scene where Holmes goes into a bar, orders a drink and

finds a clue in the little umbrella in his cocktail...' Although Keating is only credited with working on the first movie, he also assisted with the second.

The story runs for over three hours and is without any kind of tension. The re-kindling of a romance between Irene Adler and Holmes lacks credibility, partly due to Lee's stiff performance, but also because Morgan Fairchild is nearly thirty years younger and behaves like a chorus girl.

Lee was brought into the project by its

executive producer Harry Alan Towers, who had been responsible for the Fu Manchu series that Lee made in the sixties. The movie, with its slow, convoluted, interminable and very padded plot, was filmed in Luxembourg, which doubled for Vienna. One bizarre piece of casting was the pop balladeer Englebert Humperdinck as an opera singer. Picking up the idea of involving real people in Holmes' fictitious world from *The Seven-Per-Cent Solution*, 'Leading Lady' features both Sigmund Freud and Eliot Ness.

SHERLOCK HOLMES: THE GOLDEN YEARS INCIDENT AT VICTORIA FALLS

TV movie
FIRST SCREENING May 1992
PRODUCTION COMPANY Harmony Gold and
Banque Caisse, D'epargne De L'etat,
Banque Paribas, Luxembourg in association with
Silvio Berlusconi Communications
DURATION 200 minutes
(originally shown in two parts)
Colour
DIRECTOR Bill Corcoran

Sherlock Holmes (Christopher Lee), on the verge of retirement, is summoned to Windsor Castle where King Edward (Joss Ackland) engages his services to travel to Cape Town and act as a secret courier, bringing the precious diamond, the Star of Africa, back to Britain. Holmes apparently exchanges the real diamond for an exact replica before the formal handing over ceremony to ensure its safety. However, the fake stone is stolen and a man is murdered. Raffles (Alan Coates), the jewel thief, is wrongly accused of the crimes, and Holmes determines to prove his innocence and recapture the false diamond. The trail leads by train to the Victoria Falls, where the detective unmasks an intrigue involving a hidden treasure horde. Returning to England because of the sudden death of the King, Holmes apprehends the villain, who is posing as Marconi (Stephen Gurney), while he is taking moving pictures of the monarch's coffin. The detective retrieves the Star of Africa from a secret compartment in the camera. Watson (Patrick Macnee) asks Holmes whether the real or the fake stone was stolen, but Holmes says that in writing up the case he can decide.

Below: Christopher Lee, taking his second stab at Holmes on screen, after 1962's Sherlock Holmes and the Deadly Necklace.

THE SECOND STORY OF THIS MINI-SERIES — which was actually shown first — was shot entirely in Zimbabwe, and for the leading actors it was an exhausting schedule of ninety days' filming with only one day off. Lee particularly remembered the extremely high temperatures they had to endure: 'There was one sequence where everybody was having dinner in a railway carriage. It was supposed to be night and so the windows were covered with black paper — and then we had the lights, and the crew and the cast in this confined space. I was told that the temperature rose to something in the region of 130 degrees Fahrenheit.'

Macnee and Lee were at Summer Fields School in Oxford together in the early thirties, acting in the school's Shakespeare productions, and in the sixties Lee appeared in an *Avengers* episode, but this was the first time the old friends had co-starred. It was Macnee's second stab at Watson, after playing him in *Sherlock Holmes in New York* (1976). He admitted, 'I *played* it more in that movie. I think I tried to tame it more this time. I just tried to be a real human being, a doctor... he's the man who takes the viewer to the next event.' According to Macnee, he was not the first choice for the part: 'They originally wanted Nigel Stock, but he had died. They wanted Gordon Jackson and *he* died. Then they thought, "Who else is there?" and they ended up with me.' However, both scripts left little for Macnee to do but play a comic foil.

Once again the film featured a galaxy of real-life characters, including Teddy Roose-velt, Lily Langtry, King Edward and a man pretending to be Marconi, along with the fictional Raffles.

Lee hoped that there would be a third and fourth movie, but such was the poor feeling about the series — the stories were simply too long and lacking in narrative drive — that the films were edited down to three hours and went straight to video, before eventually securing airtime on television.

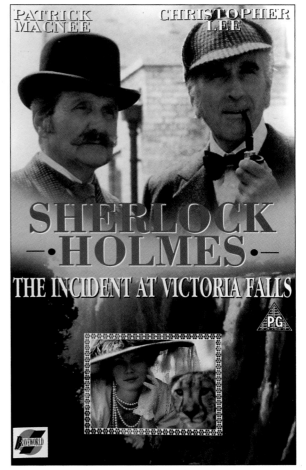

PATRICK MACNEE CHRISTOPHER LEE

SHERLOCK HOLMES
THE INCIDENT AT VICTORIA FALLS

THE LAST VAMPYRE

TV movie
First screening 27 January 1993
Production company Granada Television
Duration 108 minutes
Colour
Director Tim Sullivan

In 1782, the villagers of Lamberley burn down the manor house of the cruel St Clair family who were deemed vampires. Over a century later in 1897, the vicar of Lamberley (Maurice Denham) contacts Sherlock Holmes (Jeremy Brett). He has become concerned about Stockton (Roy Marsden), a sinister newcomer to the village and a relative of the St Clair family, who has had an unsettling effect on the community. Apparently he is capable of killing by sight: the village blacksmith drops dead at his glance. Stockton has been shown hospitality by Bob Ferguson (Keith Barron), whose young baby dies after one of the stranger's visits. Holmes and Watson (Edward Hardwicke) travel to Lamberley and the detective spends some time with Stockton, who takes him to the derelict family house. Here Holmes believes he sees a ghost, but later deduces it was the sun glinting on a broken mirror. Stockton dies when his carriage crashes into a tree and then Ferguson's maid suffers neck wounds in an attack. Holmes determines that Ferguson's adolescent son Jack (Richard Dempsey), influenced by the power of Stockton, believes himself to be a vampire and was responsible for the attack. Jack jumps to his doom before Holmes can save him.

Early in January 1992, June Wyndham Davies got a call from the programming people in London: two more two-hour Sherlocks were required, one of which would be a Christmas special. This was a surprise to her and the Granada team.

They already had three one-hour scripts in the pipeline — 'The Retired Colourman', 'The Golden Pince-Nez' and 'The Red Circle' — but nothing resembling a feature-length screenplay. Jeremy Paul was contacted: 'I was asked to write a two-hour special in three weeks. They left the choice to me. I agreed and chose 'The Adventure of the Sussex Vampire', and became consumed by the project.'

Unlike Paul's previous screenplay, based on 'The Adventure of Charles Augustus Milverton', there is even less to develop in 'The Sussex Vampire'; a weak and slender story with a most misleading title. The resulting screenplay was virtually a Holmes pastiche, with only a

himself, that he is a vampire — of a kind. Paul explained: 'There are some people who soak up the energy of others like a sponge, and draw out their resources and pocket them. Moriarty, for example, has a sort of vampirism about him.'

'The most frightening thing... is the enormous weight which has settled about Brett's once emaciated frame' — *Express*

few shreds of the original tale remaining. Jeremy Brett, fully aware that they were now sailing in uncharted territory, called it 'pretend Doyle', a concept that he would not have countenanced two years earlier. Even the script editor, Craig Dickson, admitted that with this production they had moved further from the baseline than ever before.

At the centre of the story is a newly created character, Stockton, played by Roy Marsden (then best known as Adam Dalgleish in the television adaptations of P. D. James's crime stories). Stockton manages to convince the villagers, the viewers, and to some extent Holmes

The vicar in the film was played by veteran actor Maurice Denham. The part had originally been offered to Peter Cushing, but unfortunately he had not been well enough to accept.

A great deal of *The Last Vampyre* was shot on location in the charming Cotswold village of Stanton in May 1992. This was chosen to represent Doyle's Sussex backwater of Lamberley, but the architecture and russet stonework are so typical of the Cotswolds (in Gloucestershire) that to call the film *The Sussex Vampire* would have been inappropriate. *The Lamberley Vampire* was considered but, with Lamberley sounding like an adjective describing an

affliction rather than a location, it was rejected — as was *The Cotswold Vampire*. The title that finally emerged was *The Last Vampyre*, with the archaic spelling intended to add just a touch of the Gothic to the venture.

Jeremy Brett was far from happy during the shoot: 'I'm out of my depth. You see I can't do my usual trick of bringing Doyle to rehearsal. The first week of rehearsal has always been my week for slavishly returning the script to Doyle, omitting any real departures from the canon. Now I'm not able to do that. If I make a criticism, I'm criticising [Jeremy Paul] not Doyle. It's not the canon any more; we're doing bits.'

Brett was also sad that there was no Mrs Hudson in the film. He always loved having the actress Rosalie Williams, who played Holmes's landlady, on the set; he was very fond of her: 'She is the only female I relate to as Holmes on a regular basis. Deduction is also what we're beginning to miss. I really am short on detective work. Too much of this case relies on intuition.'

At the time of shooting, Jeremy Brett

was very overweight and found it difficult moving about in the heat, weighed down as he was with his great black coat. Out in the sun he had an umbrella to keep him in the shadow, and a prop girl held a portable fan to his face to help prevent his make-up from melting. He insisted on wearing black, although Holmes would, being in the country, wear something lighter and brighter. 'Black helps to disguise my weight,' Brett admitted. 'I had to hide my fatness. I was like a great big Buddha. I cannot bear to watch myself waddle down the station platform in *Vampyre*.'

The reviews for the film were the worst the series had received to date. *The Daily Mail* headed their piece on the programme, 'Bewildering, Mr Holmes', and complained that not only was the plot all but 'impossible to unravel', but also a 'certain confusion was apparent in the physical similarity between Jeremy Brett and Roy Marsden, either or both of whom could pass for Count Dracula.'

The Daily Telegraph, while praising Brett and Hardwicke's performances as Holmes

and Watson, observed that 'it is one thing to have twenty-four carat stars, another to use them properly'. The film was seen as 'a windy piece of Victorian Gothic which respected neither the letter nor the spirit of Conan Doyle's original. Holmes' world is, above all, a rational one. To make the Great Detective grapple with characters invested with a mysterious evil which defied rational explanation was a nonsense.'

Previous page (right): *The Dracula-like Stockton (Roy Marsden).*
Above left: *Bob Ferguson (Keith Barron) mourns his infant son.*
Above right: *On location in Stanton.*
Below: *Brett is kept cool.*

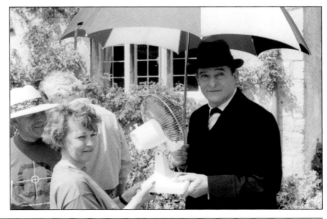

1994 BAKER STREET: SHERLOCK HOLMES RETURNS

TV movie
FIRST SCREENING 12 September 1993
PRODUCTION COMPANY Paragon Entertainment
Corporation in association with
Kenneth Johnson Productions
DURATION 97 minutes
Colour
DIRECTOR Kenneth Johnson

In the late 1890s, Sherlock Holmes (Anthony Higgins), bored now that Moriarty has been despatched, moves to San Francisco where he has himself refrigerated, to be defrosted years later in order to tackle what he considers will be the more interesting crimes of the late twentieth century. Holmes' estate, some miles from the city, is left under the care of the Hudson family, and in 1993 the current Mrs Hudson invites her friend, Doctor Amy Winslow (Debrah Farentino), to visit. Amy discovers a secret section of the wine cellar, where the body of the frozen Holmes is brought to life by a sudden power surge. Doctor Winslow takes Holmes back to San Francisco and he is soon on the trail of James Moriarty Booth (Ken Pogue), who masterminds most of the criminal activities in the city and is the descendant of Holmes' old enemy, Professor Moriarty. Holmes determines that Booth is responsible for a series of revenge murders of prominent policemen. Gradually coming to terms with the modern world, Holmes enlists the help of a streetwise youth, Zappa (Mark Adair Rios), to bring the modern Moriarty to justice.

Below: Dr Amy Winslow (Debrah Farentino) and Zappa (Mark Adair Rios) with the revived, long-haired Holmes (Anthony Higgins).

THIS MOVIE WAS THE BRAINCHILD OF KENNETH Johnson, who produced, directed and wrote the screenplay. The opening section of *1994 Baker Street: Sherlock Holmes Returns* is so similar in plot detail to the TV movie *The Return of Sherlock Holmes* (1987) that it could almost be a remake — but in style and freshness it is far superior. In essence the first twenty minutes, which involves the resuscitation of the frozen Holmes and preparing him to deal with the world of 1990s America, are setting up the basic elements of a series, of which this feature would seem to be the pilot. The 1994 Baker Street of the title is not a reference to the year, but to Amy Winslow's address in San Francisco, where Holmes settles down to do his detective work.

Holmes is played with great aplomb by Anthony Higgins, who had portrayed Rathe, the Moriarty character, in *Young Sherlock Holmes*, and had also appeared as the detective in a short-lived comedy play, *The White Glove*, which ran at the at the Lyric, Hammersmith in London for a month in 1993. He makes a striking figure gadding about San Francisco with long hair and a mixture of Victorian clothing, chinos and trainers.

While the tone of the movie is whimsical, the script strives to present us with a believable Holmes, who constantly makes a stream of brilliant, justifiable deductions about various characters. Only occasionally, for comic purposes, does he miss his target and this is because he is not yet completely *au fait* with the new world he has been reborn into. He deduces a young woman to be a prostitute because she is wearing white boots, a short skirt and heavy make-up, only to be told that she is a cheerleader.

The suggestion of a possible romance between Holmes and Winslow is handled with subtlety, and it is quite clear that this was meant to be a tantalising element of future episodes — which sadly never materialised.

SHERLOCK SELLS

ADVERTISING, MY DEAR WATSON

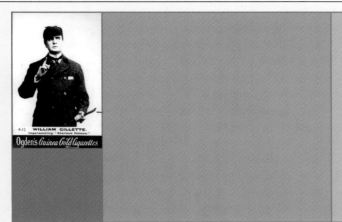

So potent is the immediately recognisable image of the Great Detective with his cape, deerstalker and magnifying glass that he has been used to advertise everything from cornflakes to mouthwash.

Above: *Gillette advertised Ogden's cigarettes.*
Below left: *Rathbone in 1946, after his last Universal Holmes film.*
Below right: *The Case of the Metal-Sheathed Elements, an educational film made for the British Electricity Council in 1972.*

As EARLY AS 1894, THE FIGURE OF SHERLOCK Holmes was being used by Beechams to sell their pills in an advertisement in the *Illustrated London News*. Since then, the famous detective and his colleague Doctor Watson have been enlisted to promote countless items of incredibly varied merchandise.

While some products, such as Ronuk Furniture Cream, Armour Corned Beef and Crunchy Nut Corn Flakes, seem strange choices to be endorsed by Holmes, cigarettes and tobacco are an obvious match. William Gillette, in his guise as the detective, appeared on one of Ogden's Guinea Gold Cigarette cards in 1916.

Shortly after finishing his last Holmes movie for Universal, in 1946, Basil Rathbone (sporting a most out-of-character moustache) appeared in a Chesterfield Cigarettes magazine advertisement wearing his Sherlock Homes costume from the film series.

The Baker Street duo have also appeared in television commercials. Perhaps the most entertaining of all were the four filmed by Esso Domestic Heating in 1970. These Canadian commercials were made in Britain, in French and English versions with two separate sets of uncredited actors playing Holmes and Watson. Each episode concerned heating problems in a large country house. In the first, 'his lordship's daughter' appears to be behaving erratically, constantly switching from a mini-dress to a maxi dress. Holmes has the solution: 'Watson, this mini-maxi mix up is caused by out-moded heating.' The young Earl of Bloomshire is fond of flowers but, as Watson tells the detective in the second commercial, 'When his young lordship woke this morning he found his bloomers blighted.'

Holmes deduces that 'the house is freezing' and enlists the aid of an Esso heating specialist. In their third Esso outing, a cry in the night leads Holmes and Watson into the old house to discover 'Sir Percy frozen in his bath.' However, the detective is certain that it is not too late to save him: 'An Esso water heater provides an almost constant supply of hot water.' The final entry in this beautifully filmed and amusing series sees Holmes and Watson playing billiards with

'his lordship'. 'Tell me Holmes, is it true that you can judge a man's character by an object that belongs to him?' asks the aristocrat. Holmes asserts that he can and, picking up one of his lordship's glass goblets, he deduces that the owner is a man of taste, but has poor water heating in the house which does not allow the glassware to be washed without leaving a smear. The answer? An Esso water heater of course.

Holmes and Watson appeared in animated form in an industrial film made for the British Electricity Council in 1972, showing how to use electricity safely and efficiently.

In 1988 the Food Lion grocery chain in

America presented the Baker Street duo in four short commercials extolling their branded products. One episode showed the pair outside in the fog when they hear a large hound coming towards them. They run off in terror because they have forgotten to bring the can opener for the Food Lion dogmeat they had brought along.

These notable examples are but features on the tip of an enormous and ever-growing Holmes advertising iceberg.

Yes! it's Elementary

ABC ALWAYS MILDER BETTER TASTING COOLER SMOKING ALL THE BENEFITS OF SMOKING PLEASURE

RIGHT COMBINATION OF THE WORLD'S BEST TOBACCOS *Properly Aged*

ALWAYS BUY CHESTERFIELD

HOUNDING HOLMES

BRINGING OUT THE ANIMAL IN SHERLOCK

Animals have always dominated the world of the cartoon film, from Mortimer (later Mickey) Mouse and Daffy Duck, to Garfield and Count Duckula. These comical creatures have often used Holmes and facets of his world to gain laughs.

WITH THE PUNNING TITLE, *Sure-Locked Holmes*, Pathe Films presented their feline charmer Felix the Cat in probably the first Holmes-related cartoon, in 1927. Felix investigates what he believes are ghosts in the house, only to discover that they are shadows made by a baby with a light.

Walt Disney got in on the act in 1937 with *Lonesome Ghosts*, in which detectives Mickey Mouse, Goofy and Donald Duck investigate a haunted house. Mickey and Goofy wear deerstalkers, while Donald retains his sailor hat.

A real oddity was the Phantasy Cartoon produced by Columbia Pictures, *The Case of the Screaming Bishop* (1944), in which Hairlock Combs and Doctor Gotsum are on the trail of a dinosaur skeleton which has disappeared from a museum.

Warner Brothers produced two Looney Tunes cartoons featuring Daffy Duck with, or in the role of, the Great Detective. In *The Great Piggy Bank Robbery* (1946) Daffy knocks himself unconscious and dreams that he is the famous sleuth Duck Twacy, who meets Sherlock Holmes while

newspaper strip *Peanuts* created by Charles M. Schultz, featured a thirty-minute episode in which Sally takes Woodstock's nest to school to talk about it in class. Snoopy turns into Sherlock Holmes in order to solve the mystery of 'The Missing Nest'.

The Chipmunks have adopted the Holmes guise in two episodes. In 'The Cruise' (1983), Alvin inadvertently helps a thief to steal some jewels and Simon, as Holmes, and Theodore, as Watson, attempt to retrieve them and capture the criminal.

investigating the theft of several piggy banks, one of which is his own. In *Deduce You Say* (1956), Daffy stars as Dorlock Holmes who, with Porky Pig as Doctor Watkins, sets out to send the villainous Shropshire Slasher back to jail. In a true comic inversion, Daffy fails miserably while the downtrodden Porky succeeds.

In 1974, the television cartoon series *It's A Mystery, Charlie Brown*, based on the

Simon and Theodore reprise their Sherlockian alter egos in 'Elementary, My Dear Simon' (1990) to challenge Moriarty and his devilish time machine.

The Chipmunks' Disney counterparts, 'the tiny but tough' *Chip 'n' Dale, Rescue Rangers*, tackled 'The Pound of the Baskervilles' in 1988. Chip's vast knowledge of Sureluck Jones detective novels comes in handy when the Rescue Rangers help a

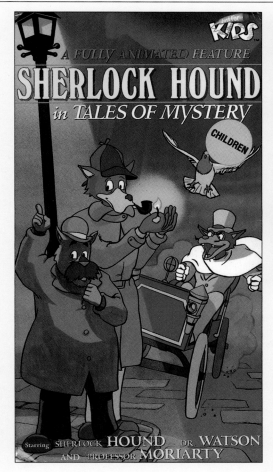

canine client to find his master's missing will in a mysterious manor house.

Staying with the Hound theme, a 1983 episode of Hanna-Barbera's *The New Scooby and Scrappy Doo Show* was titled 'The Hound of the Scoobyvilles'. The gang goes to Barkerville Hall in Scotland because the owner's sheep are disappearing. They learn of the Barkerville legend, and Scooby Doo is mistaken for the phantom Hound. Scrappy puts on a Sherlockian cape and deerstalker to solve the mystery. It turns out that the butler is behind the disappearances.

In Britain, *Henry's Cat*, a series produced by Godfrey Films for BBC Television, included two Sherlockian episodes. In 'The Case of the Pilfered Pearls' (1983), Henry's cat, having just read several Holmes stories, imagines what it would be like to be the detective. He wears a deerstalker, plays a violin and is assisted by a rabbit called Doctor Whatsis. Eventually the cat solves the mystery of Lady Penelope's missing jewellery. In a second Sherlockian outing, 'The Mystery of the Missing Santa' (1983), the sleuthing feline sets out to discover who has kidnapped Santa Claus on the night before Christmas.

In Jim Henson's *The Muppet Babies* cartoon series (1984-87), young Gonzo dons a deerstalker, an Inverness cape and carries a magnifying glass to become either Sherlock Gonzo or Inspector Gonzo in several episodes.

One of the most amusing children's cartoon series to originate from a British studio in the eighties was *Count Duckula*, featuring a reluctant vampire, voiced by David Jason, who eats broccoli sandwiches and seeks adventure. In the episode, 'All in a Fog' (1987), the Count travels to London in search of a crime to solve, and encounters Mr Sholmes and Doctor Potson.

Disney's *The New Adventures of Winnie the Pooh* touched on the Holmes theme in 'Tigger Private Eye' (1989), as Tigger starts up his own detective business and takes to wearing a cape and a deerstalker, and carrying a magnifying glass. As he does not receive any clients, he makes his own case by stealing a 'hunny' pot from Pooh.

Garfield, the irascible cat created by Jim Davis, made it to television in 1990 and one episode, 'The Hound of the Arbuckles', has the grumpy feline wanting to watch Sherlock Holmes on television rather than help his owner, Jon, look for the missing dog, Odie. Garfield falls asleep and dreams that he is Doctor Watson. He assists Holmes in finding Odie on the roof. When Garfield awakens, he finds that Odie really is on the roof.

In Japan, Sherlock Holmes was anthropomorphised into the dog star of *The Adventures of Sherlock Hound* (1984). In fact in this series all the characters,

including Watson, Moriarty and Mrs Hudson, are canines. Each episode features Sherlock — a sharp-faced, smooth-haired fox terrier type — and Dr Watson — a Skye Terrier — attempting to foil the latest evil scheme devised by the fox-like Moriarty. A few of the adventures, such as 'The Speckled Band' and 'The Blue Carbuncle', are loosely based on the Doyle canon, but in the main the stories are original and full of wit and energy. The series, dubbed into English with the voices of Larry Moss as Sherlock and Lewis Arquette as Watson, was shown on television in the Britain and released on video in America.

One Japanese cartoon film that failed to make it to either Britain or the States was the 1992 production *Mitsuge Neko Holmes no Yuurei jochu* ('Holmes the Tortoiseshell Cat'), which was based on the best-selling novel *Mitsuge Holmes to Ai no Hanataba* ('Holmes the Tortoiseshell Cat and the Loving Bunch of Flowers') by Jiro Akagawa. The forty-five-minute cartoon features the feline detective hero who decides to discover whether the police have really solved a murder which took place on an uninhabited island.

Previous page (above left): Henry's Cat, in his 1983 adventure 'The Case of the Pilfered Pearls'.
Previous page (below left), far left and left: The 1984 series The Adventures of Sherlock Hound *remains very popular, and was released on DVD in Japan in 2001.*
Previous page (right): The Pink Panther dons the deerstalker in Sherlock Pink (1976).
Above: Daffy Duck meets Sherlock in The Great Piggy Bank Robbery (1946).

THE ELIGIBLE BACHELOR

TV movie
FIRST SCREENING 3 February 1993
PRODUCTION COMPANY Granada Television
DURATION 106 minutes
Colour
DIRECTOR Peter Hammond

Driving back from a case, Holmes (Jeremy Brett) and Watson (Edward Hardwicke) pass by a mental institution and hear the inmates crying out. This depresses the detective and he suffers a series of vivid nightmares. Lord St Simon (Simon Williams) marries American heiress Hetty Doran (Paris Jefferson) in order to use her money to save his estate Glaven from his creditors. St Simon's spurned lover, actress Flora Miller (Joanna McCallum), attempts to shoot him but fails. Immediately following the wedding ceremony Hetty disappears. She is reunited with her American husband whom she thought dead. While Holmes becomes involved in the search for Hetty, he is consulted by the veiled woman of his dreams, Agnes Northcote (Anna Calder-Marshall) who claims that her sister, Helena, St Simon's second wife, was certified mad by her husband. Flora Miller impersonated her so that St Simon secured the legal papers to have Helena put away. Holmes now believes that Helena is incarcerated somewhere in Glaven. Visiting the old house he sees scenes from his nightmares including Helena who has been penned up like an animal for seven years. She exacts her revenge on St Simon by bringing part of her prison cell down upon him.

IF JEREMY BRETT HAD BEEN WORRIED ABOUT Sherlock Holmes's lack of deduction and his reliance on intuition in the script of *The Last Vampyre*, it was nothing to the concerns he felt on receiving the script for *The Eligible Bachelor*. Based on another slender Doyle tale, 'The Adventure of the Noble Bachelor', this screenplay was by another series regular, Trevor Bowen. He probably renamed the story to distance it from the original, which it hardly resembles. This ill-conceived mess, which has the air of an overblown grand opera, is the lowest point of the Granada series. It plunges Holmes into a strange melancholia and he experiences weird prophetic dreams, inexplicably connected with the main mystery he eventually comes to investigate. 'I did cut a lot of stuff out before we started filming,' Brett told me, 'but I am afraid there was still too much in that was not satisfactory.'

However, Brett's public utterances at the time of filming disguised his concern. He told *Sherlock Holmes — The Detective Magazine* that '[*The Eligible Bachelor*] is a title. But at the time of filming, he was on a manic high. He was delighted to be playing Holmes again and was determined to explore the psyche of the character further. He was even keen to do another stage play as Holmes, and kept feeding Jeremy Paul with ideas on a daily basis. Paul said, 'I listen to Jeremy and make notes. I don't want to discourage him, but nothing will come of it.'

I interviewed Jeremy Brett on the set the day before he filmed the notorious 'nightie' scene — where Holmes rushes out into Baker Street during a heavy downpour, wearing only his long white nightshirt and a thin dressing gown, to snatch up a piece of paper from the gutter which he believes is a precious clue — and he was full of enthusiasm for the sequence and excited about filming it. As he described the scene to me, he failed to see that it was

> 'The innocent Lord St Simon became the villain, thus changing the whole nature of the story. I am highly critical of this' — Dame Jean Conan Doyle.

departure. We are moving into a space we have never been in before. We now have Holmes picturing the future when he's actually on a case. It becomes really gripping. I don't know what Doyleans will think of it, but it is so very exciting.'

For years Brett had been calling himself a Doylean, fighting for fidelity to the author's character and his plots. The actor knew full well what the Doyleans would think of this outlandish script and what, in his heart of hearts, he thought too. He expressed his real opinion of the film to me in the last months of his life, by pulling a huge grimace at the mere mention of the demeaning to the character of Sherlock Holmes — at least the character as created by Arthur Conan Doyle — and that the idea had no dramatic credence and added nothing to the viewers' understanding of the convoluted plot. In other words, it was an unfortunate gimmick. Yet Brett was full of unbounded enthusiasm: 'I am really looking forward to this shot. It's going to be great fun.'

When he spoke of the sequence again in our final interview together in 1995, he groaned at the thought of it: 'Oh, the nightie scene. It's an abomination. I wish I had never done it. When I saw it, I put my

head in my hands in horror. It is so wrong.'

There was so much 'wrong' with *The Eligible Bachelor* and, despite being lushly and elegantly photographed, it was quite clear that Granada — or June Wyndham Davies at least — had lost sight of what Sherlock Holmes was all about. The press certainly thought so. While praising the production values, they were unhappy about the film as a Holmes vehicle. The review in the *Daily Express* summed up the general impression: 'Despite coaxing from the taciturn Doctor Watson and the prim

Mrs Hudson, Holmes' interest in detective work seemed to have terminally waned.'

The Sherlockian enthusiasts were more brutal in their condemnation. The *Sherlock Holmes Journal* admitted, 'it has to be said at once that attempts at critical detachment are doomed to founder beneath such a farrago of nonsense. The new plot is well nigh impossible to follow… whilst I can imagine a hypothetical twenty-first century audience deriving some pleasure from *The Last Vampyre*, let them beware of *The Eligible Bachelor*, they may actually die of laughing'.

Jeremy Brett who, in his unstable mental condition, believed he was adding new dimensions to his interpretation of Sherlock Holmes, was in fact destroying his credibility and fidelity. He was hurt by the film's reviews, but more so by the criticism of Dame Jean Conan Doyle. Brett was not only on very friendly terms with Doyle's daughter, but saw her as his guru when playing the Great Detective. Her disapprobation wounded him deeply, and he vowed never to play Sherlock Holmes again unless Doyle's stake in the plot was paramount.

Previous page (below): The ill-conceived 'nightie' scene.
Above left: The dastardly Lord St Simon (Simon Williams).
Above right: Agnes Northcote (Anna Calder-Marshall, who is married to Brett's first Watson, David Burke).
Far left: Brett with an 'urchin' inside the grounds of Manchester Town Hall, a frequent location for the Granada series.
Left: Hetty Doran (Paris Jefferson) with Lord St Simon.

THE MEMOIRS OF SHERLOCK HOLMES

FIRST SCREENING March-April 1994
PRODUCTION COMPANY Granada Television
DURATION 6 x 50 minutes
Colour
REGULAR CAST
Jeremy Brett (Sherlock Holmes),
Edward Hardwicke (Doctor Watson),
Rosalie Williams (Mrs Hudson)

After the glory days of the early Granada Holmes series, producer June Wyndham Davies now had to fight to get the last set of six films into production.

THE FINAL SERIES OF SHERLOCK HOLMES FILMS from Granada Television almost wasn't made. The year was 1993 and as far as June Wyndham Davies was aware, the programme schedulers wanted another two

feature-length movies by Christmas. She was now determined not to stretch and manipulate a meagre Conan Doyle tale into a 100-minute screenplay; instead she planned to use a straight pastiche. At least with this the critics could not complain about the mauling of a precious text. But she had not reckoned on Jeremy Brett's aversion to any non-Doyle project, particularly after the roasting the last two long films had received in the press.

Brett dug his heels in: if he was going to do Holmes again, it must be Doyle's Holmes and all the extraneous infidelities must be expunged. Davies believed that she could talk Brett around on this point, but then she received news from the programme planners in London, who by this time had lost all interest in the Sherlock Holmes films. They told her that they didn't want any more two-hour Holmes after all. So she fought to secure a place for six one-hour Sherlocks instead, but met indifference and reticence from the powers that be. As fate would have it, 'a window in the schedules' appeared for the spring of 1994. Davies grasped the nettle, despite only having just over six months to produce half a dozen one-hour films, and started preparatory work on *The Memoirs*. Elizabeth Bradley was brought in as script editor, and she admitted that her knowledge of Sherlock Holmes was weak. However, her instructions were to 'cut out the talk and concentrate on the visuals' — a statement that effectively illustrates how far Granada had moved from the benchmark set up by Michael Cox.

The series got off to a bad start. Edward Hardwicke was away appearing in the movie *Shadowlands* (1993) with Anthony Hopkins and was not available for the filming of the first episode, 'The Golden Pince-Nez'. Instead, Charles Gray returned as brother Mycroft, to fill in as Holmes's sidekick. Visually, the show is stunning. The

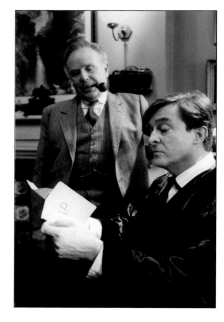

flashback scenes of the Russian Revolution belie the fact that only seventeen extras and two horses were used. The script by Gary Hopkins is fairly faithful, apart from the enforced Watson/Mycroft switch, but

the original is a weak story lacking drama and excitement, and these weaknesses were conveyed to the screen.

The second *Memoir* to be filmed was 'The Red Circle' — the only show in the series where everything went comparatively smoothly. Both Brett and Hardwicke were in attendance, Brett was in reasonable health and there were no major hold-ups in filming. Little did anyone know just how rough the production process was about to become.

The final shot of 'The Red Circle' underlines Holmes's humanity, showing him with tears in his eyes while watching the opera in the theatre where a friend of his, Firmani, was butchered. This segment

was added after filming had been completed. Composer Patrick Gowers, whose brilliant music had been used throughout all the Granada Holmes films, rang Brett after seeing a rough cut of 'The Red Circle'. He told the actor that in the closing scene, where Holmes and Watson are in a box at the opera, it appeared that the detective, eyes closed, seemed to be enjoying the music rather than remembering 'his friend Firmani'. Brett took this point and persuaded June Wyndham Davies to insert the crying shot, which Michael Cox referred to as 'embarrassing'.

'The Three Gables' was the third in the series of six *Memoirs* to be filmed but it was first to be shown both in Britain and, much later, in the United States. I talked with Brett in his caravan during location shooting of this episode. He looked unwell; he was wheezing and short of breath and still very overweight. At first our conversation took the air of a confessional: 'I know I told you the two-hour format might

be better, but of course, it's not. The ideal format for these stories is one hour. I was wrong.' Apart from the criticism of *Vampyre* and *Bachelor*, what, I wondered, had brought about this *volte-face*? 'The tricky thing technically, as an actor, is, if you're playing a man without a heart, it is very hard to sustain it realistically for two hours. People want to get underneath the shell, and this has led, on one or two occasions, to the loss of mystique of Holmes. For example, for you to hear about Holmes having a love affair with a girl — "I'm engaged to be married" — is one thing, but to actually see it [as in *The Master Blackmailer*] is something else. It exposes too much of the character. In the one-hours you have a chance to see SH at his most brilliant without peeping too far behind the scenes. So... now we're back on track. The new stories are incredibly complicated and need no padding.'

I stayed and watched the filming of the scene where Holmes faces the villainess Isadora Klein. Brett had described it to me as 'the climax of the film. Holmes is faced with the brilliant and beautiful Spanish woman. They clash rather like Tito Gobbi and Maria Callas in the second act of *Tosca*. She rushes towards him to tear his eyes out and he grabs her arm to stop her. They are very close. I am not sure how I, as Holmes, am going to react. This is new territory for me. Holmes thinks it is easier to deal with a woman than a man, but

he has forgotten the power of emotion in such an encounter. I have always to remember that sexually Holmes is a virgin.'

Sadly, Brett really was too ill to perform this scene well. He lacked sufficient breath to give the lines their full force and his movements were slow and cumbersome, like a man walking under water.

The following day he collapsed on the set and had to be rushed to hospital. The story given out at the time was that he had stayed on too long to watch a night shoot, and had caught a chill on his chest. In truth, the medically prescribed drug lithium was causing problems and water was building up in his lungs. After a few days in hospital, he emerged to complete 'The Three Gables'. He was in a wheelchair between takes and had to use oxygen to ease his breathing. Once the film was completed he was hospitalised for a month.

For June Wyndham Davies it was a nightmare scenario. Already behind schedule and with one episode having been completed without Edward Hard-

Previous page (below left): Anna (Anna Carteret) in a revolution scene from 'The Golden Pince-Nez'.
Previous page (right) and below right: Brett and Harwicke's final series was fraught with problems.
Above left: Peter Wyngarde on location for 'The Three Gables'.
Above right: Society gossip Langdale Pike (Peter Wyngarde) with Holmes.
Below left: Holmes and Watson investigate 'The Red Circle' with Inspector Gregson (Tom Chadbon).

wicke, now her leading man was out of action. The filming of the next episode, with the tragically poignant title 'The Dying Detective', had to be delayed — a very costly procedure.

Claiming that he was fit again, Brett began filming 'The Dying Detective' in October. In fact he was far from well for, apart from his physical weakness, he was rapidly sliding into one of his manic depressions. More than once he felt faint, and during the filming of one scene he collapsed into the arms of guest actor Roy Hudd. At the end-of-shoot party, Brett became very ill again, suffering what he described as a 'white out'. The next day he was in Charters Nightingale Hospital at Lisson Grove fighting for his life and sanity. The drugs had brought about lithium poisoning, causing him to swell with water retention, and had also seriously damaged his heart.

Meanwhile, back in her office at Granada, June Wyndham Davies was tearing her hair out. She had fought so hard to get this series off the ground and now her star was incapable of filming. She couldn't wait while Brett recovered. She had to press on with the next film, 'The Mazarin Stone', but her dilemma was: how do you make a Sherlock Holmes film without Sherlock Holmes? Her solution was to bring in Charles Gray once again, and move Mycroft Holmes to centre stage. For this investigation he would take on his brother's mantle of master detective.

The script for 'The Mazarin Stone' by

director Peter Hammond — Holmes tells Watson that he must be away to 'the high lands'. The idea was to inject a sense of mysticism into Holmes' absence, along with an implication that he was still tortured by the Reichenbach incident. Holmes returns at the end, following the climax of the story, when the corpulent Mycroft has retrieved the precious stone. 'Well done, brother mine,' intones a disembodied voice. We catch a glimpse of Sherlock enveloped in mist as though to indicate that he has been observing all the events from afar — up in 'the high lands'.

Brett returned to the series just before

'Neither the material — barrel scrapings from Doyle's weakest stories — nor the star's health was up to this disappointing series' — *Sherlock Holmes Gazette.*

Gary Hopkins, which also included elements from 'The Adventure of the Three Garridebs' to pad out the thin plot, had to be altered to incorporate the Mycroft character. The result was a disappointing mish-mash of elements that did not gel together.

The main story of 'The Mazarin Stone' is framed by two short scenes featuring Brett as Holmes. These were filmed later when the actor had recovered sufficiently to resume work. In the opening scene — conceived by Brett and scripted by him and

Christmas 1993. He came to the read-through of 'The Cardboard Box' attended by a nurse. June Wyndham Davies told me at the time that she had been instructed that the actor could only film on alternative days — a restriction that played havoc with the shooting schedule. 'It's not as though he has a small part!' she observed pithily.

'The Cardboard Box' is perhaps the best production of this blighted series. Brett, having lost a lot of weight, was looking more like the Sherlock of yore, if a little haggard, and Trevor Bowen's script

strengthened and deepened the drama of Doyle's original.

The opening is pleasing to see, especially as this was the last time Edward Hardwicke and Jeremy Brett appeared together as the legendary lodgers at 221B Baker Street. The Great Detective and his biographer are seated by a blazing fire in their sitting room, each smoking a pipe and conversing as old friends about a spate of grave robberies. This domestic vignette is the concentrated essence of what is so enjoyable about the stories. Hardwicke

unfailingly maintains the image of the ideal Watson in this scene, and Brett is almost back to his best, with that combination of impishness and arrogance which almost conceals the love and respect he has for his companion. There are also pleasing interchanges between Mrs Hudson and her lodger, and one wishes that Colin Jeavons as Lestrade could have made it into this final outing too.

Jeremy Brett told me that he was very pleased with the final words he uttered in this film — the final words he uttered as

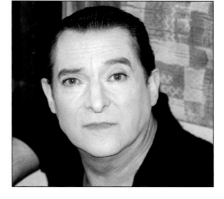

Sherlock Holmes, in fact. They were a close paraphrase of Conan Doyle's own dialogue from the story. When the tragic lovers are discovered in the river, frozen beneath a sheet of ice, Holmes turns to his old friend and says: 'What is the meaning of this, Watson? What is the object of this circle of misery and violence and fear? It must have a purpose, or else our universe has no purpose and that is unthinkable. But what? That is humanity's great problem to which reason so far has no answer.'

Shortly after completing 'The Cardboard Box', Jeremy Brett was back in hospital — a mental hospital. In his own self-effacing way he called it 'the nut house'. When *The Memoirs* was screened in Britain in March and April 1994, the man who was Sherlock Holmes failed to see his own last series, because he was in a ward where the other patients preferred to watch another channel. Jeremy Brett deferred to their choice of viewing.

Previous page (above): 'The Cardboard Box': Susan Cushing (Joanna David), Inspector Hawkins (Tom Chadbon, who in 'The Red Circle' had been Inspector Gregson — another example of the lack of care in the latter days at Granada), Watson (Hardwicke) and Holmes (Brett).

Previous page (below): Lord Cantlemere (James Villiers) and Mycroft Holmes (Charles Gray) in 'The Mazarin Stone'.

Above left: Brett and Claudine Auger discussing a scene from 'The Three Gables' with director Peter Hammond.

Above right: Filming for 'The Three Gables', with Brett looking decidedly unwell.

Middle: Brett (made up as Holmes) in his trailer, while filming 'The Three Gables'.

Left: Brett and Hardwicke with guest star Roy Hudd as the shady John Gedgrave.

MURDER ROOMS – THE DARK BEGINNINGS OF SHERLOCK HOLMES

US TITLE The Dark Beginnings of Sherlock Holmes
TV serial
FIRST SCREENING 4 and 5 January 2000
PRODUCTION COMPANY BBC TV
DURATION 2 x 60 minutes
Colour
DIRECTOR Paul Seed

Young Conan Doyle (Robin Laing), disaffected by his home life with his alcoholic father and his mother's affections for her lodger, joins Edinburgh University to study medicine. He becomes clerk to Doctor Joseph Bell (Ian Richardson), and grows suspicious of his nocturnal activities. Following Bell one night, Doyle discovers that he is helping the police with detective work. His secret discovered, the Doctor appoints Doyle as his assistant. Their first case together concerns a Mrs Canning, who has died mysteriously. Bell proves that she was gassed by her husband. Later, Bell is called to the house of Sir Henry Carlyle (Charles Dance), patron of the University, to attend to his wife. Bell diagnoses syphilis, which she contracted from her husband, who frequents a brothel in the old town where several prostitutes have been murdered. To protect his shameful secret, Carlyle was giving his wife pills that would eventually kill her. Further investigations bring Bell to the conclusion that the prostitute killer is one of Doyle's fellow students, Neill Cream (Alec Newman), who escapes capture by taking a boat to Nova Scotia, but not before poisoning Elspeth (Dolly Wells), Arthur's love. Doyle conceives the idea of an invincible detective who could have prevented her death.

IN 1999, WRITER DAVID PIRIE APPROACHED THE BBC with the idea of bringing Sherlock Holmes back to the station 'where he belonged.' But they were not interested. Despite Pirie's belief that 'the BBC and Sherlock Holmes go together', he failed to raise any interest in the project with David Thompson, head of films. Pirie explained: 'At that point I was interested in doing *A Study in Scarlet* because I always felt that a younger, more 'Oscar Wilde' Holmes had never been done. Dramatically, we've always

father and an impoverished mother forced to take in a lodger with whom she forms an alliance — the more Pirie became convinced that he had a springboard for his drama: 'While neglected at home where there was no real father figure to guide him,

been presented with the older — and at its worse — the stodgier Holmes. Sadly, this didn't appeal to David. And then one day I got a call from him. "I've had a thought," he said. "Joseph Bell. How about that?"

The suggestion immediately set Pirie's creative juices flowing. Here, he thought, was an exciting challenge — and an original take on Sherlock Holmes. The writer set about researching Conan Doyle's early life and his time spent at Edinburgh University, where he encountered Doctor Joseph Bell. The more he read of Doyle's domestic circumstances — an alcoholic, weak-minded

Doyle discovered Bell, mesmeric Bell, as a kind of mentor and surrogate father. Maybe it was imaginary. Maybe it was real. We can't know. The relationship between the two men is too obscure now, but I feel sure there was something there — that at this precise point in his life, young Arthur Conan Doyle has to find something else. Everyone says how real Sherlock Holmes is. I don't believe that something like that is created out of nothing.'

Pirie has a point. In Doyle's autobiography, *Memories and Adventures*, he records that 'Bell was a very remarkable

man in body and mind. He was thin, wiry, dark, with a high nosed acute face, penetrating grey eyes... angular shoulders... His voice was high and discordant.' He could be describing Sherlock Holmes. Certainly, that was the conceit grasped by David Pirie in *Murder Rooms*. He presents Bell not so much as an embryonic Sherlock Holmes but as a perfect replica, even giving him Holmes dialogue snatched from some of the stories.

And so Bell effectively becomes a detective hero, with the young Doyle as his assistant. However, Pirie admitted that while Bell is 'really Sherlock Holmes, Doyle cannot be Watson. He's much more troubled and much more challenging. There is more humanity in their relationship and Bell is more humane than Holmes. By the same token Doyle is less kindly, less sentimental than Watson.'

In the first episode of this two-part drama, Pirie had the difficult task of setting up the relationship between Bell and Doyle. This begins when Doyle attends one of Bell's lectures to hear him claim that he can deduce the personal details of his patients by mere observation, similar to an incident recorded in Doyle's autobiography. The young student is not impressed with these 'conjuring tricks', which he believes lack practical application. Bell, considering that he has been accused of being a charlatan, responds in true Sherlockian manner: 'Here is a simple warning. From the astrologer came the astronomer; from the alchemist came the chemist; from the mesmerist came the mental specialist. The charlatan is always the pioneer. The quack of yesterday is always the professor of tomorrow.'

For this series to work, the casting of the brilliant, enigmatic and Sherlockian

Joseph Bell had to be right. It was. Ian Richardson, stepping once more into the Holmes arena, took on the mantle of Bell. He gave a meticulous performance. *The Daily Mail* commented that 'Ian Richardson is perfectly cast... the game is really afoot' and *Variety* affirmed that 'Richardson is perfection as Bell... generating both intensity and passion.'

Although Richardson garnered most of the praise, Robin Laing also gave a very convincing portrayal as the troubled young Arthur Conan Doyle.

While the second episode was rather rushed, and the explanations somewhat submerged in the action — partly due to some hurried rewriting and editing in order bring the programme in at the specified sixty minutes — *Murder Rooms* was a great success. *The Sunday Telegraph* wrote: 'a premise with a real touch of genius... the script skilfully wove episodes from Doyle's own past into a richly textured, constantly wrong-footing plot... with a denouement as clever as anything that had gone before.'

The BBC, always on the lookout for a crowd-pleasing crime series, wasted little time in commissioning a series of Bell/Doyle adventures, and filming began in the autumn of 2000 on four ninety-minute episodes. Richardson returned as Bell, but the part of Doyle, now more mature and in medical practice, was taken by Charles Edwards. The series was good news for Holmes fans for if they couldn't have the real Baker Street sleuth himself, his creator Doyle and his inspiration Bell were a very close second.

Previous page (below left): The shadow of Sherlock Holmes?
Previous page (right): The young Arthur Conan Doyle (Robin Laing) learns from the master, Doctor Joseph Bell (Ian Richardson).
Above left: Bell and Doyle with Sir Henry Carlyle (Charles Dance).
Left: Robin Laing gives a convincing performance as the troubled young Doyle.

THE HOUND OF THE BASKERVILLES

TV movie
FIRST SCREENING 21 October 2000
PRODUCTION COMPANY Muse Entertainment Enterprises
in association with Hallmark Entertainment
DURATION 90 minutes
Colour
DIRECTOR Rodney Gibbons

Having discovered the footprints of an enormous dog by the dead body of his friend, Sir Charles Baskerville, Doctor Mortimer (Gordon Masten) is convinced that his death is connected with the old family legend of the phantom Hound. Mortimer consults Sherlock Holmes (Matt Frewer) about the safety of Sir Henry (Jason London), the heir to the estate. Holmes sends Watson (Kenneth Welsh) with Sir Henry to Baskerville Hall. Here, Sir Henry sees a strange dog stalking the grounds at night. A dinner at the Stapletons house sparks off a romance between the baronet and Beryl Stapleton (Emma Campbell), the naturalist's sister. Watson spies the butler Barrymore (Arthur Holden) signalling to Selden, the escaped convict on the moor. He is Mrs Barrymore's brother and the signal is to let him know that there is food waiting. After Selden is killed, Watson believes that there really is a phantom Hound at large. Sir Henry receives a note from Beryl asking him to meet her at Merripit house. It is a trap and Stapleton (Robin Wilcock) releases the Hound which attacks Sir Henry. Holmes appears and wounds the Hound, which turns on its master. Stapleton and the beast sink into the Grimpen Mire together.

Below: Holmes (Matt Frewer) and his sensible Watson (Kenneth Welsh), with Sir Henry Baskerville (Jason London).

THIS TELEVISION FEATURE WAS FILMED IN Montreal in the summer of 2000 and stars Matt Frewer as Holmes, although he was originally cast as Stapleton the villain. He told me that 'playing Holmes is rather like Hamlet. It's a horse that has been ridden by many jockeys and there's a certain responsibility with it — particularly to the audience, because they have certain expectations. But I think once that those preconceptions are satisfied, then you can bring your own stuff to the dance and hopefully I've done that.'

His own 'stuff' that he brought to the role included an English accent of excruciating archness. *Sherlock Holmes – The Detective* magazine noted that: '[Frewer] rollercoasters his sentences with erratic pitches of volume and varying speeds of delivery while manipulating his lean face into a series of exaggerated Bertie Wooster expressions.' It was an eccentric and controversial performance.

The twenty-two day shooting schedule was on 'a limited budget', with the cobbled streets and old buildings of Montreal doubling for Victorian London. Director Rodney Gibbons went to England for four days to capture a few location shots: 'We used Montacute House in Somerset as our Baskerville Hall. Using a computer-generated composite we placed it into the

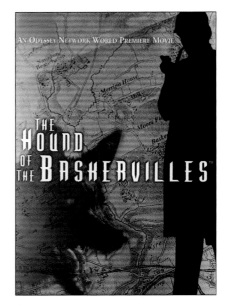

Canadian countryside.'

The Hound was a real dog, described by Frewer as 'a big, mean, jet black junkyard dog with one ear ripped up. We had one weird night with him. For a couple of shots he wore red contact lenses for effect. Looks very demonic. He lost one of the contact lenses and had everyone down on their knees searching for it while the dog relaxed in his trailer.'

What annoyed most viewers was the fact that Holmes disappears halfway through the film and only reappears at the very end (even later than in the novel), thus erasing so many dramatic moments involving the detective. Another trap the film fell into was the mismatching of Holmes' and Watson's ages. The script by Joe Wiesenfeld states clearly that Holmes is in his thirties and Watson in his fifties, when in Doyle's stories they are about the same age. Nevertheless, the best thing about the movie is Kenneth Welsh's solid and sensible Watson.

THE SIGN OF FOUR

TV movie
FIRST SCREENING 23 March 2001
PRODUCTION COMPANY Muse Entertainment Enterprises
in association with Hallmark Entertainment
DURATION 90 minutes
Colour
DIRECTOR Rodney Gibbons

India, 1856. Jonathan Small (Edward Yankie) is incarcerated for stealing the Agra treasure. Years later, Mary Morstan (Sophie Lorain) receives a lustrous pearl, along with a note beckoning her to a mysterious meeting. She consults Sherlock Holmes (Matt Frewer) and Doctor Watson (Kenneth Welsh), who accompany her and encounter Thaddeus Sholto (Marcel Jeannin), whose father served with Mary's in India. Together the two men took the treasure from Small. Major Sholto returned to England and hid the treasure in his home, Pondicherry Lodge. He confessed his secret on his deathbed, urging his twin sons to share the treasure with Mary. At Pondicherry Lodge, Holmes and Watson discover Bartholemew Sholto, killed by a poison dart and the treasure missing. Holmes sends Watson to collect Toby the tracker hound, who leads them to a boat yard, where they learn that Small and his companion Tonga took a steam launch down river in readiness to leave the country. The Baker Street Irregulars locate the launch and, despite the hindrance of Inspector Jones (Michael Peron), Holmes manages to apprehend Small, who has tipped the treasure into the river. Tonga is despatched by one of his own poisoned darts.

Below: Several scenes for the film were shot on location in the historic part of Montreal.

THE SECOND OUTING WITH MATT FREWER AND Kenneth Welsh as Holmes and Watson is more satisfying than their first. This is partly due to greater screen time being given to Holmes, allowing him more opportunity to demonstrate his detective skills. However the opening scene in Baker Street is terrible, with Frewer appearing in a strange broad lapelled tweed jacket and wearing a Tam o' Shanter while literally scraping on his violin. The Great Detective looks ridiculous. As *Scarlet Street* observed: 'He looks like he is quite prepared to play... either *Kismet* or *Brigadoon* – or both at once.'

In the novel the story climaxes with a chase down the Thames with Holmes, Watson and Inspector Athenley Jones in a police launch in hot pursuit of Jonathan Small and Tonga. However financial restraints ruled out such a spectacular finale in this production. As a result, scriptwriter Joe Wiesenfeld stages an exciting shootout on the dockside. This is just one of the interesting changes made to the original. For instance there is greater emphasis placed on Tonga's poisoned darts. Holmes realises that the potency of the poison makes the villains far more dangerous than is comprehended by the belligerent Inspector Jones. Holmes

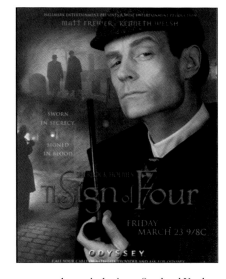

engages the pathologist at Scotland Yard to produce an antidote to the poison. (This comes as something of a surprise. One would expect Holmes to carry out the chemical work himself). The antidote proves invaluable when Watson is struck by a dart, an incident which allows the writer to show how concerned and affected Holmes is by his friend's potentially fatal wound. Indeed, pleasingly, much is made of the friendship between the two men throughout the movie with, at one point, Holmes actually apologising to Watson for his brusque manner. Writer Bert Coules observed in *Sherlock*: '...unlike some screen pairings there is real chemistry here, evidence of a real history and real affection.'

The appearance of both villains is changed significantly from the novel: Small no longer has a wooden leg, merely a damaged one and Tonga is an oriental of normal size and not Doyle's pygmy.

Scarlet Street urged viewers to stick with the film beyond the first scene, 'for it offers its own rewards, if not exactly a treasure.'

MURDER ROOMS — THE PATIENT'S EYES

TV movie
FIRST SCREENING 4 September 2001
PRODUCTION COMPANY BBC TV
DURATION 90 minutes
Colour
DIRECTOR Tim Fywell

In 1882. Arthur Conan Doyle (Charles Edwards), now a qualified doctor, has left Edinburgh University and travelled to Portsmouth to take up a medical post with an old colleague, Dr Turnavine (Alexander Armstrong), whom Doyle discovers is a charlatan. Doyle is consulted by Heather Grace (Katie Blake), a young woman who is being stalked by a demonic figure. Doyle's mentor, Joseph Bell (Ian Richardson), arrives on the scene and involves himself in the investigation. Heather was previously engaged to a Captain Horler (David Maybrick) who apparently rejected her and went off to fight in the Boer War. The pair interview Heather's uncle, who wants her to marry his friend Greenwell (Andrew Woodall). Doyle suspects that both men covet Heather's impending inheritance, but then Greenwell is murdered and Heather goes missing. Bell and Doyle find Heather in the tunnels that run underneath the wood. She is held there by Horler, disfigured and unhinged by his experiences in the war. Bell discovers that Horler killed Greenwell on Heather's instructions. Bell promises to keep her secret if Heather ensures that Horler is dealt with leniently. She leaves the town unrepentant and wealthy.

Below: Charles Edwards as the new, more mature Conan Doyle, with his mentor Joseph Bell (Ian Richardson).

DAVID PIRIE, CREATOR OF THE MURDER ROOMS format, contributed only one script to this four-part series and with it he indulged not only his love of the Holmes stories but also his passion for horror. He had scripted a darkly flamboyant version of Wilkie Collins' *The Woman in White* for the BBC in 1997, which was also directed by Tim Fywell, and now they injected the same mood of bold melodrama into the clever but rather convoluted plot of *The Patient's Eyes*. We have all the usual gothic trappings here: the lovely heroine whose life is apparently in danger, the suggestion of the supernatural provided by a ghastly apparition, various schemings of unscrupulous individuals, and murder. Added to this rich mixture were elements plucked from one of Doyle's best known Holmes tales, 'The Solitary Cyclist', in which a young woman cycles along a lonely stretch of countryside and is followed at a distance by a dark stranger also on a bicycle. In this film the stalker is a frightening hooded figure straight out of the pages of an M. R. James ghost story. It is thanks to Richardson's solid, understated performance as Bell that this rich concoction does not sink into risible pastiche.

Part of Pirie's cleverness is in using some true biographical detail in the story. For example, Doyle's trip to Portsmouth, his employment there and the eventual breakdown of his relationship with Turnavine are inserted seamlessly into his fictional confection. At one point Turnavine says of his patients, 'you must break them in early and keep 'em to heel', which is a direct quote from Doyle's autobiography.

This first episode gives the Doyle character very little to do but trot behind in Bell's footsteps, but both actors knew that they were in essence setting up the series and they were concerned that they should present themselves as individuals and not versions of Holmes and Watson. Edwards, who was perhaps a little too lean and too handsome to give us an accurate portrayal of ACD, stated that he would defend that idea that they were not just Holmes and Watson clones 'most vigorously': 'Doyle is far more a participant than Watson is. In these films Doyle comes up with many of his own ideas and solutions. Bell and Doyle are much more of an equal partnership. Doyle is a greater challenge than Watson ever was for Holmes.' However, we glimpse only a suggestion of this in *The Patient's Eyes*. The full realisation of the relationship between the two men and their equality was to come later with other writers who were not perhaps as entrenched in the Holmes genre as Pirie.

The script of *The Patient's Eyes* was turned into a novel by Pirie and was the first of his *Murder Rooms* series of books. The other titles are *The Night Calls* (2003), based on the first *Murder Rooms* script; and *The Dark Water* (2004), which is a direct sequel to the previous book but was not filmed.

MURDER ROOMS — THE PHOTOGRAPHER'S CHAIR

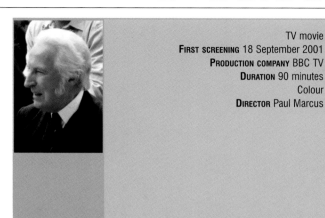

TV movie
FIRST SCREENING 18 September 2001
PRODUCTION COMPANY BBC TV
DURATION 90 minutes
Colour
DIRECTOR Paul Marcus

In 1883, Southsea. The pain that Doyle feels for his lost love Elspeth deepens. Several mutilated corpses are washed up on the beach. Each of the bodies has been asphyxiated but they also have mysterious signs of bruising around the back of the neck. Doyle is asked by Inspector Warner (Simon Chandler) to help in the investigations. Bell arrives to assist. Traces of chemicals found on the bodies lead the pair to believe that the murderer is a photographer. Doyle has become friendly with Miss Petchey (Clare Holman) a medium, whom he hopes will bring him a message from Elspeth. While Bell's detective work leads him to Mitchell (David Hayman), a talented photographer who records the street life of the poor, Doyle encounters Lord Edward Rhodes (Tim Woodward), Miss Petchey's patron, whose wife has died. He claims to have seen her spirit leave her body at the point of death. He is the murderer, carrying out his mission to try and photograph the victim's spirits as they die. He attempts to kill Doyle clamped in the photographer's chair, but Bell comes to the rescue.

Right: Joseph Bell (Richardson) returns to Edinburgh by train after helping his old pupil solve the case.

THE SCRIPT BY PAUL BILLING VERY CLEVERLY blends genuine biographical details about Doyle and Bell into a very satisfying murder mystery. It is appropriate that photography plays a central role in the plot, for Doyle was an avid photographer and wrote several articles on the subject. Similarly, after his harsh Jesuit education, he had rejected organised religion and had become 'an agnostic', as he claims in this film. He later formed an interest in spiritualism, which developed into an all-embracing passion in the closing stages of his life. This production suggests how the seeds of his convictions were sown.

Also biographical veracity is demonstrated in the tender scene where Bell confesses to Doyle how he was bereft when his wife died and initially sought the help of a medium only to discover that she was a fraud. Another effective touch is when we glimpse the photograph that Mitchell has taken of Bell and see that it resembles the famous picture of the great doctor. It also reveals that in his make up and with that white wig, how much Richardson looked like Bell.

Richardson read widely on the character of Joseph Bell and became an expert on the man. When I met him on set at Bray Studios in May 2001 he was eloquent about how his approach to the character had changed from the *Murder Rooms* pilot to the series: 'When I did *Murder Rooms* there was one tragic fact about Bell's life about which I was singularly ignorant. And that was the loss of his son. For about three hundred years the Bells had been physicians. After three daughters, Joe Bell has a son. In giving birth, his poor wife dies of peritonitis. Bell's hair goes white but he has a son. However son Benjamin was to reject the medical profession of his forbears and join the army. It was a tragic blow to Bell but he rode it out; what he found difficult to ride out was the loss of his son who fell ill with appendicitis, and died of peritonitis. Here we have a situation where Joe Bell loses a son, his hope, his future — but also his son as a medical practitioner. On the other hand we have Conan Doyle whose father is an insane alcoholic in an institution and so

to all intents and purposes is fatherless. And so the two come together and there is a special unspoken bond between them.'

This episode, the second in the series, was due to be broadcast on Tuesday 11 September 2001 but was cancelled because of the terrible events that took place in New York that day: the destruction of the Twin Towers. It is possible that this break in the rhythm of the series, and the fact that suddenly the world had more serious things to things to consider than a Victorian detective drama, may well be the reason *Murder Rooms* never fully recovered its audience and thus was not recommissioned.

MURDER ROOMS —
THE KINGDOM OF BONES

TV movie
First screening 25 September 2001
Production company BBC TV
Duration 90 minutes
Colour
Director Simon Langton

To raise the profile of his museum, Reuben Proctor (Crispin Bonham Carter), a friend of Conan Doyle, organises a public exhibition in which a recently purchased Egyptian mummy is unwrapped. Joseph Bell is engaged to perform a post mortem — but the mummy is a fake: the wrappings reveal a recently murdered corpse. In attendance is Donovan (Ian McNeice), an Irish American who invites Doyle and Bell to his mansion which is filled with antiquities, revealing his passionate interest in Celtic history. As Bell and Doyle grow nearer to the truth, a hooded figure sets fire to the laboratory while Bell is working there. He makes a last minute escape from the flames. The hooded figure is revealed as Gladys Donovan (Caroline Carver), whose father heads a cell of Fenian terrorists. Although Doyle is captured, he manages to escape but fails to save Miss Donovan's life when her horse is spooked by a circus elephant. At the climax, Doyle and Bell race to the church which Donovan, a suicide bomber, intends to blow up. Doyle tries to talk him out of it and Donovan falls to his death before he can carry out his plan.

Below and right:
Richardson and Edwards have final touches to their make-up before filming a scene.

*T*he *Kingdom of Bones* starts very well. Along with the dramatic revelation that the mummy wrappings contain a recently murdered man, we are introduced to another character from Doyle's past, one of his real-life teachers, Professor Rutherford of Edinburgh University, who became the inspiration and model for the writer's irascible Professor Challenger. Scriptwriter Stephen Gallagher observed: 'Rutherford was brilliantly played by John Sessions. If I'd known how good he was going to be I'd have made the part a lot bigger!'

On arriving at Southsea with Rutherford, Bell observes, ruefully, 'I had ten hours of him in a locked compartment on the night train – he doesn't sleep.'

The Challenger connection is hinted at in the very opening of the film when we see Doyle attending a slide show given by an explorer (played by Richardson's son, Miles) who claims that he is off to investigate a 'great unknown plateau of the South Americas... a land unseen since the world began'.

However, as the film progresses, the story becomes wilder causing the reviewer in the *Sherlock* magazine to observe that it developed into 'a boy's own caper' with the script disintegrating 'into a B movie with a preposterous climax — a sort of Victorian James Bond finale.'

This may well have been the desired effect, for Stephen Gallagher viewed the project thus: 'I loved the idea of doing Holmesian stories without all the added baggage that Sherlock Holmes has picked up over the years, but out of Conan Doyle's work I love *The Lost World* even more. So the underlying scheme of *The Kingdom of Bones* was to deconstruct *The Lost World* and scatter its elements in Doyle's imagination so that they could re-emerge as the completed work a dozen or so years later. Rather than do Holmes pastiche, I followed Doyle in adopting the more fast-moving, action-driven style of Rider Haggard in the plotting.'

One amusing visual aside occurs when Doyle goes to visit the circus camp and we see that one of the exhibits is advertised on a garish poster as: 'An unbelievable spectacle — the giant rat of Sumatra.'

However, the main interest and focus of the series remains Richardson's magnetic performance. He is so clever at suggesting the sharpness and brilliance of his mind like Sherlock Holmes, while at the same time maintaining a warmer and more attractive personality. The actor recalled an event from Bell's career to illustrate this aspect of the man: 'Bell's first and foremost object in life was the saving of life. There was an incident in his young days when he was on his rounds and came across a child who was in an advanced state of diphtheria. He had not the wherewithal to save the child's life. He couldn't perform an instant tracheotomy so he placed a tube down the boy's throat, which was filling up and choking him to death, and sucked the poison out. Unfortunately for Bell he actually swallowed some of it and was ill for a long time. He was that selfless.'

MURDER ROOMS —
THE WHITE KNIGHT STRATAGEM

TV movie
FIRST SCREENING 2 October 2001
PRODUCTION COMPANY BBC TV
DURATION 90 minutes
Colour
DIRECTOR Paul Marcus

Joseph Bell (Ian Richardson) is called in by the Edinburgh police to help solve the murder of a financier. He asks Doyle (Charles Edwards), who is visiting the city, to assist him. The investigation leads to a conflict between Bell and Lieutenant Blaney (Rik Mayall), with whom Bell has had past dealings. Blaney had proved obstructive in a previous case and now seems to delight in challenging Bell, the 'dabbling dilettante'. Bell requests Blaney be removed from the case for incompetence, but Doyle cannot understand his mentor's attitude and apparently sides with Blaney. A coolness develops between the two friends. Doyle is amazed that Bell appears to be struggling with the investigation and making mistakes. This forces Doyle to take the lead role to help out his old mentor. Ironically this strengthens the friendship. Doyle eventually explains that he supported Blaney because he suspected that he was trying to hide something. His investigations lead him to believe that Blaney is in fact the killer. With Bell he secures the evidence to prove this and faced with the truth, Blaney commits suicide.

HAVING RUN OUT OF IDEAS OF HOW TO DRAG Bell all the way from Edinburgh to Southsea, the *Murder Rooms* team decided to set this adventure on his own patch. The closeness between Bell and Doyle is established in the opening scenes which show Doyle visiting his father in the mental institution. Unwittingly the young doctor reveals that he intends to see Dr Bell while he is in Edinburgh. At this news his father throws a jealous fit, outraged to be placed in the role of 'second fiddle' by his son.

Doyle is given more detective work to do in this story and we can see how he is not only assimilating the talents of his old teacher but taking on the deductive mantle of Sherlock Holmes. There is one scene in particular in which Doyle makes a series of deductions concerning a pair of gloves in which he is able to establish that the owner is ambidextrous, smokes a great deal and does most of his smoking out of

doors. This is pure Sherlock.

Scriptwriter Daniel Boyle, who wrote many of the shows in the *Morse* series, teases the viewers in one scene where Bell is in a gent's outfitters and he picks up a deerstalker: 'I can't see an occasion but...' he ponders. He eventually presents the hat to Doyle's younger brother.

Perhaps the most interesting casting of the whole series is found in this episode with comedian Rik Mayall playing the villain — and playing him very well.

The episode closes with Doyle at his desk and a voice over revealing his thoughts about 'the strange adventures the doctor and I had been through': 'Could I ever capture them, perhaps in a series of tales, never to be recognised as the cases on which they are based? For the moment I fail. But my recollections of the doctor remain so vivid. I would see again that steely gaze, imagine him calling my name,

summoning me back to his rooms of murder. What could I not yet know was that some of the most horrifying rooms were still to be revealed.' This was obviously a set up for more stories. When I met Ian Richardson on set of *The White Knight Stratagem*, I asked if he hoped there would be a further series. He said: 'Let me be honest with you. I am too old for the part. Bell was in his late forties, very early fifties at this period and I am in my sixties. Nobody else but me seems to think that is a problem. Perhaps it isn't, but it is a thought that is constantly at the back of my mind. If there is another series, I shall be another year older at least. Having said all that, I would enjoy doing another series, provided they don't cut back on the budget and the length of time they give.' Alas, it never materialised. While the initial *Murder Rooms* two-parter garnered great praise from the press, the series passed by unnoticed.

Above left: *Richardson and Edwards pose for a picture on the cramped set of Bell's laboratory at Bray Studios.*
Above right: *Bell (Richardson) examines a specimen, hoping it will provide him with a vital clue.*

THE ROYAL SCANDAL

TV movie
FIRST SCREENING 19 October 2001
PRODUCTION COMPANY Muse Entertainment Enterprises
In association with Hallmark Entertainment
DURATION 90 minutes
Colour
DIRECTOR Peter Hammond

Holmes (Matt Frewer) is consulted by the future Kaiser of the German Empire (Robin Wilcox) to recover a compromising photograph of him and Irene Adler (Liliana Komorowska). In disguise, Holmes secures the photograph but realises that Adler is selling the plans of a secret submarine to the man she is blackmailing, the photograph being her only means of insurance. The photograph is locked away in Watson's (Kenneth Welsh) safe deposit box. Mycroft Holmes (R. H. Thomson) insists that his brother hands over the picture because it would be of great use to the British government. He refuses. Adler visits Holmes but her attempt to seduce him for the photograph fails. Holmes investigates the murder of the clerk whom he believes sold Adler the secret plans, and deduces that the body was thrown from the roof of a train. He traces the location and spies Adler passing over the last set of plans to an emissary of the Kaiser. He soon learns that he has been fooled not only by Adler but also by his brother. Adler is a double agent working for the British government and has been passing on false plans to the Germans.

Below: Holmes and Irene Adler (Liliana Komorowska).
Below left: *Kenneth Welsh as Watson.*

THE HALLMARK SERIES IMPROVES WITH THIS feature as though all involved were gaining confidence. Frewer's Holmes is gradually coming down from those strained comic heights of strange costumes (remember those Persian slippers and smoking cap from the first movie?) and even stranger face pulling exercises — in some scenes at least. Certainly Frewer's performance still irritates at times but less so than in the previous two films. In this outing we do have an almost believable and indeed human Sherlock Holmes. Maybe too human for some purists — not only crying at the opera (shades of Brett in 'The Red Circle') but also falling under the romantic spell of a beautiful woman is perhaps taking the character one step too far. However the relationship with Kenneth Welsh's excellent Watson is believable and touching. This Watson is neither a comic character nor a lap dog. He is presented as Doyle would have him: loyal, brave and with a fierce independent spirit.

Scriptwriter Joe Wiesenfeld is still sticking with Doyle for his source material but in this movie he attempts to blend two of the Holmes short stories together: 'A Scandal in Bohemia' and 'The Bruce Partington Plans'. Key dramatic elements from both narratives are used effectively but in order to help link the two plots, Irene Adler has now become an international spy and criminal misstressmind as well as an opera singer, and she is no longer from New Jersey but Poland. (That's probably because the actress playing her was Polish.) Irene's dalliance with Holmes is handled subtly and if you can take the notion of Sherlock falling in love — not a new idea, William Gillette was the first to use it — then it works reasonably well here, because it's done by suggestion and nuance rather than overtly.

The unusual but interesting aspect of the script is the way that Holmes is presented as a rather a weak character. He is fooled by Irene Adler and by his brother,

who is not only Her Majesty's Chief of Intelligence but appears to be a far tougher nut than Sherlock. Indeed Holmes refers to him as 'a caged tiger with very sharp claws.' (R. H. Thomson gives us a svelte, suave and handsome Mycroft.) Also Watson is very active in this story — he even appears in disguise — and in the mortuary when the pathologist passes judgement on how the traitor Cadogan West died, it is Watson rather than Holmes who corrects him, explaining at length his deductions. Holmes looks on beaming with pleasure like a proud father. 'Excellent Watson,' he cries when the doctor has finished. The script tends to crumble away towards the end, partly because not enough is made of the stolen submarine plans. However *The Royal Scandal* is the best in the Frewer/Welsh series so far. While sticking to Doyle as the core influence of the plot, this production attempts to do something fresh and original with the material and that is a real bonus.

THE CASE OF THE WHITECHAPEL VAMPIRE

TV movie
FIRST SCREENING 9 October 2002
PRODUCTION COMPANY Muse Entertainment Enterprises
In association with Hallmark Entertainment
DURATION 90 minutes
Colour
DIRECTOR Rodney Gibbons

One of the monks of the abbey of St Justinian the Martyr in Whitechapel is found dead, the apparent victim of a vampire. For Brother Marstoke (Shawn Laurence), this death has a horrifying resonance. Several years earlier his order founded a mission in South America where there was an outbreak of rabies. Believing that vampire bats were carriers of the disease, Marstoke had a colony of them destroyed against the wishes of a local naturalist, Dr Chagras (Neville Edwards). Soon afterwards two monks were found dead with puncture marks at the neck, apparently a revenge attack by Desmodo, the local vampire god. Marstoke believes that this demon has followed him to England. Holmes (Matt Frewer) maintains the killings are the work of a human hand but even he, when he visits the abbey and begins his investigations, begins to doubt his own convictions. He is presented with several suspects including Marstoke, Dr Chagas, who is in London to present a lecture on vampire bats, and Brother Abel (Tom Rack), a benign simpleton. It is Abel who is revealed as the murderer when Holmes in disguise sets himself up as the next victim.

Right: Welsh and Frewer in traditional garb.
Below: Holmes in disguise as a monk, hot on the trail of the killer.

HALLMARK WENT OUT ON A LIMB WITH THIS, the last of the Matt Frewer Holmes movies. They ditched Doyle altogether and went for an original screenplay written by the director Rodney Gibbons. The plot was an uneasy mix of gothic horror story and detective mystery. We are in *The Hound of the Baskervilles* and *The Scarlet Claw* territory (the murder weapon turns out to be a pronged garden weeder), where the audience are led to believe for a time that the murders may well be the work of a supernatural fiend. Brother Marstoke believes this is the case which raises the question as to why he would enlist the services of a private detective, well known for his clinical approach to crimefighting based on logic, reason and deduction and also for his marked disdain for those things that allegedly go bump in the night. Marstoke is a badly conceived

character: he states that he believes there is more than one God and he keeps relics of pagan statues in his office. Not ideal behaviour for the head monk of a Christian abbey.

This is just one of the questionable elements of this production. Take the abbey itself, situated in Renfield Place (a *Dracula* reference) in Whitechapel. Where else in the world would you find monks and nuns living together under one roof? At one point Marstoke denies having gone out from the Abbey at night. Holmes says, 'But your shoes are scuffed and covered in mud.' Surely monks wear sandals not shoes? And why, after the first murder does Holmes pronounce to Marstoke, 'Your enemy is certainly the most ruthless and resourceful of foes?' Holmes hasn't even examined the body or visited the abbey at this juncture, so what evidence prompts him to make such a claim? However, this rather overblown statement reflects the attitude of the director/writer who said of the movie: 'Every shot, every line and every scene is designed to create relentless tension and complications.'

To this viewer, it's all a bit slapdash and Frewer's Holmes is back face-pulling and elongating his words unnecessarily. He is not helped by his costume designer, Luc J. Beland. As the reviewer in *Sherlock* magazine observed, 'it is tempting to assume that Luc's middle initial stands for 'Jumblesale'.' Indeed Holmes' outfits at times veer towards the bizarre. There is one scene where he wears what one must assume is supposed to be a smoking jacket, that looks as though has been constructed from a piece of shag pile carpet. Although there are some effective moments, in the end *The Case of the Whitechapel Vampire* does fall prey to some of its own inconsistencies. It proves difficult to follow, is scarce in its clues, and troubling in some of its unchristian elements. It seems that without the 'divine intervention' at the end, when an earth tremor causes a religious statue to fall on the murderer just as he is about to shoot our detective hero, Watson would be reaching for his black arm band.

SHERLOCK — CASE OF EVIL

TV movie
FIRST SCREENING 5 August 2002
PRODUCTION COMPANY Box TV/Pueblo Films Production
DURATION 100 minutes
Colour
DIRECTOR Graham Theakston

In an attempt to save Lady DeWinter's reputation, Holmes (James D'Arcy) tracks down Professor Moriarty (Vincent D'Onofrio) and apparently shoots him dead, but his body cannot be found. Holmes had a personal vendetta against Moriarty, who had lured his bother Mycroft (Richard E. Grant) into opium addiction in his youth. Holmes gains notoriety in the press and society for ridding London of the villain. He meets Doctor Watson (Roger Morlidge) for the first time. Together, they start an investigation into the murders of several drug crimelords. Holmes becomes convinced that there one man is behind the killings — Moriarty, who plans to hold the monopoly of drug dealing in London. As he is supposedly dead, Holmes finds it hard to convince Inspector Lestrade (Nicholas Gecks) of his theory. Holmes' investigations lead him to a beautiful prostitute (Gabrielle Anwar), whom he discovers was a puppet of the Professor's, who posed as a Lady DeWinter to lure him into the plot. Holmes falls in love with her but in his final confrontation with Moriarty the villain shoots the girl. Holmes kills Moriarty who falls to his death through the clock face of Big Ben.

PRINCIPAL PHOTOGRAPHY FOR THIS MOVIE began in early November 2001 and was completed by Mid-December. The entire film was shot in Romania, with several sets, such as Baker Street, created in the Castel Film Studios, located in the little village of Snagov, famous for being the burial place of Prince Vlad Tepes, aka Dracula. CGI technology was used to add certain notable London landmarks like St Paul's Cathedral and Big Ben, which plays an important part in the finale. The film scores visually also with its wonderful street scenes, providing an interesting view of a Victorian London which is not overcrowded with extras in garish costumes.

Sherlock – Case of Evil is a bold and innovative film which presents us with a young Holmes and Watson. Not young as in the teenage version of Spielberg's movie but young as in Conan Doyle's first outing, *A Study in Scarlet*. So often film-makers have been determined or at least content to present Sherlock Holmes and his biographer as middle-aged men, ignoring

Holmes changes, the process culminating in a very telling symbolical scene where he burns all his past press cuttings, which earlier had meant so much to his vanity.

Vincent D'Onofrio gives us a smooth

'Forget all the cliches you've been used to in all Sherlock Holmes stories and movies. This is where the Legend begins.'

the fact that Doyle presented the characters initially as men in their early prime. At the very end of his career, at the time of 'His Last Bow', Holmes is referred to as a man of some sixty years.

With his youthful good looks and at times his gauchness and immature arrogance, James D'Arcy presents a very believable, feisty portrait of how the young Sherlock Holmes might have been. (Holmes 'with an L' as he points out to a police officer). Indeed, not only do Lestrade and Watson dislike this jumped up private detective on first encountering him, but so do the audience. This is the cleverness of the script by Piers Ashworth, for we see as the story progresses the character's growing and credible maturity.

and jaunty Moriarty. No dessicated, bald pated, geriatric mathematician he, but a robust and grinning malefactor with the substantial bulk of a young Orson Welles and the voice of the silky James Mason. However, the script does present him as a gangland boss — a sort of Victorian Al Capone — rather than the highly intellectual brilliant schemer that Conan Doyle gave us.

Roger Morlidge's Watson is portrayed with fire and individuality. There is no sense that this doctor is in mesmerised awe of the detective. No Nigel Bruces need apply! This Watson recognises Holmes' potential and is instrumental in moulding the brilliant but arrogant young Sherlock into a sensitive and disciplined detective, encouraging him

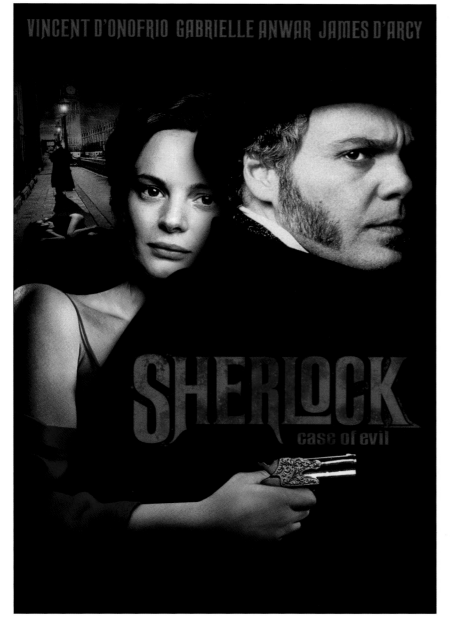

to have faith in his own ability after doubts begin to assail his confidence. This portrayal of Watson is not only the most interesting aspect of this film but the best thing to happen to the character in a long while.

However, one thing that never seems to change in a Holmes film is the character of Inspector Lestrade (Nicholas Gecks), who is at first belligerent and antagonistic towards Holmes and then grudgingly respectful at the end.

Richard E. Grant is seen briefly as a very lean Mycroft. He is also virtually a cripple, the result we must assume, judging by the eerie flashbacks, of Moriarty injecting him with drugs in his youth. Frustratingly, this aspect of the plot is never fully explained. Holmes visits his reclusive brother at the Diogenes Club and indulges in 'the old game' of deducing facts about people they observe in the street outside. This scene is a close approximation of the one featured in Doyle's 'The Greek Interpreter'.

This film also presents us with an alternative version of how Holmes and Watson meet. It is filmed in a flashy comic book style with dialogue peppered — I suspect deliberately — with anachronisms: Watson refers to an 'autopsy' and Holmes to 'serial killers' which only replaced the standard terminology of 'post-mortem' and 'mass murderers' well into the twentieth century. But with its violent, action Western-style gunfights, this movie is not just one for the new millenium, but one aimed at the youth market who wouldn't know or care about such anomalies.

As the film concludes we have the familiar set up: Holmes and Watson, who is writing up the case, are sharing rooms on Baker Street: Holmes has just been given a curly pipe by the good doctor and his aunt has sent him a deerstalker cap. As he dons the cap and sticks the pipe in his mouth, Watson takes his photograph and the iconic image is born.

The film is a radical reconstruction of the dark beginings of Sherlock Holmes, and as such is a welcome breath of fresh air.

THE HOUND OF THE BASKERVILLES

TV movie
First screening 26 December 2002
Production company Tiger Aspect Productions/BBC
Duration 100 minutes
Colour
Director David Attwood

Sir Charles Baskerville dies under mysterious circumstances. Dr Mortimer (John Nettles) believes his death is connected with the legend of the Hound of the Baskervilles and fears for the safety of the new heir, Sir Henry (Matt Day). He consults Holmes (Richard Roxburgh), who despatches Watson (Ian Hart) to accompany Sir Henry to Baskerville Hall on Dartmoor. Watson discovers Barrymore (Ron Cook) the butler signalling to a man on the moor, who turns out to be the servant's brother-in-law, Selden (Paul Kynman), an escaped convict. Watson encounters Stapleton (Richard E. Grant) and his sister Beryl (Neve McIntosh). Thinking that he is Sir Henry, Beryl tries to persuade him to return to London. Holmes discovers Holmes camping out on the moor, watching events from a distance. Following the cry of the hound they find Selden's mutilated body. He was attacked because he was wearing an old suit of clothes belonging to Sir Henry. Holmes sets a trap for the murderer Stapleton, who kills Beryl — actually his wife — because she refuses to help him. The hound is killed. Stapleton is about to shoot Holmes, who has fallen into the Grimpen Mire, when he is killed by Watson.

THIS PARTICULAR VERSION OF *THE HOUND* WAS designed as a slightly chilling post-Christmas television treat for Boxing Day 2002. To help fit in with the mood of the season, a Christmas party at Baskerville Hall was actually shoe-horned into the script and the climax on the moor takes place on Christmas Day.

Jack Tranter, BBC Controller of Drama at the time, announced that '[the film] is for an adult audience and features a genuinely frightening hound using the latest special effects technology. The film is set when it was written in 1901, in a time of great flux and change, London is welcoming in a new age of electric light and internal combustion engines while the moorland of Dartmoor is like the wild west

— bleak, inhospitable and lawless.' Sadly very little of the contrast between town and country found its way into the film, and the hound when it appeared, despite all the wizardry of the computer graphics or maybe because of it, was a terrible disappointment. And it did not glow in the dark, which is one of the most frightening aspects of the beast. As one reviewer remarked, 'Scooby Doo would not only have been more convincing, but also more frightening.'

Filming began on 8 April 2002 on the Isle of Man, with the Baker Street exteriors shot in Liverpool. The script was written by Allan Cubitt, who according to the pre-publicity pored over numerous film versions of *The Hound* looking to clarify the structure and 'discover which characters and which scenes were necessary.' Laura Lyons, along with the litigious Mr Frankland from the novel were in the end elbowed out of the way, but they were present in the original screenplay, only to fall foul of the BBC's insistence that the running time was reduced by nearly thirty minutes. However, Mrs Mortimer and the séance scene created for the 1939 Fox version were assimilated into the new script. Of course there are

bound to be changes with every new production of this tale, the writer wishing to make omissions and to inject something fresh into the project. Nevertheless, Cubitt's version is for the most part true to the Doyle novel and when it does veer off the path, it tends to improve upon the source material. The script does allow Holmes some actual detective work. For example, by collecting soil samples from the cab which has been trailing him he is able to establish that his stalker is from Dartmoor. The most impressive change is in the dramatic finale where Watson comes into his own. After the hound has been killed, he discovers that Beryl Stapleton has been hanged by her husband in one of the outbuildings. Enraged at the murder, he wreaks revenge on Stapleton by killing him.

Perhaps the most controversial aspect of the whole production is the presentation of Holmes' drug use. Shortly after Dr Mortimer has consulted him, we see Holmes inject himself; and he does so again while down on Dartmoor. This is in direct contradiction of Doyle's use of the detective's drug habit, which manifested

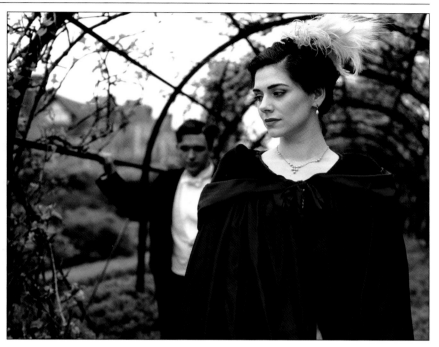

itself only when he was bored and there was no mystery on hand to occupy his mind. While on a case, he needed no further stimulation. The drug scenes add nothing to the plot or the character and just seem just like sensational dressing.

Much was made of the (comparative) youth of the leading actors. Richard Roxburgh (Holmes) was 40 and Ian Hart (Watson) was 38 at the time of filming. However they lacked chemistry. This is due perhaps to the way their relationship is presented in the script. It is laced with cynicism, mistrust and constant bickering. Watson's last words to Holmes in the movie

are, 'No, I don't trust you.'

In general, the Roxburgh/Hart duo didn't please the press or the fans. One critic remarked that Hart was seemingly so determined not to be a comic, bumbly Watson that that he made the character a grumpy, charmless and humourless fellow. The big disappointment was Roxburgh. Of all the Holmes stories, you need the right man for this one. He was 'insipid and unintense' *(The Observer)*, 'unmemorable' (*The Times*) and according to *The Daily Mail*, 'Absent for a long time. Not that one missed him very much.' Supporters of Roxburgh claim that he presented the

ideal detached reasoner. For the majority, however, he was so detached as to be absent.

Yet again Richard E. Grant was included in a Sherlock Holmes film and yet again, despite his lean aquiline looks he was not cast as Sherlock Holmes. When one of the production team was asked why he hadn't been on the top of their list when they looking for a suitable actor to play the lead, the reply was, 'He would have been far too obvious a choice.' It is disappointing that he was denied the opportunity to play Sherlock, but he certainly acted this Holmes and Watson off the screen.

Previous page left:
Holmes and Watson (Richard Roxburgh and Ian Hart) on Dartmoor — in reality the wilds of the Isle of Man.
Previous page right:
Beryl Stapleton (Neve McIntosh) and her villainous brother (Richard E. Grant).
Above left: Roxburgh as Holmes.
Above right: Sir Henry (Matt Day) attempts to woo Beryl Stapleton (Neve McIntosh)
Far Left: Taking time out from Midsommer Murders, *John Nettles as Dr Mortimer.*
Left: Dressed for the city, Richard Roxburgh as Holmes.

THE STRANGE CASE OF SHERLOCK HOLMES AND ARTHUR CONAN DOYLE

TV movie
FIRST SCREENING 27 July 2005
PRODUCTION COMPANY BBC TV
DURATION 89 minutes
Colour
DIRECTOR Cilla Ware

At the age of 33, Arthur Conan Doyle (Douglas Henshall) appears happy and successful but he harbours deep secrets and fears. He is haunted by the fact that his father is locked away in a mental institution and troubled by the notion that his detective creation, Sherlock Holmes, is overwhelming his life. When his father dies in the asylum, Doyle mysteriously and controversially kills off Sherlock Holmes. While tending to his dying wife Louise (Saskia Reeves), he is tortured by his unconsummated passion for his new love Jean Leckie (Emily Blunt). It is during this disturbed period that Doyle agrees to cooperate with a biographer called Selden (Tim McInnerny) to work on an account of the author's life. Selden interviews characters who know Doyle, including Dr Joseph Bell (Brian Cox) and Doyle's mother (Sinead Cusack) and arrives at the conclusion that despite the author's claim to the contrary, his detective was not a cold 'calculating machine' but a highly emotional man like Doyle himself. Selden helps Doyle face his demons concerning his mother's infidelity and his own betrayal of his father and then reveals himself to be Sherlock Holmes.

Right: Arthur Conan Doyle (Douglas Henshall) imprisoned by his own creation.
Below: Henshall as Doyle: a fine, convincing performance.

Such was the success of BBC Scotland's excellent three-part drama documentary on Charles Dickens (with Anton Lesser portraying the author), they decided to give Conan Doyle the same treatment. The plan was to cover Doyle's life and work in three one-hour programmes. They employed a writer to research the project and prepare a detailed treatment. At first they approved heartily of this work in progress, but then the budget was cut and the filming was reduced to one ninety minute programme. At this time the executive producer decided there was not enough of Sherlock Holmes in the mix and so another writer was sought. Stepping into the breach was Mr *Murder Rooms* himself: David Pirie. His brief was to show the influence of the character Sherlock Holmes on the mind and life of Conan Doyle. As a result, his other writings and activities were largely ignored. Pirie stated: 'I didn't just want to do a drama documentary. I wanted to really get under the skin of Arthur Conan Doyle.'

The resultant screenplay is an imagined interpretation of the facts rather than a true biographical study. Pirie said at the time of production that: 'I've always wanted to know what led him to create Holmes, a character of depth and complexity. Arthur Conan Doyle... was a very emotional man driven in ways that have never been clearly explored. As Dr

Thomas Walmsley, a psychiatrist with a particular interest in the psychology of public people, observed: "For reasons that have yet to be fully explored, there seems to have been a greater tension between the public and the private in Sir Arthur Conan Doyle than in any other public figure I have ever studied with one possible exception, the former US President Richard Nixon."'

It is true that Conan Doyle suppressed much of his private life, presenting a bluff exterior to the public, but he suffered pangs of guilt about neglecting his father who died in a mental institution, and had a suppressed love affair with Jean Leckie which he apparently refused to consummate while his first wife was alive. The film reveals not only how family and friends were shocked at the way Doyle flaunted his relationship with Jean but also how the author was tortured by the

thought of his mother's close relationship with Dr Waller, who had helped the family in many ways when Doyle's father became too ill to work. Pirie uses the character of Holmes to uncover these guilty ghosts that governed Doyle's attitude to Sherlock Holmes — a character inspired by Dr Joseph Bell who became the heroic father figure that the author lacked. It has to be said that some of the psychology applied in this programme is a little unsound and at times illogical, but it does make for a fascinating drama. One scene is particularly clever in supporting Pirie's thesis. Doyle gives Bell a watch to deduce facts about the owner, who is in fact the author's alcoholic and mentally unstable father. It is a moment transposed from *The Sign of Four* and works well in illustrating both Doyle's guilt and how he was inspired by Bell's method of analysis.

UNFILMED SHERLOCK

THE CASE OF THE UNPRODUCED PROJECTS

Over the years there have been a number of Holmes films announced but never made. It would be impossible and probably unwise to attempt to catalogue them all, but here is an entertaining and illustrative sample of some fairly recent near misses.

THE SCRIPT *SHERLOCK HOLMES AND THE Vengeance of Dracula* is perhaps the most high profile of the unmade projects. It involves Professor Moriarty unwittingly bringing the coffin carrying Dracula to London. The Count has returned to seek revenge on Professor Van Helsing and his associates. When one of them dies in mysterious circumstances, Holmes investigates. Charles Pogue, who wrote the scripts for the two Ian Richardson Holmes movies, read this screenplay and was not wholly impressed: 'For the first 30-40 pages the script isn't too bad... but then it just unravels. First with Moriarty wanting Dracula to make him an 'immortal' vampire... [And] Moriarty and Holmes ultimately joining forces to defeat Dracula, which is not a terrible idea in itself, but falls apart in practice, particularly when you add Van Helsing in the mix... Suddenly, you have three of the greatest intellects in England working together — it just dilutes

the opportunity for Holmes to be brilliant. The ending is some bizarre *fèvre* dream. They trail Dracula to some gasworks where he's going to spill his blood into the gas system and disperse it into all the gas lamps of London, thereby turning everyone into vampires... Apart from the dodgy science/magic aspect of this, let's just look at the motive! Would Dracula really want to turn everybody in London into a vampyre? [The script] just becomes an utter mishmash of logic.'

Initially Christopher Columbus was due to direct the movie but he moved on, and the script wallowed in 'development hell'. Interest was maintained for a few years, but since 2004 there has been a deafening silence.

A less sensational movie which nearly made it was *The Abbott's Cry*, written as a sequel to *The Masks of Death*. In 1986 Tyburn planned to pair Peter Cushing and John Mills again in another pensioner Holmes caper. The script by N. J. Crisp was ready and Roy Ward Baker was lined up to direct when Cushing decided that he was too ill to film. Baker, who thought the plot was better than *Masks of Death*, said, 'The story, set in the 1920s, concerns a legend which curses a certain family. It begins at night with the figure at the top [of a church] who appears to spread its wings and hurl himself to the ground. We hear him cry — the abbott's cry. Holmes is asked to investigate but as in *The Hound of the Baskervilles*, he sends Watson off to investigate.'

Other casualties include two of my own works. In 1991, a film company took up an option on my Holmes/Dracula novel, *The Tangled Skein*. Nothing came of it. Then producer June Wyndham Davies was all set

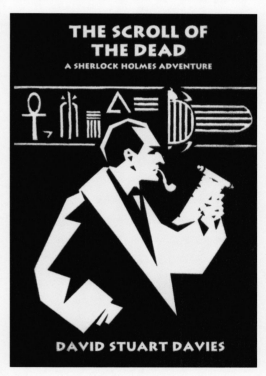

to go ahead with adapting my novel *Sherlock Holmes and the Scroll of The Dead* into a two-hour TV movie with Jeremy Brett, until Granada was told to revert to the one-hour shows. So my book was dropped.

Then there was *Elementary*, a script by Brian Helgeland which brought Moriarty, Jack the Ripper and even Buffalo Bill into the mix. Warner Brothers were developing this around 2001 but the project fizzled out. An animated Holmes series developed in the late 1970s never saw the light of day, but Carey Blyton's music for it was released on CD. And what ever happened to the TV film featuring Stephen Fry and Hugh Laurie as Holmes and Watson? Nothing. Though 'announced' by an excited press in 2004, it never actually got past the discussion stage.

SHERLOCK HOLMES AND THE CASE OF THE SILK STOCKING

TV movie
FIRST SCREENING 26 December 2004
PRODUCTION COMPANY Tiger Aspect Productions/BBC
DURATION 97 minutes
Colour
DIRECTOR Simon Cellan Jones

November, 1902. Dr Watson (Ian Hart) asks Holmes (Rupert Everett) to investigate a case that threatens to overwhelm aristocratic society. The body of a young girl has been washed up on the banks of the Thames. It is presumed that she's a prostitute. Holmes discovers a stocking wedged in her throat and he deduces that the body is that of a lady. As society prepares for the debutantes' seasonal performance, Georgina (Jennifer Moule), a young, vulnerable and heavily chaperoned young woman disappears. Scotland Yard's Inspector Lestrade (Neil Dudgeon) tries desperately to hunt down the kidnapper, but he is too late. Georgina's body is discovered, dressed in the clothes of the first victim, with a stocking lodged in her throat.

With the knowledge that a serial killer is now in operation, Holmes is galvanised into feverish action and Watson, despite his impending marriage to the beautiful Mrs Vandeleur (Helen McCrory), is drawn back to his friend's side. Holmes identifies the killer, but he has a watertight alibi. It is only when he discovers that the man in question is a twin, that he is able to act.

THE POOR CRITICAL RESPONSE AND THE disappointing viewing figures for Tiger Aspect's *The Hound of the Baskervilles*, along with Richard Roxburgh's reticence to play Holmes again, prompted the company to drop further plans to produce another

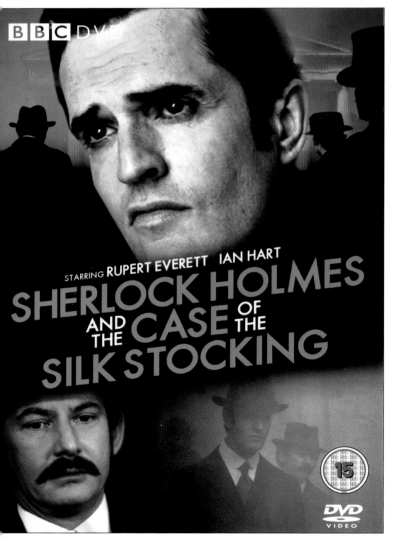

Sherlock vehicle. Scriptwriter Allan Cubitt had already been working on a fresh idea involving the detective and the character Dorian Gray, but because of the essential supernatural element at the heart of Oscar Wilde's story, he couldn't make it work.

When *The Hound* was repeated some months later it gained a much larger audience, so Tiger Aspect reversed its decision and told Cubitt to come up with a new screenplay. 'My first idea was that Jack the Ripper was back. I toyed with the idea that, about fifteen years later, around 1903, the murders started again.' This idea also failed to gel, but what Cubitt took from the exercise was the notion of Holmes tackling a serial killer. However he wanted to move the victims to the other end of the social spectrum: this time they were all to be debutantes — young aristocratic ladies making their début into society. It was also Cubitt's idea to marry Watson off in this outing: 'He marries an American widow, a psychoanalyst. No doubt that will appear to be a tremendous liberty on my part.'

It would seem that Cubitt drew a good deal of inspiration from Caleb Carr's novel *The Alienist* in his tale of a foot fetishist murderer with its elements of crime profiling and psychobabble. At one point Holmes observes, 'It's good to talk through such a traumatic experience.' The script had an uneasy contemporary feel to it, injecting a modern sadistic serial killer scenario into an Edwardian detective story.

The working title was *The Return of Sherlock Holmes*; then it became *Sherlock Holmes and the Deadly Season*, but those in power at the BBC thought it was somewhat doom-laden for a Christmas entertainment and so it became the risible

Sherlock Holmes and The Case of the Silk Stocking.

It is not a whodunnit. There are no clues presented to Holmes or the viewer in order to eliminate the suspects. In fact there are no suspects. It is up to Holmes, like a profiler, to gradually piece evidence together to build up a picture of the killer. The film is wreathed in fog, some produced by smoke machines and some added by CGI wizardry, symbolically representing the fog of the mystery Holmes is attempting to solve (whilst at the same time helping to save money by reducing the need for expensively mounted exterior scenes buzzing with extras).

Ian Hart returned to the role of Watson, still tetchy and without humour and still failing to convince us that he has a warm friendship with Holmes. However, we had a new Sherlock in Rupert Everett. Physically, he has a look and manner of Brett about him: he is tall, dark, handsome with saturnine features and a prominent nose, but producer Elinor Day was of the opinion that he was more like Rathbone. When I asked Allan Cubitt what he thought, he observed pointedly: 'I think he's very Rupert Everett to be honest.'

the sort of thing you have to face.'

Everett received mixed reviews. *The Daily Mail* stated, 'Sherlock Holmes, as reinvented by Rupert Everett, should have been a lot more special than it was'; while *The Daily Telegraph* noted that, 'Despite looking more like James Bond than Sherlock Holmes, Everett did a fine job of bringing out the man's less comfy aspects…'

While in general the reviews tended to suggest that Everett had made a reasonable if less than mesmerising stab at Holmes, they were unified in their verdict that the script was poor. It was full of anachronisms (telephones in Scotland Yard a year early, the use of phrases like 'crime scene' and 'I could murder a bottle of Monrachet') and it was peppered with second hand *bon mots* ('Save your breath to cool your porridge, Watson; I've always held that travel narrows the mind.' — all borrowed from other writers). It also broke one of the cardinal rules of crime fiction — set down by Ronald Knox — that you never use identical twins as the murderers. That's simply cheating. Nevertheless the movie did have some exciting moments and the production values were excellent. At times one could be forgiven for thinking one was watching a previously unreleased episode of the Granada series.

And certainly as Holmes he is at times rather louche, bordering on the camp. *The Daily Express* commented on the 'sexually ambiguous' nature of his performance. Everett's own ideas about Holmes did not always coincide with the scriptwriter's: 'I had a scene which illustrates Holmes' incredible untidiness. Watson returns to Baker Street to find the room a tip. You know 'he was the most untidy man that ever drove a fellow lodger to distraction' ['The Musgrave Ritual']. Now Rupert didn't want the place to be so untidy and he went around clearing things up. As a writer that's

Previous page left: The cover of the DVD, which was issued within weeks of the programme's transmission.
Previous page right: A pensive Rupert Everett as his louche version of Holmes.
Above left: A fine publicity shot of Holmes (Rupert Everett) and Watson (Ian Hart).
Above right: Another day, another hat: Rupert Everett as Holmes.
Left: Holmes considers the various locations of the stocking murders.

SHERLOCK HOLMES AND THE BAKER STREET IRREGULARS

	TV Serial
First screening	25 March and 1 April 2007
Production company	RDF Television/BBC
Duration	2 x 60 minutes
	Colour
Director	Julian Kemp

Sherlock Holmes (Jonathan Pryce) is called in by Scotland Yard to investigate the mysterious deaths of a number of police inspectors. He enlists the help of the Baker Street Irregulars. The detective suspects someone is clearing away all opposition, in order to carry out some audacious crime. When Holmes is framed for murder and placed under house arrest, it falls to the Irregulars to take on the case. But they have their own troubles: two of the gang have gone missing, and they are determined to have Holmes investigate the disappearance of their leader Jack (Benjamin Smith) and his sister Sadie (Mia Fernandez). Holmes has no choice but to agree and soon learns that the two mysteries are connected. As the Irregulars take to the streets in a series of disguises, they discover that the master criminal is Irene Adler (Anna Chancellor), who is about to pull off the crime of the century: a robbery at the London Mint. Holmes proves his innocence and there is an emotional re-union for brother and sister. With the aid of the Irregulars, Holmes traps Adler with the stolen bullion and she is arrested.

FOLLOWING THE RECENT SUCCESS OF FAMILY orientated programmes such as *Doctor Who* and *Robin Hood*, the BBC decided to return to Baker Street for a two-part serial aimed at the same kind of audience. The idea was that the show would appeal to the whole family grouping from the youngsters to the grandparents, particularly the former. Two of the writers of *Robin Hood*, Richard Kurti and Bev Doyle, were assigned the task. It was clear to them that if they were to pull in the youth audience, the Irregulars should have the lion's share of the screen time. In doing so they presented the six youngsters who make up the Irregulars as attractive, bright, gutsy and streetwise in order to appeal to teenagers of today. The writers furnished the gang with gestures and expressions that have a definite modern ring to them, for example: 'No probs', 'You're a nerd' and 'A girl is impressed with a man who has a set of wheels' (in this instance referring to roller skates). This particular bunch of Irregulars are like juvenile members of the *Mission Impossible* team, shinning up drainpipes, swapping precious stones, fooling the police and carrying out the most amazing heists for Mr 'Olmes. As director Julian Kemp observed: 'The scripts do have a contemporary feel while at same time respecting the original stories.' In essence the show is rather like the BBC's previous Irregulars series, *The Baker Street Boys* (1983), with a bigger budget and more pizzazz.

One of the plot devices, the main villain carrying out a series of inexplicable crimes as a smokescreen to hide the big heist, is similar to the one used in Rathbone's *The Adventures of Sherlock Holmes* (1939), in which another audacious robbery is planned.

The series was filmed in Dublin, where there are still plenty of Victorian locations untouched by time and the developers. It is a handsome production filmed in a fluid fast-moving style with quick, attention-holding scenes.

This show does what it says on the tin: it is entertaining for a family audience. However, as a Holmes vehicle it is faintly disappointing. Indeed, the weakest aspect of the project is the presentation of the Baker Street duo. Both characters are seen as well past middle age and somewhat staid.

Holmes is played by the wonderful actor Jonathan Pryce; but in this instance he fails to give us a mesmeric character, more of a kindly grandfather figure who plays parlour tricks with disappearing magnifying glasses. There is no dynamism or danger in his portrayal. One might argue that Pryce is playing the part purely as scripted and is giving us a bland kind of Sherlock to contrast effectively with the lively, resourceful and interesting Irregulars. Pryce stated that, 'we resisted a too stereotypical approach to Holmes. The deerstalker makes just one appearance and because it is made for family viewing smoking is discouraged.

As pipe smoking makes me nauseous, I was very happy not to light up.'

The press in general were in favour of Pryce's Sherlock. *The Hollywood Reporter* said: 'Pryce is one of those actors born to play Holmes and he uses his doleful eyes and expressive voice to good purpose with some delightful lines. When Watson says he deserves more acclaim for his work, the sleuth scornfully says the reading public is far more interested in the private lives of music hall performers than in the work of amateur detectives. 'Celebrity,' he declares,

'is the last refuge of the idiot.' Perhaps the verdict in *The Stage* hits the nail more accurately on the head: 'Jonathan Pryce chooses to play Holmes straight down the line, when other actors might have followed a quirkier route given this is a drama for, you know, kids. His take on Conan Doyle's creation adds a calm authority to proceedings that ensures things will be taken seriously.'

Watson is played by another well-respected actor, Bill Paterson. Sadly, he is given very little to do apart from establish his fondness for Battenberg cake and suggest that he still has a twinkle in his eye for the ladies.

The scriptwriters decided not to bring in the rather short-sighted, irascible Lestrade this time; instead we have a new character: the short sighted, irascible Inspector Irving played by Michael Maloney, who seems well aware that he is in a family tea-time show.

Perhaps the most interesting aspect of this production is the portrayal of Irene Adler, now seen as a kind of female Moriarty, albeit without a vast organisation. Her connection with Holmes and his apparent fondness for her adds an interesting frisson to the drama. Although she is captured at the end, the final shot of the movie seems to indicate that she is at large once more and up to mischief. This hint, along with several others, suggests that the two-parter is a pilot ready to engender a series. Pryce is very keen for that to happen: 'I hope this team can continue with what they have begun with the Irregulars.'

While Pryce's Holmes is the latest screen manifestation of Conan Doyle's universal hero, he will certainly not be the last. For over a hundred years Sherlock Holmes has proved to be an enduring and invincible film star and all the signs are that he will continue to be so.

Previous page left: Finch (Aaron Johnson) and The Master (Jonathan Pryce).
Previous page right: The elderly crimefighters: Watson (Bill Paterson) and Holmes (Jonathan Pryce).
Above left: The Baker Street Irregulars: Finch (Aaron Johnson), Tealeaf (Alice Hewkin), Sticks (Dean Gibbons), Jasmine (Megan Jones) and Sadie (Mia Ferdinand).
Top: A set of wheels comes in useful.
Above: Irene Adler (Anna Chancellor), femme fatale turned villain.
Left: Inspector Sinclair (Michael Maloney) arrests Holmes while Watson seems unmoved.

SHERLOCK HOLMES ON SCREEN

Hundreds of actors have played the character of Sherlock Holmes on the cinema and television screen. An even greater number have slapped a deerstalker on their heads and pretended to be a detective of sorts, but it would be impossible to list all the actors and actresses in this latter category. Nor is it possible to list all the productions that owe a large debt to Doyle's creation, such as the 1998 film *The Zero Effect*. However, the following filmography attempts to detail all the mainstream screen appearances of the master sleuth of Baker Street, as well as noting some of the more interesting oddities.

The films are noted thus: Title; original, alternative or literal translation title in brackets where applicable; page reference (where applicable); date of first screening; production company; country of origin; approximate duration in minutes/length in metres (with number of episodes where applicable); black and white/colour; silent/sound (where applicable); animation (where applicable); episode titles (where applicable); cast, or recurring cast followed by notable guest actors (with character names in brackets); selected technical/production credits where available: production design [Prod des], designer [Des], costume design [Cos des], set design [Set des], art direction [Art dir], editor [Ed], special effects [Sp effects], make-up, music [Mus], director of photography [Dp], screenplay [Scrp], based on/source of script [Bo], executive producer [Exec prod], associate producer [Assoc prod], producer [Prod], director [Dir].

For convenience's sake, the series of films produced by Éclair, Nordisk, Kowo Films (Germany) and Lenfilm (Soviet Union) have been grouped together under four entries, entitled Éclair, Nordisk, Sherlock Holmes and Soviet Sherlock Holmes respectively.

THE ADVENTURE OF SHERLOCK HOLMES' SMARTER BROTHER
(see pages 102-103)
14 December 1975. Roth/Jouer. USA. 91m. Colour.
Cast: Gene Wilder (Sigerson Holmes), Madeline Kahn (Jenny Hill), Marty Feldman (Sergeant Orville Sacker), Dom DeLuise (Gambetti), Leo McKern (Moriarty), Roy Kinnear (Finney), John Le Mesurier (Lord Redcliff), Douglas Wilmer (Sherlock Holmes), Thorley Walters (Dr Watson), George Silver (Bruner), Susan Field (Queen Victoria), Nicholas Smith (Hunkston), Tommy Godfrey (William), John Hollis (Moriarty's Gunman).
Selected credits: Mus: John Morris. Dp: Gerry Fisher. Scrp: Gene Wilder. Assoc prod: Charles Orme. Prod: Richard A. Roth. Dir: Gene Wilder.

THE ADVENTURE OF THE BLACK BARONET
(see pages 72-75)
26 May 1953. CBS-TV. USA. 30m. Black and white.
Cast: Basil Rathbone (Sherlock Holmes), Martyn Green (Dr Watson), Mary Howard (Lady Lavington), Anthony Drearless (Lavington), Members of the New York Baker Street Irregulars.
Selected credits: Scrp: Michael Dyne. Bo: 'The Adventure of the Black Baronet' by Adrian Conan Doyle and John Dickson Carr. Prod: Himan Brown. Dir: Robert Mulligan.

THE ADVENTURES OF SHERLOCK

HOLMES (1905)
- see *Held for Ransom*

THE ADVENTURES OF SHERLOCK HOLMES
(see pages 18-19)
1921. Stoll Picture Productions Ltd. UK. 15 x 35m. Black and white. Silent.
1 'The Dying Detective', 2 'The Devil's Foot', 3 'A Scandal in Bohemia', 4 'The Red-Headed League', 5 'A Case of Identity', 6 'The Man With the Twisted Lip', 7 'The Noble Bachelor', 8 'The Beryl Coronet', 9 'The Yellow Face', 10 'The Resident Patient', 11 'The Tiger of San Pedro', 12 'The Priory School', 13 'The Solitary Cyclist', 14 'The Empty House', 15 'The Copper Beeches'.
Recurring cast: Eille Norwood (Sherlock Holmes), Hubert Willis (Dr Watson), Madame d'Esterre (Mrs Hudson; 1, 6-8, 11, 12, 14), Arthur Bell (Inspector Lestrade; 7, 12, 14).
Notable guest actors: Cecil Humphries (Culverton Smith; 1), Harvey Barban (Mortimer Tregennis; 2), Hugh Buckler (Dr Sterndale; 2), Joan Beverley (Irene Adler; 3), Alfred Drayton (King of Bohemia; 3), Edward Arundel (Jabez Wilson; 4), H. Townsend (Spalding; 4), Edna Flugrath (Mary Sutherland; 5), Nelson Ramsey (Hosmer Angel; 5), Robert Vallis (Neville St Clair; 6), Cyril Percival (Simon; 7), Temple Bell (Hatty Doran; 7), Harry Vibart (Alexander Holder; 8), Clifford Heatherly (Grant Munro; 9), Norma Whalley (Effie Munro; 9), C. Pitt-Chatham (Dr Trevelyan; 10), Judd Green (Blessington; 10), Lewis Gilbert (Murillo; 11), George Harrington (Scott Eccles; 11), Leslie English (Dr Huxtable; 12), C.H. Croker-King (Duke of Holdernesse; 12), Violet Hewitt (Violet Smith; 13), R.D. Sylvesyter (Carruthers; 13), Allan Jeayes (Woodley; 13), Austin Fairman (Ronald Adair; 14), Madge White (Violet Hunter; 15), Lyell Johnson (Rucastle; 15).
Selected credits: Scrp: William J. Elliott, Maurice Elvey. Dir: Maurice Elvey.

THE ADVENTURES OF SHERLOCK HOLMES
(see pages 42-43)
August 1939. Twentieth Century Fox. USA. 85m. Black and white.
Cast: Basil Rathbone (Sherlock Holmes), Nigel Bruce (Dr Watson), Ida Lupino (Ann Brandon), Alan Marshal (Jerrold Hunter), Terry Kilburn (Billy the Page), George Zucco (Moriarty), Henry Stephenson (Sir Ronald Ramsgate), E.E. Clive (Inspector Bristol), Arthur Hohl (Bassick), May Beatty (Mrs Jameson), Peter Willes (Lloyd Brandon), Mary Gordon (Mrs Hudson), Holmes Herbert (Justice), George Regas (Mateo), Mary Forbes (Lady

Conyngham), Frank Dawson (Dawes), William Austin (Stranger).
Selected credits: Art dir: Richard Day, Hans Peters. Ed: Robert Bischoff. Mus: Cyril J. Mockridge. Dp: Leon Shamroy. Scrp: Edwin Blum, William Drake. Bo: *Sherlock Holmes* (play), by William Gillette. Assoc prod: Gene Markey. Exec prod: Darryl F. Zanuck. Dir: Alfred Werker.

THE ADVENTURES OF SHERLOCK HOLMES
(see pages 122-125)
24 April-5 June 1984; 25 August -29 September 1985. Granada Television. UK. 13 x 50m. Colour.
(Series 1) 1 'A Scandal in Bohemia', 2 'The Dancing Men', 3 'The Naval Treaty', 4 'The Solitary Cyclist', 5 'The Crooked Man', 6 'The Speckled Band', 7 'The Blue Carbuncle'. (Series 2) 8 'The Copper Beeches', 9 'The Greek Interpreter', 10 'The Norwood Builder', 11 'The Resident Patient', 12 'The Red-Headed League', 13 'The Final Problem'.
Recurring cast: Jeremy Brett (Sherlock Holmes), David Burke (Dr Watson), Rosalie Williams (Mrs Hudson).
Notable guest actors: Gayle Hunnicutt (Irene Adler; 1), Jeremy Kemp (Dr Roylott; 6), Natasha Richardson (Violet Hunter; 7), Patrick Newell (Blessington; 11), Eric Porter (Professor Moriarty; 12, 13).
Selected credits: Des: Mike Grimes, Tim Wilding, Margaret Coombes. Ed: Jack Dardis. Make-up: Deborah Tinsey, Susan Milton. Mus: Patrick Gowers. Dp: Mike Popley. Scrp: Alexander Baron (1), Anthony Skene (2), Jeremy Paul (3, 6), Alan Plater (4), Alfred Shaughnessy (5), Paul Finney (7). Developed for TV by John Hawkesworth. Assoc prod: Stuart Doughly. Prod: Michael Cox. Dir: Paul Annett (1, 4), John Bruce (2, 6), Alan Grint (3, 5), David Carson (7).

THE ADVENTURES OF SHERLOCK HOUND
(see pages 168-169)
1984. Rai Rever Tms. Japan. 26 x 23m. Colour. Animation.
Episode titles (in translation): 1 'The Famous Detective', 2 'The Veiled Genius, Professor Moriarty', 3 'Little Martha's Big Case', 4 'Mrs Hudson Kidnapped', 5 'The Blue Carbuncle', 6 'The Mystery of the Green Balloon', 7 'The Great Chase of the Irregulars', 8 'The Speckled Band', 9 'Treasures Under the Sea', 10 'White Cliffs of Rover', 11 'A Huge Savings Box', 12 'The Professor's Failure in the Storm', 13 'The Disappearance of a Freight Car', 14. 'The Coral Lobster', 15 'The Glittering Moriarty', 16 'The Blunder Plan in Loch Ness', 17 'The Dangerous Castle', 18 'The Monster of the Thames',

19 'The Japanese Kite Match', 20 'The Airship White Silver', 21 'Flying Fly Machine', 22 'The Parrot vs Moriarty', 23 'A Hymn for Moriarty', 24 'The Doll Changing Affair', 25 'A Slapstick Plane Race', 26 'His Last Case'.
Selected credits: Mus: Kentaroh Haneda. Prod: Yoshimitsu Takahashi. Chief Dir: Hayao Miyazaki. Some episodes were dubbed into English with the voices of: Larry Moss, Lewis Arquette, Pat Morris and Hamilton Camp.

THE ADVENTURES OF THE GREAT MOUSE DETECTIVE
- see *Basil the Great Mouse Detective*

ALFRED HITCHCOCK PRESENTS
'My Dear Watson'
21 April 1989. USA Cable Network. USA. 25m. Colour.
Cast: Brian Bedford (Sherlock Holmes), Patrick Monckton (Dr Watson), John Colicos (Inspector Lestrade).
Selected credits: Scrp: Susan Woollen. Prod: Mary Kahn. Dir: Jorge Montesi.
Watson is kidnapped and Holmes is forced to relinquish his secret files as a ransom.

ALVIN AND THE CHIPMUNKS
1 'The Cruise', 2 'Elementary, My Dear Simon'
(see pages 168-169)
(1) 1983; (2) 1990. Bagdasarian Productions in association with DIC Enterprises. USA. 13m each. Colour. Animation.
Voice cast: Ross Bagdasarian Jnr.
Selected credits: Prod: Ross Bagdasarian Jnr. Dir: Charles Nichols (1).

THE AMERICAN ADVENTURES OF SURELICK HOLMS
(aka *The Hot Adventures of Surelick Holms/ The American Adventures of Sureluck Holms/ The Gay Adventures of Sureluck Holms*)
(see pages 148-151)
1975. Hand in Hand Films. USA. 93m. Colour.
Cast: David Chandler (Holms), Frank Massey (Dr Watson).
Selected credits: Prod: Leo the Lion. Dir: Bob Ell.
Probably the first X-rated pornographic film to feature Holmes and Watson.

THE AMERICAN ADVENTURES OF SURELUCK HOLMS
- see *The American Adventures of Surelick Holms*

ARSENE LUPIN CONTRA SHERLOCK HOLMES
('Arsène Lupin vs Sherlock Holmes')
(see pages 12-15)
1910-1911. Vitascope Pictures. Germany. 2 reels. Black and white. Silent.
1 'Der Alte Sekretar' (UK 'The Old Secretaire'), 2 'Der Blaue Diamant' (UK 'The Blue Diamond'), 3 'Die Falschen Rembrandts' (UK 'The Fake Rembrandts'), 4 'Die Flucht' (UK 'Arsène Lupin's Escape'), 5 'Arsène Lupins Ende' (UK 'The Finish of Arsène Lupin').
Recurring cast: Viggo Larsen (Sherlock Holmes), Paul Otto (Arsène Lupin).
Selected credits: Dir: Viggo Larsen.

THE AVENGERS
'The Curious Case of the Countless Clues'
(see pages 148-151)
18 May 1969. An ABC-TV Production. UK. 50m. Colour.
Cast: Patrick Macnee (Steed), Linda Thorson (Tara King), Peter Jones (Sir Arthur Doyle).
Selected credits: Scrp: Philip Levene. Prod: Brian Clemens, Albert Fennell. Dir: Don Sharp.

THE BAKER STREET BOYS
(see page 118)
Mar-Apr 1983. BBC TV. UK. 8 x 30m. Colour.
1 'The Adventure of the Disappearing Dispatch Case', 2 'The Ghost of Julian Midwinter', 3 'The Adventure of the Winged Scarab', 4 'The Case of the Captive Clairvoyant'.
Recurring cast: Jay Simpson (Wiggins), Damion Napier (Beaver), Adam Woodyatt (Shiner), David Garlick (Sparrow), Debbie Norris (Queenie), Suzi Ross (Rosie), Hubert Rees (Dr Watson), Roger Ostime (Sherlock Holmes), Stanley Lebor (Inspector Lestrade).
Notable guest actors: Colin Jeavons (Professor Moriarty; 3).
Selected credits: Mus: David Epps. Scrp: Anthony Read (1, 4), Richard Carpenter (2, 3). Prod: Paul Stone. Dir: Marilyn Fox (1, 3), Michael Kerrigan (2, 4).

BASIL THE GREAT MOUSE DETECTIVE
- see *The Great Mouse Detective*

A BLACK SHERLOCK HOLMES
15 April 1918. Ebony Film Corp. USA. 13m. Black and white. Silent.
Cast: Sam Robinson (Knick Garter), Randolph Tatun (Rheum Tism, His Assistant), Gea Lewis (I Wanta Sneeze), Evon Junior (Sheeza Sneeze, a Doting Daughter), Sam Jacks (Baron Jazz).
Selected credits: Scrp: C.N. David. Dir: R.G. Phillips.
A burlesque on Sherlock Holmes with a cast of black actors.

BRAVESTAR
'Sherlock Holmes in the 23rd Century'
1989. Filmation Productions. USA. 2 x 45m. Colour. Animation.
Voice cast: Charlie Adler, Susan Blu, Pat Frayley, Ed Gilbert.
Sherlock Holmes, while fighting Moriarty at the Reichenbach Falls, is transported to the 23rd century where he assists Bravestar, a lawman living on the planet of New Texas.

THE CASEBOOK OF SHERLOCK HOLMES
(see pages 152-155)
21 February-28 March 1991. Granada Television. UK. 6 x 50m. Colour.
1 'The Disappearance of Lady Frances Carfax', 2 'The Problem of Thor Bridge', 3 'Shoscombe Old Place', 4 'The Boscombe Valley Mystery', 5 'The Illustrious Client', 6 'The Creeping Man'.
Recurring cast: Jeremy Brett (Sherlock Holmes), Edward Hardwicke (Dr Watson), Rosalie Williams (Mrs Hudson),
Notable guest actors: Cheryl Campbell (Lady Frances Carfax; 1), Daniel Massey (J. Neil Gibson; 2), Robin Ellis (Sir Robert Norberton; 3), Jude Law (Joe Barnes; 3), Peter Vaughan (Mr Turner; 4), Anthony Valentine (Baron Gruner; 5), Charles Kay (Professor Presbury; 6), Colin Jeavons (Inspector Lestrade; 6).
Selected credits: Prod des: Chris Wilkinson (1), Paul Rowan (2, 6), Steve Fineren (3, 5), Alan Price (4). Mus: Patrick Gowers. Scrp: T. R. Bowen (1), Jeremy Paul (2), Gary Hopkins (3), John Hawkesworth (4), Robin Chapman (5, 6). Developed for TV by John Hawkesworth. Prod: Michael Cox. Dir: John Madden (1), Michael Simpson (2), Patrick Lau (3), June Howson (4), Tim Sullivan (5, 6).

THE CASE OF THE FANTASTICAL PASSBOOK
1 May 1979. Martin Benson Films, commissioned by the Abbey National Building Society. UK. 33m. Colour.
Cast: Jeremy Young (Sherlock Holmes), Robert Dorning (Dr Watson), Bill Fraser (Major Grinstead).
This advertising film received the Silver Screen Award at the 12th Annual International Industrial Film Festival in Illinois.

THE CASE OF THE SCREAMING BISHOP
1944. Columbia Pictures. USA. 7m. Black and white. Animation.
Selected credits: Story: John McLeish. Prod: Charles Mintz and others. Dir: Howard Swift.

THE CASE OF THE WHITECHAPEL VAMPIRE
(see page 185)
9 October 2002. Muse Entertainment Enterprises in association Hallmark Entertainment. Canada. 90m. Colour.
Cast: Matt Frewer (Sherlock Holmes), Kenneth Welsh (Dr Watson), Shawn Lawrence (Brother Marstoke), Neville Edwards (Dr Chagas), Cary Lawrence (Sister Helen), Michael Peron (Inspector Jones), Tom Rack (Brother Abel).
Selected credits: Dp: Serge Ladouceur; Cos des: Luc J. Beland; Mus: Marc Ouellette; Selected credits: Exec Prod: Steven Hewitt, Michael Prupas; Prod: Irene Litinsky; Scrp: Rodney Gibbons; Dir: Rodney Gibbons.

CHIP N DALE: RESCUE RANGERS
'Pound of the Baskervilles'
(see pages 168-169)
1989. Walt Disney Productions. USA. 25m. Colour. Animation.
Voice cast: Corey Burton, Peter Cullen, Jim Cummings, Tres MacNeille.
Selected credits: Scrp: Eric Lewald. Prod: Tad Stones, Alan Zaslove. Dir: John Kimball, Bob Zamboni.

COUNT DUCKULA
'All in a Fog'
(see pages 168-169)
1987. Cosgrove Hall Productions. UK. 23m. Colour. Animation.
Voice cast: David Jason (Count Duckula), Barry Clayton (Narrator), Jack May, Brian Trueman, Jimmy Hibbert.

CRAZY HOUSE
(see pages 52-53)
1943. Universal Pictures. USA. 80m. Black and white.
Cast: Ole Olsen, Chic Johnson, Basil Rathbone (Sherlock Holmes), Nigel Bruce (Dr Watson)
Selected credits: Scrp: Robert Lees, Frederic I. Rinaldo. Dp: Charles Van Enger. Dir: Edward Cline.

CRIME WRITERS
'The Great Detective'
5 November 1978. BBC TV. UK. 25m. Colour.
Cast: Jeremy Clyde (Sherlock Holmes), Michael Cochrane (Dr Watson), Alex Davion (King of Bohemia/Von Bork).
Selected credits: Scrp: Mike Pavett. Prod: Bernard Adams.

THE CRUCIFER OF BLOOD
(see pages 156-157)
4 November 1991. Turner Pictures, an Agamemnon Films Production in Association with British Lion. UK. 131m. Colour.
Cast: Charlton Heston (Sherlock Holmes), Richard Johnson (Dr Watson), Susanna Harker (Irene St Clair), John Castle (Neville St Clair), Clive Wood (Jonathan Small), Simon Callow (Inspector Lestrade), Edward Fox (Alastair Ross), Kiran Shaw (Tonga).
Selected credits: Dp: Robin Vidgeon. Scrp: Fraser C.

Heston. Bo: *The Crucifer of Blood* (play), by Paul Giovanni. Prod: Fraser C. Heston. Dir: Fraser C. Heston.

DEDUCE YOU SAY
(see pages 168-169)
1956. Warner Brothers. USA. 7m. Colour. Animation.
Voice cast: Mel Blanc (Daffy Duck as Dorlock Holmes and Porky Pig as Dr Watkins).
Selected credits: Dir: Chuck Jones.

DETECTIVE
'The Speckled Band'
(see pages 86-87)
18 May 1964. BBC TV. UK. 50m. Black and white.
Cast: Douglas Wilmer (Sherlock Holmes), Nigel Stock (Dr Watson), Mary Holder (Mrs Hudson), Felix Felton (Grimesby Roylott), Diane Aulin (Helen Stoner), Marian Diamond (Julia Stoner).
Selected credits: Scrp: Giles Cooper.
Prod: David Goddard. Dir: Robin Midgley.
This series featured the adventures of a different literary detective each week. 'The Speckled Band' turned out to be the pilot programme for the 1965 Sherlock Holmes series starring Douglas Wilmer.

DRESSED TO KILL
(UK *Sherlock Holmes and the Secret Code*)
(see pages 70-71)
May 1946. Universal. USA. 72m. Black and white (colourised version available).
Cast: Basil Rathbone (Sherlock Holmes), Nigel Bruce (Dr Watson), Patricia Morison (Hilda Courtney), Edmond Breon (Julian Emery), Frederick Worlock (Col Cavanagh), Tom P. Dillon (Det Sgt Thompson), Harry Cording (Hamid), Topsy Glyn (Kilgour Child), Carl Harbord (Inspector Hopkins), Mary Gordon (Mrs Hudson), Ian Wolfe (Scotland Yard Commissioner), Patricia Cameron (Evelyn Clifford).
Selected credits: Art dir: Jack Otterson, Martin Obzina. Ed: Saul A. Goodkind. Mus: Milton Rosen. Dp: Maury Gertsman. Scrp: Frank Gruber, Leonard Lee. Exec prod: Howard S. Benedict. Prod: Roy William Neill. Dir: Roy William Neill.

DRESSED TO KILL — THE CASE OF THE PILFERED PANTIES
(see pages 148-151)
circa 1969. Playboy Flicks. USA. 7.30m.
Black and white/colour.

DR WATSON AND THE DARKWATER HALL MYSTERY
(aka *The Singular Adventure*)
(see pages 100-101)
1974. BBC TV. UK. 70m. Colour.
Cast: Edward Fox (Dr Watson), Elaine Taylor (Emily), Marguerite Young (Mrs Hudson), Christopher Cazenove (Sir Henry), Jeremy Clyde (Miles), John Westbrook (Bradshaw), Terence Baylor (Carlos), Carmen Gomez (Dolores), Anthony Langdon (Black Paul).
Selected credits: Scrp: Kingsley Amis. Prod: Mark Shivas. Dir: James Cellan Jones.

ÉCLAIR SERIES
(see pages 12-15)
1912-1913. Franco-British Film Co. Fr/UK. 8 x 40m. Black and white. Silent.
1 'The Speckled Band', 2 'The Reigate Squires', 3 'The Beryl Coronet', 4 'The Adventure of the Copper Beeches', 5 'A Mystery of Boscombe Vale', 6 'The Stolen Papers', 7 'Silver Blaze', 8 'The Musgrave Ritual'.
Recurring cast: Georges Treville (Sherlock Holmes), Mr Moyse (Dr Watson).
Selected credits: Dir: George Treville.

ELEMENTARY, MY DEAR WATSON
(see pages 100-101)
18 January 1973. BBC TV. UK. 30m. Colour.
Cast: John Cleese (Sherlock Holmes), William Rushton (Dr Watson), Josephine Tewson (Lady Cynthia), Norman Bird (Inspector Street), Chic Murray (Constable), John Wells (Prime Minister), Bill Maynard (Frank Potter), Larry Martyn (Fu Manchu), Michael Gover (Superintendent Truscott).
Selected credits: Scrp: N.F. Simpson. Prod: Barry Took. Dir: Harold Snoad.

THE ELIGIBLE BACHELOR
(see pages 170-171)
3 February 1993. Granada TV. UK. 106m. Colour.
Cast: Jeremy Brett (Sherlock Holmes), Rosalie Williams (Mrs Hudson), Simon Williams (Lord Robert St Simon), Paris Jefferson (Henrietta Doran), Anna Calder-Marshall (Helena and Agnes Northcote), Joanna McCallum (Flora Millar), Geoffrey Beevers (Inspector Montgomery), Bob Sessions (Aloysius Doran), Peter Warnock (Francis Moulton), Mary Ellis (Lady Florence), Heather Chasen (Hon Amelia St Simon), Phillada Sewell (Lady Mary), Lespeth March (Lady Blanche), Peter Graves (George Tidy), Miles Hoyle (Thomas Floutier).
Selected credits: Des: Christopher Truelove. Mus: Patrick Gowers. Scrp: T. R. Bowen. Bo: ' The Adventure of the Noble Bachelor', by Doyle. Prod: June Wyndham Davies. Dir: Peter Hammond.

THE FAMOUS ADVENTURES OF MR MAGOO
'Mr Magoo, Man of Mystery'
(see pages 148-151)
1964. UPA Picture Productions. USA. 26m. Colour. Animation.
Voice cast: Jim Backus (Magoo/Watson), Paul Frees (Sherlock Holmes/Cabbie/Jeweller), Joan Gardiner (Mrs Hudson/Helen).
Selected credits: Adapted for television by True Boardman.

FANTASY ISLAND
'Save Sherlock Holmes'
(see pages 110-111)
6 February 1982. ABC-TV. USA. 50m. Colour.
Cast: Peter Lawford (Sherlock Holmes), Donald O'Connor (Dr Watson), Ron Ely (Kevin Lansing), Ian Abercrombie (Inspector Lestrade), Camila Ashlend (Mrs Hudson), Mel Ferrer (Collingswood/ Moriarty), Ricardo Montalban (Mental Patient).
Selected credits: Scrp: Arthur C. Pierce. Prod: Arthur Rowe. Dir: Don Weiss.

FOG
- see *A Study in Terror*

THE FOUR OAKS MYSTERY
(see pages 158-159)
June 1992. Granada Television. UK. Colour.
Cast: Jeremy Brett (Sherlock Holmes), Edward Hardwicke (Dr Watson), Phyllis Calvert (Lady Cordelia).
Selected credits: Scrp: Jeremy Paul. Dir: Tim Sullivan.
A brief sequence, shown during an ITV Telethon.

THE FURTHER ADVENTURES OF SHERLOCK HOLMES
(see pages 16-17)
1922. Stoll Picture Productions Ltd. UK. 15 x 2 reels. Black and white. Silent.
1 'Charles Augustus Milverton', 2 'The Abbey Grange', 3 'The Norwood Builder', 4 'The Reigate Squires', 5 'The Naval Treaty', 6 'The Second Stain', 7 'The Red Circle', 8 'The Six Napoleons', 9 'Black Peter', 10 'The Bruce-Partington Plans', 11 'The Stockbroker's Clerk', 12 'The Boscombe Valley Mystery', 13 'The Musgrave Ritual', 14 'The Golden Pince-Nez', 15 'The Greek Interpreter'.
Recurring cast: Eille Norwood (Sherlock Holmes), Hubert Willis (Dr Watson).
Notable guest actors: Teddy Arundell (Inspector Hopkins; 1, 4, 8-14), Madame d'Esterre (Mrs Hudson; 1, 4-6, 8-13), Fred Wright (James Oldacre; 1), Hal Martin (Charles McCarthy; 2), Ray Raymond (James McCarthy; 2), Fred Raymond (John Turner; 2), Geoffrey Wilnes (Reginald Musgrave; 3), Clifton Boyne (Brunton; 3), Betty Chester (Rachel Howells; 3), Richard Atwood (Alec Cunningham; 4), Edward O'Neill (Squire Cunningham; 4), Arthur Lumley (Colonel Hayter; 4), J.R. Tozer (Latimer; 5), Robert Vallis (Wilson Kemp; 5), Cecil Dane (Melas; 5), Edith Saville (Sophy Kratides; 5), H. Wheeler (Inspector Hopkins; 5), Jack Hobbs (Percy Phelps; 6), Francis Duguid (Joseph Harrison; 6), Nancy May (Miss Harrison; 6), Fred Paul (Peter Carey; 7), Hugh Buckler (Pat Cairns; 7), Jack Jarman (John Nelligan; 7), Fred Rains (John Nelligan Sr; 7), George Foley (Charles Augustus Milverton; 8), Harry Worth (Butler; 8), Tonie Edgar Bruce (Lady Eva Bracknell; 8), George Bellamy (Beppo; 9), Jack Raymond (Pietro Venucci; 9), Alice Moffat (Lucretia; 9), Madeleine Seymour (Lady Brackenstall; 10), Lawford Davidson (Sir Eustace Brackenstall; 10), Leslie Stiles (Captain Croker; 10), Madge Tree (Theresa; 10), Cecil Ward (Lord Bellinger; 11), Dorothy Fane (Miss Hope; 11), Maria Minetti (Mrs Lucas; 11), Bertram Burleigh (Gennaro Lucca; 12), Maresco Marescini (Gorgiano; 12), Sybil Archdale (Amelia Lucca; 12), Tom Beaumont (Leverton; 12), Malcolm Todd (Cadogan West; 13), Lewis Gilbert (Mycroft Holmes; 13), Ronald Power (Colonel Walter; 13), Edward Sorley (Hugh Oberstein; 13), Olaf Hytten (Hall Pycroft; 14), Aubrey Fitzgerald (Pinner; 14), George Ridgwell (Beddington; 14), Bertram Burleigh (Hatherley; 15), Ward McAllister (Ferguson; 15), Mercy Hatton (Girl; 15).
Selected credits: Art dir: Walter W. Murton. Cam: Alfred H. Moses. Scrp: Patrick (Pointer), Frank (Kelley), L. Mannock, Geoffrey H. Malins. Dir: George Ridgewell.

GARFIELD AND FRIENDS
'The Hound of the Arbuckles'
(see pages 168-169)
1990. United Features Syndicate. USA. 8m. Colour. Animation.
Voice cast: Lorenzo Music (Garfield), Thom Huge, Greg Berger, Desiree Goyette, Frank Welker, Howie Morris, Julie Payne.
Selected credits: Scrp: Mark Evanier, Sharman DiVono. Prod: Bob Curtis, Bob Nesler. Dir: Jeff Hall, Tom Ray.

THE GAY ADVENTURES OF SURELUCK HOLMS
- see *The American Adventures of Surelick Holms*

THE GREAT MOUSE DETECTIVE
(UK *Basil, The Great Mouse Detective*, 1992 re-release *The Adventures of the Great Mouse Detective*)
(see page 140)
2 July 1986. Walt Disney/Silver Screen Partners II. USA. 74m. Colour. Animation.
Voice cast: Vincent Price (Professor Ratigan), Barrie Ingham (Basil), Val Bettin (Dr Dawson), Susanna Pollatschek (Olivia), Candy Candido (Fidget), Eve Brenner (The Mouse Queen), Alan Young (Flaversham), Laurie Main (Dr Watson), Basil Rathbone (Sherlock Holmes).
Selected credits: Mus: Henry Mancini. Scrp: Pete Young and others. Bo: *Basil of Baker Street* (books), by Eve Titus. Prod: Burny Mattinson. Dir: John Musker, Dave Michener, Ron Clements, Burny Mattinson.

THE GREAT PIGGY BANK ROBBERY
(see pages 168-169)
1946. Warner Brothers. USA. 7.40m. Colour. Animation.
Voice cast: Mel Blanc (Daffy Duck as Duck Twacy).
Selected credits: Dir: Bob Clampett.

HANDS OF A MURDERER
(Re-shown 1 August 1992 on CBS as *Sherlock Holmes and the Prince of Crime*)
(see page 147)
16 May 1990. Yorkshire International Films/Green Pond Productions Inc/Storke Enterprises Inc. UK. 97m. Colour.
Cast: Edward Woodward (Sherlock Holmes), John Hillerman (Dr Watson), Anthony Andrews

(Moriarty), Kim Thompson (Sophy), Peter Jeffrey (Mycroft Holmes), Terrence Lodge (Inspector Lestrade), Warren Clarke (Colonel Booth), Danny Newman (Wiggins), Nickolas Grace (Oberstein), Honoria Burke (Queen Victoria), Faith Kent (Mrs Hudson), Harry Audley (Farrington), David Sibley (Finch).
Selected credits: Mus: Colin Towns. Dp: Ken Westbury. Scrp: Charles Edward Pogue. Co-prod: Charles Edward Pogue. Prod: Robert E. Fuisz. Dir: Stuart Orme.

HELD FOR RANSOM
(aka *The Adventures of Sherlock Holmes*)
(see pages 12-15)
1905. Vitagraph. USA. 8m. Black and white. Silent.
Cast: Maurice Costello (Sherlock Holmes).

HENRY'S CAT
'The Case of the Pilfered Pearls', 'The Mystery of the Missing Santa'
(see pages 168-169)
1983. Godfrey Films Limited. UK. 15m each. Colour. Animation.

THE HOT ADVENTURES OF SURELICK HOLMS
- see *The American Adventures of Surelick Holms*

THE HOUND OF LONDON
(aka *Sherlock Holmes in the Hound of London*)
1993. Intrepid Productions. Canada. Colour.
Cast: Patrick Macnee (Sherlock Holmes), John Scott-Paget (Dr Watson), Colin Skinner (Inspector Lestrade), Jack Macreath (Moriarty/Rex), Sophia Thornley (Mrs Hudson).
Selected credits: Scrp: Craig Bowlsby. Dir: Peter Reynolds-Long.
This obscure, low budget TV production is not highly regarded by those who have seen it.

THE HOUND OF THE BASKERVILLES (1914, Germany)
- see *Der Hund von Baskervilles* (1914)

THE HOUND OF THE BASKERVILLES
(see pages 16-17)
8 August 1921. Stoll Picture Productions Ltd. UK. 61m. Black and white. Silent.
Cast: Eille Norwood (Sherlock Holmes), Hubert Willis (Dr Watson), Rex McDougal (Sir Henry Baskerville), Catina Campbell (Mrs Stapleton), Lewis Gilbert (John Stapleton), Robert English (Dr Mortimer), Frederick Raynham (Barryman, US: Osborne), Miss Walker (Mrs Barrymore, US: Mrs Osborne), Mme D'Esterre (Mrs Hudson), Robert Vallis (The Convict, Selden).
Selected credits: Art dir: Walter W. Murton. Ed: Leslie Britain. Dp: W. Germaine Burger. Scrp: William J. Elliot, Maurice Elvey, Dorothy Westlake. Prod: Maurice Elvey. Dir: Maurice Elvey.

THE HOUND OF THE BASKERVILLES
(see page 26)
July 1931. Gainsborough Pictures. UK. 75m. Black and white.
Cast: Robert Rendel (Sherlock Holmes), Frederick W. Lloyd (Dr Watson), John Stuart (Sir Henry Baskerville), Reginald Bach (Stapleton), Heather Angel (Beryl Stapleton), Wilfred Shine (Dr Mortimer), Sam Livesey (Sir Hugo Baskerville), Henry Hallett (Barryman), Sybil Jane (Mrs Barrymore), Elizabeth Vaughan (Laura Lyons), Leonard Hayes (Cartwright).
Selected credits: Ed: Ian Dalrymple. Dp: Bernard Knowles. Scrp: Edgar Wallace, V. Gareth Gundrey. Prod: Michael Balcon. Dir: V. Gareth Gundrey.

THE HOUND OF THE BASKERVILLES
(see pages 36-39)
31 March 1939. Twentieth Century Fox. USA. 80m. Black and white.

THE HOUND OF THE BASKERVILLES
(see pages 78-79)
4 May 1959. Hammer Films. UK. 87m. Colour.
Cast: Peter Cushing (Sherlock Holmes), André Morell (Dr Watson), Christopher Lee (Sir Henry Baskerville), Marla Landi (Cecile Stapleton), David Oxley (Sir Hugo Baskerville), Miles Malleson (Bishop Frankland), Francis De Wolff (Dr Mortimer), Ewen Solon (Stapleton), John Le Mesurier (Barryman), Sam Kydd (Perkins), Michael Hawkins (Lord Caphill), Ian Hewitson (Lord Kingsblood), Michael Mulcaster (Selden), Judi Moyens (Servant Girl), Helen Goss (Mrs Barryman).
Selected credits: Art dir: Bernard Robinson. Sup ed: James Needs. Mus: James Bernard. Dp: Jack Asher. Scrp: Peter Bryan. Exec prod: Michael Carreras. Assoc prod: Anthony Nelson Keys. Prod: Anthony Hinds. Dir: Terence Fisher.

THE HOUND OF THE BASKERVILLES
(see page 99)
22 February 1972. Universal Pictures/ABC-TV. USA. 73m. Colour.
Cast: Stewart Granger (Sherlock Holmes), Bernard Fox (Dr Watson), William Shatner (Stapleton), Ian Ireland (Sir Henry Baskerville), Anthony Zerbe (Dr Mortimer), Sally Anne Howes (Laura Lyons), Jane Merrow (Beryl Stapleton), Alan Caillou (Lestrade), Brendan Dillon (Barrymore), Arline Anderson (Mrs Barrymore).
Selected credits: Dp: Harry Wolf. Scrp: Robert E. Thompson. Prod: Stanley Kallis. Dir: Barry Crane.

THE HOUND OF THE BASKERVILLES
(see page 107)
5 November 1978. Michael White Ltd. UK. 85m. Colour.
Cast: Peter Cook (Sherlock Holmes), Dudley Moore (Watson/Mrs Holmes/Spigott), Terry-Thomas (Dr Mortimer), Kenneth Williams (Sir Henry Baskerville), Denholm Elliott (Stapleton), Hugh Griffith (Frankland), Joan Greenwood (Mrs Stapleton), Max Wall (Barrymore), Irene Handl (Mrs Barrymore), Dana Gillespie (Mary Frankland), Roy Kinnear (Selden), Spike Milligan (Constable).
Selected credits: Mus: Dudley Moore. Dp: Dick Bush, John Wilcox. Scrp: Peter Cook, Dudley Moore, Paul Morrissey. Prod: John Goldstone. Dir: Paul Morrissey.

THE HOUND OF THE BASKERVILLES
(see page 113)
3-24 October 1982. BBC TV. UK. 4 x 30m. Colour.
Cast: Tom Baker (Sherlock Holmes), Terence Rigby (Dr Watson), Nicholas Wodeson (Sir Henry Baskerville), Christopher Ravenscroft (Stapleton), Hubert Rees (Inspector Lestrade), Will Knightley (Dr Mortimer), Morris Perry (Barrymore), Michael Goldie (Selden).

Cast: Richard Greene (Sir Henry Baskerville), Basil Rathbone (Sherlock Holmes), Nigel Bruce (Dr Watson), Wendy Barrie (Beryl Stapleton), Lionel Atwill (Dr James Mortimer), John Carradine (Barryman), Barlowe Borland (Mr Frankland), Beryl Mercer (Mrs Jennifer Mortimer), Morton Lowry (John Stapleton), Ralph Forbes (Sir Hugo Baskerville), E.E. Clive (Cabby), Mary Gordon (Mrs Hudson), Peter Wiles (Roderick), Ian MacLaren (Sir Charles Baskerville), Nigel DeBrulier (Convict), Eily Malyon (Mrs Barryman), Ivan Simpson (Shepherd), John Burton (Bruce), Lionel Pape (Coroner), Denis Green (Jon).
Selected credits: Cos des: Gwen Wakeling. Set des: Thomas Little. Art dir: Richard Day, Hans Peters. Ed: Robert Simpson. Mus: Cyril J. Mockridge. Dp: Peverell Marley. Scrp: Ernest Pascal. Assoc prod: Gene Markey. Prod: Darryl F. Zanuck. Dir: Sidney Lanfield.

Selected credits: Scrp: Alexander Baron. Prod: Barry Letts. Dir: Peter Duguid.

THE HOUND OF THE BASKERVILLES
(see page 117)
13 May 1983. Mapleton Films. UK. 99m. Colour.
Cast: Ian Richardson (Sherlock Holmes), Donald Churchill (Dr Watson), Martin Shaw (Sir Henry Baskerville), Denholm Elliott (Dr Mortimer), Brian Blessed (Geoffrey Lyons), Eleanor Bron (Mrs Barrymore), Glynis Barber (Beryl Stapleton), Nicholas Clay (Stapleton), Ronald Lacey (Inspector Lestrade), Edward Judd (Barrymore), Connie Booth (Laura Lyons), David Leyton (Sir Charles Baskerville).
Selected credits: Scrp: Charles Pogue. Prod: Otto Plaschkes. Dir: Douglas Hickox.

THE HOUND OF THE BASKERVILLES
(see pages 144-145)
31 August 1988. Granada Television. UK. 105m. Colour.
Cast: Jeremy Brett (Sherlock Holmes), Edward Hardwicke (Dr Watson), Raymond Adamson (Sir Charles Baskerville), Neil Duncan (Dr Mortimer), Ronald Pickup (Barrymore), Rosemary McHale (Mrs Barrymore), Kristoffer Tabori (Sir Henry Baskerville), Edward Romfourt (Purser), James Faulkner (Stapleton), Philip Dettmer (Pageboy), Stephen Tomlin (Perkins), Fiona Gillies (Beryl Stapleton), Bernard Horsfall (Frankland), Donald McKillop (Vicar of Grimpen), William Ilkley (Selden), Myrtle Devenish (Countrywoman), Elizabeth Spender (Laura Lyons), Donald Bisset (Manservant).
Selected credits: Des: James Weatherup, Chris Bradshaw. Mus: Patrick Gowers. Scrp: Trevor Bowen. Exec prod: Michael Cox. Prod: June Wyndham Davies. Dir: Brian Mills.

THE HOUND OF THE BASKERVILLES
(see page 178)
21 October 2000. Muse Entertainment Enterprises in association with Hallmark Entertainment. Canada. 90m. Colour.
Cast: Matt Frewer (Sherlock Holmes), Kenneth Welsh (Dr Watson), Jason London (Sir Henry Baskerville), Gordon Masten (Dr Mortimer), Robin Wilcock (Jack Stapleton), Emma Campbell (Beryl Stapleton), Arthur Holden (Barrymore), John Dunn-Hill (Frankland).
Selected credits: Cos des: Renee April. Des: Jean Baptiste Tard. Dp: Eric Cayla. Scrp: Joe Wiesenfeld. Exec prod: Steve Hewitt, Michael Prupas. Prod: Irene Litinsky. Dir: Rodney Gibbons.

THE HOUND OF THE BASKERVILLES
(see page 188)
26 December 2002. Tiger Aspect Productions for the BBC. UK. 100m. Colour.
Cast: Richard Roxburgh (Sherlock Holmes), Ian Hart (Dr Watson), Matt Day (Sir Charles Baskerville), Richard E. Grant (Stapleton), Neve McIntosh (Beryl Stapleton), John Nettles (Mortimer), Ron Cook (Barrymore), Liza Tarbuck (Mrs Barrymore), Geraldine James (Mrs Mortimer), Danny Webb (Lestrade), Paul Kynman (Selden).
Selected Credits: Dp: James Welland; Mus: Rob Lane; Prods: Greg Brennan, Gareth Neame, Sally Woodward Gentle, Rebecca Eaton & Steve Christian; Scrp: Allan Cubitt; Dir: David Atwood.

THE HOUSE OF FEAR
(see pages 58-59)
16 March 1945. Universal Pictures. USA. 69m. Black and white.
Cast: Basil Rathbone (Sherlock Holmes), Nigel Bruce (Dr Watson), Aubrey Mather (Alastair), Gavin Muir (Chalmers), Dennis Hoey (Inspector Lestrade), Paul Cavanagh (Simon Merrivale),

Holmes Herbert (Alan Cosgrove), Dick Alexander (Ralph King), Cyril Delevanti (Stanley Raeburn), Wilson Benge (Guy Davies), Harry Cording (John Simpson), David Clyde (Alex MacGregor), Florette Hillier (Alison MacGregor), Sally Shepherd (Mrs Monteith).
Selected credits: Ed: Ray Snider. Mus dir: Paul Sawtell. Dp: Virgil Miller. Scrp: Roy Chanslor. Prod: Roy William Neill. Dir: Roy William Neill.

DER HUND VON BASKERVILLES

(see pages 12-15)
(USA *The Hound of the Baskervilles*)
June 1914. Vitascope Pictures. Germany. 4 reels. Black and white. Silent.
Cast: Alwin Neuss (Sherlock Holmes), Friedrich Kuhne (Stapleton), Hanni Weiss (Laura Lyons), Erwin Fichtner (Lord Henry Baskerville), Andreas Van Horne (Barrymore).
Selected credits: Prod des: Hermann Warm. Dp: Karl Freund. Scrp: Richard Oswald. Dir: Rudolph Meinert.

DER HUND VON BASKERVILLES

('The Hound of the Baskervilles')
1929. Erda-Film-Produktions. Germany. 2382 metres. Black and white. Silent.
Cast: Carlyle Blackwell (Sherlock Holmes), Georges Seroff (Dr Watson), Alexander Murski (Sir Hugo Baskerville), Betty Bird (Beryl Stapleton), Robert Garrison (Frankland), Fritz Rasp (Stapleton), Alma Taylor (Mrs Eliza Barrymore), Erich Ponto, Valy Arnheim, Livio Pavenelli, Carla Bartheel, Jaro Furth.
Selected credits: Scrp: Herbert Juttke, Georges C. Klaren. Dir: Richard Oswald.
The last silent Sherlock Holmes film.

DER HUND VON BASKERVILLES

(see pages 34-35)
('The Hound of the Baskervilles')
January 1937. Ondra-Lamac-Film. Germany. 82m. Black and white.
Cast: Bruno Guttner (Sherlock Holmes), Fritz Odemar (Dr Watson), Peter Moss (Lord Henry Baskerville), Friedrich Kayssler (Lord Charles Baskerville), Fritz Rasp (Barrymore), Lilly Schonborn (Mrs Barrymore), Erich Ponto (Stapleton), Ernst Rotmund (Dr Mortimer), Alice Brandt (Beryl Vendeleure), Gertrude Walle (Holmes' Landlady), Paul Rehkopf (Convict), Hanna Waag (Lady Baskerville), Artur Malkowski (Lord Baskerville), Klaus Pohl, Ika Thimm, Ernst Schaah, Kurt Lauermann, Horst Bitt.
Selected credits: Mus: Paul Huhn. Dp: Willy Winterstein. Scrp: Carla von Stackelberg. Dir: Karel Lamac.

THE INTERIOR MOTIVE

(see pages 100-101)
7 October 1975. Kentucky Educational Television/ WKLE/Channel 46. UK. 15m. Colour.
Cast: Leonard Nimoy (Sherlock Holmes), Burt Blackwell (Dr Watson).
Selected credits: Scrp: Richard L. Smith. Prod: George Rasmusson. Dir: George Rasmusson.

IT'S A MYSTERY CHARLIE BROWN

(see pages 168-169)
1974. Lee Menderson-Bill Melendez Production in association with Charles M. Schulz Creative Associates and United Artists. USA. 22m. Colour. Animation.
Voice cast: Todd Barbee (Charlie Brown), Melanie Kahn (Lucy), Stephen Shea (Linus), Donna Forum (Peppermint Patti)
Selected credits: Mus: Vince Guaraldi. Scrp: Charles Schulz.

THE LAST ADVENTURES OF SHERLOCK HOLMES

(see pages 16-17)
1923. Stoll Picture Productions Ltd. UK. 15 x 2 reels. Black and white. Silent.

1 'Silver Blaze', 2 'The Speckled Band', 3 'The Gloria Scott', 4 'The Blue Carbuncle', 5 'The Engineer's Thumb', 6 'His Last Bow', 7 'The Cardboard Box', 8 'The Disappearance of Lady Frances Carfax', 9 'The Three Students', 10 'The Missing Three-Quarter', 11 'The Mystery of Thor Bridge', 12 'The Stone of Mazarin', 13 'The Dancing Men', 14 'The Crooked Man', 15 'The Final Problem'.
Recurring cast: Eille Norwood (Sherlock Holmes), Hubert Willis (Dr Watson), Madame d'Esterre (Mrs Hudson; 1, 4, 10, 11), Tom Beaumont (Inspector Gregory; 1, 5-8, 12, 15).
Notable guest actors: Sam Austin (Silas Brown; 1), Knighton Small (Colonel Ross; 1), Sam Marsh (Straker; 1), Lewis Gilbert (Dr Grimesby Roylott; 2), Cynthia Murtagh (Helen Stoner; 2), Jane Graham (Julia Stoner; 2), Fred Raynham (James Trevor; 3), Reginald Fox (Victor Trevor; 3), Laurie Leslie (Jack Prendergast; 3), Ray Raymond (Evans; 3), Douglas Payne (Peterson; 4), Sebastian Smith (Henry Baker; 4), Gordon Hopkirk (James Ryder; 4), Bertram Burleigh (Hatherly; 5), Henry Latimer (Colonel Lysander Stark; 5), Nelson Ramsey (Von Bork; 6), Kate Gurney (Martha; 6), John Butt (James Browner; 7), Hilda Anthony (Mary Browner; 7), Eric Lugg (Alec Fairbairn; 7), Maud Wulff (Miss Cushing; 7), David Hawthorne (Hon Philip Green; 8), Evelyn Cecil (Lady Frances Carfax; 8), Cecil Morton York (Holy Peters; 8), William Lugg (Soames; 9), A. Harding Steerman (Bannister; 9), L. Verne (Gilchrist; 9), Hal Martin (Cyril Overton; 10), Cliff Davies (Lord Mount-James; 10), Albert E. Rayner (Dr Leslie Armstrong; 10), Leigh Gabell (Godfrey Staunton; 10), A.B. Imeson (Mr Gibson; 11), Violet Graham (Miss Dunbar; 11), Noel Grahame (Mrs Gibson; 11), Harry J. Worth (Inspector; 11), Lionel d'Aragon (Count Sylvius; 12), Laurie Leslie (Merton; 12), Frank Goldsmith (Hilton Cubitt; 13), Wally Bosco (Slaney; 13), Dezma du May (Mrs Cubitt; 13), Jack Hobbs (Henry Wood; 14), Gladys Jennings (Mrs Barclay; 14), Percy Standing (Professor Moriarty; 15).
Selected credits: Art dir: Walter W. Murton. Ed: Challis N. Sanderson. Dp: Alfred H. Moses. Scrp: Geoffrey H. Malins, P.L. Marnock. Dir: George Ridgewell.

THE LAST VAMPYRE

(see pages 164-165)
27 January 1993. Granada Television. UK. 108m. Colour.
Cast: Jeremy Brett (Sherlock Holmes), Edward Hardwicke (Dr Watson), Roy Marsden (John Stockton), Keith Barron (Bob Ferguson), Yolanda Vazquez (Carlotta), Maurice Denham (Reverend Merridew), Richard Dempsey (Jack Ferguson), Juliet Aubrey (Dolores), Jason Hetherington (Michael), Elizabeth Spriggs (Mrs Mason).
Selected credits: Des: Christopher J. Bradshaw. Mus: Patrick Gowers. Scrp: Jeremy Paul. Bo: 'The Sussex Vampire', by Doyle. Prod: June Wyndham Davies. Dir: Tim Sullivan.

LELICEK VE SLUZBACH SHERLOCKA HOLMESE

('Lelicek in the Service of Sherlock Holmes')
(see pages 34-35)
1932. Elektafilm AS. Czechoslovakia. 65m. Black and white.
Cast: Martin Fric (Sherlock Holmes), Vlasta Burian (Frantisek Lelicek and Fernando XXIII, King of Portorico), Fred Bulin (Holmes' Servant, James), Lida Baarova (Queen Kralovna).
Selected credits: Dp: Otto Heller, Jan Stallich. Scrp: Vaclav Wasserman, Hugo Vavrise. Prod: Jan Reiter. Dir: Karel Lamac.

THE LIMEJUICE MYSTERY OR WHO SPAT IN GRANDFATHER'S PORRIDGE

(see pages 148-151)
1930. Associated Sound Film Industries. UK. 8.30m. Black and white. Animated marionettes.
Selected credits: Mus: Phillip Braham. Dir: Jack Harrison.

Silent action with musical soundtrack, featuring the characters Herlock Sholmes and Anna Went Wrong.

LONESOME GHOSTS

(see pages 168-169)
1937. Walt Disney Productions. USA. Colour. Animation.
Voice cast: Walt Disney (Mickey Mouse), Pinto Colvig (Goofy), Clarence Nash (Donald Duck).
Selected credits: Prod: Burt Gillett.

THE LOSS OF A PERSONAL FRIEND

(see pages 148-151)
1987. UK. 15m. Colour.
Cast: Peter Harding (Sherlock Holmes), Ian Price (Dr Watson), Miss McKinnley (Maggie Ellis).
Selected credits: Mus: Keith Anderson. Scrp: N.G. Bristow. Prod: Michael Ostrow. Dir: N.G. Bristow.
This film was shown once on Sky Television in the UK during the late eighties with no acknowledgement of its source.

LOST IN LIMEHOUSE OR LADY ESMERELDA'S PREDICAMENT

1932. Radio Pictures, A Masquers' Presentation (Produced by The Masquers' Club of Hollywood). USA. 20m. Black and white.
Cast: Olaf Hytten (Sheerluck Jones), Charles McNaughton (Hodson), Laura La Plante (Esmerelda), John Sheenan (Sir Marmaduke Rakes).
Selected credits: Story: Walter Weemes. Dir: Otto Brower.

MAGNUM, P.I.

'Holmes is Where the Heart Is'
(see pages 110-111)
8 March 1984. CBS-TV. USA. 50m. Colour.
Cast: Patrick Macnee (Sherlock Holmes), John Hillerman (Higgins/Dr Watson), Tom Selleck (Magnum), Maurice Roeves (Hopkins), George Cheung (Victor Ching/Moriarty).
Selected credits: Scrp: Judy Burns, Jay Higely.

DER MANN, DER SHERLOCK HOLMES WAR

('The Man Who Was Sherlock Holmes')
(see pages 34-35)
July 1937. UFA. Germany. 113m. Black and white.
Cast: Hans Albers (Sherlock Holmes), Heinz Rühmann (Dr Watson), Marieluise Cladius (Mary Berry), Hansi Knotteck (Jane Berry), Hilde Weissner (Madame Ganymar), Siegfried Schürenberg (Monsieur Lapin), Paul Bildt (The Man Who Laughed [Sir Arthur Conan Doyle])
Selected credits: Mus: Hans Sommer. Dp: Fritz Arno. Scrp: Robert A. Stemmle, Karl Hartl. Prod: Alfred Greven. Dir: Karl Hartl.

THE MAN WHO DISAPPEARED

- see *The Man With the Twisted Lip*

THE MAN WITH THE TWISTED LIP

(aka *The Man Who Disappeared*)
(see pages 72-75)
1950. Dryer-Weenolsen Productions. UK. 35m. Black and white.
Cast: John Longden (Sherlock Holmes), Campbell Singer (Dr Watson), Beryl Baxter (Doreen St Clair), Walter Gotell (Luzatto), Hector Ross (Neville St Clair).
Selected credits: Prod/Dir: Richard M. Grey.

THE MASKS OF DEATH

(see page 121)
23 December 1984. Tyburn Films. UK. 90m. Colour.
Cast: Peter Cushing (Sherlock Holmes), John Mills (Dr Watson), Anne Baxter (Irene Adler), Ray Milland (Home Secretary), Anton Diffring (Von Felseck), Gordon Jackson (Inspector MacDonald), Jenny Laird (Mrs Hudson), Susan Penhaligon (Miss Derwent), Russell Hunter (Alfred Coombs).
Selected credits: Mus: Philip Martel. Scrp: N.J. Crisp. Bo: Story by John Elder (Anthony Hinds). Prod: Norman Pridgen, Kevin Francis. Dir: Roy Ward Baker.

THE MASTER BLACKMAILER

(see pages 160-161)
2 January 1992. Granada Television. UK. 108m. Colour.
Cast: Jeremy Brett (Sherlock Holmes), Edward Hardwicke (Dr Watson), Robert Hardy (Charles Augustus Milverton), Norma West (Diana, Lady Swinstead), Gwen Ffrangcon-Davies (The Dowager), Serena Gordon (Lady Eva Blackwell), Sarah McVicar (The Hon Charlotte Miles), David Mallinson (Colonel Dorking), Brian Mitchell (Harry, Earl of Dovercourt), Colin Jeavons (Inspector Lestrade), Sophie Thompson (Agatha), Rosalie Williams (Mrs Hudson), Nickolas Grace (Bertrand).
Selected credits: Des: Christopher Truelove. Mus: Patrick Gowers. Scrp: Jeremy Paul. Prod: June Wyndham Davies. Dir: Peter Hammond.

THE MEMOIRS OF SHERLOCK HOLMES

(see pages 172-175)
7 March 1994-11 April 1994. Granada Television. UK. 6 x 50m. Colour.
1 'The Three Gables', 2 'The Dying Detective', 3 'The Golden Pince-Nez', 4 'The Red Circle', 5 'The Mazarin Stone', 6 'The Cardboard Box'.
Recurring cast: Jeremy Brett (Sherlock Holmes), Edward Hardwicke (Dr Watson), Charles Gray (Mycroft Holmes), Rosalie Williams (Mrs Hudson).
Notable guest actors: Claudine Auger (Isadora Klein; 1), Peter Wyngarde (Langdale Pike; 1), Mary Ellis (Lady Maberley; 1), Benjamin Pullen (Duke of Lomond; 1), Gary Cady (Douglas Maberley; 1), Caroline Blakiston (Dowager Duchess of Lomond; 1), Michael Graham (Haines-Johnson; 1), Emma Hardwicke (Dora; 1), Richard Bonneville (Victor Savage; 2), Susannah Harker (Adelaide Savage; 2), Jonathan Hyde (Culverton Smith; 2), Roy Hudd (John Gedgrave; 2), Trevor Bowen (Charles Damant; 2), Frank Finlay (Professor Coram/Segius; 3), Nigel Planer (Inspector Hopkins; 3), Christopher Guard (Willoughby Smith; 3), Anna Carteret (Anna; 3), Kathleen Byron (Mrs Marker; 3), Daniel Finlay (Vladimir; 3), Betty Marsden (Mrs Warren; 4), Kenneth Connor (Mr Warren; 4), Tom Chadbon (Inspector Gregson; 4), Jon Finch (Count Sylvius; 5), Phyllis Calvert (Agnes Garrideb; 5), Sebastian Shaw (Nathan Garrideb; 5), James Villiers (Lord Cantlemere; 5), Joanna David (Susan Cushing; 6), Ciaran Hinds (Jim Browner; 6), Deborah Findlay (Sarah Cushing; 6), Lucy Whybrow (Mary Browner; 6).
Selected Credits: Des: Michael Young (1, 3, 6), Christopher Truelove (2, 5), Christopher Pemsel (4). Mus: Patrick Gowers. Scrp: Jeremy Paul (1, 4), T.R. Bowen (2), Gary Hopkins (3, 5), William Humble (6). Prod: June Wyndham Davies. Dir: Peter Hammond (1, 3, 5), Sarah Hellings (2, 4, 6).

THE MISSING REMBRANDT

(see page 27)
August 1932. Twickenham Film Studios Ltd. UK. 84m. Black and white.
Cast: Arthur Wontner (Sherlock Holmes), Ian Fleming (Dr Watson), Francis L. Sullivan (Baron von Guntermann), Miles Mander (Claude Holford), Jane Welsh (Lady Violet Lumsden), Minnie Rayner (Mrs Hudson), Dino Galvani (Carlo Ravelli), Philip Hewland (Inspector Lestrade), Herbert Lomas (Manning), Anthony Hollis (Marquis De Chaminade), Takase (Chang Wu).
Selected credits: Dp: Basil Emmott. Scrp: Cyril Twyford, H. Fowler Mear. Bo: 'Charles Augustus Milverton', by Doyle. Prod: Julius Hagen. Dir: Leslie Hiscott.

MORIARTY

- see *Sherlock Holmes* (1922)

THE MUPPET BABIES

(see pages 168-169)
1984–87. A Marvel Production in association with Henson Associates/CBS TV. USA. 23m per episode. Colour. Animation.
Relevant episodes include: 'The Case of the Missing Chicken' (1984), 'Once Upon an Egg Timer' (1985), 'Of Mice and Puppets' (1986), 'The Muppet Broadcasting Company' (1986), 'Plan Eight From Outer Space' (1987)'.
Voice cast: Russi Taylor (Gonzo), Frank Welker (Beaker), Dave Coulier (Bunsen).
Selected credits: Scrp: Lois Becker, Mark Stratton. Prod: Roy Allen Smith, Hank Sayoran, Bob Richardson.
The episode 'The Muppet Broadcasting Company' features Dr Bunsen Honeydew and his assistant Beaker playing 'Sherlock Bunsen' and 'Dr Beaker' in a radio drama.

MURDER AT THE BASKERVILLES

- see *Silver Blaze* (1937)

MURDER BY DECREE

(see pages 108-109)
2 February 1979. Ambassador Films/Famous Players/Avco Embassy Pictures. Canada. 120m. Colour.
Cast: Christopher Plummer (Sherlock Holmes), James Mason (Dr Watson), David Hemmings (Inspector Foxborough), Susan Clark (Mary Kelly), Anthony Quayle (Sir Charles Warren), John Gielgud (Prime Minister), Frank Finlay (Inspector Lestrade), Donald Sutherland (Robert Lees), Genevieve Bujold (Annie Crook), Betty Woolf (Mrs Hudson), Iris Fry (Elizabeth Stride), Geoffrey Russell (Home Secretary), Roy Lansford (Sir Thomas Spivey), Victor Langeley (Prince of Wales).
Selected credits: Des: Harry Pottle. Mus: Carl Zittrer, Paul Zaza. Dp: Reginald H. Morris. Scrp: John Hopkins. Bo: *The Ripper File* (TV series), by John Lloyd and Elwyn Jones. Exec prod: Len Herberman. Prod: Rene Dupon, Bob Clark. Dir: Bob Clark.

MURDER ON THE BLUEBELL LINE

(see pages 148-151)
1 April 1987. BBC TV. UK. 35m. Colour.
Cast: Hugh Fraser (Sherlock Holmes), Ronald Fraser (Dr Watson).
Selected Credits: Scrp: John Lynch. Dir: John Lynch. A documentary, based on *The Piltdown Inquest* (1986).

MURDER ROOMS - THE DARK BEGINNINGS OF SHERLOCK HOLMES

(US *The Dark Beginnings of Sherlock Holmes*)
(see pages 176-177)
4 and 5 January 2000. BBC Television. UK. 2x60 m. Colour.
Cast: Ian Richardson (Joseph Bell), Robin Laing (Arthur Conan Doyle), Charles Dance (Sir Henry Carlyle), Alec Newman (Neill Cream), Dolly Wells (Elspeth Scott).
Selected credits: Mus: Jim Parker; Scrp: David Pirie; Prod: Ian Madden; Dir: Paul Seed.

MURDER ROOMS — THE KINGDOM OF BONES

(see page 182)
25 September 2001. BBC Television. UK. 90m. Colour.
Cast: Ian Richardson (Joseph Bell), Charles Edwards (Arthur Conan Doyle), John Sessions (Professor Rutherford), Simon Chandler (Inspector Warner), Ian McNeice (Heyward Donovan), Caroline Carver (Gladys Donovan), Crispin Bonham-Carter (Reuben Proctor), Innes Doyle (Ben McLeod), Miles Richardson (Everard Im Thurn).
Selected credits: Mus: John Lunn; Scrp: Stephen Gallagher; Prod: Alison Jackson; Dir: Simon Langton.

MURDER ROOMS — THE PATIENT'S EYES

(see page 180)
4 September 2001. BBC Television. UK. 90m. Colour.
Cast: Ian Richardson (Joseph Bell), Charles Edwards (Arthur Conan Doyle), Alexander Armstrong (Turnavine), Andrew Woodall (Greenwell), Dragan Micanovic (Coatley), Simon Chandler (Inspector Warner).
Selected credits: Mus: John Lunn; Scrp: David Pirie; Prod: Alison Jackson; Dir: Tim Fywell.

MURDER ROOMS — THE PHOTOGRAPHER'S CHAIR

(see page 181)
18 September 2001. BBC Television. UK. 90 m. Colour.
Cast: Ian Richardson (Joseph Bell), Charles Edwards (Arthur Conan Doyle), Clare Holman (Miss Petchey), Tim Woodward (Rhodes), Simon Chandler (Inspector Warner), Roger Lloyd Pack (Dr Ibbotson), David Hayman (Mitchell), Claire Harman (Elspeth).
Selected credits: Mus: John Lunn; Scrp: Paul Billing; Prod: Alison Jackson; Dir: Paul Marcus.

MURDER ROOMS — THE WHITE KNIGHT STRATAGEM

(see page183)
2 October 2001. BBC Television. UK. 90m. Colour.
Cast: Ian Richardson (Joseph Bell), Charles Edwards (Arthur Conan Doyle), Rik Mayall (Blaney), Hugh Ross (Doyle Senior), Ronald Pickup (Sir John Starr), Annette Crosbie (Margaret Booth), Anton Lesser (Milburn).
Selected credits: Mus: John Lunn; Scrp: Daniel Boyle; Prod: Alison Jackson: Dir: Paul Marcus.

MY GRANDFATHER'S CLOCK

1934. MGM. USA. 17m. Colour.
Cast: Charles Judels (Philo Holmes), Franklin Pangborn (Dr Watkin), William Tannen, Pauline Brooks.
Selected credits: Technicolor phot: Ray Rennahan. Lyrical continuity: Felix E. Feist. Mus: Felix E. Feist. Scrp: Felix E. Feist. Dir: Felix E. Feist.

THE NEW ADVENTURES OF WINNIE THE POOH

'Tigger, Private Eye'
(see pages 168-169)
1989. Walt Disney Television Animation Productions. USA. 12m. Colour. Animation.
Voice cast: Jim Cummings, Tim Hoskins, Paul Winchell, Peter Cullen, John Fiedler, Nicholas Melody.
Selected credits: Prod: Karl Geurs. Dir: Karl Geurs.

THE NEW SCOOBY AND SCRAPPY DOO SHOW

'The Hound of the Scoobyvilles'
(see pages 168-169)
1983. Hanna-Barbera Productions/ABC-TV. USA. 10m. Colour. Animation.
Voice cast: Casey Kasem (Shaggy), Don Messick (Scooby).
Selected credits: Scrp: Gene Ayres. Prod: Art Scott.

1994 BAKER STREET: SHERLOCK HOLMES RETURNS

(see page 166)
12 September 1993. Paragon Entertainment Corporation in association with Kenneth Johnson Productions. USA. 97m. Colour.
Cast: Anthony Higgins (Sherlock Holmes), Debrah Farentino (Dr Amy Winslow), Mark Adair Rios (Zappa), Joy Coghill (Mrs Hudson), Julian Christopher (Detective Griffin), Ken Pogue (James Moriarty Booth), John Wardlow (Old Man Moriarty), Daniel Chambers (Mr Hudson), Norman Armour (Father Moriarty).
Selected credits: Mus: Janes Di Pasquale. Scrp: Kenneth Johnson. Exec prod: Jon Slan. Assoc prod: Susan Apling. Prod: Kenneth Johnson. Dir: Kenneth Johnson.

NORDISK SERIES

(see pages 12-15)
The Nordisk studios (The Great Northern Film Company) in Denmark produced a series of black and white Silent films featuring Sherlock Holmes (often, but not always, played by Viggo Larsen) between 1908 and 1911.

SHERLOCK HOLMES I
SHERLOCK HOLMES IN DANGER OF HIS LIFE

(Original title: *Sherlock Holmes i Livsfare*)
1908. Nordisk. Black and white. Silent
Cast: Viggo Larsen (Sherlock Holmes), Holger Madsen (Raffles), Gustav Lund (Moriarty).
Selected credits: Scrp: Viggo Larsen. Dir: Viggo Larsen.

SHERLOCK HOLMES II
RAFFLES' ESCAPE FROM PRISON

(Original title: *Raffles Flugt fra Fængslet*)
1908. Nordisk. Black and white. Silent
Cast: Viggo Larsen (Sherlock Holmes), Holger Madsen (Raffles).
Selected credits: Scrp: Viggo Larsen. Dir: Viggo Larsen.

SHERLOCK HOLMES III
THE THEFT OF THE STATE DOCUMENT

(Original title: *Det Hemmelige Dokument* ['The Secret Document']/aka *Sherlock Holmes in the Gas Cellar*)
1908. Nordisk. Black and white. Silent
Cast: Einar Zangeberg (Sherlock Holmes).
Selected credits: Scrp: Viggo Larsen. Dir: Viggo Larsen.

SHERLOCK HOLMES IV
THE THEFT OF THE DIAMONDS

(Original title: *Sangerindens Diamanter* ['The Singer's Diamonds'])
1909. Nordisk. Black and white. Silent
Cast: Viggo Larsen (Sherlock Holmes).
Selected credits: Scrp: Viggo Larsen. Dir: Viggo Larsen.

SHERLOCK HOLMES V
CAB NO. 519 or THE LEGACY ROBBERY

(Original title: *Droske Nr. 519*)
1909. Nordisk. Black and white. Silent
Cast: Viggo Larsen (Sherlock Holmes), Elith Pio (The Heir).
Selected credits: Scrp: Viggo Larsen. Dir: Viggo Larsen.

SHERLOCK HOLMES VI
THE GREY DAME or THE GREY LADY or OF SHERLOCK HOLMES' MEMORIES

(Original title: *Den Grå Dam* or *Af Sherlock Holmes Opleveser VI*)
1909. Nordisk. Black and white. Silent
Cast: Viggo Larsen (Sherlock Holmes), Gustav Lund (Lord Beresford), Elith Pio (Willy, Lord Beresford's Son), Poul Welander (John, Lord Beresford's Nephew).
Selected credits: Scrp: Viggo Larsen. Dir: Viggo Larsen.

THE BOGUS GOVERNESS

(Original title: *Den Forklædte Guvernante* or *Den Forklædte Barnepige*)
1910. Nordisk. Black and white. Silent
Cast: Otto Lagoni (Sherlock Holmes), Poul Welander (The Father).

A CONFIDENCE TRICK

(Original title: *Sherlock Holmes i Bondefangerkløer* ['Sherlock Holmes in the Hands of the Confidence Men'] or *Den Stjaalne Tegnebog* ['The Stolen Wallet'])
1910. Nordisk. Black and white. Silent
Cast: Otto Lagoni (Sherlock Holmes).

THE BLACK HAND or
THE BLACKMAILERS

(Original title: *Den Sorte Haand* or *Mordet i Baker Street* ['Murder in Baker Street'])
1910. Nordisk. Black and white. Silent
Cast: Otto Lagoni (Sherlock Holmes), Axel Boesen (The Rich Mr X). Ingeborg Rasmussen (Mrs X),
Poul Welander (The Villain), Erik Crone (The Boy Dick).
Selected credits: Dir: Holger Rasmussen.

THE STOLEN LEGACY or THE MILLION DOLLAR BOND

(Original title: *Milliontestamentet* or *Millionobligationen* or *Den Stjålne Millionobligation*)
1910. Nordisk. Black and white. Silent
Cast: Alwin Neuss (Sherlock Holmes), Einar Zangenberg (Dr Mors), Mrs Zangenberg (The Countess), Anton Seitzberg (Billy), Victor Fabian (A Police Constable).

HOTEL THIEVES

(Original title: *Hotelrotterne* or *Hotelmysterierne* or *Sherlock Holmes' Sidste Bedrifter*)
1910. Nordisk. Black and white. Silent
Cast: Einar Zangenberg (Sherlock Holmes), H.C. Nielsen (The Villain).

THE BLACK HOOD or
THE CONSPIRATORS

(Original title: *Den Sorte Hætte*)
1911. Nordisk. Black and white. Silent
Cast: Lauritz Olsen (Sherlock Holmes), Otto Lagoni (Harry Clarke, Leader of the Black Hood Gang).
Selected credits: Scrp: Ravn Jonson. Dir: William Augustinus.

THE OTHER SIDE

(see pages 158-159)
2 August 1992. BBC TV. UK. 50m. Colour.
Cast: Frank Finlay (Sir Arthur Conan Doyle), Richard E. Grant (Sherlock Holmes), Cathryn Harrison (Madame Moshel).
Selected credits: Mus: Rob Hadleigh. Scrp: David Aston.

O XANGO DE BAKER STREET

October 2001. Sky Light Cinema Foto and Art Ltda. Brazil. 118m. Colour.
Cast: Joaquim de Almeida (Sherlock Holmes), Anthony O'Donnell (Dr Watson), Maria de Medieros (Sarah Bernhardt).
Selected credits: Mus: Edu Lobo; Scrp: Marcus Bernstein, Miguel Faria Jnr, Patricia Melo from the novel by Jo Soares; Dir: Miguel Faria Jnr.

PARAMOUNT ON PARADE

(see page 22)
Holmes sequence: 'Murder Will Out (A Travesty of Detective Mysteries)'
April 1930. Paramount Pictures. USA. 102m. Black and white.
Cast: Clive Brook (Sherlock Holmes), Philo Vance (William Powell), Warner Oland (Dr Fu Manchu), H. Reeves-Smith (Dr Watson), Eugene Pallette (Sgt Heath), Jack Oakie (The Victim).
Selected credits: Sup dir: Elsie Janis. Exec prod: David O. Selznick. Sequence dir: Frank Tuttle.

THE PEARL OF DEATH

(see pages 56-57)
August 1944. Universal Pictures. USA. 67m. Black and white.
Cast: Basil Rathbone (Sherlock Holmes), Nigel Bruce (Dr Watson), Evelyn Ankers (Naomi Drake), Miles Mander (Giles Conover), Rondo Hatton (The Creeper), Dennis Hoey (Lestrade), Mary Gordon (Mrs Hudson), Ian Wolfe (Amos Holder), Charles Francis (Digby).
Selected credits: Art dir: John B. Goodman, Martin Obzina. Ed: Jay Snyder. Mus: Frank Skinner. Dp: Virgil Miller. Scrp: Bertram Millhauser. Bo: 'The Adventure of the Six Napoleons', by Doyle. Prod: Roy William Neill. Dir: Roy William Neill.

PRIVATE EYE POPEYE

(see pages 148-151)
1954. Paramount Pictures. USA. 6.30m. Colour. Animation.
Voice cast: Jack Mercer (Popeye).
Selcted credits: Dir: Max Fleischer.

THE PRIVATE LIFE OF
SHERLOCK HOLMES

(see pages 94-97)
28 October 1970. Mirisch Production Co/United Artists/Phalanx/Sir Nigel. USA. 125m. Colour.
Cast: Robert Stephens (Sherlock Holmes), Colin Blakely (Dr Watson), Irene Handl (Mrs Hudson), Christopher Lee (Mycroft Holmes), Genevieve Page (Gabrielle Valladon), Stanley Holloway (First Gravedigger), Clive Revill (Rogozhin), Tamara Toumanova (Petrova), Mollie Maureen (Queen Victoria), George Benson* (Inspector Lestrade). [* Cut from the release print.]
Selected Credits: Prod des: Alexander Trauner. Art dir: Tony Inglis. Ed: Ernest Walter. Mus: Miklos Rozsa. Dp: Christopher Challis. Scrp: Billy Wilder, I.A.L. Diamond. Assoc prod: I.A.L. Diamond. Prod: Billy Wilder. Dir: Billy Wilder.

PROFESSOR LIGHTFOOT
AND DR TWIDDLE

(see pages 148-151)
1953. CBS-TV. Canada. 13 x 15m. Black and white.
1 'The Haunted House', 2 'Mix-up in Mexico', 3 'Terror by Train', 4 'A-feudin' and A-fightin'', 5 'Inside India', 6 'Trapped in a Trunk', 7 'The Hatchet Man', 8 'Net of Fate', 9 'Out West', 10 'A Case of Hypnosis', 11 'Darkest Africa', 12 'Room for a Night', 13 'Thief in the Night'.
Cast: Trained chimpanzees.
Recurring voice cast: Paul Frees (Sherlock Holmes). Daws Butler (Dr Watson).

PURSUIT TO ALGIERS

(see pages 62-63)
October 1945. Universal Pictures. USA. 65m. Black and white.
Cast: Basil Rathbone (Sherlock Holmes), Nigel Bruce (Dr Watson), Marjorie Riordan (Sheila), Rosalind Ivan (Agatha Dunham), Martin Kosleck (Mirko), Rex Evans (Gregor), John Abbott (Jodri), Frederic Worlock (Prime Minister), Morton Lowry (Sanford), Wee Willie Davis (Gubec), Gerald Hamer (Kingston), Wilson Benge (Clergyman), Leslie Vincent ([King] Nikolas).
Selected credits: Art dir: John B. Goodman, Martin Obzina. Ed: Saul A. Goodkind. Mus: Frank Skinner. Dp: Paul Ivano. Scrp: Leonard Lee. Prod: Roy William Neill. Dir: Roy William Neill.

REICHENBACH FALLS

(see page 131)
1 March 2007. BBC Scotland. UK. 75m. Colour.
Cast: Alex Newman (John Buchan), John Sessions (Joseph Bell), Richard Wilson (Conan Doyle).
Selected Credits: Scrp: James Major from an idea by Ian Rankin; Prod: Gaynor Holmes; Dir: John McKay.

REMINGTON STEELE

'Steele's Gold'
(aka 'Elementary Steele')
22 May 1984. NBC-TV. USA. 49m. Colour.
Cast: Pierce Brosnan (Remington Steele), Stephanie Zimbalist (Laura), Peter Evans (Sherlock Holmes), Keone Young (Mr Moto).
Selected credits: Scrp: Michael Gleason. Prod: Gareth Davis. Dir: Robert Butler.

THE RETURN OF
SHERLOCK HOLMES

(see page 22)
25 October 1929. Paramount. USA. 79m. Black and white. Silent/Sound.
Cast: Clive Brook (Sherlock Holmes), H. Reeves-Smith (Dr Watson), Harry T. Morey (Professor Moriarty), Donald Crisp (Sebastian Moran), Betty Lawford (Mary Watson), Phillips Holmes (Roger Longmore), Hubert Ducre (Roger).
Selected credits: Ed: Helene Turner. Dp: William Steiner Jr. Scrp: Basil Dean, Garrett Fort. Prod: David O. Selznick. Dir: Basil Dean, completed by Clive Brook.

THE RETURN OF
SHERLOCK HOLMES

(see pages 136-139)
9 July-20 August 1986; 6 April-27 April 1988.
Granada Television. UK. 11 x 50m. Colour.
(Series 1) 1 'The Empty House', 2 'The Abbey
Grange', 3 'The Musgrave Ritual', 4 'The Second
Stain', 5 'The Man With the Twisted Lip', 6 'The
Priory School', 7 'The Six Napoleons'. (Series 2)
8 'The Devil's Foot', 9 'Silver Blaze', 10 'Wisteria
Lodge', 11 'The Bruce-Partington Plans'.
Recurring cast: Jeremy Brett (Sherlock Holmes),
Edward Hardwicke (Dr Watson), Rosalie Williams
(Mrs Hudson; 1, 4-6, 9, 11), Colin Jeavons (Inspector
Lestrade; 1, 4, 7),
Notable guest actors: Patrick Allen (Colonel
Sebastian Moran; 1), Paul Lacoux (Hon Ronald
Adair; 1), Paul Williamson (Inspector Hopkins; 2),
Conrad Phillips (Sir Eustace Brackenstall; 2), Anne
Louise Lambert (Lady Mary Brackenstall; 2), Oliver
Tobias (Captain Croker; 2), Michael Culver
(Reginald Musgrave; 3), James Hazeldine (Richard
Brunton; 3), Patricia Hodge (Lady Hilda Trelawney
Hope; 4), Stuart Wilson (Hon Trelawney Hope; 4),
Clive Francis (Neville St Clair/Hugh Boone; 5),
Eleanor David (Mrs St Clair; 5), Terence Longdon
(Isa Whitney; 5), Denis Lill (Inspector Bradstreet; 5,
11), Alan Howard (Duke of Holdernesse; 6),
Nicholas Gecks (James Wilder; 6), Eric Sykes
(Horace Harker; 7), Marina Sirtis (Lucretia; 7),
Steve Plytas (Venucci; 7), Emile Wolk (Beppo; 7),
Gerald Campion (Morse Hudson; 7), Denis Quilley
(Leon Sterndale; 8), Peter Barkworth (Colonel Ross;
9), Malcolm Storry (Inspector Gregory; 9), Freddie
Jones (Inspector Baynes; 10), Donald Churchill
(Scott Eccles; 10), Charles Gray (Mycroft Holmes;
11), Jonathan Newth (Colonel Valentine Walter; 11),
Amanda Waring (Violet Westbury; 11), Sebastian
Stride (Cadogan West; 11), Geoffrey Bayldon
(Sidney Johnson; 11).
Selected credits: Des: Margaret Coombes (1, 6),
Tim Wilding (2, 4, 5, 7, 10), Michael Grimes (3, 8),
Alan Price (9), Alan Pickford (11). Mus: Patrick
Gowers. Scrp: John Hawkesworth (1, 4, 5, 9,11),
T. R. Bowen (2, 6), Jeremy Paul (3, 10), Alan Plater
(6), John Kane (7), Gary Hopkins (8). Exec prod:
Michael Cox. Prod: June Wyndham Davies.
Dir: Howard Baker (1), Peter Hammond (2, 10),
David Carson (3, 7), John Bruce (4), Patrick Lau (5),
John Madden (6), Ken Hannam (8), Brian Mills (9),
John Gorrie (11).

THE RETURN OF
SHERLOCK HOLMES
(see page 141)
10 January 1987. CBS Entertainment. USA. 100m.
Colour.
Cast: Michael Pennington (Sherlock Holmes),
Margaret Colin (Miss Jane Watson), Lila Kaye
(Mrs Houston), Connie Booth (Violet Morstan),
Nicholas Guest (Toby), Barry Morse (Carter
Morstan), Paul Maxwell (Hopkins), Sheila Brand
(Kitty).
Selected credits: Scrp: Bob Shayne. Prod: Nick
Gillot. Dir: Kevin Connor.

THE RETURN OF THE WORLD'S
GREATEST DETECTIVE
(see pages 100-101)
June 1976. Universal Studios. USA. 78m. Colour.
Cast: Larry Hagman (Sherman Holmes), Jenny
O'Hara (Dr Joan Watson), Nicholas Colsanto
(Lt Tinker), Helen Verbit (Mrs Hudson),
Ivor Francis (Spiner).
Selected credits: Scrp: Roland Kibbee, Dean
Hargrove. Prod: Roland Kibbee. Dir: Dean Hargrove.

UN RIVALE DE
SHERLOCK HOLMES
(USA *Rival Sherlock Holmes*)
(see pages 12-15)
1908. Societa Anonima Ambrosio. Italy. 1 reel.
Black and white. Silent
Cast: Unknown

THE ROBBERY AT THE
RAILROAD STATION

(see pages 148-151)
26 February 1912. Champion Film Company. USA.
Black and white. Silent.
Stars two unnamed actors as Sherlocko and Watso
from a contemporary comic strip.

ROTTERDAM – AMSTERDAM
1918. Messter-Film. Germany. 1145 metres.
Black and white. Silent.
Cast: Viggo Larsen (Sherlock Holmes).
Selected credits: Scrp: Richard Hunter.
Dir: Viggo Larsen.

THE ROYAL SCANDAL
(see page 184)
19 October 2001. Muse Entertainment Enterprises in
association Hallmark Entertainment. Canada. 90m.
Colour.
Cast: Matt Frewer (Sherlock Holmes), Kenneth
Welsh (Dr Watson), Liliana Komorowska (Irene
Adler), R. H. Thomas (Mycroft Holmes), Daniel
Brochu (Wiggins), Robin Wilcox (Crown Prince).
Selected credits: Dp: Serge Ladouceur; Cos des: Luc
J. Beland; Mus: Marc Ouellette; Exec Prod: Steven
Hewitt, Michael Prupas; Prod: Irene Litinsky; Scrp:
Joe Wiesenfeld; Dir: Rodney Gibbons.

THE SCARLET CLAW
(see pages 54-55)
June 1944. Universal Pictures. USA. 74m.
Black and white.
Cast: Basil Rathbone (Sherlock Holmes),
Nigel Bruce (Dr Watson), Gerald Hamer
(Potts/Tanner/Alistair Ransom), Paul Cavanagh
(Lord Penrose), Arthur Hohl (Emile Journet),
Miles Mander (Judge Brisson), Kay Harding
(Marie Journet), David Clyde (Sergeant Thompson),
Ian Wolfe (Drake), Victoria Horne (Nora), George
Kirby (Father Pierre), Frank O'Connor (Cab
Driver), Harry Allen (Storekeeper).
Selected credits: Art dir: John B. Goodman, Ralph
M. Delacy. Ed: Paul Landres. Sp effects: John P.
Fulton. Dp: George Robinson. Mus: Frank Skinner.
Scrp: Edmund L. Hartmann, Roy William Neill.
Original story: Paul Gangelin, Brenda Weisberg.
Prod: Roy William Neill. Dir: Roy William Neill.

THE SCARLET RING
- see *A Study in Terror* (1933)

EIN SCHREI IN DER NACHT
('A Scream in the Night')
1915. Decla. Germany. 3 reels. Black and white.
Silent.
Cast: Alwin Neuss (Sherlock Holmes).
Selected credits: Scrp: Paul Rosenhayn.
Dir: Alwin Neuss.

THE SEVEN-PER-CENT SOLUTION
(see pages 104-105)
24 October 1976. Universal Pictures. USA. 113m.
Colour.
Cast: Nicol Williamson (Sherlock Holmes),
Robert Duvall (Dr Watson), Alan Arkin (Sigmund
Freud), Vanessa Redgrave (Lola Deveraux),
Laurence Olivier (Professor Moriarty), Jeremy Kemp
(Baron Von Leinsdorf), Charles Gray (Mycroft
Holmes), Alison Leggatt (Miss Hudson), Joel Grey
(Lowenstein), Samantha Eggar (Mary Morstan
Watson), Gertan Klauber (Amin Pasha).
Selected credits: Prod des: Ken Adam. Mus: John
Addison. Dp: Oswald Morris. Scrp: Nicholas Meyer.
Bo: Novel by Nicholas Meyer. Prod: Herbert Ross.
Dir: Herbert Ross.

SHERLICK HOLMES
(see pages 148-151)
1976. Taurus Productions Blue Video. USA. 90m.
Colour.
Cast: Harry Reems (Sherlick Holmes), Zebedy
Colt (Dr Watson), Annie Sprinkle, Candy Love,
Bobby Astyr, Elvera.
Selected credits: Scrp: Bear Wilson. Prod: Ralph
Ell. Dir: Tim McCoy.

SHERLOCK — CASE OF EVIL
(See page 186)
5 August 2001. Box TV/Pueblo Films Production.
USA. 100m. Colour.
Cast: James D'Arcy (Sherlock Holmes), Roger
Morlidge (Dr Watson), Vincent D'Onofrio
(Professor Moriarty), Gabrielle Anwar (Rebecca
Doyle), Richard E. Grant (Mycroft Holmes),
Nicholas Gecks (Inspector Lestrade).
Selected credits: Dp: Lukas Strebel; Mus: Mike
Moran; Prod: Tim Bradley; Scrp: Piers Ashworth;
Dir: Tim Bradley.

SHERLOCK HOLMES
1908. Projectograph. Hungary. 1 reel.
Black and white. Silent.
Cast: Bauman Karoly (Sherlock Holmes).

SHERLOCK HOLMES
1909. Italia Film Company. Italy. Black and white.
Silent.
Cast: unknown.

SHERLOCK HOLMES
(see pages 12-15)
May 1916. Essanay Film Mfg Co. USA. 64m.
Black and white. Silent.
Cast: William Gillette (Sherlock Holmes), Edward
Fielding (Dr Watson), Ernest Maupain (Professor
Moriarty), Marjorie Kay (Alice Faulkner), William
Pestance (Prince), Stewart Robbins (Benjamin
Foreman), Grace Reals (Madge Larrabee), Buford
Hampden (Little Billy), Fred Malatesta (McTague).
Selected credits: Scrp: H.S. Sheldon, William
Gillette. Bo: *Sherlock Holmes* (play), by
William Gillette. Dir: Arthur Bethelt.

SHERLOCK HOLMES
Kowo Films. Germany. Black and White. Silent.
A series of nine films produced between
1917–1919.

DER ERDSTROMMOTOR
('The Earthquake Motor')
1917.
Cast: Hugo Flink (Sherlock Holmes).
Selected credits: Scrp: Paul Rosenhayn.
Dir: Karl Heinz Wolff.

DIE KASETTE
('The Casket')
1917.
Cast: Hugo Flink (Sherlock Holmes).
Selected credits: Scrp: Paul Rosenhayn.
Dir: Karl Heinz Wolff.

DER SCHLANGENRING
('The Snake Ring')
1917.
Cast: Hugo Flink (Sherlock Holmes).
Selected credits: Scrp: Paul Rosenhayn.
Dir: Karl Heinz Wolff.

DIE INDISCHE SPINNE
('The Indian Spider')
1917.
Cast: Hugo Flink (Sherlock Holmes).
Selected credits: Scrp: Paul Rosenhayn. Dir: Karl
Heinz Wolff.

WAS ER IM SPIEGEL SAH
('What He Saw in the Mirror')
1918.
Cast: Ferdinand Bonn (Sherlock Holmes).
Selected credits: Dir: Karl Heinz Wolff.

DIE GIFTPLOMBE
('The Poisoned Seal')
1918.
Cast: Ferdinand Bonn (Sherlock Holmes).
Selected credits: Dir: Karl Heinz Wolff.

DAS SCHICKSAL DER
RENATE YONGK
('The Fate of Renate Yongk')

1918.
Cast: Ferdinand Bonn (Sherlock Holmes).
Selected credits: Scrp: Werner Bernhardy.
Dir: Karl Heinz Wolff.

DIE DOSE DES KARDINALS
('The Cardinal's Snuffbox')
1918.
Cast: Ferdinand Bonn (Sherlock Holmes).
Selected credits: Scrp: Otto Schubert-Stevens.
Dir: Karl Heinz Wolff.

DER MORD IM SPLENDID HOTEL
('Murder in the Hotel Splendid')
1919.
Cast: Kurt Brenkendorff (Sherlock Holmes).
Selected credits: Dir: Karl Heinz Wolff.

SHERLOCK HOLMES
(UK *Moriarty*)
(see pages 18-19)
1 May 1922. Goldwyn Pictures. USA. 136m.
Black and white. Silent.
Cast: John Barrymore (Sherlock Holmes),
Roland Young (Dr Watson), Gustav von Seyffertitz
(Professor Moriarty), Carol Dempster (Alice
Faulkner), Hedda Hopper (Madge Larrabee),
William H. Powell (Forman Wells), Louis Wolheim
(Craigin), John Willard (Inspector Gregson),
Reginald Denny (Prince Alexis), Anders Randolf
(Larrabee).
Selected credits: Dp: J. Roy Hunt. Scrp: Marion
Fairfax, Earle Browne. Bo: *Sherlock Holmes* (play), by
William Gillette. Prod: F.J. Godsol. Dir: Albert
Parker.

SHERLOCK HOLMES
(see pages 28-29)
11 November 1932. Fox. USA. 68m. Black and white.
Cast: Clive Brook (Sherlock Holmes), Reginald
Owen (Dr Watson), Miriam Jordan (Alice Faulkner),
Ernest Torrence (Professor Moriarty), Howard Leeds
(Billy the Page), Alan Mowbray (Inspector Gore-
King), Herbert Mundin (Pub Keeper), Montague
Shaw (Judge), Arnold Lucy (Chaplain), Lucien
Prival (Hans, the Hun), Roy D'Arcy (Manuel Lopez),
Stacey Fields (Tony Ardetti), Edward Dillon
(Ardetti's Henchman), Robert Graves Jr (Gaston
Roux), Brandon Hurst (Secretary to Erskine),
Claude King (Sir Albert Hastings), Ivan Simpson
(Faulkner).
Selected credits: Ed: Margaret Clancy. Dp: George
Barnes. Scrp: Bertram Millhauser. Prod: William Fox.
Dir: William K. Howard.

SHERLOCK HOLMES
(see pages 72-75)
1951. BBC TV. UK. 6 x 30m (some programmes
overran). Black and white.
1 'The Empty House', 2 'A Scandal in Bohemia', 3
'The Dying Detective', 4 'The Reigate Squires', 5
'The Red-Headed League', 6 'The Second Stain'.
Recurring cast: Alan Wheatley (Sherlock Holmes),
Raymond Francis (Dr Watson), Bill Owen (Inspector
Lestrade; 1, 3, 5, 6), Iris Vandeleur
(Mrs Hudson; 1, 3, 4, 6).
Notable guest actors: Henry Oscar (Culverton Smith;
3), Sebastian Cabot (Jabez Wilson; 5), John Le
Mesurier (Eduardo Lucas; 6).
Selected credits: Scrp: C. A. Lejeune. Prod/Dir:
Ian Atkins.

SHERLOCK HOLMES
(see pages 76-77)
1953-1954. Guild Films. USA. 39 x 30m.
Black and white.
1 'The Case of the Cunningham Heritage',
2 'The Case of Lady Beryl', 3 'The Case of the
Pennsylvania Gun', 4 'The Case of the Texas
Cowgirl', 5 'The Case of the Belligerent Ghost',
6 'The Case of the Shy Ballerina', 7 'The Case of
the Winthrop Legend', 8 'The Case of Blind Man's
Bluff', 9 'The Case of Harry Croker', 10 'The
Mother Hubbard Case', 11 'The Case of the Red-
Headed League', 12 'The Case of the Shoeless

Engineer', 13 'The Case of the Split Ticket', 14 'The
Case of the French Interpreter', 15 'The Case of the
Singing Violin', 16 'The Case of the Greystone
Inscription', 17 'The Case of the Laughing Mummy',
18 'The Case of the Thistle Killer', 19 'The Case of
the Vanished Detective', 20 'The Case of the Careless
Suffragette', 21 'The Case of the Reluctant
Carpenter', 22 'The Case of the Deadly Prophecy',
23 'The Case of the Christmas Pudding', 24 'The
Case of the Night Train Riddle', 25 'The Case of the
Violent Suitor', 26 'The Case of the Baker Street
Nursemaids', 27 'The Case of the Perfect Husband',
28 'The Case of the Jolly Hangman', 29 'The Case of
the Imposter Mystery', 30 'The Case of the Eiffel
Tower', 31 'The Case of the Exhumed Client', 32
'The Case of the Impromptu Performance', 33 'The
Case of the Baker Street Bachelors', 34 ' The Case of
the Royal Murder', 35 'The Case of the Haunted
Gainsborough', 36 'The Case of the Neurotic
Detective', 37 'The Case of the Unlucky Gambler',
38 'The Case of the Diamond Tooth', 39 'The Case
of the Tyrant's Daughter'.
Recurring cast: Ronald Howard (Sherlock Holmes),
Howard Marion Crawford (Dr Watson), Archie
Duncan (Inspector Lestrade).
Notable guest actors: Pierre Gay (Ralph
Cunningham; 1), Ursula Howells (Jan; 1), Paulette
Goddard (Lady Beryl; 2), Peter Copley (Lord Beryl;
2/John Winthrop; 7), Gregore Aslan (Jocko Farrady;
8), David Oxley (Haterley; 12), Harris [Harry] Towb
(Brian O'Casey; 13), Tony Wright (John Cartwright;
16), Michael Gough (Russell Partridge; 27), Basil
Dignam (Sir Arthur Treadley; 29), Richard
O'Sullivan (Andy Finwick; 32).
Selected credits: Scrp: Sheldon Reynolds (1, 2, 3, 8,
20, 25), Charles M. and Joseph Early (4, 17-19, 27,
30, 34-36), Charles M. Early (5, 6, 17), Harold J.
Bloom (7, 9, 12), Lou Morheim (10, 11, 13, 14, 23,
24, 28, 31, 33, 36-38), Kay Krause (15), Hamilton
Keener (26), Roger E. Garris (29, 32, 34, 39),
Gertrude and George Fass (16, 21, 22). Prod: Sheldon
Reynolds. Dir: Jack Gage (1, 2, 7, 10, 20), Sheldon
Reynolds (3, 5, 6, 8, 9, 11, 17, 22, 26, 38), Steve Previn
(4, 12-16, 18, 19, 21, 23, 24, 25, 27-37, 39).

SHERLOCK HOLMES
(see pages 86-87)
1965. BBC TV. UK. 12 x 50m. Black and white.
1 'The Illustrious Client', 2 'The Devil's Foot', 3 'The
Copper Beeches', 4 'The Red-Headed League',
5 'The Abbey Grange', 6 'The Six Napoleons',
7 'The Man With the Twisted Lip', 8 'The Beryl
Coronet', 9 'The Bruce-Partington Plans', 10
'Charles Augustus Milverton', 11 'The Retired
Colourman', 12 'The Disappearance of Lady Frances
Carfax'.
Recurring cast: Douglas Wilmer (Sherlock Holmes),
Nigel Stock (Dr Watson), Peter Madden (Inspector
Lestrade; 6, 7, 9-12), Enid Lindsey (Mrs Hudson; 9,
11, 12).
Notable guest actors: Peter Wyngarde (Baron
Gruner; 1), Rosemary Leach (Kitty Winter; 1),
Patrick Troughton (Mortimer Tregennis; 2), Patrick
Wymark (Jephro Rucastle; 3), Nyree Dawn Porter
(Lady Brackenstall; 5), Anton Rogers (Hugh
Boone/Neville St Clair; 7), David Burke (Sir George
Burnwell; 8), Derek Francis (Mycroft Holmes; 9),
Maurice Denham (Josiah Amberley; 11), Joss
Ackland (Philip Green; 12).
Selected credits: Scrp: Giles Cooper (1, 2, 6, 9),
Vincent Tisley (3, 12), Anthony Read (4), Clifford
Witting (5, 10), Ian Reed (7, 11), Nicholas Palmer
(8). Prod: David Goddard. Dir: Peter Sasdy (1),
Max Varnel (2, 8), Gareth Davies (3, 6), Peter
Duguid (4), Peter Creegan (5), Eric Taylor (7),
Shawn Sutton (9, 12), Philip Dudley (10),
Michael Haus (11).

SHERLOCK HOLMES
(see pages 134-135)
10 October 1967-17 March 1968. TV. Germany. 6 x
50m. Black and white.
1 'Das Gefleckte Band', 2 'Sechsmal Napoleon',
3 'Die Liga der Rotharigen', 4 'Die Bruce-Partington
Plane', 5 'Das Beryl Diaden', 6 'Das Haus bei den

Blutbuchen'.
Recurring cast: Erich Schellow (Sherlock Holmes),
Paul Edwin Roth (Dr Watson).
Selected credits: Scrp: based on the originals
used by the BBC for the Douglas Wilmer series.
Dir: Peter May.

SHERLOCK HOLMES AND A STUDY IN SCARLET
(see page 119)
1984. Pacific Arts. Australia. 45m. Colour. Animation.
Voice cast: Peter O'Toole (Sherlock Holmes), Earle
Cross (Dr Watson).
Selected credits: Mus: John Stuart. Scrp: John King.
Prod: Eddy Graham.

SHERLOCK HOLMES AND DR. WATSON
(see pages 110-111)
1979-80. Filmways. USA. 24 x 25m. Colour.
1 'A Motive for Murder', 2 'The Case of the Speckled
Band', 3 'Murder on a Midsummer's Eve', 4 'Four
Minus Four Is One', 5 'The Case of the Perfect
Crime', 6 'The Case of Harry Rigby', 7 'The Case of
Blind Man's Bluff', 8 'A Case of High Security',
9 'The Case of Harry Crocker', 10 'The Case of the
Deadly Prophecy', 11 'The Case of the Baker Street
Nursemaids', 12 'The Case of the Purloined Letter',
13 'The Case of the Final Curtain', 14 'The Case of
the Three Brothers', 15 'The Case of the Body in the
Case', 16 'The Case of the Deadly Tower', 17 'The
Case of Smith & Smythe', 18 'The Case of the
Luckless Gambler', 19 'The Case of the Shrunken
Heads', 20 'The Case of Marauder's Millions', 21
'The Case of the Travelling Killer', 22 'The Case of
the Other Ghost', 23 'The Case of the Sitting
Target', 24 'The Case of the Close-Knit Family'.
Recurring cast: Geoffrey Whitehead (Sherlock
Holmes), Donald Pickering (Dr Watson),
Patrick Newell (Inspector Lestrade), Kay Walsh
(Mrs Hudson).
Notable guest actors: Norman Bird (Denham; 1),
Victoria Tennant (Julia Stoner; 2), Melissa Stribling
(Mrs Langley; 2), Sue Lloyd (Elizabeth Neale; 3),
Cheryl Kennedy (Sarah Bailey; 6), John Carson
(Vickers; 7), Derek Bond (Sir Charles; 8), Robert
Gillespie (Charlie Willis; 9), Richard Greene (Lord
Brompton; 12), Glynis Barber (Meredith Stanhope;
14/Sophie; 23), Catherine Schell (Lady Tarleton;
16), Geoffrey Bayldon (Hadlock; 16), Bernard
Bresslaw (Hubert Smythe; 17), Derren Nesbitt
(George Wharton; 18), Simon Oates (James
McIntyre; 19), David Buck (Vincent Chesney; 20).
Selected credits: Scrp: Sheldon Reynolds, Joe
Moreheim, Tudor Gates and others (many scripts
were re-worked by Reynolds from his original 1954-
1955 Sherlock Holmes series). Prod: Sheldon
Reynolds. Dir: Sheldon Reynolds (1-4), Ronald
Stevens (5), Val Guest (6, 11-14, 19, 20-22, 24),
Peter Sasdy (7), Roy Ward Baker (8, 15-18), Freddie
Francis (9, 10), Aurelio Crugnola (23).

SHERLOCK HOLMES AND THE BAKER STREET IRREGULARS
(see pages 194-195)
25 March and 1 April 2007. RDF Television for the
BBC. UK. 2x60m. Colour.
Cast: Jonathan Pryce (Sherlock Holmes), Bill
Paterson (Dr Watson), Anna Chancellor (Irene
Adler), Michael Maloney (Inspector Stirling), Aaron
Johnson (Finch), Dean Gibbons (Sticks), Benjamin
Smith (Jack), Mia Fernandez (Sadie), Alice Hewkin
(Tealeaf), Megan Jones (Jasmine).
Selected Credits: Dp: Ciaran Tanham; Mus: Debbie
Wiseman Prod: Andy Rowkey; Scrp: Richard Kurti
and Bev Doyle; Dir: Julian Kemp.

SHERLOCK HOLMES AND THE BASKERVILLE CURSE
(see pages 119)
1984. Pacific Arts. Australia. 70m. Colour. Animation.
Voice cast: Peter O'Toole (Sherlock Holmes),
Earle Cross (Dr Watson).
Selected credits: Mus: John Stuart. Scrp:
Eddy Graham. Prod: Eddy Graham.

SHERLOCK HOLMES AND THE CASE OF THE MISSING LINK

(see pages 158-159)
15 October 1992. ITV. UK. 25m. Colour.
Cast: Reece Dinsdale (Sherlock Holmes), Gerald Horan (Dr Watson), Paul Darrow (Sir Arthur Conan Doyle).
Selected credits: Scrp: Neil Crombie.
A science documentary in which Holmes and his creator investigate the theory of 'the missing link.'

SHERLOCK HOLMES AND THE CASE OF THE SILK STOCKING

(see page 192)
26 December 2004. Tiger Aspect Productions for the BBC. UK. 97m. Colour.
Cast: Rupert Everett (Sherlock Holmes), Ian Hart (Dr Watson), Neil Dudgeon (Lestrade), Jonathan Hyde (George Pentney), Helen McCrory (Mrs Vandeleur), Guy Henry (Mr Bilney).
Selected Credits: Dp: David Katznelson; Prod; Elinor Day; Scrp: Allan Cubitt; Dir: Simon Cellan Jones.

SHERLOCK HOLMES AND THE DEADLY NECKLACE

(Original title: *Sherlock Holmes und das Halsband des Todes*)
(see pages 84-85)
1962 (UK dubbed version February 1968). Constantin Film Verleih of Berlin. Germany. 86m. Black and white.
Cast: Chistopher Lee (Sherlock Holmes), Thorley Walters (Watson), Senta Berger (Ellen Blackburn), Hans Söhnker (Professor Moriarty), Hans Nielson (Inspector Cooper), Edith Schultze-Westrum (Mrs Hudson).
Selected Credits: Ed: Ira Oberberg. Mus: Martin Slavin. Scrp: Curt M. Siodmak. Bo: *The Valley of Fear*, by Doyle (supposedly). Prod: Artur Brauner. Dir: Terence Fisher (with Frank Winterstein).

SHERLOCK HOLMES AND THE GREAT MURDER MYSTERY

(see pages 12-15)
1908. Crescent Films Mfg Co. USA. 1 reel. Black and white. Silent.
Cast: unknown.

SHERLOCK HOLMES AND THE PRINCE OF CRIME

- see *Hands of a Murderer*

SHERLOCK HOLMES AND THE SECRET CODE

- see *Dressed to Kill*

SHERLOCK HOLMES AND THE SECRET WEAPON

(see pages 46-47)
December 1942. Universal Pictures. USA. 68m. Black and white.
Cast: Basil Rathbone (Sherlock Holmes), Nigel Bruce (Dr Watson), Lionel Atwill (Professor Moriarty), Dennis Hoey (Lestrade), Mary Gordon (Mrs Hudson), William Post Jr (Dr Franz Tobel), Karen Verne (Charlotte Eberli), Holmes Herbert (Sir Reginald).
Selected credits: Art dir: Jack Otterson. Ed: Otto Ludwig. Mus: Frank Skinner. Dp: Lester White. Scrp: Edward T. Lowe, W. Scott Darling, Edmund L. Hartmann. Bo: 'The Adventure of the Dancing Men', by Doyle. Adaptation by W. Scott Darling, Edmund L. Hartmann. Assoc prod: Howard Benedict. Dir: Roy William Neill.

SHERLOCK HOLMES AND THE SIGN OF FOUR

(see pages 119)
1984. Pacific Arts. Australia. 48m. Colour. Animation.
Voice cast: Peter O'Toole (Sherlock Holmes), Earle Cross (Dr Watson).
Selected credits: Mus: John Stuart. Scrp: Eddy Graham. Prod: Eddy Graham.

SHERLOCK HOLMES AND

THE VALLEY OF FEAR

(see pages 119)
1984. Pacific Arts. Australia. 48m. Colour. Animation.
Voice cast: Peter O'Toole (Sherlock Holmes), Earle Cross (Dr Watson).
Selected credits: Mus: John Stuart. Scrp: Norma Green. Prod: Eddy Graham.

SHERLOCK HOLMES AND THE VOICE OF TERROR

(see pages 44-45)
18 September 1942. Universal Pictures. USA. 65m. Black and white.
Cast: Basil Rathbone (Sherlock Holmes), Nigel Bruce (Dr Watson), Evelyn Ankers (Kitty), Reginald Denny (Sir Evan Barham), Henry Daniell (Sir Alfred Lloyd), Montagu Love (General Jerome Lawford), Thomas Gomez (Meade), Olaf Hytten (Admiral Fabian Prentiss), Leyland Hodgson (Captain Ronald Shore), Hillary Brooke (Jill Grandis), Mary Gordon (Mrs Hudson), Arthur Blake (Crosbie), Harry Stubbs (Taxi Driver).
Selected credits: Art dir: Jack Otterson. Ed: Russell Schoengarth. Mus: Frank Skinner. Dp: Woody Bredell. Scrp: Lynn Riggs. Adaptation: Robert D. Andrews, John Bright. Bo: 'His Last Bow', by Doyle. Assoc prod: Howard Benedict. Dir: John Rawlins.

SHERLOCK HOLMES AUF URLAUB

('Sherlock Holmes on Leave')
1916. Vitascope Pictures. Germany. 3 reels. Black and white. Silent.
Cast: Alwin Neuss (Sherlock Holmes).
Selected credits: Scrp: Karl Schonfeld. Dir: Karl Schonfeld.

SHERLOCK HOLMES BAFFLED

(see pages 12-15)
1900 (copyrighted 1903). American Mutoscope and Biograph Company. USA. 35 seconds. Black and white. Silent.
Cast: unknown.

SHERLOCK HOLMES CONTRA DR MORS

1914. Vitascope. Germany. Black and white. Silent.
Cast: Ferdinand Bonn (Sherlock Holmes), Erich Kahne (Dr Mors).
Selected credits: Scrp: Richard Oswald.

SHERLOCK HOLMES CONTRA PROFESSOR MORYARTY or DER ERBE VON BLOOMROD

(see pages 12-15)
('The Heir of Bloomrod')
April 1911. Vitascope. Germany. 2 reels. Black and white. Silent.
Cast: Viggo Larsen (Sherlock Holmes), Paul Otto (Professor Moriarty).
Selected credits: Dir: Viggo Larsen.

SHERLOCK HOLMES: DIE GRAUE DAME

('Sherlock Holmes: The Grey Lady')
(see pages 34-35)
1937. Neue Film KG. Germany. 90m. Black and white.
Cast: Hermann Speelmans (Jimmy Ward), Maria Iretzkaja (Trude Marlen), Elisabeth Wendt (Lola), Edwin Jurgensen (Baranoff), Theo Shall (Harry Morrel), Ernst Karchow (Inspector Brown), Werner Finck (John, Ward's Servant), Werner Scharf (Jack Clark), Hans Halden (James Hewitt), Henry Lorenzen (Archibald Pepperkorn), Reinhold Bernt (Wilson), Eva Tinschmann (Frau Miller).
Selected credits: Scrp: Erich Engels, Hans Heur. Bo: *Die Tat des Unbekannten* ('The Deed of the Unknown'; play), by Miller-Puzika. Dir: Erich Engels.

SHERLOCK HOLMES FACES DEATH

(see pages 50-51)
September 1943. Universal Pictures. USA. 68m. Black and white.

Cast: Basil Rathbone (Sherlock Holmes), Nigel Bruce (Dr Watson), Hillary Brooke (Sally Musgrave), Dennis Hoey (Inspector Lestrade), Milburn Stone (Captain Vickery), Arthur Margetson (Dr Sexton), Halliwell Hobbes (Brunton), Gavin Muir (Phillip Musgrave), Frederick Worlock (Geoffrey Musgrave), Gerald Hamer (Lanford), Vernon Downing (Clavering), Olaf Hytton (Captain Mackintosh), Minna Phillips (Mrs Howells), Mary Gordon (Mrs Hudson).
Selected credits: Art dir: John Goodman, Harold MacArthur. Ed: Fred Feitchans. Mus: Frank Skinner. Dp: Charles Van Enger. Scrp: Bertram Millhauser. Prod: Roy William Neill. Dir: Roy William Neill.

SHERLOCK HOLMES IN CARACAS

(see pages 134-135)
1992. Big Ben Productions/Tiuna Films/Foncine. Venezuela. Colour.
Cast: Jean Manuel Montesinos (Sherlock Holmes), Gilbert Dacournan (Dr Watson).
Selected credits: Bo: 'The Sussex Vampire', by Doyle (loosely). Dir: Juan E. Fresnan.

SHERLOCK HOLMES IN NEW YORK

(see page 106)
18 October 1976. Twentieth Century Fox. USA. 100m. Colour.
Cast: Roger Moore (Sherlock Holmes), Patrick Macnee (Dr Watson), John Huston (Moriarty), Charlotte Rampling (Irene Adler), Gig Young (Mortimer McGraw), David Hudleston (Insp Lafferty), Signe Hasso (Fraulien Reichenbach), Leon Ames (Furman), Jackie Coogan (Hotel Proprieter), Marjorie Bennett (Mrs Hudson), Geoffrey Moore (Scott Adler).
Selected credits: Mus: Richard Rodney Bennett. Scrp: Alvin Sapinsky. Prod: John Cutts. Dir: Boris Sagal.

SHERLOCK HOLMES IN THE HOUND OF LONDON

- see *The Hound of London*.

SHERLOCK HOLMES IN THE 22nd CENTURY

(see pages 158-159)
Series 1: 1999; Series 2: not shown. Scottish Television. UK. 26 x 21m. Colour. Animation.
(Series 1) 1 'The Fall and Rise of Sherlock Holmes', 2 'The Crime Machine', 3 'The Hounds of the Baskervilles', 4 'The Resident Patient', 5 'The Scales of Justice', 6 'The Adventure of The Dancing Men', 7 'The Crooked Man, 8 'The Adventure of the Empty House', 9 'The Deranged Detective', 10 'The Silver Badge', 11 'The Sign of Four', 12 'The Adventure of the Sussex Vampires', 13 'The Musgrave Ritual'. (Series 2) 14 'The Five Orange Pips', 15 'The Adventure of the Beryl Board', 16 'The Secret Safe', 17 'The Adventure of the Mazarin Chip', 18 'The Red-Headed League', 19 'The Adventure of the Second Stain', 20 'A Case of Identity', 21 'The Adventure of the Engineer's Thumb', 22 'The Man With the Twisted Lip', 23 'The Gloria Scott', 24 'The Adventure of the Six Napleons', 25 'The Adventure of the Creeping Man', 26 The Adventure of the Blue Carbuncle'.
Recurring voice cast: Jason Gray Stanford (Sherlock Holmes), John Payne (Dr Watson), Akiko Morison (Inspector Beth Lestrade), Viv Leacock (Wiggins), Richard Newman (Professor James Moriarty).
Selected credits: Exec prod: Elizabeth Partyka. Dir: Scott Heming.

SHERLOCK HOLMES IN WASHINGTON

(see pages 48-49)
April 1943. Universal Pictures. USA. 71m. Black and white.
Cast: Basil Rathbone (Sherlock Holmes), Nigel Bruce (Dr Watson), George Zucco (Richard Stanley/Heinrich Hinkle), Marjorie Lord (Nancy Partridge), Henry Daniell (William Easter),

John Archer (Lt Peter Merriam), Gavin Muir (Bert Lang), Edmund MacDonald (Det Lt Grogan), Thurston Hall (Senator Henry Babcock), Don Terry (Howe), Holmes Herbert (Mr Ahrens), Gerald Hamer (Alfred Pettibone/John Grayson), Mary Forbes (Beryl Pettibone), Mary Gordon (Mrs Hudson).

Selected credits: Art dir: Jack Otterson. Ed: Otto Ludwig. Mus: Frank Skinner. Dp: Lester White. Scrp: Bertram Millhauser, Lynn Riggs. Assoc prod: Howard Benedict. Dir: Roy William Neill.

SHERLOCK HOLMES NÄCHLICHE BEGEGNUNG

('Sherlock Holmes's Nocturnal Encounter')
1916. Vitascope. Germany. 4 reels. Black and white. Silent.
Cast: Alwin Neuss (Sherlock Holmes).

SHERLOCK HOLMES'S FATAL HOUR

- see *The Sleeping Cardinal*

SHERLOCK HOLMES SOLVES 'THE SIGN OF THE FOUR'

(UK *The Sign of Four*)
1913. Thanhouser. USA. 2 reels. Black and white. Silent.
Cast: Harry Benham (Sherlock Holmes).

SHERLOCK HOLMES: THE GOLDEN YEARS INCIDENT AT VICTORIA FALLS

(see page 163)
May 1992. Harmony Gold and Banque Caisse, D'epargne De L'etat, Banque Paribas, Luxembourg in association with Silvio Berlusconi Communications. USA. 200m (originally shown in two parts). Colour.
Cast: Christopher Lee (Sherlock Holmes), Patrick Macnee (Dr Watson), Jenny Seagrove (Lily Langtry), Claude Akins (Rooseveldt), Richard Todd (Lord Roberts), Joss Ackland (King Edward), Sunitha Singh (Marharani), Claudia Udi (Amelia Morrison), John Indi (Khumalo), Stephen Gurney (Glugliamo Marconi), Antony Fridjhon (Mavroplois), Neil McCarthy (James Morrison), Dale Cutts (Van Meer), Pat Pillay (Chondra Sen), Alan Coates (Stanley Bullard), Kenway Baker (Inspector Lestrade).
Selected credits: Scrp: Bob Shayne. Bo: Story by Gerry O'Hara. Exec prod: Harry Alan Towers. Prod: Frank Agrama, Norman Siderow, Daniele Loranzano. Dir: Bill Corcoran.

SHERLOCK HOLMES: THE GOLDEN YEARS SHERLOCK HOLMES AND THE LEADING LADY

(see page 162)
August 1992. Harmony Gold and Banque Caisse, D'epargne De L'etat, Banque Paribas, Luxembourg in association with Silvio Berlusconi Communications. USA. 200m (originally shown in two parts). Colour.
Cast: Christopher Lee (Sherlock Holmes), Patrick Macnee (Dr Watson), Jerome Willis (Mycroft Holmes), Morgan Fairchild (Irene Adler), John Bennett (Sigmund Freud), Englebert Humperdinck (Opera Singer).
Selected credits: Scrp: Bob Shayne. Exec prod: Harry Alan Towers. Prod: Frank Agrama, Alessandro Tasca, Daniele Loranzano. Dir: Peter Sasdy.

SHERLOCK HOLMES UND DAS HALSBAND DES TODES

- see *Sherlock Holmes and the Deadly Necklace*

THE SIGN OF THE FOUR (1913)

- see *Sherlock Holmes Solves 'The Sign of Four'*

THE SIGN OF FOUR

(see pages 16-17)
1923. Stoll Picture Productions Ltd. UK. 5 reels. Black and white. Silent.

Cast: Eille Norwood (Sherlock Holmes), Arthur Cullin (Dr Watson), Isobel Elsom (Mary Morstan), Madame d'Esterre (Mrs Hudson), Norman Page (Jonathan Small), Fred Raynham (Prince Kahn), Humberston Wright (Dr Sholto), Arthur Bell (Insp Athenley Jones), Henry Wilson (Pygmy).
Selected credits: Art dir: Walter M. Murton. Dp: John J. Cox. Scrp: Maurice Elvey. Dir: Maurice Elvey.

THE SIGN OF FOUR

(see page 30)
September 1932. Associated Radio Pictures. UK. 75m. Black and white.
Cast: Arthur Wontner (Sherlock Holmes), Ian Hunter (Dr Watson), Isla Bevan (Mary Morstan), Graham Soutten (Jonathan Small), Miles Malleson (Thaddeus Sholto), Kynaston Reeves (Bartholemew Sholto), Herbert Lomas (Major Sholto), Gilbert Davies (Inspector Anthenley Jones), Togo (Tonga), Claire Greet (Mrs Hudson).
Selected credits: Dp: Robert de Grasse. Scrp: W.P. Lipscomb. Exec prod: Basil Dean. Prod: Rowland V. Lee. Dir: Graham Cutts.

THE SIGN OF FOUR

(see page 116)
13 May 1983. Mapleton Films. UK. 90m. Colour.
Cast: Ian Richardson (Sherlock Holmes), David Healy (Dr Watson), Thorley Walters (Major John Sholto), Joe Melia (Jonathan Small), Cherie Lunghi (Mary Morstan), Terence Rigby (Insp Layton), Clive Merrison (Bartholomew Sholto), Richard Heffren (Thaddeus Sholto), John Pendric (Tonga).
Selected credits: Mus: Harry Rabinowitz. Scrp: Charles Pogue. Prod: Otto Plaschkes. Dir: Desmond Davis.

THE SIGN OF FOUR

(see pages 142-143)
29 December 1987. Granada Television. UK. 100m. Colour.
Cast: Jeremy Brett (Sherlock Holmes), Edward Hardwicke (Dr Watson), Jenny Seagrove (Mary Morstan), John Thaw (Jonathan Small), Ronald Lacey (Thaddeus and Bartholomew Sholto), Emrys James (Atheley Jones), Kiran Shah (Tonga), Robin Hunter (Major Sholto), Gordon Gostelow (Sherman), Terence Skelton (Captain Morstan).
Selected credits: Des: Tim Wilding. Mus: Patrick Gowers. Scrp: John Hawkesworth. Exec prod: Michael Cox. Prod: June Wyndham Davies. Dir: Peter Hammond.

THE SIGN OF FOUR

(see page 179)
23 March 2001. Muse Entertainment Enterprises in association with Hallmark Entertainment. Canada. 90m. Colour.
Cast: Matt Frewer (Sherlock Holmes), Kenneth Welsh (Dr Watson), Sophie Lorain (Mary Morstan), Marcel Jeannin (Thaddeus and Bartholomew Sholto), Edward Yankie (Jonathan Small), Michael Peron (Inspector Jones), Noel Burton (Professor Morgan), Fernando Chien (Tonga).
Selected credits: Dp: Eric Cayla. Scrp: Joe Wiesenfeld. Exec prod: Steven Hewitt, Michael Prupas. Prod: Irene Litinsky. Dir: Rodney Gibbons.

SILVER BLAZE

(USA *Murder at the Baskervilles*)
(see page 33)
July 1937. Twickenham Film Productions Ltd. UK. 71m. Black and white.
Cast: Arthur Wontner (Sherlock Holmes), Ian Fleming (Dr Watson), Lyn Harding (Professor Moriarty), Lawrence Grossmith (Sir Henry Baskerville), Judy Gunn (Diana Baskerville), Arthur Macrae (Jack Trevor), Arthur Goullet (Col Sebastian Moran), Martin Walker (John Straker), Eve Gray (Mrs Straker), John Turnbull (Inspector Lestrade), Robert Horton (Col Ross), Minnie Rayner (Mrs Hudson), Ronald Shiner (Stableboy).
Selected credits: Art dir: James Carter. Dp: Sidney Blythe. Scrp: Arthur Macrae, H. Fowler Mear, Arthur Wontner. Prod: Julius Hagen. Dir: Thomas Bentley.

SILVER BLAZE

(see pages 100-101)
27 November 1977. Highgate Associates for Harlech Television. UK. 25m. Colour.
Cast: Christopher Plummer (Sherlock Holmes), Thorley Walters (Dr Watson), Basil Henson (Colonel Ross), Gary Wilson (Inspector Gregory), Richard Beale (Straker), Barry Treham (Silas Brown), Josie Kidd (Mrs Straker), Donald Burton (Fitzroy Simpson).
Selected credits: Mus: Paul Lewis. Scrp: Julian Bond. Prod: William Deneen. Dir: John Davies.

THE SINGULAR ADVENTURE

- see *Dr Watson and the Darkwater Hall Mystery*

SIR ARTHUR CONAN DOYLE'S SHERLOCK HOLMES

(see pages 90-91)
1968. BBC TV. UK. 16 x 50m. Colour.
1 'The Second Stain', 2 'A Study in Scarlet', 3 'The Dancing Men', 4 'The Hound of the Baskervilles' (two parts). 5 'The Boscombe Valley Mystery', 6 'The Greek Interpreter', 7 'The Naval Treaty', 8 'The Mystery of Thor Bridge', 9 'The Musgrave Ritual', 10 'Black Peter', 11 'Wisteria Lodge', 12 'Shoscombe Old Place', 13 'The Solitary Cyclist', 14 'The Sign of Four', 15 'The Blue Carbuncle'.
Recurring cast: Peter Cushing (Sherlock Holmes), Nigel Stock (Dr Watson), Grace Arnold (Mrs Hudson; 2, 3, 7-11, 14, 15), George A. Cooper (Inspector Gregson; 2, 6), William Lucas (Inspector Lestrade; 1, 2).
Notable guest actors: Daniel Massey (Trelawney Hope; 1), Cecil Parker (Lord Bellinger; 1), Derek Waring (Henri Fournaye; 1), Maxwell Reed (Hilton Cubitt; 3), Gary Raymond (Sir Henry Baskerville; 4), Peter Woodthorpe (Wilson Kemp; 6), Dennis Price (Lord Holdhurst; 7), Corin Redgrave (Percy Phelps; 7), Peter Bowles (Joseph Harrison; 7), Juliet Mills (Grace Dunbar; 8), Georgia Brown (Rachel; 9), Derek Francis (Scott Eccles; 11), Nigel Green (Sir Robert Norberton; 12), Edward Woodward (Mason; 12), Charles Tingwell (Carruthers; 13), John Stratton (Insp Athenley Jones; 14), Paul Daneman (Bartholemew Sholto; 14), Ann Bell (Mary Morstan; 14), Frank Middlemass (Peterson; 15).
Selected credits: Mus: Alan Fogg. Scrp: Jennifer Stuart (1), Hugh Leonard (2, 4), Michael and Mollie Hardwicke (3, 14), Bruce Stewart (5), John Gould (6, 7), Harry Moore (8), Alexander Baron (9, 11), Richard Harris (10), Donald Tosh (12), Stanley Miller (13, 15). Prod: William Sterling. Dir: Henry Safran (1-3), Graham Evans (4), Viktors Ritelis (5, 9, 13), David Saire (6), Antony Kearney (7, 8, 10), Roger Jenkins (11), William Bain (12, 15), William Sterling (14).

THE SLEEPING CARDINAL

(USA *Sherlock Holmes' Fatal Hour*)
(see page 25)
March 1931. Twickenham Film Studios Ltd. UK. 84m. Black and white.
Cast: Arthur Wontner (Sherlock Holmes), Ian Fleming (Dr Watson), Minnie Rayner (Mrs Hudson), Leslie Perrins (Ronald Adair), Jane Welsh (Kathleen Adair), Norman McKinnell (Col Henslowe/Prof Robert Moriarty), Philip Hewland (Inspector Lestrade), Louis Goodrich (Col Sebastian Moran).
Selected credits: Dp: Sidney Blythe. Scrp: Cyril Twyford, H. Fowler Mear, Leslie S. Hiscott, Arthur Wontner. Bo: 'The Final Problem' and 'The Adventure of the Empty House', by Doyle. Prod: Julius Hagen. Dir: Leslie Hiscott.

SOVIET SHERLOCK HOLMES

(see pages 134-135)

SHERLOCK HOLMES AND DR WATSON

1979. Lenfilm movie studio for Central Television. Leningrad.
1 'Acquaintance', 2 'Bloody Inscription'.
Recurring cast: Vasily Livanov (Sherlock Holmes), Vitaly Solomin (Dr Watson), Borislav Brondukov

(Lestrade), Boris Kluyev (Mycroft Holmes), Rina Zelenaya (Mrs Hudson).
Selected credits: Mus: Vladimir Dashkevtich. Bo: *A Study in Scarlet* (1, 2), 'The Adventure of the Speckled Band' (1), by Doyle. Dir: Igor Maslennikov.

THE ADVENTURES OF SHERLOCK HOLMES AND DR WATSON
1980. Lenfilm movie studio for Central Television. Leningrad.
1 'The Master Blackmailer', 2 'Deadly Fight', 3 'Hunt for the Tiger'.
Selected credits: Bo: 'The Adventure of Charles Augustus Milverton' (1), 'The Final Problem' (2), 'The Adventure of the Empty House' (3), by Doyle.

THE ADVENTURES OF SHERLOCK HOLMES AND DR WATSON
1981. Lenfilm movie studio for Central Television. Leningrad.
'The Hound of the Baskervilles' (2 episodes).

THE ADVENTURES OF SHERLOCK HOLMES AND DR WATSON
1983. Lenfilm movie studio for Central Television. Leningrad.
'The Treasures of Agra' (2 episodes).
Selected credits: Bo: *The Sign of Four* (1, 2), 'A Scandal in Bohemia' (1), by Doyle.

THE ADVENTURES OF SHERLOCK HOLMES AND DR WATSON
1986. Lenfilm movie studio for Central Television. Leningrad.
'20th Century Begins' (2 episodes).
Selected credits: Bo: 'The Adventure of the Engineer's Thumb' (1), 'The Adventure of the Second Stain' (1), 'His Last Bow' (2), 'The Adventure of the Bruce-Partington Plans' (2), by Doyle.

THE SPECKLED BAND
(see page 23)
March 1931. British and Dominion Studios. UK. 90m. Black and white.
Cast: Raymond Massey (Sherlock Holmes), Athole Stewart (Dr Watson), Lyn Harding (Dr Grimesby Rylott), Angela Baddeley (Helen Stonor), Nancy Price (Mrs Staunton), Marie Ault (Mrs Hudson), Joyce Moore (Violet Stonor).
Selected credits: Dp: Freddie Young. Scrp: W.P. Lipscomb. Bo: *The Speckled Band* (play) and 'The Adventure of the Speckled Band' (story), by Doyle. Prod: Herbert Wilcox. Dir: Jack Raymond.

SPIDER WOMAN
(see pages 52-53)
January 1944. Universal Pictures. USA. 62m. Black and white.
Cast: Basil Rathbone (Sherlock Holmes), Nigel Bruce (Dr Watson), Gale Sondergaard (Adrea Spedding), Dennis Hoey (Inspector Lestrade), Vernon Downing (Norman Locke), Alec Craig (Radlik), Arthur Hohl (Adam Gilflower), Mary Gordon (Mrs Hudson), Harry Cording (Fred Garvin), Angelo Rossitto (Pygmy).
Selected credits: Mus: Frank Skinner. Art dir: John B. Goodman. Ed: James Gibbon. Mus: Frank Skinner. Dp: Charles Van Enger. Scrp: Bertram Millhauser. Bo: elements from several Doyle stories, including 'The Adventure of the Speckled Band', *The Sign of Four*, 'The Adventure of the Devil's Foot', 'The Adventure of the Dying Detective', 'The Final Problem' and 'The Adventure of the Empty House'. Prod: Roy William Neill. Dir: Roy William Neill.

STAR TREK: THE NEXT GENERATION
(see pages 110-111; 158-159)
Paramount. USA. 4 x 45m. Colour.
11 November 1987, 7 'Lonely Among Us'.
10 December 1988, 29 'Elementary, Dear Data'.
13 January 1991, 85 'Data's Day'.
25 January 1993, 138 'Ship in a Bottle'.

Recurring cast: Patrick Stewart (Jean Luc Picard), Jonathan Frakes (Riker), Brent Spiner (Data), Michael Dorn (Worf), Marina Sirtis (Troi), LeVar Burton (Geordi LaForge), Gates McFadden (Dr Crusher; 7, 138).
Notable guest actors: Daniel Davis (Professor Moriarty; 29, 138), Diana Muldaur (Dr Pulaski; 29), Dwight Shultz (Lt Barclay; 138).
Selected credits: Scrp: D. C. Fontana (7), Brian Alan Lane (29), (Harold Apter and Ronald D. Moore (85), Rene Echevarria (138). Dir: Cliff Bole (7), Rob Bowman (29), Robert Weimer (85), Alexander Singer (138).

THE STRANGE CASE OF SHERLOCK HOLMES AND ARTHUR CONAN DOYLE
(see page 190)
27 July 2005. BBC Scotland. UK. 89m. Colour.
Cast: Douglas Henshall (Arthur Conan Doyle), Tim McInnerny (Selden), Brian Cox (Dr Joseph Bell), Sinead Cusack (Mrs Doyle), Saskia Reeves (Louise Doyle), Emily Blunt (Jean Leckie), Allan Corduner (Greenhough-Smith), Anthony Calf (Bryan Charles Waller), John Bett (Charles Doyle).
Selected Credits: Dp: John Rhodes; Mus: Malcolm Lindsay; Prod: Richard Downes; Scrp: David Pirie; Dir: Cilla Ware.

THE STRANGE CASE OF THE END OF CIVILISATION AS WE KNOW IT
(see pages 100-101)
18 September 1977. ITV. UK. 55m. Colour.
Cast: John Cleese (Arthur Sherlock Holmes), Arthur Lowe (Dr William Watson), Ron Moody (Dr Gropinger), Joss Ackland (Both Presidents of the USA), Denholm Elliott (English Delegate), Josephine Tewson (Miss Hoskins), Stratford Johns (Commissioner of the Police), Connie Booth (Mrs Hudson), Dudley Jones (Hercule Poirot), Luie Caballero (Columbo), Mike O'Malley (Sam Spade), Joseph Brady (Ironside), Paul Chapman (McCloud).
Selected credits: Scrp: Joe McGrath, Jack Hobbs. Dir: Joe McGrath.

A STUDY IN SCARLET
(see pages 12-15)
October 1914. The Samuelson Mfg Co Ltd. UK. 4 reels. Black and white. Silent.
Cast: James Bragington (Sherlock Holmes), Fred Paul (Jefferson Hope), Agnes Glynne (Lucy Ferrier), Harry Paulo (Brigham Young), James Le Fre (John Ferrier).
Selected credits: Scrp: Harry Engholm. Prod: G.B. Samuelson. Dir: George Pearson.

A STUDY IN SCARLET
(see pages 12-15)
December 1914. Gold-Seal Universal. USA. 20m. Black and white. Silent.
Cast: Francis Ford (Sherlock Holmes), Jack Francis (Dr Watson).
Selected credits: Scrp: Grace Cunard. Dir: Francis Ford.

A STUDY IN SCARLET
(aka *The Scarlet Ring*)
(see page 31)
April 1933. World Wide. USA. 75m. Black and white.
Cast: Reginald Owen (Sherlock Holmes), Warburton Gamble (Dr Watson), Anna May Wong (Mrs Pike), Alan Dinehart (Thaddeus Merrydew), June Clyde (Eileen Forrester), J. M. Kerrigan (Jabez Wilson), Alan Mowbray (Inspector Lestrade), Wyndham Standing (Captain Pyke), Halliwell Hobbes (Malcolm Dearing), Tempe Piggit (Mrs Hudson), Tetsu Komai (Ah Yet).
Selected credits: Scrp: Robert Florey. Continuity and dialogue: Reginald Owen. Prod: Burt Kelly, Samuel Bischoff, William Saal. Dir: Edwin L. Marin.

A STUDY IN TERROR
(USA *Fog*)
(see pages 88-89)

4 November 1965. Compton/Sir Nigel Films. UK. 95m. Colour.
Cast: John Neville (Sherlock Holmes), Donald Houston (Dr Watson), Robert Morley (Mycroft Holmes), Frank Finlay (Lestrade), John Fraser (Edward Osbourne, Lord Carfax), Anthony Quayle (Dr Murray), Barbara Leake (Mrs Hudson), Barbara Windsor (Annie Chapman), John Cairney (Michael), Adrienne Corri (Angela Osbourne), Cecil Parker (Prime Minister), Dudley Foster (Home Secretary), Judi Dench (Sally), Georgia Brown (Singer), Terry Downes (Chunky), Christiane Maybach (Polly Nichols), Peter Carsten (Max Steiner), Charles Regnier (Joseph Beck), Jones (Duke of Shires), Kay Walsh (Cathy Eddowes), Edina Ronay (Mary Kelly), Avis Bunnage (Landlady), Patrick Newell (PC Benson), Norma Foster (Liz Stride).
Selected credits: Ed: Henry Richardson. Art dir: Alex Vetchinsky. Mus: John Scott. Dp: Desmond Dickinson. Scrp: Donald and Derek Ford. Exec prod: Herman Cohen. Prod: Henry E. Lester. Dir: James Hill.

SURE-LOCKED HOLMES
(see pages 168-169)
1927. Pathe Film Exchange. USA. Black and white. Animation. Silent.
Selected credits: Animator: Otto Messmer. Prod: Pat Sullivan.
Starring Felix the Cat.

TALES OF THE RODENT SHERLOCK HOLMES
(see pages 148-151)
1990. BBC TV. 7 x 30m. Colour.
Cast: Roland Rat (Sherlock Holmes), Kevin the Gerbil (Dr Watson), Roy Sampton (McDreadful).
Notable guest actors: Barbara Windsor (Irene Wilson), Mollie Sugden, Bernard Bresslaw.
Selected credits: Scrp: Colin Bostock-Smith, Dominic MacDonald, David Claridge. Prod: Steve Haggard.

TERROR BY NIGHT
(see pages 68-69)
1 February 1946. Universal Pictures. USA. 60m. Black and white.
Cast: Basil Rathbone (Sherlock Holmes), Nigel Bruce (Dr Watson), Alan Mowbray (Major Duncan Bleek/Col Sebastian Moran), Dennis Hoey (Inspector Lestrade), Renee Godfrey (Vivian Vedder), Mary Forbes (Lady Margaret Carstairs), Billy Bevan (Train Attendant), Frederic Worlock (Professor Kilbane), Boyd Davis (Inspector McDonald), Skelton Knaggs (Sands), Gerald Hamer (Mr Shallcross), Janet Murdoch (Mrs Shallcross).
Selected credits: Art dir: John B. Goodman. Ed: Saul A. Goodkind. Mus: Frank Skinner. Dp: Maury Gertsman. Scrp: Frank Gruber. Prod: Roy William Neill. Dir: Roy William Neill.

THEY MIGHT BE GIANTS
(see page 98)
9 March 1971. Universal Pictures. USA. 88m on release. Colour.
Cast: George C. Scott (Justin Playfair), Joanne Woodward (Dr Mildred Watson), Jack Gilford (Wilbur Peabody), Lester Rawlins (Blevins Playfair), Rue McClanahan (Daisy), Ron Weyand (Dr Strauss).
Selected credits: Mus: John Barry. Dp: Victor Kemper. Scrp: James Goldman. Bo: Play by James Goldman. Prod: John Foreman. Dir: Anthony Harvey.

THE THREE GARRIDEBS
(see pages 72-75)
27 November 1937. NBC. USA. 30m. Black and white.
Cast: Louis Hector (Sherlock Holmes), William Podmore (Dr Watson), Arthur Maitland (John Garrideb), James Spottswood (Nathan Garrideb), Violet Besson (Mrs Hudson), Eustace Wyatt (Inspector Lestrade), Selma Hall (Mrs Saunders).
Selected credits: Scrp: Thomas H. Hutchinson. Prod: Robert Palmer.

The first dramatisation of Sherlock Holmes on television.

TOUHA SHERLOCKA HOLMESE
('The Longing of Sherlock Holmes')
(see pages 134-135)
3 March 1972. Bararandov Studio. Prague. Czech.
109m. Colour.
Cast: Radovan Lukavsky (Sherlock Holmes), Vaclav Voska (Dr Watson), Vlasta Fialova (Lady Abraham), Marie Rosukova (Lady Oberon), Bohus Zahorsky (Maestro), Josef Patocka (Sir Arthur Conan Doyle).
Selected credits: Scrp: Ilja Hurnik, Stepan Skalsky. Dir: Stepan Skalsky.

THE TREASURE OF ALPHEUES T. WINTERBORN
26 December 1980. CBS-TV (Children's Mystery Theatre). USA. 45m. Colour.
Cast: Keith McConnell (Sherlock Holmes), Laurie Main (Dr Watson).
Selected credits: Scrp: Kimmer Ringwald. Bo: Novel by John Bellairs (although Holmes and Watson do not appear in the book). Prod: Diane and Paul Asselin. Dir: Murray Golden.

THE TRIUMPH OF SHERLOCK HOLMES
(see page 32)
February 1935. Real Art Productions Ltd. UK. 84m. Black and white.
Cast: Arthur Wontner (Sherlock Holmes), Ian Fleming (Dr Watson), Lyn Harding (Professor Moriarty), Minnie Rayner (Mrs Hudson), Leslie Perrins (John Douglas), Jane Carr (Ettie Douglas), Charles Mortimer (Inspector Lestrade), Michael Shepley (Cecil Barker), Ben Weldon (Ted Balding), Roy Emerton (Boss McGinty), Wilfred Caithness (Colonel Sebastian Moran).
Selected credits: Scrp: H. Fowler Mear, Cyril Twyford. Bo: *The Valley of Fear*, by Doyle. Prod: Julius Hagen. Dir: Leslie Hiscott.

TWO SLEUTHS
(see pages 148-151)
Series 1: 1911-1912. Biograph; Series 2: 1912-1913. Keystone. USA. Black and white. Silent.
(Series 1) 1 '$500,000 Reward', 2 'Trailing the Counterfeiters', 3 'Their First Divorce Case' 4 'Caught With the Goods' 5 'Their First Kidnapping Case'. (Series 2) 6 'At It Again', 7 'A Bear Escape', 8 'The Stolen Purse' 9 'The Sleuth's Last Stand' 10 'The Sleuths at the Floral Parade', 11 'Their First Execution'.
Recurring cast: Fred Mace (Sherlock Holmes), Mack Sennett (Sherlock Holmes; except 6).
Selected credits: Dir: D.W. Griffith.

THE VALLEY OF FEAR
(see pages 12-15)
May 1916. The Samuelson Mfg Co Ltd. UK. 6 reels. Black and white. Silent.
Cast: H. A. Saintsbury (Sherlock Holmes), Arthur M. Cullen (Dr Watson), Booth Conway (Moriarty), Daisy Burrell (Ettie Shafter), Jack Macaulay (McGinty), Cecuil Mannering (John McMurdo).
Selected credits: Scrp: Harry Engholm. Prod: G.B. Samuelson. Dir: Alexander Butler.

WITHOUT A CLUE
(see page 146)
21 February 1988. ITC/Eberhardt Stirdivant Production. UK. 107m. Colour.
Cast: Michael Caine (Sherlock Holmes/Reginald Kincaid), Ben Kingsley (Dr Watson), Jeffrey Jones (Inspector Lestrade), Paul Freeman (Professor Moriarty), Lysette Anthony (Leslie Giles), Nigel Davenport (Lord Smithwick), Pat Keen (Mrs Hudson), Peter Cook (Greenhough Smith), Tom Killick (Sebastian), Matthew Savage (Wiggins).
Selected credits: Des: Brian Ackland Snow. Ed: Peter Tanner. Mus: Henry Mancini. Dp: Alan Hume. Scrp: Gary Murphy, Larry Strawther. Exec prod: Dennis A. Brown. Prod: Marc Stirdivant. Dir: Thom Eberhardt.

THE WOMAN IN GREEN
(see pages 60-61)
15 June 1945. Universal Pictures. USA. 68m. Black and white.
Cast: Basil Rathbone (Sherlock Holmes), Nigel Bruce (Dr Watson), Hillary Brooke (Lydia Marlowe), Paul Cavanagh (Sir George Fenwick), Henry Daniell (Professor Moriarty), Eve Amber (Maude), Sally Shepherd (Crandon), Matthew Boulton (Inspector Gregson), Mary Gordon (Mrs Hudson).
Selected credits: Art dir: John B. Goodman, Martin Obzina. Ed: Edward Curtiss. Sp effects: John P. Fulton. Mus: Frank Skinner. Dp: Virgil Miller. Scrp: Bertram Millhauser. Prod: Roy William Neill. Dir: Roy William Neill.

YOUNG SHERLOCK
(see page 112)
Oct-Dec 1982. Granada Television. UK. 1 x 50m, 7 x 30m. Colour.
1 'The Young Master', 2 'The Gypsy Calls Again', 3 'The Riddle of the Dummies', 4 'The Singular Thorn', 5 'The Woman in Black', 6 'The Gass Cutter's Hand', 7 'The Unexpected Visitors', 8 'The Eye of the Peacock'.
Recurring cast: Guy Henry (Sherlock Holmes), June Barry (Mrs Turnbull), Heather Chasen (Aunt Rachel), Christopher Villiers (Jasper Moran), John Fraser (Uncle Gideon), Tim Brierly (John Whitney), Lewis Fiander (Ranjeet).
Selected credits: Mus: Paul Lewis. Scrp: Gerald Frow. Prod: Pieter Rogers. Dir: Nicholas Ferguson.

YOUNG SHERLOCK HOLMES
(UK *Young Sherlock Holmes and the Pyramid of Fear*)
(see pages 132-133)
4 December 1985. Amblin Entertainment for Paramount. USA. 109m. Colour.
Cast: Nicholas Rowe (Sherlock Holmes), Alan Cox (John Watson), Sophie Ward (Elizabeth), Anthony Higgins (Rathe/Moriarty), Susan Fleetwood (Mrs Dribb), Freddie Jones (Cragwich), Nigel Stock (Waxflatter), Roger Ashton-Griffiths (Lestrade), Earl Rhodes (Dudley), Brian Oulton (Master Sneigrove), Patrick Newell (Bently Bobster), Michael Hordern (Voice of Older Watson).
Selected credits: Mus: Bruce Broughton. Dp: Stephen Goldblatt. Scrp: Chris Columbus. Exec prod: Steven Spielberg, Kathleen Kennedy, Frank Marshall. Prod: Mark Johnson. Dir: Barry Levinson.

YOUNG SHERLOCK HOLMES AND THE PYRAMID OF FEAR
- see *Young Sherlock Holmes*

DER ZEICHEN DER VIER
('The Sign of Four')
(see pages 134-135)
1974. Germany. 55m. Colour.
Cast: Rolf Becker (Sherlock Holmes), Roger Lumont (Dr Watson), Gila von Weiterhausen.
Selected credits: Bo: *The Sign of Four* by Doyle.

SELECTED BIBLIOGRAPHY
Bunson, Matthew E. *The Sherlock Holmes Encyclopedia* (Pavilion,1995).
Cox, Michael *A. Study in Celluloid* (Rupert Books, 1999).
Crowe, Cameron *Conversations With Wilder* (Alfred A. Knopf, 1999).
Davies, David Stuart *Holmes of the Movies* (New English Library, 1976).
Davies, David Stuart *Bending the Willow* (Calabash Press, 1996).
De Waal, Ronald B. *The Universal Sherlock Holmes* (Metropolitan Toronto Reference Library, 1994).
Druxman, Michael B., *Basil Rathbone His Life and His Films* (Barnes, 1975).
Eyles, Allen *Sherlock Holmes, A Centenary Celebration* (John Murray, 1986).
Haydock, Ron *Deerstalker* (Scarecrow Press Inc, 1978).
Kelley, Gordon E. *Sherlock Holmes, Screen and Sound Guide* (Scarecrow Press Inc, 1994).
Pohle, Robert W. Jnr, and Hart, Douglas C. *Sherlock Holmes on Screen* (Barnes, 1977).
Pointer, Michael *The Public Life of Sherlock Holmes* (David and Charles, 1975).
Rathbone, Basil *In and Out of Character* (Doubleday and Co, 1962).
Steinbrunner, Chris and Michaels, Norman *The Films of Sherlock Holmes* (Citadel, 1978).